New directions for equity
in mathematics education

New directions for equity in mathematics education

Edited by

WALTER G. SECADA
University of Wisconsin, Madison

ELIZABETH FENNEMA
University of Wisconsin, Madison

LISA BYRD ADAJIAN
University of Wisconsin, Madison

Published in collaboration with the National Council of Teachers of Mathematics

CAMBRIDGE
UNIVERSITY PRESS

Published by the Press Syndicate of the University of Cambridge
The Pitt Building, Trumpington Street, Cambridge CB2 1RP
40 West 20th Street, New York, NY 10011-4211, USA
10 Stamford Road, Oakleigh, Melbourne 3166, Australia

510, 71

N 532

First published 1995

Printed in the United States of America

Library of Congress Cataloging-in-Publication Data
New directions for equity in mathematics education / edited by Walter
G. Secada, Elizabeth Fennema, Lisa Byrd Adajian
    p. cm.
Includes bibliographical references and index.
ISBN 0-521-47152-4 – ISBN 0-521-47720-4 (pbk.)
1. Mathematics – Study and teaching – United States. 2. Minority
students – Education – United States. 3. Minority students –
Education – Mathematics. I. Secada, Walter G. II. Fennema,
Elizabeth. III. Adajian, Lisa Byrd.
QA13.N49   1995
510'.71–dc20   94-19250
                                    CIP

A catalog record for this book is available from the British Library.

ISBN 0-521-47152-4 Hardback
ISBN 0-521-47720-4 Paperback

To the memory of
Deborah A. Carey
friend, colleague, and collaborator

Contents

vii

Part III

Contributors

Michael W. Apple
Department of Curriculum and
  Instruction
University of Wisconsin, Madison

Lisa Byrd Adajian
National Center for Research in Mathe-
  matical Sciences Education
Wisconsin Center for Education
  Research
University of Wisconsin, Madison

Patricia B. Campbell
Campbell–Kibler Associates
Groton, Massachusetts

Deborah A. Carey
Department of Curriculum and
  Instruction
University of Maryland at College Park

Thomas P. Carpenter
Department of Curriculum and
  Instruction
University of Wisconsin, Madison

Suzanne K. Damarin
Department of Educational Policy and
  Leadership
The Ohio State University

Elizabeth Fennema
Department of Curriculum and
  Instruction
University of Wisconsin, Madison

Megan L. Franke
Department of Education
University of California, Los Angeles

Marilyn Frankenstein
College of Public and Community
  Service
University of Massachusetts, Boston

Laurie E. Hart
Department of Elementary Education
University of Georgia

Harvey B. Keynes
School of Mathematics
University of Minnesota

Lena Licón Khisty
College of Education
University of Illinois at Chicago

Gloria Ladson-Billings
Department of Curriculum and
  Instruction
University of Wisconsin, Madison

Gilah C. Leder
Graduate School of Education
La Trobe University
Bundoora, Victoria
Australia

Barbara Scott Nelson
Education Development Center
Newton, Massachusetts

Ann S. Rosebery
TERC
Cambridge, Massachusetts

Walter G. Secada
National Center for Research in Mathe-
  matical Sciences Education
Wisconsin Center for Education
  Research
University of Wisconsin, Madison

Edward A. Silver
Learning Research and Development
  Center
University of Pittsburgh

ix

Margaret Schwan Smith
Learning Research and Development
    Center
University of Pittsburgh

George M. A. Stanic
Department of Elementary Education
University of Georgia

William Tate
Department of Curriculum and
    Instruction
University of Wisconsin, Madison

Beth Warren
TERC
Cambridge, Massachusetts

Acknowledgments

We would like to thank Margaret Powell for her technical editing of this book. Deborah Stewart coordinated final proofreading. Kathleen Steele handled numerous clerical and administrative tasks. Without the expert and cheerful help of these three people, the manuscript would have been less than it is and it would never have made it to press.

The preparation of the book was supported by the National Center for Research in Mathematical Sciences Education through a grant from the Office of Educational Research and Improvement, United States Department of Education (grant number R117G10002), and by the Wisconsin Center for Education Research, University of Wisconsin, Madison. The opinions expressed in this publication do not necessarily reflect the views of the National Center for Research in Mathematical Sciences Education, the Office of Educational Research and Improvement, or the Wisconsin Center for Education Research.

Introduction

*Walter G. Secada, Elizabeth Fennema, and
Lisa Byrd Adajian*

The purpose of this book is to move scholarship on the nature of equity in mathematics education into lines of inquiry that incorporate alternative conceptions of equity, new methods of inquiry, or some developments that extend the classical boundaries of work in this field. Presumably, as efforts in new directions begin to take hold, their results will inform evolving policy and practice so that these might proceed in a more equitable way.

Our efforts are not meant to suggest that previous work no longer applies or that we somehow consider it out of date. Indeed, many of these chapters trace their genesis to classical notions of equity: that is, equity thought of in terms of equality (or inequality) of educational opportunity; as a quantitative construct; or as focused on the inputs, processes, or outcomes of education. Such research has had and will continue to have a major impact not just in scholarship, but also in the arenas of public policy and practice. For example, work on differential student achievement (Secada, 1992), drop-out (Arias, 1986; National Center for Education Statistics, 1992; Rumberger, 1987), course taking and careers (Chipman & Thomas, 1987; National Science Foundation, 1986; Oakes, 1990a), tracking (Gamoran 1987, 1991; Gamoran & Mare, 1989; Oakes, 1985, 1990b), and teacher–student interactions (Fennema, 1990; Peterson & Fennema, 1985) will continue to inform work in equity.

We saw our challenge, however, in terms of recent developments. Scholarly inquiry has begun to focus on new areas through research in cognitive psychology; by making problematic such classically held notions as race, gender, social class, and even the goals of schooling itself; by using poststructural analyses and semiotics; by incorporating a range of perspectives and voices that have been previously unheard; and, in brief, by asking new kinds of questions from different points of view.

The United States, where much of our work is situated, and other countries find themselves confronted with new social realities based on the demographics of their school-aged population. Worldwide, education is in a time of ferment where often contradictory calls for reform are commonplace. These calls range from notions of restructuring the classroom,

1

school, and district to efforts that would incorporate elements of competition and choice in schooling that heretofore has been thought of as a free, universally available public service. And, finally, some fundamental notions about equity are becoming more qualitatively textured, more explicitly value-laden, and more linked to notions of fairness than has been the case in the past.

If equity as an area of scholarly inquiry is to continue to grow and develop, we reasoned that it needs to take account of, and to become situated in, developments in scholarly methodology and in the critical contemporary issues facing education. Research on equity should anticipate new social questions and new directions in research and policy, rather than lagging behind and then having to play intellectual catch-up; it should question what might come to be; and equity-based inquiry should become an integral part of the agenda from the start.

It was these challenges that we had in mind when, in the spring of 1991, the National Center for Research in Mathematical Sciences Education (NCRMSE) commissioned a series of papers from mathematics educators whose work in one form or another touched upon the education of girls, ethnic and cultural minorities, bilingual students, and the economically disadvantaged. We asked these individuals to think about their work and to situate it in our paradigm so that it might provide new insights into the nature of equity in the present contexts of demography and reform. Initial drafts of the chapters by Harvey Keynes, Marilyn Frankenstein, Gilah Leder, Patricia Campbell, Suzanne Damarin, Lena Khisty, and Beth Warren and Ann Rosebery were presented at a seminar series sponsored by NCRMSE. Subsequently, we added to that collection the chapters by Edward Silver, Margaret Schwan Smith and Barbara Scott Nelson; Deborah Carey, Elizabeth Fennema, Thomas P. Carpenter, and Megan L. Franke; Gloria Ladson-Billings, Walter Secada, William Tate, and George Stanic and Laurie Hart. The result is the present volume.

The book is organized, roughly, in three parts. The first – comprising Chapters 1 through 7 – addresses a wide range of cultural issues, broadly construed. Three chapters report on projects – Quantitative Understanding: Amplifying Student Achievement and Reasoning (QUASAR, Silver, Smith, & Nelson), University of Minnesota Talented Youth Mathematics Program (UMTYMP, Keynes), and Cognitively Guided Instruction (CGI, Carey, Fennema, Carpenter, & Franke) – that are designed to enhance how students experience mathematics as a school subject. In these programs, efforts are consciously made to address the backgrounds, needs, and interests of diverse student populations. All three projects are cognizant of the reform movement in mathematics education as exemplified, in part, by recent publications of the National Council of Teachers of Mathematics (1989, 1991) and the National Research Council (1989), and they provide evidence that it is possible to teach in ways that the reformers endorse, as well as in ways that make mathematics come alive to a wide range of students.

Teachers are key players in QUASAR and CGI; Gloria Ladson-Billings describes characteristics of teachers who are successful in teaching African American students. Beyond the mathematics classroom, she documents how these teachers show personal interest in their students, maintain high standards and a commitment to their students' success not just in mathematics but also in life, and display excitement in the subject that helps breathe life into what so easily proves dull and uninteresting.

The final three chapters in the first part, by Walter Secada, Marilyn Frankenstein, and William Tate, show how social and cultural analyses of mathematics education can acquire a critical edge. Secada argues that many barriers to incorporating equity into the current reforms can be characterized and traced to particular norms and beliefs that are part of the way that the mathematics education community constitutes itself. Marilyn Frankenstein provides a critical analysis of social class and describes her efforts to incorporate that analysis into her teaching of adult students. William Tate argues that much of the current push for a national test in mathematics, even if voluntary, can be traced to notions of merit that were intended to grant legitimacy to the original social structures, slavery in particular, in American society.

The second part of the book – Chapters 8 through 11 – is oriented to issues of gender. Gilah Leder's analysis alerts us to how psychosocial processes in classrooms can disempower people who are otherwise very competent. Patricia Campbell's review of successful out-of-school programs for girls (from diverse social class and ethnic backgrounds) in mathematics and science provides suggestions for how in-school reform efforts might be shaped to make mathematics more girl-friendly. Suzanne Damarin's analysis draws from recent developments in feminist scholarship to ask if there might be such a thing as feminist mathematics. George Stanic and Laurie Hart use classical work on gender as the basis for an anthropological study of the culture and beliefs found in a single mathematics classroom. They conclude that race and gender interact in ways that render some of the assumptions by which we generalize across racial groups highly problematic.

The third major part of this book, composed of Chapters 12 and 13, looks at language and mathematics. Lena Khisty explores the nature of discourse in Spanish-speaking bilingual teachers' mathematics classes and finds that features of what has come to be known as the mathematics register can constrain the successful negotiation of meaning in those classrooms. Beth Warren and Ann Rosebery describe their work on staff development and scientific sense making among bilingual teachers of Haitian-Creole–speaking students.

A close reading of the chapters shows a variety of themes and settings that cut across these groupings. For example, like much of the current educational reform movement, the chapters by Secada, Frankenstein, Tate, and Damarin provide a critique of current practice but also do more. These chapters push beyond the boundaries set by the reform movement to critique many of the tenets of the reform itself. The chapters by Keynes and Campbell are set firmly in out-of-school settings that provide different perspectives on ways by which those settings might inform efforts to make learning in-school more like learning out-of-school (Resnick, 1987).

The chapters by Ladson-Billings, Leder, Stanic and Hart, and Khisty look very closely at teachers, teaching, and the dynamics of classrooms. As in these chapters, teachers are central in Chapter 1 on QUASAR (by Silver et al.) and Chapter 2 on CGI (by Carey et al.), as well as in Chapter 13 on Cheche Konnen (by Warren and Rosebery). But also, these chapters describe very complex in-school programs that combine curriculum, teaching, and assessment in ways that support student reasoning and engagement in worthwhile content. The three chapters also address issues of teacher empowerment and the re-skilling of teachers (Apple, 1982, 1986). QUASAR, CGI, and Cheche Konnen include strong staff development components that equip teachers to learn about mathematics and science as sense-making activities and to use that information in their practice.

Beyond their settings and topics, these chapters provide and illuminate deeper themes that should interest anyone who is concerned about the quality of school mathematics in general: the critical importance of maintaining student interest in mathematics; the role that cultural and linguistic referents (broadly construed) play in maintaining that interest; the centrality of teachers, their knowledge, and beliefs not just about mathematics but also about their students and about the purposes of schooling; and the social contexts in which and for which we are educating students.

Also, there are tensions across these chapters and we invited Michael Apple, who has written about the current school mathematics reform movement (Apple 1992a, 1992b), to end this book with his reflections on some of those tensions. How, we must wonder, might scholarly inquiry, policy-making, and practice proceed in light of these insights? Are there not contradictions between programs and perspectives that accept the reform agenda as given and seek to build on that versus those perspectives that critique the reform? That such questions become necessary as one reads these chapters indicates the diversity of thought in the field of equity. This is a sign of health – a sign that the field is poised to move forward. It is in the debates engendered by these tensions as they become more explicit that we should develop the subtlety of thought and the kinds of inquiry that will enable us to understand how opportunity is unequally distributed in this society, the role that mathematics and education play in that stratification, and how we might reclaim the aegis of educational reform to include the creation of a fairer social order as a legitimate goal.

References

Apple, M. (1982). *Education and power*. Boston, MA: Routledge & Kegan Paul.

(1986). *Teachers and text*. Boston, MA: Routledge & Kegan Paul.

(1992a). Do the standards go far enough? Power, policy, and practice in mathematics education. *Journal for Research in Mathematics Education, 23*(5), 412–431.

(1992b). Thinking more politically about the challenges before us: A response to Romberg. *Journal for Research in Mathematics Education, 23*(5), 438–440.

Arias, M. B. (1986). The context of education for Hispanics: An overview. *American Journal of Education, 95*(1), 26–57.

Chipman, S. F., & Thomas, V. G. (1987). The participation of women and minorities in mathematical, scientific, and technical fields. In E. Z. Rothkopf (Ed.), *Review of research in education* (Vol. 14, chapter 9, pp. 387–430). Washington, DC: American Educational Research Association.

Fennema, E. (1990). Teachers' beliefs and gender differences in mathematics. In E. Fennema & G. Leder (Eds.), *Mathematics and gender* (pp. 169–187). New York: Teachers College Press.

Gamoran, A. (1987). The stratification of high school learning opportunities. *Sociology of Education, 60*, 135–165.

(1991). Schooling and achievement: Additive versus interactive models. In S. W. Raudebush & W. J. Douglas (Eds.), *Schools, classrooms, and pupils: International studies of schooling from a multilevel perspective* (pp. 37–52). New York: Academic Press.

Gamoran, A., & Mare, R. D. (1989). Secondary school tracking and educational inequality: Compensation, reinforcement, or neutrality? *American Journal of Sociology, 94*, 1146–1183.

National Center for Education Statistics, United States Department of Education. (1992). *The condition of education 1992*. Washington, DC: United States Government Printing Office.

National Council of Teachers of Mathematics. (1989). *Curriculum and evaluation standards for school mathematics*. Reston, VA: Author.

(1991). *Professional standards for teaching mathematics*. Reston, VA: Author.

National Research Council. (1989). *Everybody counts*. Washington, DC: National Academy Press.

National Science Foundation. (1986). *Women and minorities in science and engineering* (NSF 86–301). Washington, DC: Author.

Oakes, J. (1985). *Keeping track: How schools structure inequality*. New Haven, CT: Yale University Press.

(1990a). Opportunities, achievement, and choice: Women and minority students in science and mathematics. In C. B. Cazden (Ed.), *Review of Research in Education* (Vol. 16, pp. 153–222). Washington, DC: American Educational Research Association.

(1990b). *Multiplying inequalities: The effects of race, social class, and tracking on opportunities to learn mathematics and science*. Santa Monica, CA: Rand Corporation.

Peterson, P. L., & Fennema, E. (1985). Effective teaching, student enjoyment of classroom activities, and sex-related differences in learning mathematics. *American Educational Research Journal, 22*, 309–335.

Resnick, L. B. (1987). Learning in school and out. *Educational Researcher, 16*(9), 13–20.

Rumberger, R. W. (1987). High school dropout: A review of issues and evidence. *Review of Education Research, 57*, 101–121.

Secada, W. G. (1992). Race, ethnicity, social class, language, and achievement in mathematics. In D. Grouws (Ed.), *Handbook of research on mathematics teaching and learning* (pp. 623–660). New York: Macmillan.

Part I

1   The QUASAR Project: Equity concerns meet mathematics education reform in the middle school

Edward A. Silver, Margaret Schwan Smith, and Barbara Scott Nelson

QUASAR (Quantitative Understanding: Amplifying Student Achievement and Reasoning) is an educational reform project aimed at fostering and studying the development and implementation of enhanced mathematics instructional programs for students attending middle schools in economically disadvantaged communities. The focus on mathematics is important because of the unacceptably low mathematics achievement of American students, which has been documented in many national and international assessments, and because of the current interest of educators and policymakers in mathematics education reform. The student population targeted for special attention in this project is important because demographic trends predict that we will see in coming decades an increasingly large proportion of our society composed of persons who are the least well served by the current educational system: racial and ethnic minorities and the economically disadvantaged.[1]

The QUASAR project has a particular focus on mathematics education – a relatively narrow but important slice of the educational pie – but it also relates to a more general agenda of equity and social justice. The potential of this country's cultural diversity has not been fully developed, because all children have not been given reasonable opportunity to learn mathematics and other school subjects that would open the doors to employment and further education. The disastrous implications of this situation were noted by the National Research Council in *Everybody Counts,* a report to the nation on the state of mathematics education:

Because mathematics holds the key to leadership in our information-based society, the widening gap between those who are mathematically literate and those who are not coincides, to a frightening degree, with racial and economic categories. We are at risk of becoming a divided nation in which knowledge of mathematics supports a productive, technologically powerful elite while a dependent, semiliterate majority, disproportionately Hispanic and Black, find economic and political power beyond reach. Unless corrected, innumeracy and illiteracy will drive America apart. (1989, p. 14)

9

Thus, QUASAR can be seen as part of a broader set of efforts to create a society that offers opportunity to each of its members to be successful and to contribute to the social and economic good. Demographic trends indicate that continued underinvestment in the education of the poor, disproportionate numbers of whom are members of racial or ethnic minority groups, will exacerbate the current achievement gaps between groups in this society and between students in the United States and their counterparts in other industrialized societies.[2]

This chapter describes the context and content of instructional reform efforts within the project. A brief overview and history of QUASAR is provided, after which some aspects of the current crisis in mathematics education are reviewed, with particular focus on the situation in schools serving poor communities. The low levels of student participation and achievement in mathematics are discussed, as is the relationship between these data and the forms of instructional practice that currently characterize mathematics education in this country. A case is made that mathematics instructional practice needs to be reformed by inventing forms of instruction that develop greater student understanding, blend basic skills with high-level thinking and reasoning, and encourage open communication among students and their teachers about mathematical ideas. Finally, glimpses of instructional practices in QUASAR schools and classrooms are provided to illustrate how these challenges are being addressed.[3] The examples portray the interplay between equity concerns and mathematics education reform, with particular focus on two equity issues: (a) increasing access for all students to high-quality mathematics instruction that challenges them to think and reason and not simply to memorize and repeat, and (b) increasing the relevance of mathematics for children by connecting it more deeply to their lives and their cultures and by building on the strengths of knowledge and ways of knowing that children bring to school with them.

The QUASAR Project: A brief overview

The QUASAR Project was launched in the fall of 1989, as a demonstration that it was both feasible and responsible to implement instructional programs that foster the acquisition of mathematical thinking and reasoning skills by students attending middle schools in economically disadvantaged communities (Silver, 1989). A fundamental premise of the project was that low levels of participation and performance in mathematics by females, ethnic minorities, and the poor were not due primarily to a lack of ability or potential but rather to educational practices that denied access to meaningful, high-quality experiences with mathematics learning. QUASAR was initiated with a clear focus on students in economically disadvantaged communities and a conviction that these students could be assisted to learn a broader range of mathematical content, acquire a deeper understanding of mathematical ideas, and improve their ability to reason and solve complex problems, if effort, imagination, and reasonable financial resources were applied.

Design principles underlying the QUASAR Project

QUASAR rests on the premise that it is both necessary and possible to develop mathematics education in a way that serves all students well and provides avenues for them to develop their intellectual potential. Moreover, in its design, the project posits that it is possible for such a mathematics education to be consistent with the results of the past few decades of research on learning, which has suggested that all learners actively construct their own knowledge, even in complex intellectual domains such as mathematics. This view of learners as active constructors of knowledge suggests the intellectual bankruptcy of previous, deficit-based models of achievement and suggests a new vision of education. In this view, the task of teachers and schools is not to detect and remediate students' deficits, but rather to identify and nurture sources of competence in students. In this view, the job of teachers and schools is to provide the support and materials with which each student not only refines and makes more mathematically sophisticated his or her own constructs and means of building knowledge but also appropriates and uses mathematical or general academic concepts, principles, and processes contributed by others. The intended result is a form of education that serves all students far better.

QUASAR has focused on individual schools – rather than districts or individual teachers – as the starting point for systemic educational reform. School-based program innovations require that many components of the educational system be addressed in a coordinated fashion, including staff development, ongoing teacher support, curriculum revision, and alignment of assessment and instruction. Moreover, it is from school-based innovations that districts can adapt successful approaches for wider implementation; this process of spreading activation and influence to other schools will be tracked in the project.

Adaptation is an important design feature of the project. Too little is known about the spread of programmatic initiatives beyond the boundaries of the mathematics program at a single school. After the initial project sites have designed, implemented, and refined their instructional approaches, the project will encourage the emergent programs, practices, and principles to be applied and adapted to a broader range of educational settings. QUASAR staff and the partners at the development sites will share accumulated knowledge and experience with personnel at the adaptation sites and assist them in shaping appropriate programs tailored to their specific needs.

The QUASAR reform strategy combines elements of "top down" and "bottom up" approaches to school change. In the tradition of "top down" reform efforts, the importance of coherent general principles as guides for reform is recognized, and all project sites have affirmed the general goals of curriculum breadth, deeper student understanding, and emphasis on high-level thinking and reasoning. Local project sites have also developed plans that incorporate a shared set of focal activities: staff development, ongoing teacher support, curriculum development or revision, and alignment of student assessment with instructional practice. On the other hand, recognizing the power of "bottom up" approaches to reform and the importance of tying reform efforts closely to the nuances of local conditions, QUASAR does not encourage or support reforms imposed from a distance. Rather, the project encourages and supports reform efforts that are designed and implemented by those who live or work in the affected communities. In working with locally based collaborative teams, QUASAR seeks not only to build on the strengths of each member of the partnership, but also to weave the programs deeply into the educational and social fabric of the schools and surrounding communities in order to build their capacity to face fundamental challenges and to solve their own educational problems.

QUASAR is not only a practical school demonstration project; it is also a complex research study of educational change and improvement. The project's research design has been heavily influenced by evidence – accumulated from several decades of research on school reform – that school change must be treated as a *process* rather than as a *product* (e.g., Lieberman, 1986). Therefore, the project seeks to study programmatic activities as they occur rather than waiting until an appropriate moment in time to render a summative judgment about the effectiveness of the reform efforts. Project researchers aim at the identification of critical features of successful programs by studying several different approaches being taken to accomplish the general instructional program goals; examining the implementation of these programs in schools and in teachers' classrooms; assessing the impact of the programs on teachers' instructional practices, knowledge, and beliefs; evaluating the impact of the programs on student performance by devising new assessment tools to measure students' growth in mathematical reasoning and problem solving; and ascertaining conditions that appear to facilitate or inhibit the success of these instructional reform efforts. Through its extensive research effort, the project aims to identify programs, practices, and principles that can guide effective mathematics instruction for middle school students.[4]

QUASAR sites and programs

School sites and their surrounding communities constitute the operational heart of project activities. QUASAR has begun its work with a small number of educational partnerships centered around middle schools located in economically disadvantaged areas. In particular, six geographically dispersed sites are serving as initial development environments for teachers and administrators from a middle school, working in collaboration with "resource partners" from a local university or education agency, to develop, implement, and modify innovative mathematics instructional programs for middle school students. In line with the general goals of the project, the mathematics curriculum at these sites includes a broad range of mathematical topics that stretch beyond the traditional middle school menu of computation with whole numbers and fractions (e.g., geometry, statistics, and probability). Instructional practices used at the sites to support the goals of thinking, reasoning, and problem solving include the use of mathematical tasks that allow multiple entry points, multiple solution paths, and multiple modes of demonstrating competence; a focus on concrete grounding of mathematical ideas through the use of visual and iconic representations; an emphasis on communication featuring enhanced levels of discourse between teachers and students and among students; and creation of classroom communities that value thinking and reasoning and provide a safe environment for students.

QUASAR sites can be described, at least in part, in terms of the basic criteria used in site selection. During the 1989–1990 school year, four sites were chosen using a four-stage process: nomination, acknowledgment of interest, formal written application, and site visitation. Two additional sites were added during the 1990–1991 school year to complete the set of six development sites. The process began with about 200 nominees and included 42 formal applications. The chosen sites had applications that satisfied the four basic selection criteria: (a) a partnership involving a middle school serving an economically disadvantaged community and one or more resource partners committed to working in collaboration with the school staff to enhance the mathematics program; (b) a plan for enhancing the mathematics program by placing a greater emphasis on reasoning and problem solving – a plan based on sound principles or solid evidence of prior work and one that appeared to have the potential for rapid implementation; (c) a school whose climate and general functioning appeared to support and allow the principal and faculty to focus attention on program innovation and academic achievement; and (d) clear interest on the part of the school mathematics faculty in undertaking these instructional program reforms. The sites also satisfied additional selection criteria by varying with respect to geographic location, ethnicity of student population, and instructional program plans, and by featuring schools that were "as typical as possible" in order to facilitate adaptation.

With sites in California, Georgia, Massachusetts, Oregon, Pennsylvania, and Wisconsin, the geographic dispersal is clear. Across the six sites there is considerable diversity in the ethnicity and race of the student populations, with two sites serving predominantly African American students, two serving primarily Hispanic or Latino students, and the other two sites having more cultural diversity in their student populations. Although school climate and general functioning were selection criteria, it is important to note that QUASAR schools are quite typical of public schools serving poor communities, in that they are constrained in their educational efforts by significant problems beyond their control and direct influence. The vast majority of QUASAR students come from families who have annual incomes of less than $20,000 and who qualify for free or reduced-cost lunch programs; many live in low-income housing projects located in the school communities. For many students, their basic needs are often not being met in the areas of health care, housing, transportation, and economic and personal security. As a consequence, many students are not able to attend school regularly, do not have available energy and attentiveness to focus squarely on an academic agenda, or are not sufficiently free of family and other responsibilities to study well at home.

QUASAR teachers are ordinary people engaged in extraordinary efforts to develop enhanced instructional programs for their students under very difficult circumstances. They are typical of middle school mathematics teachers all over the country in that the majority have elementary certification with limited formal training and background in mathematics, with many completing only a mathematics methods course in college. There is also predictable diversity among project teachers—many are novice teachers with no more than 5 years of experience, whereas others have more than 20 years of experience; most are eager to participate in efforts to change mathematics instruction, but others see little need for change; many share background experiences and racial or ethnic identities similar to those of their students, and a few do not. Although typical in the ways just noted, most teachers in project schools are exceptional among middle school mathematics teachers in their commitment to improving the life chances of their students and in their willingness to exert extra effort to accomplish that goal. In their efforts, teachers are supported by their resource partners, who provide guidance and a sustained reflective presence; by their principals, who try to buffer the project from outside influences that would destroy it before it could become fully established; and by each other, drawing strength from the solidarity that develops as they work together to build new forms of instructional practice that work well for their students.

In recognition of the complexity of the goals of the project, activities at QUASAR sites are focused on a number of different areas, including curriculum development and modification, staff development and ongoing teacher support, classroom and school-based assessment design, and outreach to parents and the school district at large. It is beyond the scope of this chapter to describe these efforts in detail. Suffice it to say that instructional improvement efforts are being supported by a network of interrelated activities that attempt to develop the capacity of the school and the teachers to provide an enhanced mathematics program for each child. For example, in the area of teacher staff development and ongoing support, project sites are characterized by a diverse set of activities that include: regularly scheduled meetings at which teachers can discuss instructional goals and share the results of their implementation efforts; frequent interactions between teachers and their resource partner(s); specially designed courses or formal staff development sessions on topics of interest to the teachers; "retreats" to provide time for reflection and extended discussion of progress; and participation in professional meetings and conferences.

Partners at QUASAR sites are engaged in efforts that reside at the intersection of attempts to reform mathematics education and increase educational equity. In their programmatic work, they are attempting to increase students' access to strong, nonremedial curricula and instruction; their confidence and competence in using mathematics to solve problems; their interest in mathematics; their ability to "make sense" of mathematics; and their competence in communicating about it, especially with respect to reasoning and constructing mathematical arguments. Although the work is not yet completed, the struggles to achieve these goals are noteworthy. As is seen in greater detail in the next section, these intended outcomes represent a sharp departure from the current situation in this country.

The QUASAR Project: Context and challenges

QUASAR has been undertaken in response to a sense of crisis in mathematics education. Low rates of student participation in elective mathematics courses, poor student performance on national and international assessments, and inadequate instructional quality have gained widespread attention. Each of these issues relates not only to the general quality of the nation's educational system but also to matters of equity. Fortunately, there is reason to be hopeful that the problems can be addressed in efforts that combine attention both to improving the quality of the mathematical experiences offered to the nation's students and to increasing the relevance of those experiences to their lives and cultures. After a review of the situation that has led to the sense of crisis in education, attention is given to the opportunities afforded by current mathematics education reform efforts and the challenges therein. The discussion is limited to those issues that relate most directly to QUASAR.

Inadequacies in student performance and mathematics instructional quality

If there is a general crisis in mathematics education in the nation, then the situation for those least well served by the current system is even more desperate. Embedded in this brief review of the current state of mathematics achievement and instructional quality is special attention to features that pertain to matters of equity.[5]

Low participation rates and poor performance. Data available from the recent National Assessment of Educational Progress (NAEP) mathematics assessments (Dossey, Mullis, Lindquist, & Chambers, 1988; Mullis, Dossey, Owen, & Phillips, 1991) indicate that too few students are electing to take advanced mathematics courses and studying mathematics throughout their high school years. The NAEP data suggest that, for the nation as a whole, only 9 of every 100 graduating high school students completes 4 years of college preparatory mathematics and is thereby prepared adequately for the study of calculus in college. In disadvantaged urban communities, the participation rate in advanced mathematics courses is even worse: Only 5 of every 100 students completes 4 years of college preparatory mathematics. In these urban schools serving economically disadvantaged communities, students take very little mathematics at all. In fact, four of five students take no math beyond the minimum required for graduation, which may be as little as 2 years of prealgebra coursework. Furthermore, although the college-attending rates of minority and majority students are almost identical for students who have taken algebra and geometry in high school (Pelavin & Kane, 1990), NAEP data indicate that less than half the students in urban schools take any mathematics beyond a year of algebra, and one in five do not study algebra at all.

With respect to performance, results of national and international assessments (Bourque & Garrison, 1991; Robitaille & Garden, 1989) have provided sobering statistics regarding the impoverished state of American students' mathematical proficiency, especially with respect to complex tasks and problem solving. Not only are there too few American students performing at the highest levels on these assessments, but there are too few females, ethnic minorities, and students from poor communities in the group of high-performing students. In fact, the vast majority of students are achieving at levels substantially below international standards.

From an equity perspective, not all the news concerning mathematics performance has been gloomy. For example, it has been reported that minority students have narrowed the achievement gap in standardized test performance (Congressional Budget Office, 1987) and on the NAEP (Mullis, Owen, & Phillips, 1990) over the past two decades. In fact, these analyses have shown that minority students have improved at a faster rate than their white counterparts. Secada (1992a) carefully reviewed the evidence that has been presented to support these claims and concluded that the story is less clear than it appears at first glance. For example, the validity of conclusions drawn from the achievement test data base is compromised by the "Lake Wobegon" effect reported by Cannell (1989), who found that virtually all states and school districts used the same type of norm-referenced achievement test scores to report that their students were performing above the national average. The NAEP data are likewise unclear in their implications, since the pattern of change for various minority groups does not appear to be the same over the past few assessment administrations. Matthews, Carpenter, Lindquist, and Silver (1984) reported a consistent pattern of gains for minority students on all types of questions (e.g., knowledge, skills, understanding, and problem solving) on the NAEP assessment between 1978 and 1982; whereas, the gains reported for the 1986 assessment were limited to lower-level questions, and primarily to African American students and not Hispanic students. Moreover, the magnitude of the observed changes in NAEP has been fairly small.

Despite uncertainty about the uniformity and magnitude of the changes in performance of minority students, the evidence does suggest that some improvements have occurred. Nevertheless, despite the positive outcome of reducing intergroup performance differences, the NAEP gains have generally come from improved performance only on those portions of tests related to factual knowledge and basic calculation skills; little change has been found for portions of the test measuring higher-level mathematical outcomes (Secada, 1992b). The good news is that the observed improvements almost certainly indicate that the additional financial support, made available through Chapter 1 to schools serving economically disadvantaged communities, has been used to an advantage, and that the students in these programs have learned what they have been taught (Birman, 1987). On the other hand, the lack of improvement on more complex tasks suggests that the available instruction has been focused only on low-level objectives. This inference is supported by data, discussed later in this chapter, regarding the instructional practices utilized in many high schools attended by predominantly ethnic minority and poor students. These instructional practices may be sufficient to support the narrowing of performance differences on tasks requiring only basic factual knowledge or on routine computational skills, but they are unlikely to lead to improved performance on more complex tasks that require mathematical reasoning and problem solving.

Collectively, these data point to the need to improve mathematics course enrollment and mathematics achievement for all American students, with a special emphasis in poor communities on increasing the level of students' participation and performance in a mathematics sequence that takes them at least as far as algebra and geometry. However, since the trajectory for high school participation and performance in mathematics is set prior to ninth grade (Oakes, 1990b), it is imperative that these issues be addressed not only at the high school level but also in middle school mathematics programs, which are QUASAR's target. Beyond equalizing opportunities for course enrollment, it is also important to enhance the quality of instruction students receive in mathematics courses.

Inadequacies of conventional mathematics instructional practice. As many studies have suggested (e.g., Porter, 1989; Stodolsky, 1988), conventional mathematics instruction emphasizes whole-class instruction, with students listening to a teacher's explanation and watching the teacher work sample problems, followed by students working alone on problems presented in their textbooks or on worksheets, the goal of which is to produce stylized answers to narrowly prescribed questions for which there is a single answer that is already known by the teacher, and that can and will be validated only by teacher approval. This script for conventional mathematics instruction is virtually identical to that reported in several studies conducted in the 1970s and summarized by Fey (1981).

Few instructional innovations appear to have taken firm hold in mathematics instruction. In the area of cooperative learning, for example, despite clear evidence that the use of cooperative learning can increase elementary and middle school student mathematics achievement (Slavin, 1989; Webb, 1989), mathematics teachers generally appear to make little use of truly collaborative learning opportunities for their students. Self-reported data obtained from teachers and students sampled by NAEP (Mullis et al., 1991) indicate that students and teachers differ in reporting the frequency with which students work in small groups in mathematics class. Although the responses of the mathematics teachers surveyed would indicate that about half of the nation's students worked in small groups in mathematics class at least once a week, only slightly more than one-fourth of the students indicated that they worked in small groups that frequently. The discrepancy may be due to the fact that classrooms may be organized so that students sit at tables with other students, thereby leading teachers to report a fairly high rate of having students working in groups, even though each student's work may actually be done in isolation from the others at the table, thereby leading them to report less frequent actual collaborative work.

In general, the NAEP data show that instructional practices in mathematics classes tend to consist of having students work problems from their textbooks or from worksheets. Few opportunities are provided for students to engage in extended exploration of mathematical topics, since fewer than 30% of students or teachers report any instance of working on a mathematical investigation or project during the year. Moreover, instruction appears to emphasize paper-and-pencil proficiency, since only 19% of students in Grade 8 are allowed unrestricted use of calculators during mathematics class, and only 34% are ever allowed to use a calculator on a mathematics test.

Another glimpse at conventional school mathematics instruction can be obtained by inference from the reported tendency of students to perceive school mathematics as a domain that is disconnected from sense making and the world of everyday experience (Resnick, 1988; Schoenfeld, 1991). Silver, Shapiro, and Deutsch (1993) found that, when middle school students were asked to provide interpretations for an answer to a division problem dealing with a real-world situation, their responses dealt more with technical concerns than with sense making. Many students proposed answers that involved a fraction of a bus (even though they knew that buses do not have fractional parts), apparently because the technical process of computation produced a fractional answer. Students' dissociation of sense making from mathematical activity was evident not only from the responses they provided but also from the explanations they did not give, since reports from the students' teachers suggested that some children engaged in more sense making than was evident in their written responses. Apparently, students did not see their "sensible" answers (e.g., using a minivan could serve as a practical representation for a "fractional part" of a full bus) as having validity in the context of responding to a mathematics problem. The requirement that mathematics should make sense was apparently not a feature of students' mathematics instruction. The results reported by Silver et al. (1993) also identified another deficiency of conventional mathematics teaching: Students had difficulty providing explanations of their reasoning or justifications for their answers. Explanations and interpretations, in oral or written form, are not a regular feature of instructional activities in mathematics classrooms.

Inadequacies in conventional instructional practices are closely tied to limitations in curriculum content at the middle school level. Conventional mathematics instruction for elementary and middle school students has generally focused narrowly on the teaching and learning of computational skills involving whole numbers and rational numbers. In a national survey of instructional practices in middle school education, Epstein and MacIver (1989) found a "conservative emphasis on basic skills and a lack of attention to creating learning opportunities that are more responsive to the characteristics of early adolescents" (p. 31). Moreover, in basic subject areas, they found that "the most frequent instructional approaches emphasize drill and practice . . . more passive than active learning, and more attention to teaching strategies than to learning strategies" (p. 33). At all educational levels, "drill-to-kill" or "assembly-line" instruction, consisting of repetitive drill-and-practice on basic computation and other routine procedures, has characterized school mathematics, especially in impoverished urban and rural schools.[6]

Despite a few notable success stories, the content and conduct of mathematics education and compensatory education in poor communities has typically been inadequate to enhance the life chances of the students attending these schools. Deficiencies in conventional instructional practice are also linked to typical school organizational practices, such as the practice of "tracking" students into academic classes and programs of study in order to produce homogeneous student groups with respect to certain measure(s) of mathematical ability, usually standardized test scores. Data obtained from teachers sampled by NAEP (Mullis et al., 1991) indicate that nearly two-thirds of the nation's schools engage in tracking, since they assign eighth-grade students to different mathematics classes according to ability. In practice, disproportionate numbers of students from poor communities are relegated to the "remedial track" by the current educational system (Oakes, 1990a). In lower-track classes, students receive less actual instruction than their peers in nonremedial classes, and the instruction they do receive almost exclusively emphasizes low-level knowledge and skills (Oakes, 1985).

A major report on middle school education, *Caught in the Middle* (California State Department of Education, 1987), argued that the assignment of "at risk" students, who are deficient in basic skills, to extensive blocks of remedial instruction often fails because it reinforces negative self-perceptions by emphasizing students' past failures and deprives them of cognitive stimulation:

Students who have even the most acute deficiencies in basic skills need to experience the intellectual excitement of high-order thought processes. Instructional time devoted to basic skills deficiencies should never preempt the opportunity of students to explore the cutting edges of thought and feelings embedded in the subject matter of the core curriculum. (p. 67)

An excessive emphasis on lower-level school mathematics instruction in poor communities ignores not only students' needs for a richer diet of more thoughtful mathematical experiences, but also the needs and desires of many teachers who wish to see their students attain greater mathematical power through the solving of difficult problems and through mastery of challenging material that spans a broad range of mathematical topics. In schools serving poor communities, teachers and students alike have been trapped for too long in a web of poor preparation, low expectations, and limited resources.

In order to improve the situation for students attending schools in economically disadvantaged areas, it will not be enough to provide more of what they now receive. Special efforts must be made to ensure that enhanced forms of mathematics instruction reach those schools as well. Some laudable efforts have been based on the so-called effective schools approach (Edmonds, 1979; Sizemore, 1987), but the mathematical targets toward which these efforts have been directed involve a focus on basic computational skills rather than on problem solving, reasoning, and higher-level thinking. Although these prior efforts and successes are likely to be informative about general school climate and instructional leadership issues, they are far less likely to provide detailed guidance about instructional practices that will promote alternative forms of mathematics instruction that blend attention to basic skills with a focus on higher-level thinking, reasoning, and problem solving; nor are they likely to be informative about the forms of staff development and ongoing support that will be needed in urban schools to bolster and solidify these kinds of instructional changes. Knapp and Turnbull (1990) examined the premises that underlie conventional approaches to teaching "disadvantaged students" and suggested that the limitations inherent in attempts to use conventional "best practices" achieve the goals of increased understanding and problem solving in the area of mathematics. More recently, Knapp, Shields, and Turnbull (1992) reported the results of an empirical investigation of mathematics teaching in 140 classrooms in 15 schools serving "the children of poverty" and reached the following conclusion: "By comparison with conventional practices, instruction that emphasizes meaning and understanding is more effective in inculcating advanced skills, is at least as effective at teaching basic skills, and engages students more extensively in academic learning" (p. i).

A response to the crisis: New goals and increased relevance

The findings already discussed – low rates of participation in mathematics courses, poor performance on assessments of mathematical proficiency, insufficient availability of high-quality mathematics instruction – have contributed to the current sense of crisis in mathematics education. In response to this crisis, increasing the achievement of all U.S. students in the area of mathematics has been promulgated as a national education goal. Discussions regarding the goal of increased student achievement are not being limited to conventional, low-level mathematical goals. In fact, the national discussions have generally supported the goals of the mathematics education reform movement, as represented in the *Curriculum and Evaluation Standards for School Mathematics* (1989) and *Professional Standards for Teaching Mathematics* (1991), both issued by the National Council of Teachers of Mathematics (NCTM). These documents have influenced educators and policy makers to address the goals of increased participation, improved performance, and enhanced instructional quality in a manner consistent with the spirit of the more general mathematics education reform efforts. The complex challenge is to move forward on an agenda simultaneously aimed at achieving equity and access to good mathematics instruction, while redefining the nature of such instruction.

New goals for mathematics education. Current reform efforts are based on a vision of school mathematics that emphasizes thinking, reasoning, problem solving, and communication rather than memorization and repetition. The school mathematics reform agenda takes as a fundamental premise that children construct their knowledge and that a goal of education is to empower all students to be confident solvers and posers of mathematical problems. Thus, these efforts are aimed at an education that is different in kind from the conventional forms of school mathematics instruction described earlier. Although there is a strong desire to have students learn more mathematics, the intent of the current reform effort is not simply to give students more of what they are now offered in mathematics. It will be insufficient for students to take more mathematics courses, if those courses teach content that is too limited, if they fail to connect mathematics to students' life experiences, and if they fail to empower students to use mathematics in a wide variety of settings.

The reform efforts in mathematics are connected to efforts in other subject areas to create new forms of literacy (Resnick, 1987). It is essential not only that students be able to read, write, and perform basic arithmetic procedures, but also that they know when and why to apply those procedures, to make sense out of complicated situations, and to develop strategies for formulating and then solving complex problems. As a result of such a high-literacy education, students would be expected not only to execute algorithms and recall factual knowledge but also to impose meaning and structure on new situations, to generate hypotheses and critically examine evidence, and to select the most appropriate from among a repertoire of strategic alternatives. These students would be better able to take their place in a citizenry that will undoubtedly need to change frames of reference in meeting the challenges of the new century, as the intellectual and technical requirements of jobs and occupations change[7] and as changing social conditions require new social or economic alignments.

Contemporary efforts at school mathematics reform take as a fundamental premise that children are active constructors of their own knowledge and that social interaction and communication is at the heart of meaningful learning. Thus, it is essential that these reform efforts address the connection between the mathematics taught in school and the lives of the children who are asked to learn it. A summary of this perspective on mathematics education is provided by Ernest (1991):

School mathematical knowledge must reflect the nature of mathematics as a social construction: Tentative, growing by means of human creation and decision-making, and connected with other realms of knowledge, culture and social life. . . . it is to be embedded in student culture and the reality of their situation, engaging them and enabling them to appropriate it for themselves. (pp. 207–208)

If our goal is an education that helps students to use their minds well, rather than simply teaching them to perform a certain algorithmic behavior at appropriate times, then educational practices must embrace, affirm, and begin with the content and structure of what students bring to the enterprise. Thus, because of not only the constructivist underpinnings of the mathematics education reform agenda but also the practical demands of providing rich learning opportunities for diverse populations of children, increased pedagogical emphasis must be placed on assisting learners to become engaged in mathematical activity that is embedded in the learner's social and political context (Mellin-Olsen, 1987).

Cognitive and cultural issues are related to school mathematics reform. Although the increasingly multicultural character of U.S. society and its public school population has not escaped the attention of most educators and policymakers, there is no general agreement about the instructional implications of this multiculturalism for mathematics or any other school subject. Thus, in general, schools continue to offer an education that relates closely to cognitive skills and tasks that are more congruent with what is considered the American "mainstream" (i.e., the white middle class) than with other American subcultures. Moreover, instructional practices in schools are seldom designed to embrace the strengths that culturally diverse children bring with them to school, nor do they regularly provide bridges that would enable children from distinct subcultures to develop fluency in both their own and the mainstream cultures. Such fluency would support agility in moving back and forth between mainstream culture and that of home and community, thereby making it possible, for children who wish to do so, to succeed in both.

An example of the incongruity that can occur in schooling is provided by Leap (1988) in a study of culturally linked approaches to mathematics problem solving among fifth- and sixth-grade youngsters of the Ute tribe of northeastern Utah. Among the findings was the observation that students often reacted to the degree of reality they perceived in the situation described in the word problem before deciding how (or whether) to solve it. When a Ute student was asked to determine how much money his brother would have to spend on gasoline if he wanted to drive his pickup truck from the reservation to Salt Lake City, the student did not attempt to solve the problem as it was posed. Instead, he assessed the truth value of the problem and answered, "My brother does not have a pickup truck." Evidently, assessments of truth value are a common part of everyday life on the reservation and affect decisions about personal conduct as well as about tribal affairs more generally. The willingness to engage with mathematical problems that contain hypothetical, or counterfactual, situations would seem to be a requirement for success in a mathematics education that stresses problem solving. This example illustrates that making such education accessible to culturally diverse populations requires helping students negotiate transitions among frames of reference.

Heath (1983) eloquently describes the differences in cultural patterns – language use, space and time orderings, problem-solving techniques, sense of social fabric, and interactional rules – between two Piedmont (Appalachia) communities, and analyzes how growing up in each community prepares children in very different ways for what lies ahead in school. Although Heath's analysis is somewhat limited by her sacrifice of differences among individuals within each community in favor of treating individuals as relatively complete carriers of the culture, language, and thinking patterns associated with the community in which they live, her analysis is nevertheless compelling and informative. Furthermore, she explores ways in which school life could be conducted so as to help these students "code switch," thereby essentially becoming bicultural and increasing their opportunities for success in mainstream American society.

Concerns about cognitive–cultural mismatch are also at the heart of some disagreements regarding the most effective ways to teach children of color.[8] For example, Delpit (1988) has argued that disagreements between black and white educators over skills training versus process-oriented approaches to language arts and reading instruction essentially represent a plea on the part of black educators to make the codes of mainstream culture – discourse patterns, interactional styles, and spoken and written language codes – explicit to students so they can master and use them in order to advance in mainstream society, if they choose to do so. Delpit argues that process-oriented, progressive educational techniques can, in their indirectness, seem not to teach anything, but rather to hide the codes even further. The issue, she argues, is not whether basic skills or higher-order thinking skills should be taught, but that both be taught, be seen as taught, as alternative codes that students can adopt at will as matters of personal choice or in response to task demands.[9]

The multicultural dimension of school mathematics reform. Addressing the cognitive–cultural educational interface will require increased attention both to children's characteristic ways of thinking and reasoning in different settings, including their everyday lives in their home communities, and to the contexts provided by those everyday lives for the exploration of mathematics. Secada (1991) has argued, for example, that the inclusion (or exclusion) of certain contexts in the mathematics curriculum provides (or withholds) affirmation of the legitimacy of those contexts for exploring mathematical ideas:

Unless the mathematics curriculum includes real contexts that reflect the lived realities of people who are members of equity groups and unless those contexts are rich in the sorts of mathematics which can be drawn from them, we are likely to stereotype mathematics as knowledge that belongs to a few privileged groups. (p. 49)

This notion can be actualized in a wide range of approaches, including making systematic efforts to find appropriate mathematical problem contexts in the everyday lives of children; connecting mathematics to topics or persons in history, art, music, or other areas of cultural relevance to the ethnic and social groups to which children belong; and using mathematics to analyze problems of deep concern and relevance to members of various ethnic or social communities, such as the analysis of systematic patterns of racism in housing, banking, or colonialist foreign policy decisions (Shan & Bailey, 1991).

These ideas about weaving the cultural backgrounds and life experiences of students into the fabric of the school mathematics curriculum are compatible with the suggestions of many educators who have advocated the need for a multicultural curriculum for culturally diverse student populations. For example, Gay (1988) points out that conventional school tasks have been conducive to providing learning opportunities for Caucasian students, and that it is equally important to provide non-Caucasian learners with opportunities and experiences that are as conducive to their successful learning. Moreover, she underscores the importance of selecting and using instructional materials that are representative of a wide variety of different ethnic and cultural group experiences.

Further indication that the mathematics education reform perspective may be successfully merged with the cultural concerns of educators of children of color can be drawn from recent work by Ladson-Billings (1990, 1992). Her analyses of effective elementary school teachers of African American students in urban schools suggests the importance of "culturally relevant" teaching, in which important characteristics of the students and their local community culture are linked to classroom instructional practice and expectations for student outcomes. Among the characteristics of culturally relevant teaching that Ladson-Billings identifies are a teacher's belief that all children can succeed, an orientation toward helping students develop their own ways of knowing and understanding rather than "telling" and "putting knowledge into" the students, and a vision of the class as a community of learners for whom knowledge is viewed critically and within which students are encouraged to learn collaboratively. Although Ladson-Billings has not focused on the characteristics of successful teaching of mathematics per se, one can certainly see a close affinity between many of the characteristics of successful teachers of urban African American children that she has identified and ideas espoused in the mathematics education reform documents and in some descriptions of innovative mathematics teaching in nonurban settings (e.g., Lampert, 1986, 1990; National Council of Teachers of Mathematics, 1991).[10]

Summary

Improving the mathematical proficiency of all American students requires fundamental changes in the way that mathematics education is conducted in the nation's classrooms – changes that involve not only enriching instruction by expanding the range of pedagogical strategies employed and the range of topics and skills taught, but also finding ways to connect the desired outcomes to children's natural ways of thinking and reasoning and to their lives and experiences outside of school. From an equity perspective, the challenge is to provide a new form of education in *all* schools, with special attention to those schools serving the children of greatest need.

Despite the obvious need to do so, it will undoubtedly be quite difficult to make changes in instructional practice that both respond to the concerns identified and align with the goals and standards of the school mathematics reform movement. Many of the complex challenges are identified in this chapter. In addition, at the middle school level, there are a few additional challenges. For example, imperfect student performance in the area of basic arithmetic skills creates public pressure for substantial attention to these topics in the middle school. Thus, it will be necessary to invent forms of instruction that blend experience with basic-level and higher-level mathematical tasks. Moreover, teachers at the middle school level often lack substantial background and training in mathematics, so the development of new teaching styles to assist students in solving more challenging mathematical problems will undoubtedly be difficult. In addition, teachers often lack the knowledge and experience that may be required to make salient the relevance of mathematics to the lives of the students they teach. Thus, it is essential that substantial attention be given to the needs of teachers as well as those of students. Despite these challenges, it is clear that much must be done and much can be done. The examples provided in the next section illustrate some of the possibilities.

Improving the accessibility, quality, and relevance of middle school mathematics instruction: Examples from QUASAR schools

The examples discussed in this section are faithful reproductions of actual occurrences.[11] They have been chosen to illustrate key points in the narrative. They are representative not in the sense that they are "typical" practices seen every day in every classroom in every QUASAR school, but rather in the sense that they are illustrative of the kinds of efforts being made by teachers to provide a mathematics education that is fundamentally different in kind from that which has generally been provided to middle school students in poor communities in the nation. Our use of these examples is not intended to convey the message that an ideal state has been achieved in these classrooms, nor that every classroom in every school would produce such examples. QUASAR is definitely a story of "work in progress" – of the struggle to change instruction in ways that are fundamentally different from conventional practice. Instead of choosing examples that illustrate the frustrations and defeats inherent in the struggle to change – and there are such cases – we have selected from the many examples that illustrate successes and possibilities. Although many of our choices focus on teachers and instructional practice rather than on students and learning outcomes, the major motivation for these instructional change efforts is to increase the learning opportunities and successes of students.

Increasing access to high-quality mathematics instruction

In response to low student participation rates in academic mathematics coursework at the secondary school level and the disastrous consequences for students' life chances, teachers and resource partners at schools involved in the QUASAR Project have committed themselves to preparing students either to take and pass college preparatory mathematics courses in secondary school, or to enroll in and successfully complete suitable technical career training. The goal of preparing middle school students so that they have increased access to "gateway" (e.g., nonremedial) mathematics experiences in the secondary school was frequently mentioned in the applications received from schools wishing to participate in the QUASAR Project. For example, an application from one of the selected sites asserted: "By influencing mathematics achievement and attitudes towards mathematics at the middle school level, greater numbers of historically underrepresented students can become better prepared for more challenging mathematics coursework in high school and beyond."

Detracking: Removing the barriers and opening the doors. In order to increase student access at the secondary school level, it is not sufficient to upgrade the quality of the content and instruction only for some classes and some students. Therefore, efforts at QUASAR sites are being made to ensure broad access to enhanced instructional program elements. Rather than assuming that only a few students can be successful, the operating assumption in QUASAR programs is that virtually all children can learn the content of middle school mathematics sufficiently well to pursue a challenging mathematics program at the secondary school level successfully. Since most of the children enter these middle schools with substantial deficits in reading comprehension and arithmetic computation as measured by performance on standardized tests, the assumption underlying these programs is quite revolutionary and the challenges are numerous.

As noted in the earlier discussion of current instructional practice, it is quite common at the middle school level for students to be tracked into different classes on the basis of presumed ability. In these different tracks, students pursue different curricula or the same curricula at markedly different speeds. This practice has led to unequal opportunity for children in the lower tracks to pursue courses with higher-level goals and objectives. The generally pernicious effects of these practices were discussed earlier in the chapter, and the extensive research on this topic has been elegantly summarized by Oakes (1992). Of particular importance is the finding that instruction in lower-track courses tends to omit any treatment of challenging material, thereby further denying students access to high-quality mathematics. Thus, project sites are decreasing the number of academic tracks so as to provide more students with intellectually challenging tasks and high-quality instruction.

Prior to beginning the QUASAR Project, many of the sites, like the vast majority of middle schools in the country, engaged in fairly extensive academic tracking. The abolition of academic tracking was one of the early goals of most project sites. In remarks that are fairly typical of the ideas expressed by people at a number of the sites at the outset of the project, the authors of one site's application expressed the view that tracking based on ability was undesirable for the school's student population because the school's own tracking policies had worked to the cognitive and affective detriment of too many students: "The self-esteem level and, consequently, the achievement level of students in the lower tracks has suffered greatly." In a comment that reflects the thinking of many QUASAR teachers fairly well, a teacher at one of the sites noted that "a lot of the kids that are classified as lost, or turned off, or unintelligent, or whatever, really have some powerful ideas and some powerful ways of thinking, and exposing the other kids to that and them to the ways the other kids think is just too powerful to overlook."

Despite the conviction of most site participants that tracking should be eliminated, there exist political and educational realities that prevent complete implementation of this belief. At most of the sites, it has been standard practice to identify a high-ability group that is designated to take algebra in eighth grade. In most cases, this practice began many years ago in order to prevent migration of academically talented students to magnet schools outside the community. Even after the inception of the QUASAR Project at these school sites, the "advanced" group has continued to exist, thereby creating an upper-level track. Nevertheless, other tracks have been eliminated at the schools. Moreover, site participants expect that, as the regular mathematics classes place greater emphasis on high-level mathematics, the remaining distinctions among tracks will blur and eventually disappear, as it becomes clear that all students are receiving a strong academic mathematics program.

Addressing mathematics instruction in special classes. Another way to decrease tracking is by offering all children, even those who receive instruction in "special service" programs, a similar diet of mathematics instruction that includes a broad range of curriculum and an emphasis on understanding, reasoning, and problem solving. As a result of state or federal mandates, schools are often required to offer differentiated services to some students with special needs (e.g., Chapter 1, special education, or bilingual education). If teachers in these special programs work with their colleagues who teach mainstream mathematics classes, they may also be able to provide richer mathematical experiences for their students. At QUASAR sites, special-program teachers are often involved in staff development activities and in meetings to discuss program philosophy, goals, and progress. Early experience suggests that this can have a beneficial impact on teachers and students.

As would be expected, all QUASAR schools are eligible to provide Chapter 1 services to a substantial portion of their student populations. Thus, Chapter 1 is an important component of the mathematics instruction available to students in QUASAR schools. Several sites have been designated as School-Wide Projects because of the large number of students eligible to receive Chapter 1 services. At other sites, the number of students eligible for Chapter 1 services may be three or four times greater than the number actually being served.

Unlike conventional Chapter 1 instruction, which is often disconnected from the mainstream mathematics instruction that students receive, the Chapter 1 instruction at several QUASAR sites involved teachers who work closely with their colleagues who are teaching mainstream mathematics classes. By keeping abreast of the activities and emphases in the curriculum of the mainstream classes, the Chapter 1 teachers are better able to help students engage in challenging mathematical tasks. One tactic that has been used with success involves the Chapter 1 teacher "preteaching" difficult material in order to assist students in developing deeper understanding of concepts or better computational fluency related to topics that are about to be taught in mainstream instruction. After this preteaching, the Chapter 1 students are better able to participate fully in the regular class activity and achieve success.

As the following story illustrates, efforts are also being made to provide richer instructional opportunities for students enrolled in special education classes. Ms. Jones,[12] the teacher of special education classes at one QUA-SAR site, has been participating in mathematics-staff development activities since the beginning of the project. These activities include: attending workshops designed to introduce teachers to new materials that serve to improve both pedagogical and content knowledge; participating in meetings with colleagues to discuss curriculum, read research reports, and reflect on their practice; and engaging in formal and informal opportunities to talk with colleagues and resource partners about what students know and are able to do mathematically. Her involvement in these activities has had bidirectional impact. Although not a member of the core mathematics faculty, Ms. Jones apparently affected her colleagues through the questions and concerns she raised in discussions, as the following quote from one of them illustrates: "Her questions led me to see some other ways to help kids understand. And we came up with manipulatives also which will help her kids. . . . It was helpful to me and to her." As a result of her interaction with the other mathematics teachers, Ms. Jones altered her instructional program to include activities that involve more than computational proficiency, which is typically the focus of mathematics instruction in special education classes.

Beyond the benefits that accrue to Ms. Jones and her colleagues, it is clear that her students have also benefited. The value for the children in her classes became evident in an unsolicited letter sent to the school's principal by an academic specialist whose job involves traveling throughout the school district to test and evaluate children receiving special education services. The letter writer indicated that students tested at this middle school differed in several ways from their peers at other middle schools in the district: (a) They tended to score higher than other students on the mathematics subtests; (b) they understood more readily what was asked of them; (c) they appeared to be more confident; and (d) numerous students achieved "spectacular skills, way beyond their potential or cognitive level." Although it is not possible to validate the accuracy of these claims, it appears reasonably certain that the mathematical performance of Ms. Jones's special education students is exceptional in some important ways.

Although there are some clear successes evident in a story such as this, it should not be assumed that attempts to provide challenging tasks and high-quality mathematics instruction throughout the school do not encounter serious challenges. For example, not all special program teachers are willing to devote their attention to innovative instruction or to increasing their own knowledge of mathematics content. Moreover, significant challenges must also be met in the regular mathematics classes. As schools develop organizational ways to reduce tracking, teachers find themselves challenged to meet the needs of increasingly heterogeneous groups of students in their mathematics classes. Therefore, in addition to removing institutional barriers, it is important to focus on the nature of the instructional environments in which students are asked to learn mathematics and on the new forms of instructional practice needed to support that learning.

Improving the quality of mathematics instruction:
Building communities of learners

In her review of research on teaching high-level thinking and reasoning skills, Resnick (1987) concluded that developing higher-order cognitive abilities requires shaping a disposition to thought through participation in social communities that value thinking and independent judgment. This suggests a view of mathematics classrooms as communities of collaborative, reflective practice, in which students are challenged to think deeply about and to participate actively in engaging the mathematics they are learning. As Silver, Kilpatrick, and Schlesinger (1990) have argued, "Within communities, the need for communication is obvious. Within mathematical communities, communication in the form of discussion, argument, proof, and justification is natural" (p. 23). In such communities, students would be expected not only to listen but also to speak mathematics themselves, as they discuss observations and share explanations, verifications, reasons, and generalizations. In such classrooms, students would have opportunities to see, hear, debate, and evaluate mathematical explanations and justifications. These classrooms, as Silver et al. have noted, become places in which "the emphasis is less on memorizing procedures and producing answers and more on analyzing, reasoning and becoming convinced" (1990, p. 38). Thus, such classroom communities represent a new vision of mathematics education – a vision compatible with the precepts of the contemporary reform documents and aimed at eradicating the legacy of conventional instructional practices, as well as allowing equitable access to high-quality mathematics instruction and challenging content for all students.

As the preponderance of instructional data discussed earlier reveals, such classroom communities of mathematical practice are relatively rare in American schools. They have been described in a few places (e.g., Lampert, 1986; National Council of Teachers of Mathematics, 1991), but such descriptions have generally not been drawn from schools serving the children of greatest need. There is reason to believe that all students can benefit from learning in classroom communities in which higher-level thinking and communication are emphasized. A recent examination of the educational practices used with linguistically and culturally diverse student populations found that collaboration and communication were key elements of effective instructional practice at all levels of the educational system and that the curriculum contained a blend of both challenging and basic academic material (Garcia, 1991). Surely, exceptional examples of such instruction exist today in some classrooms in some schools in some communities in the

United States, but the challenge is to make this kind of mathematics instruction the norm rather than the exception. The experiences of teachers in QUASAR schools in their efforts to create such communities will not only be informative about the nature of classroom communities of mathematical practice but also be an important component of any convincing demonstration that this view of mathematics education can be beneficial for all students.

Cooperative groups: Fostering communication and collaboration. In QUASAR classrooms, many teachers are using cooperative learning groups as a means of fostering cooperation and communication among students to cope with the wide range of student abilities and prior achievements in their school's detracked mathematics instructional program. In cooperative groups, students at different levels of mathematical knowledge and understanding can work collaboratively to solve problems and explore ideas. In the cooperative groups, students have opportunities to communicate their ideas to other students, and they also get to hear the ideas of their peers.

At one site, the students in Ms. Newman's class spend most of their time working within a four-person, mixed-ability group. In order to foster diverse interactions and avoid social problems that may arise in long-term groupings, Ms. Newman changes group membership periodically. The groups have well-defined rules for behavior and roles (e.g., reader, recorder), which usually rotate among group members over time. In Ms. Newman's class, the rules and norms for group functioning are designed to help students work with a high degree of cooperation and self-sufficiency. For example, each group gets only one copy of an assignment (rather than each member having a copy); raising a hand to ask a question of the teacher indicates that this is a question that no one in the group can answer (and the teacher often checks this before answering a query); and raising a hand to answer a question asked by the teacher means that everyone in the group can answer the question (and so the teacher may call on anyone in the group and not just the person whose hand is raised). Each member of a group is responsible for understanding the tasks on which the group is working, and, after completion of the assignment, each member must be able not only to provide a final answer but also to explain the strategies and reasoning that led to the final group answer. To one of Ms. Newman's favorite questions, "What do you have to do to understand?" her students respond, "Communicate!"

At another QUASAR site, Mr. Henderson also uses cooperative groups in his mathematics classes. Students in his school, where mathematics achievement on a locally administered standardized test ranges from the 15th to the 98th percentile, are grouped heterogeneously for mathematics instruction. Posters, prominently displayed in Mr. Henderson's classroom, provide slogans that remind students of the value of collaboration: "One for all – all for one" and "Many hands make the burden light." Other posters in the room display statements that students are encouraged to use when working together in cooperative groups: "Good answer," "You can do it," "Tell us how you would do it," "Where are you stuck?" "You're on the right track," "Give it a try," "We'll help you through it," "Believe in yourself," "What is the problem asking for?" and "You're not a quitter." Making effective use of cooperative groups in such settings, however, requires more than arranging diverse groups of students around tables and displaying inspirational posters on classroom walls. Attention must be paid not only to the organization and inspiration of students in the room but also to the kinds of mathematical tasks being used.

QUASAR teachers in cooperative groups frequently use tasks that have multiple entry points, multiple solution paths, and often more than one correct answer. The mathematics tasks used in conventional instruction focus on well-rehearsed procedures for obtaining a single correct solution and emphasize only reading, writing, and computation as the major vehicles for learning. In contrast, tasks used in project classrooms often draw on a greater diversity of students' abilities and talents. The tasks often allow successful completion through use of a wider range of intelligences (Gardner, 1982) and intellectual skills, including visual and spatial acuity, nonverbal representational skills, logical reasoning, and written and oral communication skills.

Consider the following summary of one of Mr. Henderson's class sessions devoted to the topic of surface area and volume. Each group was given a set of 24 cubes and asked to construct a rectangular solid, or box, using all 24 cubes; to draw a sketch of the solid that they constructed; to find the area, surface area, and dimensions of the box they constructed; and to record their results. After a brief presentation and discussion of the task, Mr. Henderson set the groups to work, as he circulated around the room checking on the process of each group. Once a group completed a cycle for one solid, they were encouraged to continue the process with a different solid. When sufficient progress had been made, members of each group presented their results, which were compiled in a table (Figure 1.1).

Students were then asked to make a generalization about the solids and the compiled data in the table. A student noted that longer boxes had greater surface areas than shorter, more compact boxes, and the class agreed with this analysis. Mr. Henderson asked the class to explore how the surface area would be affected if a "compact" rectangular solid were cut in half and the two halves were placed end-to-end to make it longer, or if one of the "long" solids were cut and reassembled to be more compact. After exploration in small groups, followed by whole-class discussion, the class concluded that the surface area (a) increases as the height decreases

Dimensions	Surface Area	Volume
1 x 1 x 24	98	24
1 x 2 x 12	76	24
1 x 3 x 8	70	24
1 x 4 x 6	68	24
2 x 2 x 6	56	24
2 x 3 x 4	52	24

Figure 1.1. Dimensions and surface areas for rectangular solids with volume 24.

and the length and width increase and (b) decreases as the length, width, and height become numerically closer. Mr. Henderson then asked students to speculate about the smallest surface area possible for a 24-cube rectangular solid, if they were allowed to "cut up" the cubes. After some discussion, the group came to the conclusion that a cube would have the smallest possible surface area. The lesson concluded with students writing in journals about the relationship between volume and surface area.

This task illustrates several features of the kind of mathematics instruction teachers are striving for in QUASAR classrooms. It was exploratory in nature. It involved the integration of basic skills (multiplication and/or addition in calculating volume and surface area) with higher-level processes (making and testing conjectures, making judgments, and forming generalizations based on patterns in data). The task also accommodated multiple modalities of information processing and answer production, since it involved spatial, visual, written, and oral communication: Students used three-dimensional cubes to build boxes, made two-dimensional sketches of the boxes, recorded observations in a chart, discussed observations orally, and recorded conclusions in written form in a journal. The task was accessible to all students in the class, yet it offered sufficient challenge for the most able students in the class. The organization of students into cooperative groups allowed students with different abilities and interests to bring their knowledge and talents to bear on the completion of the task.

Supporting mathematical thinking and communication. Unfortunately, a crucial ingredient in implementing new forms of instructional practice successfully was not salient in the above example in Mr. Henderson's class.

Simply putting students into cooperative learning groups to work on tasks that are open to multiple routes of exploration is insufficient to ensure that they will learn. Whether in small groups or in large group discussions, a critical aspect of building classroom learning communities for students is the creation of an atmosphere of trust and mutual respect. Without such an atmosphere, students will be reluctant to posit their tentative ideas and hypotheses, to question assertions that are puzzling to them, or to share their alternative interpretations. The students in Mr. Henderson's class were willing to share their hypotheses and have them tested by their peers. How is such a classroom environment established?

In their efforts to create an atmosphere conducive to learning, teachers at QUASAR schools are often supported by schoolwide efforts to create trust and mutual respect. Such efforts are probably essential in creating a generally supportive environment within which the mathematics teachers can create classroom communities where mathematical ideas are explored freely, where students need not fear error or ridicule. In classrooms of middle school students, who are self-conscious and socially anxious anyway, the building of an open atmosphere of trust and respect is no small challenge, especially since there is a tension between encouraging students to question each other's ideas and assertions and yet demanding that students respect each other as persons. In these classroom communities, it becomes acceptable to criticize someone's ideas but not to criticize the person. The combination of a supportive environment in the school and within the mathematics classroom allows students to develop greater confidence in themselves as learners and deeper respect for themselves and others as human beings. These outcomes are vitally important for students whose lives outside of school are often filled with the negative images projected by the larger society on the culturally diverse. In addition to the affective value that school and classroom support provides for students, there are also cognitive payoffs when students are able to use their minds freely in exploring and exchanging their mathematical ideas with their teacher and their peers.

Another QUASAR teacher, Ms. Healy, has also worked hard to establish an atmosphere of mutual trust and respect in her classroom, in which she says her students "feel safe to make what we would call mistakes" and so that the "fear of wrong answers goes away." She expects her students to take risks by expressing their ideas openly in class, to make presentations of their solutions and their reasoning, and to ask questions if they do not understand another student's presentation. Ms. Healy openly acknowledges, to students and observers alike, that these expectations can be "scary" for the members of her class, so she offers consistent support. She emphasizes that there are no "dumb questions" in her classroom and that it is acceptable to struggle with ideas and to be unsure.

In Ms. Healy's class, the focus is not on "getting the right answer in the

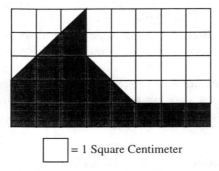

□ = 1 Square Centimeter

Figure 1.2. Homework problem on metric area measure.

right way," but rather on students communicating and trying to make sense of mathematics together as a community. In her role as facilitator, Ms. Healy tries to help the group achieve consensus through a give-and-take process that often involves several students sharing their thinking at the overhead projector, amid debate and questioning by peers. In this classroom, students are supported as they take substantial responsibility for their own learning.

Learning to question and coming to understand. One lesson observed in Ms. Healy's classroom reveals some facets of community building that may encourage students to share their ideas and to seek clarification until they reach suitable levels of understanding. After a session in which students explored area and linear measure using metric units, Ms. Healy gave her class as homework problems four irregular shapes, one of which is shown in Figure 1.2, in which the area was to be determined in square centimeters and square millimeters.

On the day following the homework assignment, the class began with a student (Ellen) at the overhead projector explaining her solution and her strategy for finding the area (in square centimeters) of the shape in Figure 1.2. She explained that she "just counted" to obtain 17½ cm² and pointed to each square or half square as she counted up to a total of 17½ squares. In response to a student question regarding the counting of the half squares, Ellen indicated that she knew that "two halves make a whole," and that the diagonal line divided a square into two halves. The class unanimously agreed that Ellen's solution was correct and that the area could also be correctly represented as 17.5 cm². There was, however, far less unanimity regarding the matter of expressing the area in square millimeters. Many students indicated that they had difficulty on the homework and voiced confusion, so Ms. Healy asked students to work with their partners to determine the solution. Students had a variety of materials available to them, including centimeter square pieces, metric rulers, and calculators.

As students worked with partners, Ms. Healy conversed with various student pairs, asking them to explain and justify their work. After a few minutes, Ms. Healy asked a student, Larry, to explain his solution. Larry indicated that he obtained the answer of 170 by multiplying 17 by 10, because for "every one centimeter there is 10 millimeters." Six students indicated that they also had obtained the answer 170, but most students did not get the same answer. Ms. Healy encouraged students to ask Larry questions about his reasoning and solution process. One student questioned the use of 17 rather than 17.5, to which Larry responded that he "dropped the .5" because it was "more complicated" and reiterated that you just multiply by 10 because "a centimeter is equal to 10 millimeters." Another student thought that multiplication was the correct idea, but that the factor should be 100 rather than 10, since each centimeter square was 10 mm x 10 mm. This student argued that the answer should be 1,750 mm². Yet another student returned to the assertion that 17 was easier to deal with than 17.5, and argued that it wasn't, since "you just move the decimal over when you multiply by 10." The class then discussed whether the decimal point would move to the right or the left after the number was multiplied by 10. Occasionally, Ms. Healy asked questions to attempt to steer "off track" discussion back to what she judged to be the important mathematical issues.

After deciding the direction of the "moving decimal point," another student, Natalie, returned to an observation made previously by another student and asserted that each square centimeter was actually 100 square millimeters, after which Ms. Healy asked her to explain her reasoning. At the overhead projector, Natalie illustrated her assertion with a 10 X 10 square, which she asked her classmates to think of as one square centimeter "blown up" to make it clear that it was also a 10 mm X 10 mm square (see Figure 1.3). Natalie argued that since each centimeter square was equivalent to 100 mm squares, 17.5 cm² was equivalent to 1,750 mm². After Natalie completed this explanation, another student said: "Bravo, Bravo! I agree with you one hundred percent!" However, there was still some disagree-

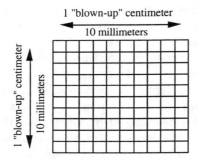

Figure 1.3. "Blow-up" model of a centimeter square.

ment in the class. Ms. Healy indicated that "it's okay to think differently," and allowed even further discussion. Despite the fact that some students were frustrated and asked Ms. Healy to "just tell us the answer so we can move on," she refused to do so. She insisted that it was crucial for the class to reach agreement about the matter under discussion and dispute, or else the rest of the assignment would be pointless.

The class eventually reached consensus around Natalie's approach, but only after further discussion of the differences between linear and area measure, which was the intended focus of the lesson sequence. As students began to articulate their misunderstandings, it became clear that they were applying rules of linear measure (one centimeter equals 10 millimeters) to area measure. At one point, Natalie returned to the overhead projector to demonstrate that the measure of the length was indeed 10 times larger in millimeters, but she pointed out that there are two lengths – one on each side of the square – so that the measure of the area of the square in square millimeters is actually 10 x 10 bigger in square millimeters. She went on to show that this could also be related to the "move the decimal point" explanation, since 10 x 10 was 100 and corresponded to moving the decimal point two decimal places, one place for each 10. Ms. Healy then provided some additional activities to reinforce Natalie's explanation.

Several things are noteworthy about this vignette from Ms. Healy's classroom. First, the students were engaged in debate about mathematical assertions, and they used mathematical argumentation to support differing positions. Ms. Healy showed that she valued student ideas by listening carefully to students' explanations. The students, in turn, listened to each other respectfully, though they were not always convinced of another's point. Second, the activity was more about sense making than about generating answers. Throughout the activity just discussed, the teacher's focus remained on helping students develop a conceptual understanding of the relationship between linear and area measure. Rather than providing a set of rules and procedures to be remembered, Ms. Healy insisted that students explain their thinking and make sense of the mathematics involved in the problem.

In a conventional mathematics classroom, a teacher would be expected to provide a "rule" for converting from square centimeters to square millimeters, to present it to the students, work an example or two, and then have students practice the rule on a set of assigned problems. From that perspective, it was clearly "inefficient" to spend so much time on this single problem. By so doing, however, Ms. Healy was encouraging students to persevere in understanding a problem and in obtaining a sensible solution, which are both important goals in the learning of mathematics. Although painful and difficult at times, such meandering journeys to mathematical outcomes that make sense for students have benefits that can be measured in terms of both cognitive growth and dispositional outcomes. Students in Ms. Healy's class have responsibility for their own learning, and they know that their learning depends on their continuing to question until they understand. In Ms. Healy's classroom, she and her students have formed a community in which they work together to develop shared understandings about mathematics. Students felt comfortable sharing their thinking, and they were comfortable challenging each other's ideas. Ms. Healy and her students have created a community in which explanation, questioning, argumentation, and sense making are a normal part of mathematics class. It is interesting to note that many features of Ms. Healy's class – a nonthreatening atmosphere, connected discourse, broad participation with self-selected turns – have been identified as characteristic of effective instruction for linguistically diverse learners (Garcia, 1991; Goldenberg, 1991).

Building communities of linguistically diverse learners. Despite encouraging evidence that learning communities can be successfully created for linguistically diverse student populations, teachers face special challenges in creating safe and supportive environments in these situations. In special "bilingual mathematics" classes, the teacher and students share more than one language and must negotiate meaning within dialogue that often moves freely between languages. In regular mathematics classes populated at least in part by children whose native language is not English, the challenges are even greater. In addition to providing an excellent discussion of many issues related to bilingualism and the instructional emphases in current mathematics education reform efforts, Secada (1992a) provides a compelling discussion of the ways in which students with limited proficiency in English can be "left out" of the discourse in communication-rich mathematics classes, even when the lesson is being conducted by an exceptional mathematics teacher. Children may feel most comfortable expressing their ideas in a language other than English, and this may be a language with which the teacher has little or no fluency.

At one QUASAR site, an effort has been made to employ mathematics teachers who speak Spanish, which is the first language of the majority of students attending the middle school. Conversations among students and between teachers and students in many classrooms, not only those officially designated bilingual, are often conducted in Spanish or involve discourse that moves freely back and forth between English and Spanish. Locally developed mathematics instructional materials are prepared and provided simultaneously to all students in both languages (on the same page or on separate pages), thereby affording students the option of reading and/or responding in either language. More recently, an effort has also been made to have some commercial materials, which are already prepared in English, translated into Spanish for use at the school. The availability of mathematics problems in both languages affords students an opportunity to choose the language with which they are most comfortable or to combine their use of languages. For example, it is not uncommon to see an English response to a Spanish task (or vice versa), or a response that contains elements of both languages.

At another QUASAR site, where students speak a variety of languages and most of the teachers speak only English, Mr. Edwards works with the students in his classroom to develop a shared meaning of mathematics vocabulary and relies on students working together to provide translations to classmates and to the teacher, as discourse often moves among several languages. In this setting, Mr. Edwards is working hard to respect the needs of many children to express their ideas in other languages, to provide an environment that supports such expression by the children, and to assure that the ideas being communicated are in a form that can be understood by him and by other students in the classroom community. Even in settings that are not officially multilingual, teachers face a similar issue because children often have informal ways of expressing themselves that may be unfamiliar to the teacher. It would be easy but unwise for those of us interested in mathematics education reform to minimize the challenges that such situations present. As teachers struggle to create supportive classroom environments in which children can express their mathematical ideas freely, they are redefining schooling in revolutionary ways that honor rather than devalue children's non–school-based language and experience.

Enhancing the relevance of school mathematics

Within the QUASAR Project, teachers are attempting to make mathematics more relevant to the lives and cultures of their students. In this section, some examples of these attempts are presented. Three areas are described: (a) building upon problem-solving skills developed and used in students' lives outside of school; (b) relating mathematics to students' interests; and (c) connecting mathematics to the cultural heritage of students.

Building upon students' life experiences. In their application to become part of the QUASAR Project, teachers at one selected site noted that their "mathematics instruction did not consider, nor did it utilize, the cultural background of their student population," nor did it capitalize on the array of problem-solving skills students brought with them from their home environments. In the first year of the project at that school, explicit attention to students' nonschool knowledge and problem solving surfaced in an interesting way. Teachers had administered an open-ended task (shown here), which had been sent as practice task to help students prepare for the administration of the QUASAR Cognitive Assessment Instrument.[13]

Yvonne is trying to decide whether she should buy a weekly bus pass. On Monday, Wednesday, and Friday, she rides the bus to and from work. On Tuesday and Thursday, she rides the bus to work, but gets a ride home with her friends. Should Yvonne buy a weekly bus pass? Explain your answer.

Busy Bus Company Fares
One Way $1.00
Weekly Pass $9.00

At a subsequent meeting, teachers met to discuss their students' performance, which had some surprising aspects. In particular, many students indicated that Yvonne should purchase the weekly pass rather than paying the daily fare, which the teachers believed to be the more economical choice. Curious about this unexpected answer to what the teachers believed to be a rather straightforward question – a multistep arithmetic story problem involving multiplication of whole numbers – they decided to discuss the problem in class and ask students to explain their thinking. The ensuing discussion with students provided an interesting illustration of their application of out-of-school knowledge and problem-solving strategies to a mathematics problem. Many students argued that purchasing the weekly pass was a much better decision because the pass could allow many members of a family to use it (e.g., after work and in the evenings), and it could also be used by a family member on weekends. Students' reasoning about this problem – situated in the context of urban living and the cost-effective use of public transportation – demonstrated to the teachers that there was more than one "correct" answer to this problem.[14] This experience made it clear to the teachers that if their goal was assessing what students know and are able to do, then it was essential that students not only provide answers but also explain their thinking and reasoning. The experience with the Busy Bus Company problem illustrates that increasing the relevance of school mathematics to the lives of children involves more than merely providing "real world" contexts for mathematics problems; real world solutions for those problems must also be considered. Until the forms of reasoning and problem solving that are developed and used in out-of-school settings are brought into close contact with the forms of reasoning and problem solving being developed in school mathematics, attempts at increased relevance are doomed to failure. Moreover, unless different forms of reasoning and problem solving are considered in school, there will be little chance for students to come to understand the conditions that optimize the application of each form.

In addition to considering problems and solutions that relate to the lives of the children, it is also possible to use instructional practices that build on the life experiences of the student population. At one site, which serves a predominantly Latino population, students spend most of their class time exploring mathematical tasks in small groups or pairs. Teachers and resource partners feel that the extensive use of cooperative learning builds on cultural values and expectations by promoting team work rather than individual accomplishment; by encouraging students to help each other in a noncompetitive environment the way they would be expected to help a sibling, and by fostering the oral communication of ideas, which is an important feature of their culture.

Relating mathematics to students' interests. Other attempts to increase the relevance of mathematics to the lives of children involve making contact with activities that children find enjoyable and interesting, such as games, stories, dramatic play, and music. For example, most children, even early adolescents, enjoy having someone read stories to them. Beyond its relevance to the "culture of childhood," storytelling is also an important feature of the oral tradition of many cultural groups. Dramatic, storylike settings can also be used to provide contexts for mathematical exploration or problem solving. An excerpt from the instructional activity at one QUASAR site illustrates the way in which storytelling can be integrated with mathematical problem solving. Ms. Bensen gave a dramatic reading in story form of the logic puzzle, "A Mathematical Tug of War" (Burns, 1982), to her eighth-grade students. In the first round of the contest that forms the context for this problem, four (equally strong) acrobats are pitted against five (equally strong) grandmas in a tug-of-war, and the result is a draw. In the second round, one of the acrobats and two of the grandmas are pitted against Ivan the wonder dog, and the result is another draw. The students are challenged to determine the result of the final round of this contest, in which Ivan and three of the grandmas will oppose the four acrobats. The students were directed to solve the problem, and then to prepare a written explanation of their method, reasoning, and a justification of their solution. Ms. Bensen read the solutions at home that evening and then invited some students to present their solutions to the entire class the next day.

Although this problem has only one clearly correct answer, the students used a variety of strategies to solve it. Some students solved the problem using diagrams and pictures to depict a series of equivalent substitutions that could be used to determine the final outcome; their diagrams and pictures were often aesthetically pleasing and artistically rich. Other students provided natural language descriptions of their thinking, using deductive reasoning based on the equivalent quantities in the problem. This verbal, deductive approach was used by Stephanie, whose solution is shown here:

> Three grandmas and Ivan is against 4 acrobats. Ivan is as strong as two grandma's and 1 acrobat. So in the last contest really its five grandmas and one acrobat. In the first contest it was five grandma's against four acrobats. The grandmas and acrobats had the same amount of strength. In the second contest Ivan had the same amount of strength as two grandma's and one

acrobat. As we have stated Ivan is as strong as two grandma's and one acrobat. He already has three grandma's on his team, so its five grandma's and one acrobat when you substituted grandmas and acrobats for Ivan. So its five grandmas and one acrobat against four acrobats. I have seen that five grandmas are as strong as four acrobats but the grandma's have one extra acrobat on their team. Since the five grandmas are as strong as four acrobats but the extra acrobat pulls the four acrobats over the line. So I know that the team with Ivan and the three grandmas will be the winners.

Finally, some other students employed more formal algebra-style approaches (e.g., Michael's solution, shown below), in which relationships among quantities were represented with equations involving invented notation.

(Rd. 1)	$4\,a = 5\,g$
(Rd. 2)	$I = 2\,g, 1\,a$
(Rd. 3)	$I, 3\,g\,?\,4\,a$

$$\text{If } I = 2\,g, 1\,a \text{ (Rd. 2)}$$
$$I, 3\,g = 2\,g + 3\,g, 1\,a = 5\,g, 1\,a$$
$$\text{If } 5\,g = 4\,a \text{ (Rd. 1)}$$
$$5\,g, 1\,a > 4\,a$$

From the information given, I came to the conclusion that Ivan is an equivalent of 2 grandmas and 1 acrobat, plus 3 grandmas. That means you add the 2 grandmas and 3 grandmas, giving 5 grandmas, plus the remaining acrobat. So 5 grandmas and 1 acrobat will overpower 4 acrobats.

In this instructional excerpt, the integration of storytelling and mathematical problem solving provided an engaging context in which students sought to solve a complex mathematical problem, to explain and justify in writing the thinking and reasoning they used, and to experience multiple approaches to the problem via the presentation and discussion of solutions in class. In addition, their work on the problem allowed students to use approaches that were compatible with their strengths and interests, such as visually based solutions for students with artistic interest and talent. Students who used less sophisticated procedures were able to see more elegant or powerful solutions demonstrated and made available for inspection and discussion. Since this was also true in the case of the Busy Bus Company problem, this instructional approach illustrates not only an attempt to increase the relevance of mathematics instruction but also the provision of mathematical activities and problems that allow a variety of solution methods, so as to build both on children's strengths and on their natural ways of thinking and reasoning.

The example just discussed shows how a mathematical problem can be embedded in a dramatic, storylike setting to engage children's attention. Many stories, poems, and other forms of literature can be used to stimulate mathematical investigation and problem solving, even if they are not already stated in the form of a mathematics problem. For example, teachers at several sites have used many of the poems from anthologies, such as *Where the Sidewalk Ends* (Silverstein, 1974), as opportunities for thinking, reasoning, and problem solving, as well as for student self-expression.

In one instructional episode, students in Ms. Norton's class were presented with the poem entitled "Smart" (Silverstein, 1974), which begins with a man giving his son a $1 bill, and then describes various monetary exchanges made by the boy. Mathematics enters into consideration of this poem because the monetary exchanges successively increase the number of coins he possesses but decrease the value of the collection. In fact, after the final exchange, he has only five pennies (and a speechless father!) left. After a dramatic reading of the poem by Ms. Norton, who also taught reading to these students, they were asked to respond to a variety of mathematics and language activities based on the poem: to provide examples that show whether or not the child in the story understood the value of money; to draw a picture of the sequence of money trades occurring in the story; to devise a strategy to help this young man better understand the value of money; to explain whether or not the boy's dad was speechless because, as the boy asserts in the poem, he was so proud of his son; and to rewrite the poem so that it is mathematically correct. Kendra's poem, with correct monetary exchanges for $2, illustrates one student's response to the rewriting of the original poem, which began with $1.

> Smarter Than Before
> My dad gave me 2 dollar bills
> cause I'm his smartest daughter
> and I swapped them for 8 shiny quarters
> cause 8 quarters are the same as 2 dollars.
>
> Just then, along came Myesha
> and just cause she kind,
> she gave me 6 quarters and 5 dimes
> for that is the same as mine.
>
> I took the coins to Arica Thomas
> down at Lee's Store.
> The fool gave me 2 quarters, 1 dollar, and 5 dimes
> Oh, that's the same as before.
>
> And then I went and showed my dad
> He smiled and I saw his teeth.
> He closed his eyes and gave me a big hug,
> Too proud of me to speak.

Beyond connecting to storytelling and dramatic reading, activities such as this can more generally provide interesting contexts for connecting mathematics and literature; for stimulating children's interest in reading, writing, and mathematics; and for engaging children in thinking about situations in which mathematics can be applied.

In addition to literature and poetry, many students are interested in music, and this interest can provide opportunities for students to think creatively about mathematics. In many of the communities in which QUASAR schools are located, "rap" music is popular with many, though not all, students. At several sites, rap music is used occasionally in mathematics instruction as a vehicle for promoting classroom communication.[15] Students are sometimes asked to write rap songs that incorporate mathematics topics from recent lessons. At one site, students also wrote rap songs as a means of expressing their feelings about the new kind of mathematics instruction they were encountering in QUASAR classrooms.

Games are also of interest to middle school students. In addition to being interesting and enjoyable, games provide rich contexts in which children can explore mathematical ideas or practice mathematical skills (Bright, Harvey, & Wheeler, 1985). Some games can also serve as a means of relating mathematics to the cultural or ethnic roots of the children and/or to their lives outside of school. At a staff development session, teachers at a school with a primarily African American student population were introduced to Wari, an African game reputed to be one of the best and oldest in the world (Zaslavsky, 1973).

Games have often fallen short of their potential as teaching tools in mathematics because children can play games without focusing on the mathematics or on the reasoning strategies (Bright et al., 1985). Therefore, since the mathematical concepts and skills (counting and basic concepts of greater than, less than, or equal to) are familiar to middle school students, QUASAR teachers have used Wari as a context in which to focus children's attention on the reasoning and thinking that is embedded in skillful playing of the game. Thus, it provides another opportunity to integrate higher-level and basic-level mathematical thinking.

Use of such recreational pastimes as Wari, which is also known as Mancala, serves the dual purpose of providing an interesting context for exploring mathematical reasoning and content and of exposing children to some aspects of their cultural heritage. For example, as Haggerty (in Zaslavsky, 1973) remarked about the game Wari:

In addition to its value . . . as a means of developing the intuitive abilities so important to problem-solving, there is another outcome equally valuable. This outcome is the recognition of the close identification of the game throughout the history of civilization with the development of systems of numeration and the concept and ideas of number. (p. 131)

Since games, like stories, are a ubiquitous feature of the heritage of all cultural groups, they can be used by thoughtful teachers to serve these dual goals in mathematics classrooms.

Connecting mathematics to students' cultural heritage. As the Wari example suggests, another way that teachers are attempting to develop a multicultural emphasis is by connecting mathematics to historical topics and persons of relevance to the ethnic groups to which children belong. The motivation for such multicultural connections is often related to affective and social rather than cognitive outcomes. As Secada (in press) has suggested, attempts to connect children to persons and topics from their cultural heritage often become ends in themselves and do not actually help children learn and use mathematics. From a mathematics instructional perspective, one would seek culturally relevant materials that could lead not only to positive affective outcomes but also to higher levels of engagement and enhanced learning by students. Multicultural connections are being used in this way at some sites.

At one QUASAR school located in a district that has made a major commitment to the infusion of African American studies into the curriculum, some teachers have been examining ways to develop connections that not only enhance students' knowledge and appreciation of their own cultural heritage but also enrich their mathematics learning. The school district has mandated the use of the African American Baseline Essays (Hilliard & Leonard, 1990)[16] and has facilitated their use by distributing curriculum guides that note explicit connections between topics treated in the essays and specific units or topics in the curriculum in various subject areas, including mathematics. For example, an essay on Egyptian numerals, which includes a discussion of the use of symbols for numbers, is suggested as a component of a mathematics unit on numeration. The essays also highlight the lives of African Americans such as Benjamin Bannaker by providing biographical sketches and examples of the mathematics with which they are associated, to show the rich legacy of mathematical ideas, quantitative thinking, and invention in African American culture. This has led to the expansion of some activities and the creation of new ones. For example, at the suggestion of the site's resource partner, Ms. Jackson used *Africa Counts* (Zaslavsky, 1973) as a source to expand the treatment of Muhammad ibn Muhammad, an 18th-century African astronomer and mathematician. Instead of merely assigning her students a brief biography, Ms. Jackson had students actively investigate magic squares, a mathematical topic explored by this historical figure. In addition to providing the historical–cultural linkage, the assignment provided a useful context for blending the practice of basic arithmetic skills with more complex reasoning skills, such as generalizing.

At another site with a large number of Latino students, teachers have focused on Latin America by working on interdisciplinary units, such as *The Second Voyage of the Mimi* (Bank Street College Project in Science and Mathematics, 1989), that involve mathematics as well as social studies, science, and language. In *The Second Voyage of the Mimi,* the ancient Mayan culture provides a context for exploring astronomy and archaeology, as well as mathematics. The study of Mayan mathematics, embedded in a larger unit on numeration, required students to articulate and apply their understanding of the base-10 number system. In addition to helping students develop a deeper understanding of place value, the experience with *The Second Voyage of the Mimi* provided them with a connection to their culture and an opportunity for students to learn more about the work of scientists.

Although these examples show that efforts are being made to increase the relevance of mathematics to the lives of children, teachers at project sites will undoubtedly continue to struggle with the challenging task of trying to change what and how they teach, as well as making it more relevant to the student population. Many of the changes being made in instructional practice (e.g., use of small-group work, more open-ended problem solving, emphasis on oral and written explanations and justifications of solutions) can be expected to naturally lead to an increased connection between mathematics and children's ways of thinking and reasoning outside of school, but responses to cultural diversity are somewhat more complex. Not surprisingly, the challenges are especially great in those schools in which the student population is culturally diverse, thereby complicating the notion of cultural relevance, or in situations in which there is a mismatch between the cultural background and daily life experience of the teachers and that of their students, thereby limiting the resources and knowledge readily available to the teachers. At one QUASAR site that has both features, the teachers and resource partners developed a plan for a series of workshops and meetings during the school year with experts on cultural diversity and with knowledgeable professionals in the local community to raise teachers' awareness of multicultural issues, to encourage them to infuse multiculturalism into the mathematics curriculum, to give information and resources for such infusion, and to provide opportunities for discussion and ongoing support for implementation during the school year. The teachers now clearly believe that it is worth the effort to find ways to provide high-quality mathematics instruction that is also reasonably well connected to the cultural heritage of their students.

QUASAR, equity, and mathematics education reform: Some final comments

If the current rhetoric about improving the mathematics achievement of American students is to be translated into action, then serious efforts will need to be made in promoting new forms of mathematical literacy and numeracy throughout the school population. The goal must be to offer all students the opportunity to take academically challenging courses at all educational levels. If these efforts succeed, then the benefits to society in the form of a better-skilled work force and a more enlightened citizenry will be substantial. As a nation we can no longer afford to have only a small portion of our students using their minds well in reasoning about quantitative situations.[17] Nor can we afford to lose the advantages of diversity.

QUASAR is a project that offers students attending middle schools in economically disadvantaged communities an enhanced mathematics instructional program. The brief glimpses into QUASAR classrooms have revealed teachers and students who are beginning to redefine what it means to know and be able to do mathematics. No longer is knowing defined solely as getting a numerically correct answer through use of prescribed procedures passed from teachers to students. Rather, emphasis is placed on understanding, which is fostered through the oral and written communication of ideas and the active participation of students as they think, reason, and construct new knowledge. Some problems used in these classrooms are open to multiple interpretations and strategies, and they may have more than one answer. Other tasks build on students' natural ways of thinking and reasoning as well as on their nonschool experiences. In their classrooms, many teachers have created communities of collaborative practice where thinking and reasoning are valued and where being able to explain your thinking and justify your reasoning is treated as being at least as important as arriving at a "correct" solution. In these classrooms, students are exploring and making sense of the mathematics they are learning.

The classroom episodes also reveal a broadening of the curriculum beyond the narrow range of topics and skills that have generally been the focus of middle school instruction. In Mr. Henderson's lesson on geometry, students explored the relationship between surface area and volume and looked for generalizations. In Ms. Bensen's class, students explored algebraic relationships between quantities in both informal and more formal ways. Topics such as algebra and geometry are often omitted from the middle school curriculum, in favor of continued rehearsal of the material taught in earlier grades (Flanders, 1987). An expanded curriculum not only provides students with a more adequate foundation for secondary school mathematics, but also affords them an opportunity to discover the interrelated nature of mathematical knowledge and to provide contexts for the use of basic arithmetic concepts and skills.

The glimpses into QUASAR classrooms and schools presented in this chapter provide some early evidence that it is possible to offer high-quality mathematics instruction to all children, not simply to those fortunate enough to live in affluent circumstances. It is important to note, however, that these successes should be tempered by other evidence, in this project and elsewhere, that fundamental changes in instructional practice proceed slowly and unevenly and that these efforts are severely constrained by factors beyond the control of the participants, such as school district policies and general economic conditions that often threaten to crush fledgling reform efforts. It would be incorrect to assume that the creation of the classroom communities found in these examples occurs easily, at uniform rates of speed, or equally well at each QUASAR site, or even that the classroom communities share characteristics that are immediately visible. In some classes, students appear to control the mathematical discourse much of the time, but in other classes the teacher appears to exert more control, and the relative amounts of time spent in each mode may vary among different teachers within a site and even across mathematical topics within a single teacher's classroom. Individual differences among teachers have an important mediating influence on the processes of creating and orchestrating classroom communities. Some teachers are better able to adjust their teaching to accommodate more student-centered discourse than are other teachers, and teachers also differ in their willingness to do so.

QUASAR teachers and resource partners are engaged in the hard work of bringing the rhetoric of mathematics education reform into contact with the realities of urban schooling. Although the types of classrooms described here are at the heart of the vision portrayed by current reform documents, they represent a new frontier in mathematics education in urban middle schools, where innovation is usually late in arriving, short in duration, and not available to all students. Early in the life of the project, representative teachers and resource partners assembled in Pittsburgh for a meeting to share stories of their work, their accomplishments, their failures, and their frustrations. At this meeting, they began to call the QUASAR Project the "revolution of the possible." Revolutions are rarely easy, but this one is necessary if we are to make progress in enhancing mathematics education for all students.

Acknowledgments

Preparation of this chapter was supported by a grant from the Ford Foundation (grant number 890-0572) for the QUASAR Project. Any opinions expressed herein are those of the authors and do not necessarily represent the views of the foundation. We would like to acknowledge the assistance of Catherine Brown, Carol Parke, Michele Saulis, Marcia Seeley, and Mary Kay Stein in identifying some of the QUASAR Project examples used herein, and for feedback on an earlier draft of this paper. We also wish to thank Iris Carl, Michaele Chappell, Ruth Cossey, Gilberto Cuevas, Elizabeth Fennema, Barbara Grover, Edward McDonald, Leslie Salmon-Cox, and William Tate for their comments on an earlier version.

Notes

1 QUASAR is designed as an intervention aimed at middle schools serving poor communities, regardless of the ethnic or racial membership of the population being served. Even though one cannot equate members of racial or ethnic minority groups with the poor, the high proportion of racial and ethnic minorities who live in poor urban areas leads to the fact that the children attending QUASAR schools are primarily, though not exclusively, members of racial or ethnic minority groups.

2 Conservative estimates put the proportion of educationally disadvantaged students in today's schools at one-third (Pallas, Natriello, & McDill, 1989). In the next 30 years, all social conditions that today serve as indicators of educational disadvantage are expected to increase: The number of children in poverty is expected to increase 37%, the number of children not living with both parents is expected to increase 30%, and the number of children living with poorly educated mothers is expected to increase 56%.

3 Our use of classroom examples is intended to illustrate key points under discussion rather than to reflect a complete analysis of these episodes.

4 The research aspects of the QUASAR Project are not a major focus in this chapter, so we have omitted an extensive presentation from that perspective. Descriptions of the research design and methodology being employed to examine teachers' instructional practices can be found in Stein, Grover, and Silver (1991a,b). A description of an approach being taken to assess student cognitive outcomes with respect to problem solving, reasoning, and communication can be found in Lane (1993) and Silver and Lane (1993a). There are, however, important equity-related issues embedded in the research aspects of the project. For example, efforts are made to ensure racial and ethnic balance among the observers who document classroom activity at the project sites, and students who are identified for special observation in classrooms are drawn from a pool that is balanced for gender, ability, and ethnicity. In our use of performance assessments to measure students' cognitive growth, efforts are made to ensure the fairness of the performance assessments across ethnic and language subgroups, such as the use of bilingual assessment booklets. For a more complete treatment of equity issues related to QUASAR's assessment, see Silver and Lane (1993b).

5 This chapter focuses on matters of educational equity as they relate to the economically disadvantaged. Given the disproportionate number of racial and ethnic members living in poverty at this time, our discussion deals primarily with the issues of poverty and cultural diversity. There are important gender-related equity issues in the area of mathematics education. Moreover, there is a gender-related dimension to the education of students in economically disadvantaged communities, since there has been a rapid increase in the number of poor households headed by African American or Hispanic females, and almost all of the increase in children born into poverty between 1980 and 1990 has been from these households (Hodgkinson, 1985, 1992). Nevertheless, space does not permit a full treatment of gender in this chapter. The reader is referred to Leder (this volume) for an excellent summary of gender issues as they pertain to mathematics education.

6 Our critique of conventional instructional practices in economically disadvantaged communities is not meant to deny or ignore the difficulties and challenges

presented in these settings. Urban and poor schools usually serve populations whose needs are not adequately met in the areas of health care, housing, transportation, and economic and personal security, thereby making it difficult for students and teachers to focus on academic work. Moreover, these schools tend to experience large class sizes and high rates of turnover among teachers, support staff, and administrators, thereby making consistency in instruction difficult. The situation in urban and poor schools is even more problematic because of inequities in current methods of funding public education in the United States (Kozol, 1991), which often provide schools serving students with the greatest needs with far fewer dollars to support educational services than schools serving students who live in more economically privileged communities. These consequences of poverty make urban education extremely challenging, and their ultimate solutions almost certainly lie in changes in social and economic policy, and not merely in changes in instructional practice. Despite these obstacles, however, there are some urban schools that, with courage, tenacity, ingenious leadership, and dedicated staff, have managed to create conditions conducive to good academic education, at least for a period of time (e.g., Grant, 1988; Meier, 1992).

7 Although various reports and projections (e.g., Commission on the Skills of the American Workforce, 1990; Johnston & Packer, 1987; Mishel & Teixeira, 1991) differ markedly in their estimates of the degree of labor shortage or skills mismatch that America may face in the next several decades, the reports are unanimous in their calls for a general upgrading of the quality of the education of the workforce. Of special concern in all of these analyses is the poor cognitive-skills performance of American students and workers when compared with that of their counterparts in countries with which the United States competes economically.

8 In addition to analyses of cognitive mismatch, there is also a substantial literature analyzing the alienation from school felt by many students because they have lost faith in the capacity of school to prepare them for adult life. These students do not share the values, life experience, or style of the staff (Metz, 1988), and may perceive a need to reject important aspects of their own racial or cultural identity in order to exhibit behaviors that are rewarded in schools (Fordham & Ogbu, 1986). Cognitive mismatch may well be a contributing factor in such alienation (Erickson, 1987), or it may be that alienation is interwoven with fundamental epistemological differences between mainstream views of knowledge as entity versus subcultural views of knowledge as experience (Murrell, 1989). In either case, the social and political disjunctions that alienation produces are certainly serious. This chapter focuses on the contribution that could be made by a well-conceived, cognitively based, school reform agenda; thus, the larger topic of alienation is not pursued. Its absence should not be taken as an indication that we misunderstand its importance.

9 Delpit (1988) also asserts that the skills/process debate is about power – about who gets to participate in determining what is best for poor children and children of color. Given the absence of any significant role for minority educators in the formation of the NCTM *Curriculum and Evaluation Standards* (1989) or the NCTM *Professional Standards for Teaching Mathematics,* (1991) the power issue may loom large in attempts to implement the NCTM goals in urban, predominantly minority communities.

10 The overlap between Ladson-Billings' findings and the current mathematics

education reform rhetoric is not complete. In particular, Ladson-Billings identifies some characteristics of successful teachers that are rarely, if ever, mentioned in mathematics education reform discussions, such as teachers' viewing themselves as part of the community, viewing their teaching as giving something back to the community, and viewing teaching as being passionate and artistic with respect to content rather than aloof and technical.

11 To ensure the fidelity of the reproduced examples to actual occurrences, primary source materials (e.g., artifacts of the application process, audiotapes of interviews, and videotapes of classroom instruction) were used whenever possible, and validated secondary source material (e.g., observers' accounts of classroom instruction, transcriptions of interviews) were used at other times. Moreover, drafts of this paper were shared with other members of the QUASAR Project staff who are knowledgeable about all data related to project site activity. In some cases, additional discussions were held with teachers to clarify aspects of the examples presented here. Most of the examples are drawn from data collected during the second year of implementation at sites.

12 In order to preserve anonymity, all names used to denote teachers in this chapter are pseudonyms.

13 The QUASAR Cognitive Assessment Instrument (QCAI) consists of a set of open-ended tasks that assess mathematical reasoning, mathematical problem solving, the understanding of mathematical concepts, and communication of mathematical explanations or justifications. See Lane (1993) or Silver and Lane (1993a) for additional information on the QCAI.

14 The developers intended this task to have more than one correct solution, depending on the nature and quality of the explanation and reasoning provided. Thus, the children's response came as less of a surprise to the task developers than it did to the teachers.

15 The occasional use of rap as a communication and verbal interaction medium in QUASAR classrooms should not be interpreted as a blanket endorsement of rap music. Although a powerful medium for communication in African American and other minority communities and capable of being used to the educational benefit of children (Willis, 1989), specific aspects of the content of some rap music (e.g., advocacy of violence against police, use of racial epithets) have created considerable justifiable controversy (Marriott, 1993).

16 Although the essays have generally been criticized for historical inaccuracy, the mathematics component has not been subject to this critique (Martel, 1991).

17 QUASAR is not alone in its effort to meet the challenges described. Other projects are also working to improve the life chances of American students. For example, many schools are involved in projects that focus on upgrading curriculum and instruction in general (e.g., accelerated schools); improving the quality of the content and pedagogy in mathematics at the elementary school level (e.g., Project Impact); increasing access to academic mathematics courses in high school (e.g., Equity 2000); promoting parental involvement and school-based support systems (e.g., School Development Project); and providing experience-based approaches to mathematics learning (e.g., The Algebra Project).

References

Bank Street College Project in Science and Mathematics. (1989). *The second voyage of the Mimi* [video/multimedia]. Pleasantville, NY: Sunburst.

Birman, B. F. (1987). *The current operation of the Chapter 1 program: Final report for the national assessment of Chapter 1*. Washington, DC: Office of Educational Research and Improvement, United States Department of Education.

Bourque, M. L., & Garrison, H. H. (1991). *The levels of mathematics achievement: Initial performance standards for the 1990 NAEP mathematics assessment, Vol. 1: National and state summaries*. Washington, DC: National Assessment Governing Board.

Bright, G. W., Harvey, J. G., & Wheeler, M. M. (1985). Learning and mathematics games. (*Journal for Research in Mathematics Education Research Monograph Series No. 1.*) Reston, VA: National Council of Teachers of Mathematics.

Burns, M. (1982). *Math for smarty pants*. Boston: Little, Brown.

California State Department of Education. (1987). *Caught in the middle*. Sacramento, CA: Author.

Cannell, J. J. (1989). *The "Lake Wobegon" report: How public educators cheat on standardized achievement tests*. Albuquerque, NM: Friends for Education.

Commission on the Skills of the American Workforce. (1990). *America's choice: High skills or low wages*. Rochester, NY: National Center on Education and the Economy.

Congressional Budget Office. (1987, August). *Educational achievement: Explanations and implications of recent trends*. Washington, DC: United States Government Printing Office.

Delpit, L. D. (1988). The silenced dialogue: Power and pedagogy in educating other people's children. *Harvard Educational Review, 58,* 280–298.

Dossey, J. A., Mullis, I. V. S., Lindquist, M. M., & Chambers, D. L. (1988). *The mathematics report card*. Princeton, NJ: National Assessment of Educational Progress.

Edmonds, R. R. (1979). Effective schools for the urban poor. *Educational Leadership, 37,* 15–27.

Epstein, J. L., & MacIver, D. J. (1989). *Education in the middle grades: Overview of a national survey on practices and trends*. Baltimore, MD: Center for Research on Elementary and Middle Schools, Johns Hopkins University.

Erickson, F. (1987). Transformation and school success: The policies and culture of educational achievement. *Anthropology and Education Quarterly, 18,* 335–356.

Ernest, P. (1991). *The philosophy of mathematics education*. London: Falmer.

Fey, J. T. (1981). *Mathematics teaching today: Perspectives from three national surveys*. Reston, VA: National Council of Teachers of Mathematics.

Flanders, J. R. (1987). How much of the content in mathematics textbooks is new? *Arithmetic Teacher, 35,* 18–23.

Fordham, S., & Ogbu, J. (1986). Black students' school success: Coping with the burden of "acting white." *Urban Review, 18,* 1–31.

Garcia, E. (1991). *Education of linguistically and culturally diverse students: Effective instructional practices* (Educational Practice Report: 1). Santa Cruz: University of California, Santa Cruz, National Center for Research on Cultural Diversity and Second Language Learning.

Gardner, H. (1982). *Frames of mind: The theory of multiple intelligences*. New York: Basic.

Gay, G. (1988). Designing relevant curricula for diverse learners. *Education and Urban Society, 20*(4), 327–340.

Goldenberg, C. (1991). *Instructional conversations and their classroom application* (Educational Practice Report: 2). Santa Cruz: University of California, Santa Cruz, National Center for Research on Cultural Diversity and Second Language Learning.

Grant, G. (1988). *The world we created at Hamilton High*. Cambridge, MA: Harvard University Press.

Heath, S. B. (1983). *Ways with words: Language, life, and work in communities and classrooms*. Cambridge University Press.

Hilliard, A., & Leonard, C. (Eds.). (1990). *African American baseline essays*. Portland, OR: Portland Public Schools.

Hodgkinson, H. L. (1985). *All in one system: Demographics of education, kindergarten through graduate school*. Washington, DC: Institute for Educational Leadership.

(1992). *Demographic look at tomorrow*. Washington, DC: Institute for Educational Leadership.

Johnston, W. B., & Packer, A. E. (1987). *Workforce 2000: Work and workers for the 21st century*. Indianapolis, IN: Hudson Institute.

Knapp, M. S., Shields, P. M., & Turnbull, B. J. (1992). *Academic challenge for the children of poverty. Summary report*. Washington, DC: United States Department of Education, Office of Policy and Planning.

Knapp, M. S., & Turnbull, B. J. (1990). *Better schooling for the children of poverty: Alternatives to conventional wisdom* (Vol. 1: Summary). Washington, DC: Office of Planning, Budget, and Evaluation, United States Department of Education.

Kozol, J. (1991). *Savage inequalities: Children in America's schools*. New York: Crown.

Ladson-Billings, G. (1990). Like lightning in a bottle: Attempting to capture the pedagogical excellence of successful teachers of black students. *Qualitative Studies in Education, 3*, 335–344.

(1992). Culturally relevant teaching: The key to making multicultural education work. In C. Grant (Ed.), *Research and multicultural education: From the margins to the mainstream* (pp. 106–121). London: Falmer.

Lampert, M. (1986). Knowing, doing, and teaching multiplication. *Cognition and Instruction, 3*, 305–342.

(1990). When the problem is not the question and the solution is not the answer: Mathematical knowing and teaching. *American Educational Research Journal, 27*(1), 29–64.

Lane, S. (1993). The conceptual framework for the development of a mathematics assessment instrument for QUASAR. *Educational Measurement: Issues and Practice, 12*(2), 16–23.

Leap, W. L. (1988). Assumptions and strategies guiding mathematics problem solving by Ute Indian students. In R. R. Cocking & J. P. Mestre (Eds.), *Linguistic and cultural influences on learning mathematics* (pp. 161–186). Hillsdale, NJ: Erlbaum.

Lieberman, A. (Ed.) (1986). *Rethinking school improvement: Research, craft and concept*. New York: Teachers College Press.

Marriott, M. (1993, January 24). Rap's embrace of "nigger" fires bitter debate. *New York Times*, pp. 1, 11.

Martel, E. (1991). How valid are the Portland baseline essays? *Educational Leadership, 49*, 20–23.

Matthews, W., Carpenter, T. P., Lindquist, M. M., & Silver, E. A. (1984). The third national assessment: Minorities and mathematics. *Journal for Research in Mathematics Education, 15*, 165–171.

Meier, D. (1992). Reinventing teaching. *Teachers College Record, 93*(1), 594–609.

Mellin-Olsen, S. (1987). *The politics of mathematics education*. Dordrecht, The Netherlands: D. Reidel.

Metz, M. (1988). Some missing elements in the educational reform movement. *Educational Administration Quarterly, 24*(4), 446–460.

Mishel, L., & Teixeira, R. A. (1991). *The myth of the coming labor shortage: Jobs, skills and incomes of America's Workforce 2000*. Washington, DC: Economic Policy Institute.

Mullis, I. V. S., Dossey, J. A., Owen, E. H., & Phillips, G. W. (1991). *The state of mathematics achievement: NAEP's 1990 assessment of the nation and the trial assessment of the states*. Washington, DC: National Center for Education Statistics.

Mullis, I. V. S., Owen, E. H., & Phillips, G. W. (1990). *Accelerating academic achievement: A summary of findings from 20 years of NAEP*. Princeton, NJ: Educational Testing Service.

Murrell, P. C., Jr. (1989, March). *Coping in the culture of power: Resilience as a factor in black students' academic success*. Paper presented at the annual meeting of the American Educational Research Association, San Francisco.

National Council of Teachers of Mathematics (1989). *Curriculum and evaluation standards for school mathematics*. Reston, VA: Author.

(1991). *Professional standards for teaching mathematics*. Reston, VA: Author.

(1992). *The road to reform in mathematics education: How far have we traveled?* Reston, VA: Author.

National Research Council. (1989). *Everybody counts*. Washington, DC: National Academy of Sciences.

Oakes, J. (1985). *Keeping track: How schools structure inequality*. New Haven, CT: Yale University Press.

(1990a). *Multiplying inequalities: The effect of race, social class, and tracking on opportunities to learn mathematics and science*. Santa Monica, CA: Rand Corporation.

(1990b). Opportunities, achievement, and choice: Women and minority students in science and mathematics. In C. B. Cazden (Ed.), *Review of research in education* (Vol. 16, pp. 153–222). Washington, DC: American Educational Research Association.

(1992). Can tracking research inform practice? Technical, normative and political considerations. *Educational Researcher, 21*(4), 12–21.

Pallas, A. M., Natriello, G., & McDill, E. L. (1989). The changing nature of the disadvantaged population: Current dimensions and future trends. *Educational Researcher, 18* (5), 16–23.

Pelavin, S. H., & Kane, M. (1990). *Changing the odds: Factors increasing access to college*. New York: College Entrance Examination Board.

Porter, A. C. (1989). A curriculum out of balance: The case of elementary school mathematics. *Educational Researcher, 18*(5), 9–15.

Resnick, L. B. (1987). *Education and learning to think*. Washington, DC: National Academy of Sciences.

(1988). Treating mathematics as an ill-structured discipline. In R. I. Charles & E. A. Silver (Eds.), *Research agenda for mathematics education, Vol. 3: The teaching and assessing of mathematical problem solving* (pp. 31–60). Hillsdale, NJ/Reston, VA: Erlbaum / National Council of Teachers of Mathematics.

Robitaille, D., & Garden, R. (Eds.) (1989). *The IEA study of mathematics II: Contexts and outcomes of school mathematics*. Oxford: Pergamon.

Schoenfeld, A. H. (1991). On mathematics as sense-making: An informal attack on the unfortunate divorce of formal and informal mathematics. In J. F. Voss, D. N. Perkins, & J. W. Segal (Eds.), *Informal reasoning and education* (pp. 311–343). Hillsdale, NJ: Erlbaum.

Secada, W. G. (1991). Agenda setting, enlightened self-interest, and equity in mathematics education. *Peabody Journal of Education, 66* (2), 22–56.

(1992a). Evaluating the mathematics education of LEP students in a time of educational change. In *Proceedings of the National Research Symposium on Limited English Proficient Student Issues: Focus on Evaluation and Measurement* (Vol. 2, pp. 209–256). Washington, DC: Office of Bilingual Education and Minority Languages Affairs, United States Department of Education.

(1992b). Race, ethnicity, social class, language, and achievement in mathematics. In D. A. Grouws (Ed.), *Handbook of research on mathematics teaching and learning* (pp. 623–660). New York: Macmillan.

(in press). Toward a consciously multicultural mathematics curriculum. In F. R. Batiz (Ed.), *Reinventing urban education: Multiculturalism and the social context of schooling*. New York: IUME Press, Teachers College, Columbia University.

Shan, S., & Bailey, P. (1991). *Multiple factors: Classroom mathematics for equality and justice*. Staffordshire, England: Trentham.

Silver, E. A. (1989). QUASAR. *Ford Foundation Letter, 20*, 1–3.

Silver, E. A., Kilpatrick, J., & Schlesinger, B. (1990). *Thinking through mathematics*. New York: College Entrance Examination Board.

Silver, E. A., & Lane, S. (1993a). Assessment in the context of mathematics instruction reform: The design of assessment in the QUASAR project. In M. Niss (Ed.), *Assessment in mathematics education and its effects* (pp. 59–70). London: Kluwer Academic.

(1993b, March). *Balancing considerations of equity, content quality, and technical excellence in designing, validating and implementing performance assessments in the context of mathematics instructional reform: The experience of the QUASAR project.* Paper presented at the Symposium on Equity and Educational Testing and Assessment, Washington, DC.

Silver, E. A., Shapiro, L. J., & Deutsch, A. (1993). Sense-making and the solution of division problems involving remainders: An examination of students' solution processes and their interpretations of solutions. *Journal for Research in Mathematics Education, 24*(2), 117–135.

Silverstein, S. (1974). *Where the sidewalk ends.* New York: Harper & Row.

Sizemore, B. A. (1987). The effective African-American elementary school. In G. W. Noblit & W. T. Pink (Eds.), *Schooling in social context: Quantitative studies* (pp. 175–202). Norwood, NJ: Ablex.

Slavin, R. E. (1989). Cooperative learning and student achievement. In R. E. Slavin (Ed.), *School and classroom organization* (pp. 129–156). Hillsdale, NJ: Erlbaum.

Stein, M. K., Grover, B. W., & Silver, E. A. (1991a, October). *A methodology for studying teacher change within a mathematics education reform project.* Paper presented at a presession entitled "Methodologies for studying teacher change in the reform of school mathematics" at the annual meeting of the North American chapter of the International Group for the Psychology of Mathematics Education, Blacksburg, VA.

(1991b). Changing instructional practice: A conceptual framework for capturing the details. In R. G. Underhill (Ed.), *Proceedings of the Thirteenth Annual Meeting of the North American Chapter of the International Group for the Psychology of Mathematics Education* (pp. 36–41). Blacksburg, VA: Virginia Polytechnic & State University.

Stodolsky, S. (1988). *The subject matters: Classroom activity in mathematics and social studies.* University of Chicago Press.

Webb, N. M. (1989). Peer interaction and learning in small groups. *International Journal of Educational Research, 13*(1), 21–39.

Willis, M. G. (1989). Learning styles of African American children: A review of the literature and interventions. *Journal of Black Psychology, 16*(1), 47–65.

Zaslavsky, C. (1973). *Africa counts.* Boston: Prindle, Weber & Schmidt.

2   Can equity thrive in a culture of mathematical excellence?

Harvey B. Keynes

The University of Minnesota Talented Youth Mathematics Program (UM-TYMP) is a statewide program aimed at providing an alternative educational experience for Minnesota's most mathematically talented students. The Program and home schools identify students in Grades 5–8 who have scored above the 95th percentile on any standardized mathematics test and invite them to take part in a qualifying examination. From approximately 1,400 students who test annually, about 140–150 are invited to participate.

The Program provides an intense academic environment and a different culture of mathematics via a sequence of specially designed accelerated mathematics courses. UMTYMP students attend a 2-hour class one afternoon each week, after school, for 30 weeks from September through May. The students average 8 to 10 hours of weekly homework to be completed in school during release time from the regular mathematics program, or at home. During the first 2 years (the high school component), students study customized UMTYMP programs in Algebra (equivalent to Algebra I and Algebra II) in the first year, and Geometry/Mathematical Analysis in the second year. The high school component is taught by outstanding certified high school mathematics teachers and undergraduate teaching assistants, many of whom graduated from the Program. As mandated by a 1984 Minnesota state law, 2 full years of high school mathematics credit in Algebra I/II is to be granted for completion of the first year UMTYMP Algebra, and 1 year's credit each in Geometry and Math Analysis for the second year UMTYMP course.

Following the high school component, the students study calculus of one and several variables, linear algebra, and differential equations in the college component. This component consists of special university honors courses created for the UMTYMP students by the School of Mathematics at the University of Minnesota. Since most program participants ultimately pursue careers in widely varying areas of mathematics, science, engineering, and technology, the courses provide carefully monitored problem-solving curricula that are taught by senior faculty from the University of Minnesota and from local colleges at the outreach sites. In the first year,

57

differential and integral calculus are studied. In the second, sequences, series, and linear algebra are covered. A third year explores linear analysis – a course in multivariable calculus using linear algebra and geometry. For students still in high school, a fourth-year topics course in advanced undergraduate mathematics is offered.

Since students graduate from high school at several points in the UM-TYMP program, the courses are designed so that at the end of each year, students may easily move into regular university courses. A student earns eight to ten University of Minnesota undergraduate mathematics credits in calculus for successful completion of each year of UMTYMP calculus. These credits are regularly transferred to other colleges and universities.

Several years ago, a Program self-study identified a need to address wider participation of females and students of color. We believed that we could design intervention and support activities that would enable us to seriously address the issue of equity while maintaining the intellectual thrust and integrity of the UMTYMP academic program. The results of these efforts have had a major effect on increasing the participation of the targeted groups of students, as well as our creating significant improvements in the Program. The overall intent of this chapter is to illustrate how a program for very talented mathematics students evolved simultaneously in such a way as to also address equity and excellence. We will describe how UMTYMP identified issues of equity that existed in the specific educational environments in which the Program operates, and, based on educational research and best practice, developed ways to address these problems with interventions suitable to the Program's goals. Most important, we will show that these support activities and interventions have clearly resulted in more equitable outcomes.

In this chapter, we first provide an overview of UMTYMP's goals, design, and content, and describe some of its unusual student-centered features. We then summarize the influence and outcomes of the Program regarding the students. Turning to equity, we will present some of the special issues facing female students and students of color, and the Program's philosophy and rationale behind the design of the intervention activities. We then will provide descriptions of the different interventions and how we designed strategies for implementing them. Next, we provide a report on the initial outcomes of these efforts in addressing both equity issues and overall program improvement, and outline our plans to maintain a long-term evaluation of these interventions, as well as to measure their effectiveness. We conclude with a description of several possible directions and activities for addressing remaining equity concerns.

Program goals, design, and content

In this section, we provide a broad overview of the design and structure of UMTYMP. This description deals mainly with general aspects rather than specific details; the latter can be found in Keynes (1991).

The overall goal of UMTYMP is to provide an intense, mathematically challenging, and dynamic academic program for mathematically talented and motivated students in a highly supportive and success-oriented environment. The curriculum is under constant discussion and revision by Program personnel in order to reflect the best current ideas about all subjects, from algebra through calculus. While classes are accelerated beyond the standard school schedule, the content, teaching styles, and support activities available to the students are designed to enable virtually *all* students chosen for participation to be highly successful. Program emphasis is on work habits and homework as key features and measures of successful participation, rather than solely on classroom participation testing. An important element is to give students a sense of participating in a culture of mathematics and a sense of how this culture can help them in their careers and lives. Although the Program's size and crisp pace require some level of bureaucracy, the intellectual and curricular decisions are made at the grass-roots level; namely, by the highly qualified and motivated high school and university teaching staff.

Both curricula and textbooks in any subject can be revised or replaced in any year. The process involves a cooperative search and a report prepared by the teaching staff. As a result, textbooks and curricula in the high school courses tend to change about once every 2 or 3 years. The Program encourages and supports "risk taking" at the curricular level when the intellectual goals of the students will be better served. For example, the current geometry text, S. Lang and G. Murrow's *Geometry, A High School Course* (1988), reflects a modern and different approach to geometry, which challenges both the students and teaching staff. To support the teachers in making this choice, UMTYMP provided its own summer in-service opportunities and additionally compensated teachers who served on homework and examination development teams.

We cannot overemphasize the importance of a broad and deep support system that has been developed for the students and their families by the Program as a result of its equity efforts. These supports cover social and attitudinal factors as well as academic issues, and may be characterized as high-level nurturing that is intended to motivate all students to succeed at their highest levels of capability. Although these interventions were initially developed in connection with the activities designed to increase female participation, their marked successes have led to their institutionalization into the entire Program.

One important aspect is the Program's concern with giving high visibility to the "perks" associated with being interested in and working hard for achievement in mathematics. These opportunities, described in a later section, include the special admission procedures for UMTYMP students at several major universities and the striking success of UMTYMP students in science, mathematics, and engineering majors at prestigious colleges. Opportunities for academic-year enrichment activities are also provided. Family interest in college achievements of UMTYMP graduates and the special opportunities for UMTYMP participants seem to be major factors in their support of the Program.

To illustrate the alignment of the goals of the Program with the major goals of the National Council of Teachers of Mathematics (NCTM) *Curriculum and Evaluation Standards for School Mathematics* (1989), we provide the following chart. Listed under each standard (1–11) are the Program features that address these goals.

UMTYMP and the NCTM standards

Standards	UMTYMP
1. Mathematics as problem solving	· Curriculum emphasis on the process of solving problems. · Challenging problems are an important part of all homework. · Applications of mathematics are emphasized.
2. Mathematics as communication	· Provides exposure to a wide variety of mathematical concepts. · Mathematical notation is used in a manner consistent with collegiate mathematics. · Students are required to write in good English.
3. Mathematics as reasoning	· Geometry is approached through several proof patterns (synthetic, transformational, analytic). · Concepts and conceptual reasoning are expected in all courses, ranging up to some proofs in college-level courses. · Conceptual problems are an integral part of all classroom discussions and homework.
4. Mathematical connections	· Total curriculum is intertwined with algebraic, geometric, and analytic approaches to mathematics. · Calculus is unified and presents multivariable calculus utilizing linear algebra, analysis, and geometry.

UMTYMP and the NCTM standards (cont.)

Standards	UMTYMP
5. Algebra	· Two years of algebra covered in the first year are followed by significant use of algebraic approaches.
6. Functions	· Functions and the functional approach is a common thread running through all UMTYMP courses. Algebra is taught from an applications point of view, leading to the formation of functions. The transformation view of geometry further develops the functions concept. Mathematical analysis is approached as a study of classes of functions. Calculus is based on a more detailed analysis of functions, and functions are applied in a variety of ways. The approach in linear algebra is based on the geometry and regularity of linear transformations.
7. Geometry from a synthetic perspective	· Although the second-year geometry component is the main point at which these topics are covered, a geometric perspective and emphasis is a common major thread in algebra, math analysis, and calculus. In linear algebra, the entire curriculum rests heavily on geometric descriptions in 2- and 3-space.
8. Geometry	· Geometry from an algebraic perspective.
9. Trigonometry	· The algebra courses study trigonometric ideas from triangles in a variety of problems. In math analysis, the functional approach to trigonometry is emphasized. Trigonometric functions and ideas of periodicity continue to be heavily used in all of the calculus courses.
10. Statistics	· The constructions and studies of tables, charts, and graphs is taught in algebra, as well as in other areas of statistics. The current algebra texts put increased emphasis on statistics.
11. Probability	· All of the topics of probability proposed in the *Standards* are covered in algebra. Probabilistic problems and approaches are used in geometry, math analysis, and in all of the calculus courses.

The challenges of educating UMTYMP students

The students who qualify for the Program and elect to participate are usually quite complex and highly motivated. Beyond their obvious abilities in mathematics, they frequently display behaviors and learning styles that are not readily encouraged in the normal classroom. The guideline of performance – a score in the 95th percentile or above on some national mathematics achievement examination – to take the UMTYMP Qualification Examination allows latitude on the part of the school and the mathematics teachers to encourage some students and discourage others. The Program has found that parent and self-identification of students is frequently as reliable as school identification, and has moved toward a more open system that allows nearly all students who wish to take the qualifying examination to do so. Surprisingly, despite the more open system and Program adjustment of the qualifying examination on a yearly basis, overall scores have continued to rise – rather dramatically so in the last few years.

A poor school identification technique will frequently emphasize characteristics primarily of work or study habits and classroom behaviors to test students for UMTYMP, instead of more meaningful characteristics. In particular, some students are identified for special mathematical talent on the basis of knowing the answers, copying and memorizing well, and being attentive and cooperative in class. Other students, who are independent, frequently uninterested due to boredom, and either withdrawn or academically disruptive, are ignored. These identification anomalies may be due to both discipline and management issues, as well as to the conflict of such students' behavior with a teacher's personal values. The experience of UMTYMP shows that the misidentification issue is far more prevalent for females than for males. Initial experience in seeking larger populations of students of color indicates that similar problems of identification also occur in their case.

Noting the characteristics of the students who most successfully participate in UMTYMP, the Program classes are designed to help these types of learners. Some of these characteristics – intensity, complexity, ability to draw inferences, and a self-critical nature – demand that a class designed for these students encourage variations of teaching style and individualized approaches to accommodate the large variety of personalities and learning styles of the students. It is a very special challenge to the teachers of UMTYMP to create this type of atmosphere within the classroom and still cover the mathematics planned within a 2-hour period. This task would be daunting if the Program followed the standard format of a typical high school class. The UMTYMP teachers quickly learn that alternative formats are far more successful with these students. We will describe some of the common features that emerge in most of these classes, independent of the different teaching styles of the staff. They typify some of the alternate teaching strategies that can enhance learning for students who are bright, but often frustrated.

The high school classes typically consist of students in Grades 7–9 who study all of UMTYMP Algebra in the first year and Geometry/Math Analysis in the second year. To cover 2 years of high school mathematics in 60 classroom hours of instruction (including about 8 hours of testing) would be virtually impossible without significant changes in instructional philosophy. In these classes, only the central ideas and most significant types of problems are actually presented. Experience has shown that the routine topics – a large portion of the usual curriculum – are learned by these students without any formal classroom instruction. Moreover, different students learn different aspects of the subject through deliberate self-instruction. Thus, only occasionally does the entire class attentively follow the teacher discussion. Frequently, students are working at their desks on their own, or discussing a problem with a neighbor, while the teacher explains a concept. Even eating snacks while working does not seem to interfere with learning. The teaching assistant in the class may be talking to a few students about a confusing concept or a difficult problem while all this is happening. Students can be intensely "on task" at one moment and diverted at the next. Many of the rules for classroom participation frequently seem to be ignored. Yet, from all this seeming confusion and lack of structure, these students master large amounts of substantial content extremely well. Much of it is due to the work ethic and extensive effort necessary to complete the challenging homework assignments each week. The classes provide motivation and some catalytic ideas. The students put it all together themselves.

The use of technology by this group of students is also very unusual. If time were not such an important factor and better computing facilities were available, these students could probably benefit from increased use of technology. But even within the Program constraints, some productive uses of graphing calculators are now being introduced. An alternate course, aimed to attract more students of color and economically disadvantaged students, is developing a curriculum for algebra, geometry, and math analysis that totally integrates the TI-81 graphing calculator into the course. Preliminary results in the first two years were very positive. In the regular courses, many students will buy a graphing calculator and use it as a tool on their own, as needed. Classroom sets of TI-81s are available for use with several special lessons created by the instructor. The students find little difficulty in integrating this technology at whatever level is comfortable to them individually. The important thing is to guide them into discovering good mathematical ideas with technology and not to use it simply as a fast computational tool. Because the use of graphing calculators and their integration into the curriculum has proved so advantageous, the Program will require the purchase of graphing calculators for all students in the algebra and calculus classes beginning in the 1993–1994 academic year. Scholarship funds will be available to ensure that financially needy students will be issued calculators.

The UMTYMP classes represent a wide range of ages and maturity levels. A typical algebra class consists of a few fifth- and sixth-grade students together with seventh and eighth graders, and some fairly immature males with some quite mature females. Yet, all generally learn the material very well. This happens because the teachers encourage each student to approach the subject in a style that best suits her or him as an individual. The students are respected not on the basis of their age or maturity, but on the basis of what they contribute to the class. Thus, a sixth grader who works intensely on her own, but who comes up with her share of answers, earns her place in the class.

The key to successful teaching within UMTYMP is recognition of the teacher as a facilitator of learning, rather than simply as an expositor of good curriculum. These students have an enormous capacity to learn and will absorb ideas like sponges if properly motivated and encouraged. Material that is not directly covered or that is dropped from the curriculum is usually learned at some point in the context of another topic or a rich example. By the end of the course, most students have mastered the major concepts and techniques very well. They are well prepared for the challenging UMTYMP calculus courses that they begin after the high school algebra and mathematics component, and for their future collegiate mathematics and science course work.

The influence and outcomes of UMTYMP for its students

If the major outcome of special programs for mathematically talented students were solely to provide a more supportive environment for learning, it might be difficult to defend the need for these programs against a variety of equally deserving programs for other populations. Fortunately, UMTYMP has accumulated evidence indicating a deeper influence on its students. One expected measure of success would be the performance of students and the choice of courses and majors in educational programs subsequent to their involvement in the UMTYMP programs. Another good long-term measure is their success in obtaining undergraduate degrees in science, mathematics, and engineering, and their choices of careers. Since many factors can influence the choices made by these students, it is also useful to have made a record of anecdotal information and self-evaluations by the participants about the specific influences of UMTYMP over a period of time. Because data has been gathered for only a relatively short period, it is not yet possible to make definitive statements about long-term impacts. But a preliminary analysis does indicate certain deep influences and effects of UM-TYMP on its participants. In this section, we will deal primarily with UMTYMP as a model of what can be accomplished by appropriate programming for talented students.

In order to maintain longitudinal information about its students and alumni, UMTYMP has recently developed an extensive database. The alumni database tracks students during their academic career(s) and their working career(s). The information for the database is obtained through annual questionnaires sent to all students who have completed at least 2 years of the UMTYMP college program (or one year in the smaller outreach programs). Once a student has responded to an inquiry, the UMTYMP office annually sends a listing of the information on file and requests that the person make any changes to update the information. This information includes the student's major(s), their college or university, student address, degrees completed, and past and present employers. Currently, there is information about 359 alumni in this database. Recent information is very accurate. The overall database is extensive and complex, and the large number of fields allows many types of reports to be generated. The quality and size of this database make it an excellent resource for longitudinal information about talented mathematics students and their progress, following intensive mathematics.

To provide a background for a discussion about UMTYMP's influence on its students, it is useful to review some general attitudes about programs for talented students. A pervasive belief of the American public is that innate intelligence and ability are the keys that unlock all doors. If a student has the native intelligence, then there is little need to do anything educationally for her, since she will make it anyway. Exciting curricula and hard work will do little to change the outcomes. In mathematics, a corollary of this attitude is the belief stated in *Everybody Counts* (National Research Council, 1989, p. 10) that "learning mathematics requires special ability, which most students do not have." Although this myth has continued to plague efforts to provide a rich curriculum for all students, it particularly allows many schools to justify the attitude that virtually any mathematics program serves their talented students well, since these students will survive no matter what educational experiences they have. This attitude, together with frequent instances of staff and public concerns about the elitist nature of special programs for the talented, serves to relieve many schools of carefully evaluating the need and potential of these programs.

The growing body of evidence associated with these issues shows that many of these beliefs are unfounded. An ETS study reported in the *Chronicle of Higher Education* (1992, p. A25) showed that even among high-ability 1980 high school seniors, less than one-half (49%) obtained college degrees within 7 years of graduation. Although there can be many reasons for nongraduation, the lack of appropriate, high-quality school programs was identified as one important cause. In mathematics, the influence of participating in appropriate K–12 programs seems to be even more pronounced. Although it is difficult to correlate program participation with career outcomes, one useful measure is the choice of majors in mathematics and the sciences. In fall, 1989, among all freshmen entering college, only 2.2% chose mathematics or the physical sciences as an interest for a possible major, with 0.6% and 0.4% choosing mathematics and physics respectively (*Chronicle of Higher Education*, 1990, p. A33). The figure in mathematics dropped to one-half of 1% in 1990 – about one-ninth the peak population of 4.6% in 1970. Even restricting the population to the most talented high school students shows little improvement. A recent sample of high school seniors in the top 10% of their class, according to *Who's Who Among American High School Students* (Twenty-second Annual Survey of High Achievers, 1991), showed that in this population, only 2.4% chose mathematics as an intended major. In contrast, 23% of UMTYMP male graduates and 12% of its female graduates actually major in mathematics, and 20% of the males and 21% of female graduates major in physics, as illustrated in Tables 2.1.1 and 2.1.2.

Since UMTYMP espouses a culture of mathematics with its students and with their families, it is not unexpected that many participants are very active in mathematics competitions and summer programs targeted at talented students. Student success in these activities indicates that the Program provides them with a substantial mathematics background and, more important, an interest in pursuing new directions. In 1991–1992, 9 of the top 10 participants in the Minnesota portion of the American High School Mathematics Examination were students from UMTYMP. Eighteen of the 30 Minnesota team members in the American Regional Mathematics League (ARML) were in UMTYMP. The Program frequently sends two students each year to the prestigious Rickover Summer Institutes. In the summer of 1991, two UMTYMP students (one male and one female) were chosen to be among the 24 students to participate in an NSF-funded 2-week summer ARML program in Russia. Based on special UMTYMP efforts to stress cooperative aspects of competitions, female students are now showing more interest in participating in competitions. Involvement of UMTYMP female students in summer enrichments and research programs has also increased.

Looking at collegiate admissions of alumni, Table 2.2 indicates that the overall success of UMTYMP graduates in gaining admission to the best schools is quite high.

Schools such as Stanford, the California Institute of Technology, the Massachusetts Institute of Technology (MIT), and Harvard actively recruit UMTYMP graduates based on their excellent academic performances. Many of these institutions offer very attractive scholarship and financial aid packages to UMTYMP students. The University of Minnesota benefits

Table 2.1.1. *UMTYMP alumni surveys – Current majors of males*

Current Major	Under-graduate	Graduate	Total	%
Mathematics	43	6	49	23
Physics	38	4	42	20
Computer science	22	3	25	12
Electrical engineering	22	2	24	11
Aerospace engineering	7	1	8	4
Chemistry	7	1	8	4
Economics	7	1	8	4
Mechanical engineering	6	2	8	4
Chemical engineering	7	0	7	3
Engineering (unspecified)	7	0	7	3
English	7	0	7	3
Philosophy	6	1	7	3
Music	5	0	5	2
Medicine	2	2	4	2
Astronomy/astrophysics	3	0	3	1
Biology	3	0	3	1
Political science	3	0	3	1
Biochemistry	2	1	3	1
Mathematics education	2	1	3	1
Statistics	2	1	3	1
Business	2	0	2	1
Education	2	0	2	1
History	2	0	2	1
Material sciences	2	0	2	1
Psychology	2	0	2	1
Russian area studies	2	0	2	1
Law	0	2	2	1
American literature	1	0	1	.5
American studies	1	0	1	.5
Biomedical engineering	1	0	1	.5
Civil engineering	1	0	1	.5
Computer engineering	1	0	1	.5
East Asian studies	1	0	1	.5
Engineering physics	1	0	1	.5
Geology	1	0	1	.5
German	1	0	1	.5
Microbiology	1	0	1	.5
Natural sciences	1	0	1	.5
Sociology	1	0	1	.5
Actuarial science	0	1	1	.5
Ecology	0	1	1	.5
Genetics	0	1	1	.5
Rabbinical	0	1	1	.5
Other	19	1	20	10
Undecided	12	1	13	6
Total	256*	34*	290*	

209 males responded – 177 undergraduates, 32 graduates
* Some alumni have multiple majors

Table 2.1.2. *UMTYMP alumni surveys – current majors of females*

Current major	Under-graduate	Graduate	Total	%
Physics	8	1	9	21
Biology	6	1	7	16
Mathematics	4	1	5	12
Chemistry	4	0	4	9
Economics	3	0	3	7
Chemical engineering	2	1	3	7
English	2	1	3	7
Biochemistry	2	0	2	5
Political science	2	0	2	5
Computer science	1	0	1	2
Education	1	0	1	2
Electrical engineering	1	0	1	2
Engineering (unspecified)	1	0	1	2
German	1	0	1	2
History	1	0	1	2
Japanese	1	0	1	2
Japan studies	1	0	1	2
Medicine	1	0	1	2
Music	1	0	1	2
Physical science ed.	1	0	1	2
Psychology	1	0	1	2
Science	1	0	1	2
Studio arts	1	0	1	2
Theater arts	1	0	1	2
Health services	0	1	1	2
Molecular biology	0	1	1	2
Statistics	0	1	1	2
Other	0	1	1	2
Undecided	3	0	3	7
Total	51*	9	60*	

43 females responded – 34 undergraduates, 9 graduates
*Some alumni have multiple majors

significantly from the Program – 45 of the 245 alumni currently in college attend the university. About 20 percent of the graduate students (8/41) in the alumni database do their graduate work at the university.

Returning to the examination of the majors of alumni (Tables 2.1.1 and 2.1.2), the initial data indicate that UMTYMP helps to open up the pipelines for its female graduates dramatically. Approximately 70% (30 of 43) of the females responding to the survey are majoring in some field of mathematics, science, or engineering; 40% are pursuing degrees in more than one major.

Table 2.2. *UMTYMP alumni surveys – current colleges/universities of alumni*

College/university	Total	Undergraduate		Graduate	
		Male	Female	Male	Female
University of Minnesota – Twin Cities	45	34	3	5	3
Stanford University	23	17	5	1	0
Carleton College	14	13	1	0	0
MIT	14	10	4	0	0
Harvard University	11	10	0	1	0
Cal Tech	10	9	0	1	0
University of Wisconsin – Madison	9	5	3	1	0
Princeton University	6	5	0	1	0
University of California – Berkeley	6	3	1	1	1
University of Chicago	6	3	1	2	0
Rensselaer Polytechnic Institute	4	4	0	0	0
Duke University	4	1	2	1	0
University of Pennsylvania	4	3	0	1	0
Cornell University	4	0	1	1	2
North Dakota State University	3	3	0	0	0
Oberlin College	3	3	0	0	0
St. Olaf	3	3	0	0	0
Wellesley College	3	0	3	0	0
Columbia University	3	2	0	0	1
Dartmouth University	3	1	1	1	0
Johns Hopkins University	3	1	1	1	0
Purdue University	3	2	0	1	0
Yale University	3	1	1	1	0
Brigham Young University	2	2	0	0	0
Gustavus Adolphus	2	1	1	0	0
Harvey-Mudd	2	2	0	0	0
Iowa State University	2	2	0	0	0
Macalester College	2	2	0	0	0
Northwestern University	2	2	0	0	0
St. John's University	2	2	0	0	0
Swarthmore College	2	2	0	0	0
Williams College	2	2	0	0	0
University of St. Thomas	2	1	0	1	0
University of Washington	2	0	0	2	0
Others (1 each)	36	19	5	10	2
Total	245	170	33	33	9

203 undergraduates responded – 170 males, 33 females
42 graduates responded – 33 males, 9 females

Others – Undergraduate male (1 each): Anoka AVTI, Brown, Case Western Reserve, Drake, George Washington, Hamline, Houston, Indiana, Le Tourneau, University of Minnesota – Duluth, University of Minnesota – Morris, University of

Table 2.2. (*cont.*)

Missouri – Columbia, Notre Dame, St. Cloud State, St. Scholastica, Taylor, Valparaiso, University of Washington, Washington University, St. Louis

Others – Undergraduate female (1 each): Concordia, Michigan State, Rice, Sarah Lawrence, Wesleyan

Others – Graduate male (1 each): University of Arizona, UCLA, University of California – San Diego, Carnegie Mellon, University of Colorado, Ecole Polytechnique Lausanne, Jewish Theological Seminary, Moorhead State, National Technological University, William Mitchell

Others – Graduate female (1 each): St. Mary's, University of Tokyo

The statistics for male alumni are equally impressive: 80% are majoring in some field of mathematics, science, or engineering, and 39% are pursuing degrees in more than one major. Looking at the data on undergraduate degrees and jobs for 1981–1986 UMTYMP alumni (Tables 2.3.1 and 2.3.2), the record for female alumni continues to be impressive.

Eighty percent (12 of 15) have undergraduate degrees in mathematics, sciences, or engineering, and 62% (5 of 8) are currently employed in scientific jobs. Similar statistics also hold for male alumni: 80% have scientific undergraduate degrees and 54% (13 of 24) are currently employed in the sciences.

There are some additional influences that are more difficult to quantify, but that appear to be rather significant. In alumni surveys, female graduates especially attest to the importance of UMTYMP in their intellectual growth and in developing self-confidence. In a recent survey that brought 183 responses, 80 graduates provided additional comments, with 32 supportive and 34 highly supportive of the Program. Only six comments were critical. Turning to parents of UMTYMP students, the Program's specific efforts to involve them as advocates for their children has resulted in a very high level of parent support for the Program. Finally, the dynamic nature of the UMTYMP curriculum and the involvement in its development by the teacher leaders in the high school teaching staff have had a significant effect on the UMTYMP teachers' personal views of mathematics and teaching styles, and an overall positive influence in the Minnesota secondary teaching community with respect to developing programs for mathematically talented students.

Incorporating equity into UMTYMP: Blending equity and excellence

We have already noted a widely held belief that all programs for talented students are "elitist." Although we question many aspects of this percep-

Table 2.3.1. *UMTYMP alumni surveys – degrees obtained by 1980–1981 to 1985–1986 alumni*

	Male alumni					Female alumni	
Degree obtained	Under-graduate	Graduate	Total	%	Degree obtained	Under-graduate	%
Mathematics	14	2	16	35	Mathematics	6	40
Physics	9	1	10	22	Computer Science	3	20
Electrical engineering	6	1	7	15	Biochemistry	1	7
Biology	5	0	5	11	Chemisty	1	7
Chemistry	5	0	5	11	Chemical engineering	1	7
Computer science	3	0	3	7	Civil engineering	1	7
Economics	3	0	3	7	Electrical engineering	1	7
Aerospace engineering	2	0	2	4	English	1	7
Mechanical engineering	2	0	2	4	Family practice & community health	1	7
Civil Engineering	1	1	2	4	Genetics	1	7
Biochemistry	1	0	1	2	History	1	7
Biomedical engineering	1	0	1	2	Italian	1	7
Business administration	1	0	1	2	Mechanical engineering	1	7
Genetics	1	0	1	2	Molecular biology	1	7
Geology & geophysics	1	0	1	2	Music	1	7
Music	1	0	1	2	Total	22*	
Political science	1	0	1	2			
Religious studies	1	0	1	2			
Other	2	3	5	11			
Total	60*	8	68*				

46 males responded – 46 with undergraduate degrees, 8 with graduate degrees

15 females responded – all with undergraduate degrees

* Some alumni have degrees in multiple disciplines

Table 2.3.2. *UMTYMP alumni surveys – job profiles for 1980–1981 to 1985–1986 alumni*

Job profile	Male	Female	Total
Engineer	6	2	8
Actuarial	2	1	3
Business – managerial	2	0	2
Computer programming	2	0	2
Military	2	0	2
Scientific research	1	1	2
Advertising	0	1	1
Bookkeeping	1	0	1
Business – sales	1	0	1
Composer/musician	1	0	1
Computer design	1	0	1
Financial market	1	0	1
Medical research	1	0	1
Mother – full time	0	1	1
Paralegal	0	1	1
Police officer	1	0	1
Teacher	1	0	1
Unemployed	1	1	2
Total	24	8	32

32 Alumni responded – 24 males, 8 females

tion, it has been historically true that these programs primarily involved white and, more recently, Asian males as participants. Nearly all programs are now looking at increasing the participation of females and students of color in their activities. Questions are consistently raised about whether such interventions can be accomplished only by lowering expectations and standards of excellence. The experience of UMTYMP in several intervention programs, described in this section, has shown that expectations and standards for excellence can be maintained and even improved while dealing with equity. A key role that programs for talented students can play is to change the expectation in our society about the mathematical capabilities of students of color and females. Demonstrating that they can succeed in a program whose standards and expectations are high changes the mathematics expectations for *all* students of color and females, most especially within the K–12 teaching community. This principle is eloquently expressed in *Everybody Counts* (National Research Council, 1989): "Equity for all requires excellence for all; both thrive when expectations are high" and has been the guiding approach in UMTYMP. Thus, while maintaining the historical strength of the Program and curriculum, UMTYMP succeeded in designing a variety of support, social, and counseling activities that improved the learning environment and atmosphere for capable students needing these interventions. Moreover, the interventions were designed so that the most successful would be used to change the Program for all UMTYMP students. Hence, the general principle asserting that successful activities that address equity frequently lead to improvement and strengthening of the overall program remains true when applied to programs for talented students.

A frequently underrecognized aspect of participation in UMTYMP is the self-confidence and intellectual maturity gained by the students. As an indication of the importance of these factors, it is useful to examine some observations reached by Sheila Tobias (1990). She notes that for college students, first-year experiences in courses make a big difference in choices of majors. Female students are more affected than males by this indicator. Enjoying a mathematics or science course more than other courses turns out to be a significant predictor of decisions on a major. Finally, Tobias found that the earlier calculus is studied, the greater the chance of success in college science courses. If we accept these conclusions, they provide some good reasons for the exceptional success of UMTYMP graduates in mathematics, science, and engineering majors. Their background and attitudes, including the intellectual discipline and time management learned through participation in UMTYMP, have led to positive experiences in UMTYMP calculus while still in high school, followed by productive and enjoyable experiences in advanced mathematics and science courses in their freshman year in college. Many more talented females and students of color might be successful at scientific and technical majors if they have opportunities in programs such as UMTYMP.

In designing intervention activities for UMTYMP, we wanted all participants to have the same benefits and opportunities that made the Program so valuable to its initial student population. Moreover, the Program recognizes how critical family support is to success in UMTYMP, and the positive benefits that a supportive school environment provides. Thus, we looked at many ways to improve school and social environments, means of improving family support, study habits, counseling needs, and in general at ways to provide a more sympathetic learning environment. We were convinced that many students who were currently not in the Program had the intellectual ability to deal with mathematics at the level that UMTYMP expected. Following the models of the most successful intervention programs, we wanted the new atmosphere of the Program to draw out the interest and motivation of a greater number of students by having them discover for themselves the benefits and rewards, as well as the sacrifices, associated with the long-term culture of mathematics engendered by UMTYMP. We took the position that these interventions should be carefully evaluated and that Program personnel should try to identify what worked best and for what reasons. We also wanted students and their families to be involved in the decisions about what types of interventions they felt would work best. Further, we took care to note student attitudinal shifts and anecdotal information that also indicated changes, but are more difficult to quantify. We planned to identify and retain only those interventions that we found to be most effective.

Although the interventions used were initially designed to affect female students, we emphasized those that could affect all UMTYMP students. As mentioned earlier, we regarded the improvement of the Program for all students as an important secondary effect of our intervention. We also believed that interventions that increased female participation would contribute to the creation of a similar UMTYMP project for students of color that would be as successful. Our results to date have clearly indicated that such approaches can be developed and can succeed quite admirably.

The Bush Foundation Intervention Program to Increase Female Participation

Several factors seemed to be prominent in inhibiting female participation in the Program: notable were the lack of an appropriately supportive environment – both in school and at home – and of appropriate family expectations of career goals for mathematically talented students. All too frequently, one family would indifferently request withdrawal of a daughter performing near the top of her class, whereas another tenaciously pleaded to keep enrolled a son struggling with the content. It was also apparent that inconsistent and sometimes negative messages from the schools regarding participation in UMTYMP affected females more severely than males. Finally, issues affecting personal esteem – lack of self-confidence, lack of involvement in even cooperative competitions – played a prominent role.

Cultural attitudes also have a very critical part. There is the stigma of being typed as a "nerd" for a talented student who actively pursues a special academic program. This is especially true in mathematics and the sciences, subjects in which large numbers of students from all strata continue to have difficulties. A fear of social isolation and lack of friendships if one is too advanced or too good in mathematics can easily influence students not to pursue appropriately challenging course work. This is a particularly important issue when providing advanced course work for gifted female students in their early teen years. A UMTYMP female student who is beginning 9th or 10th grade and is studying college-level calculus may face serious social problems with peers, boys and girls, who do not hold mathematics achievement in high regard.

Prior to our introduction of the Bush Intervention Program, several main features regarding female participation in UMTYMP were evident. Students were primarily chosen to participate in the qualifying examination by school identification, and program statistics indicated that the schools did not do as well at identifying mathematically talented female students as they did with male students. Even when a female student qualified, she was more likely to turn down admission than her male counterpart. Once in the Program, given equal ability and equal grades, female persistence was lower. Finally, the overall performance of female students was below the overall performance of male students.

Based on this information, the Program developed five goals for improvement of female participation. These were:

1. Increase female interest in testing for UMTYMP (40% or more girls).
2. Increase the quality of the total female applicant pool (percentage qualified should equal the percentage testing).
3. Increase female participation in UMTYMP (30% or more girls).
4. Increase female retention in UMTYMP (retention rate of girls equal to that of boys).
5. Improve female achievement within UMTYMP (performance and grade distribution for girls comparable to that of boys).

A local Minnesota foundation, the Bush Foundation, offered funding to support large-scale projects to improve female participation and success in mathematics. With a major Bush grant awarded in 1988, UMTYMP created a series of interventions that included social, cultural, and counseling activities, as well as changes in Program recruitment and UMTYMP class structure. We briefly describe some of these interventions to support each goal.

A great deal of attention was given to the first two goals: increasing female interest in testing for UMTYMP and increasing the quality of the total female applicant pool. Two key intervention strategies emerged. First, prior UMTYMP data had suggested that females in seventh grade or below who had scored within 5 points of qualification and retested the following year had a higher qualification rate than the average student who tested. Based on this observation, UMTYMP created a series of social and enrichment activities designed to maintain interest in the Program during the academic year and encourage retesting for UMTYMP during the next year. This practice has proved so successful that the above group was expanded to include females within 10 points of qualifying. A special spring examination was created, and a 3-week summer enrichment institute was developed. This group of interventions has proved to be equally successful in recruiting an increased number of students of color; separate funding from the NSF Young Scholars Program's Early Alert Initiative and the Department of

Energy's PREP program helps support its continuation (further detail is provided in a subsequent section). A second important intervention was the development of a new early (spring) registration procedure. This process relieved much of the pressure on the schools to identify students early in the fall and provided many more opportunities for families to choose to have a son or daughter tested, even if the schools were not encouraging. The new registration procedures definitely helped improve both the number and quality of first-time female testers.

To address the next two goals – increasing female participation and increasing female retention – a broad variety of programmatic interventions and changes were developed. Balancing the structure of UMTYMP with the need for a critical population of females within each class, the Program decided that classes with 50% enrollment of each sex would be most desirable. Classes with this gender balance have proved to support strongly increased female participation and retention, and all classes in the high school component are now about 40% female, reflecting overall female participation. Orientation materials and meetings were improved so that important materials were in the hands of students and parents earlier, and smaller meetings made more personal contact possible. A full-time female Program counselor and coordinator is now available to oversee all of these changes and manage the social, cultural, and counseling intervention activities developed. This individual has played a crucial role in the success of the Bush Intervention Program and other equity activities.

Additional staff also enabled UMTYMP to create regular Tuesday study sessions for students wanting to spend additional time on UMTYMP courses. These study group sessions are handled by UMTYMP teaching assistants (TAs) and encourage students to work together in study groups. The TA is available to help as needed. A study session is viewed as a cooperative learning effort in a supportive environment where ideas and problems can be shared. Students are encouraged to come with as much of the homework completed as possible and be prepared to share ideas, problems, and concepts with which they are having difficulty, or that they wish to discuss in more detail. Some students attend regularly and indicate that these study sessions are an important factor in their success.

Finally, a study skills workshop was instituted to help students adjust to the special requirements of UMTYMP participation. Held on the first Saturday of October, it covers the study habits, homework, and test skills necessary to succeed in the Program.

Social events became a key component of the interventions directed at female retention. While the socialization initially began with female-only events, student demand soon resulted in coed activities. Once comfortable with being in UMTYMP, most females wanted to be part of coeducational functions. Social functions included bowling parties, pizza outings, and movies. Also, group study parties for major UMTYMP examinations became popular social components.

To support the perspective that UMTYMP provides not only a mathematics education but encourages a culture of mathematics, older students participate in several social events that focus on college and career information. One such event is a calculus luncheon that features a social hour followed by male and female alumni presentations on the impact of UMTYMP on their college experiences. A college night providing extensive information about colleges, credits for UMTYMP course work, special admission opportunities for UMTYMP graduates, and individual counseling opportunities is also provided. Included are discussions about attending all-female colleges. Finally, the annual Learning Styles Workshop and Mathematics Fun Fair are typical of the quarterly Saturday enrichment activities that round out the cultural experience of the younger UMTYMP students.

In addressing the fifth goal, improving female achievement within the UMTYMP Program, it is difficult to specify precisely which interventions have had the greatest impact on female achievement. One that has certainly helped to reveal and correct academic problems early is the monthly telephone call to all female Algebra and Geometry/Math Analysis students. Teaching assistants in all UMTYMP Algebra and Geometry/Math Analysis classes were required to contact their female students once a month for the first 3 months. These calls served to monitor student progress while they also produced suggestions for improving the Program. The calls are designed to make students more comfortable in initiating telephone contact with their TAs and in seeking help with difficult mathematics problems over the phone. These calls have proved to be very valuable to both parents and students and are now made to all students in the Program.

In an effort to sustain parental involvement, UMTYMP has opened a variety of academic-year activities to both parents and students. These include the Learning Styles Workshop, Mathematics Fun Fair, and the College Night program. The academic progress of all students is monitored by the UMTYMP counselor, and there is continued emphasis on regular counseling contacts with the parents. The continued involvement of parents as a key component of the UMTYMP support system has been one of the major successes of the various interventions.

Some interventions have not been as successful. A program was initiated for selected schools in which key female teachers would develop some mathematical enrichment activities for and encourage participation in UMTYMP by their most mathematically talented students. Due to the difference in environments at the various schools, this program never developed sustained support among the schools or teachers. Moreover, the female students involved in this intervention did not perform significantly better on the UMTYMP qualifying examination than the general student. Thus, the intervention was canceled. Although we still believe that personal contacts at school would have a positive impact on UMTYMP, other types of school support need to be established.

Cray Technology-Intensive Alternative Course: Addressing
the needs of students of color and economically
disadvantaged students

Program personnel have always been aware of the possibility that many highly capable students might benefit from variations on the standard UM-TYMP curriculum. In fact, some of the successful students currently enrolled in UMTYMP found it helpful to repeat portions of a course already completed, or withdraw from the Program for some portion of the year. A slower-paced period, or the opportunity to enrich their background in some aspect of a subject, is often quite beneficial. Both prior to and following these periods, the students progress without difficulty through the standard UMTYMP courses. Sometimes they return as stronger students after this period of change.

Another challenge for the Program is the admission of capable and motivated students who subsequently discover serious gaps in their mathematical skills or major problems with their study habits. With intense help and major extra efforts on the students' part, they succeed in the Program. But handling the extra work on top of the already heavy demands of the regular curriculum can be too burdensome, and frequently these students are forced to withdraw.

To address both of these situations, and with the support of Cray Research and several other high-technology corporations, UMTYMP developed an alternative course. The new course maintains the same standards and basic curriculum as the current 2-year high school program, but provides a more enriched and more customized program over a 3-year period. The somewhat slower pace allows more time to enrich standard topics, provides additional background on an individualized basis when necessary, and somewhat lessens the heavy homework commitment of the regular program. An additional tutorial class each week encourages group work and appropriate study habits, provides focused activities on higher-level problem-solving skills, and generally provides necessary assistance and support. This model enables the Program to accept capable students whose admission scores may reflect background gaps or study skills deficiencies. However, students completing the alternative curriculum are expected to be able to handle the regular UMTYMP Calculus program as well as the other students. Finally, the flexibility and individualization of the alternative program and special features, such as community-based tutorial workshops, are designed to encourage greater participation in UMTYMP by students of color and economically disadvantaged students. The opportunity to work individually with motivated and talented students and shape some of the skills necessary to succeed in UMTYMP provides another important dimension of equity.

The recent emergence of graphing calculators in the secondary curriculum provided another direction for this alternative model. With the availability of the more user-friendly second-generation graphing calculator (e.g., the TI-81) and the general availability of better software, it was decided to emphasize technology in this alternative course. Computers will be used for classroom demonstrations, and the new materials will follow the guidelines suggested by the NCTM *Standards* (1989).

In many ways, the alternative course can be viewed as the strongest course of the UMTYMP high school component. It incorporates many of the practices and features that are known to support student success, such as workshops, technology-based curricula, opportunities for special help, and others. It is a very expensive program to run, and the Program staff needs to examine possibilities for maintaining it in the face of flat or declining funding. Some students and families view the 3-year alternative as less desirable than the standard 2-year program. Hence, students who are considering the alternative course and whose qualifying scores are sufficiently strong are always given the option to participate in the standard program. A sizable number tend to take the standard option. Finally, all recruiting efforts for the underrepresented and economically disadvantaged students are aimed at participation in the basic 2-year UMTYMP Program, and not particularly in the alternative course. The latter is intended to increase student options in the Program and to extend it to as broad an audience as possible.

With the experience and knowledge acquired from the Bush Intervention Program, UMTYMP initiated a variety of activities during 1990–1991 to ensure that the 1991–1992 pilot class would indeed achieve broader representation among students of color. Special contacts and commitments were sought from the schools, community organizations, and families. These included school visits, community visits (including churches and recreational groups), and parent meetings. Some groups of parents of students of color already in UMTYMP met with the Program staff to provide information on how well the Program was currently serving their students and how to structure new supports. Their strong belief in the value of UMTYMP and their active support of their children's involvement in the Program were striking and instrumental in motivating Program personnel to pursue the alternative model.

Most of 1990–1991 was devoted to gaining credibility in the various communities and identifying a pool of potential students for the alternative pilot. African American students in UMTYMP were interviewed by reporters from the major African American newspapers. Fifteen community organizations were contacted, nearly all of which were excited about the opportunity on behalf of the students they served. Some were exceptionally supportive. The Boys and Girls Clubs offered to have their tutors identify gifted children and offered the use of their clubs for testing and class purposes. Overall, the African American community was the most enthusiastic and most willing to provide significant support. UMTYMP has continued to work in identifying key leaders and organizations in the Hispanic and Native American communities. In general, we are convinced that the community linkage and support are essential features if this program is to be successful.

The Program tried some different approaches to the schools. In addition to Minneapolis and St. Paul, the eight suburban districts in the area with the largest minority populations were contacted via mathematics department chairs, principals, and PTAs. Twenty-four schools identified 150 students. Some individual schools, including a science and mathematics magnet elementary school in St. Paul, provided outstanding support and encouragement for the participation of their students. Teachers and principals were generally very enthusiastic and appreciative of UMTYMP's efforts. Several counselors also became involved and were excited about the opportunities offered their students of color.

Telephone calls to parents proved to be quite helpful. They appreciated the personal interaction and the opportunity to discuss their children's futures, although some were concerned about having their students identified as a "student of color." Overall, the parents were eager to assist and support their students' participation in UMTYMP.

A special spring admission test, held at various community sites, was administered in April 1991. One hundred fifty-eight (158) students registered for the examination, and 20 students were identified as eligible to participate in the 1991–1992 course. Forty percent of the eligible students were girls. A residential summer enrichment institute was offered to these students in 1991; 18 of the 20 students who qualified in the spring attended. The enrichment institute enabled the students to meet one another and the instructor, and to become familiar with the graphing calculator. It allowed the students to begin to understand how UMTYMP functions, to become familiar with its approaches and its curriculum expectations, and to study some interesting enriched mathematics topics. The institute was regarded as extremely successful by both the students and their parents, and it is now incorporated as part of the preparticipation intervention program.

For a variety of reasons, 5 of the original 20 students chose not to participate in the 1991–1992 alternative course. However, five additional students of color were identified from the fall admission test and readily accepted the invitation to participate in the Cray Alternative Course. Thus, the Program overall identified 25 eligible students and enrolled 20 in the alternative course, and 1 in the regular program. (Four declined to participate in either.) Thirty near-qualifiers were also identified.

The ethnic breakdown for the 1991–1992 alternative course is given below. Note that 30% (6 of 20) of the participating students were female.

	Male	Female
African American	5	3
White	2	1
Asian/Pacific Islander	2	1
Hispanic	5	1

As a result of UMTYMP's efforts via the Cray Alternative Course, significant progress was made in the overall testing of increased numbers of students from underrepresented groups. Combining all tests in 1991, 251 (up from 165 in 1990) minority students tested for UMTYMP (54 African American, 18 Hispanic, 9 Native American, 124 Asian, and 36 other). This number represents 14% of the total UMTYMP testing population and exceeds overall state percentages for these groups.

UMTYMP has repeated these successes in 1992. Additional emphasis was placed on including economically disadvantaged students. In the spring of 1992, 190 students (85 females and 105 males) tested for the Cray Alternative Course. From this group, 20 students were selected for participation in the 1992–1993 class. Efforts continued throughout the summer and fall to identify additional underrepresented and economically disadvantaged students, as well as a new pool of near-qualifiers. The final ethnic breakdown for the class is given below.

	Male	Female
African American	1	2
Asian/Pacific Islander	4	0
Hispanic	3	1
Native American	2	1
Other (Guyanese, East Indian)	0	2
White (economically disadvantaged)	2	0

Thus, in 1992, the Program overall identified 25 eligible students, enrolling 18 in the alternative course, and 4 in the regular program.

The Cray Alternative Course has provided UMTYMP with opportunities to utilize innovative methods of teaching. The instructor for the 1991–1992 class, a Presidential Award nominee who is highly proficient in the use of technology in the classroom, has developed a new customized algebra curriculum based on extensive use of the TI-81 graphing calculator. Students in the Technology Intensive Alternative course are lent a calculator for their use during the year. The instructor has access to two overhead projectors for the TI-81 to use in demonstrations of mathematical concepts. This allows him to ask deeper questions, pose new types of problems, and, in general, provide a visual method of understanding the mathematical concepts. A measure of success for this approach is that the Algebra I final grade average in the alternative course matched the average for the standard UMTYMP algebra classes. The success of the underrepresented students in a program with such high standards has been particularly striking.

Preparticipation intervention activities: The Early Alert Initiative

We briefly noted earlier the success of an academic year and summer institute of social and enrichment activities in encouraging students who nearly qualified for UMTYMP to retest and participate successfully in the Program. This particular intervention has proved so advantageous that UM-TYMP developed, with external funding, a more extensive, ongoing program to encourage greater participation by females, students of color, and economically disadvantaged students. We briefly describe this Early Alert Initiative, or EAI, for these populations here.

Students scoring within 10 points of the qualifying score on the UM-TYMP examination are called near-qualifiers. The EAI targets sixth-, seventh-, and, in some special cases, eighth-grade female, underrepresented, and economically disadvantaged near-qualifiers. The reason for selecting this group (female students electing to retest) is its significance as a positive factor on subsequent qualification and successful participation in UM-TYMP. Between 1988 and 1991, girls who scored within 10 points of qualification and were retested the following year demonstrated a dramatic increase in their scores (more so than males with the same scores) and had a much better chance than first-time testers to qualify for UMTYMP. The intervention activities for females were designed to maintain their interest in UMTYMP by providing a year of enrichment activities culminating in an exciting summer program.

Based on this background, we determined that a specially designated set of interventions based on a broad set of objectives should be available to near-qualifier students. These objectives are:

1. To provide a comfortable, interesting setting for the target students to learn and enjoy mathematics, to become more aware of its applications, and to understand its role in society.
2. To provide opportunities for targeted students to become familiar with mathematical problem solving in a stimulating, small-group environment.
3. To expose students to innovative mathematics and research methodology.
4. To create a mathematics environment that facilitates one-on-one interaction between students and highly successful faculty, business people, and researchers.
5. To help students become aware of communication problems in mathematics and improve their communication skills.

6. To provide information on the nature of mathematics so that students will better understand career opportunities in mathematics and related areas.
7. To address social and cultural issues facing talented female students, students of color, and economically disadvantaged students.
8. To expose students to a variety of careers and disciplines that rely upon mathematics – for example, engineering, chemistry, and physics.
9. To enhance UMTYMP information dissemination highlighting the value of mathematics programs that provide enrichment in mathematics and its applications.
10. To prepare and encourage target students to test and participate in UMTYMP.
11. To identify larger numbers of target students.

These objectives are achieved through a series of academic-year programs culminating in a 3-week summer institute. This program not only provides a broad enrichment experience in mathematics and science, but it also helps prepare students for qualification in UMTYMP.

The academic-year schedule consists of a once-a-month program for the targeted near-qualifying students. Some current UMTYMP algebra students participate to provide peer tutoring, a social context, and motivation for participation in UMTYMP. To support a positive social and family context for learning, parents are encouraged to attend activities and asked to help their children carry out their commitment to the Program. Participating students are required to attend at least six out of nine events, the September orientation program being mandatory for both students and their parents.

While the initial September activity is basically social, it includes an orientation for the students and their families as a means of informing them of the Program, its expectations and goals, and the type of mathematics to be covered. Subsequent meetings emphasize small-group instructional activities, research-oriented interactive demonstrations, career exploration, faculty interactions, tours and demonstrations, informal mentoring, and question periods. Each event involves a directed group activity, a demonstration or tour, and time for lunch or dinner.

Students who have attended at least six of the nine events during the academic year can participate in a 3-week commuter summer enrichment institute in late June and early July. The summer enrichment institute follows the same format as previously successful UMTYMP summer programs. The institute emphasizes mathematics and related topics as a culture and method of scientific inquiry, mathematics as a career enabler, and mathematical thinking as a challenging but exciting opportunity for each participant.

Curriculum for the institute usually includes the following features:

1. Close interactions with senior research mathematics faculty, graduate students, and undergraduate students.

2. Innovative content material and instructional approaches.
3. Small-group problem solving and group interactions.
4. Hands-on computer and calculator activities.
5. Introduction to research approaches and methodology.

There are also career-exploration activities with professionals that include discussions on cultural and social barriers, as well as discussions of college options and costs. An exciting final week of hands-on computer visualization activities at the research-oriented, NSF-supported Geometry Center is currently under development.

The pool of targeted near-qualifiers continues to grow each year. For 1992–1993, 168 students from the targeted groups were designated as near-qualifiers. However, the nature of the Early Alert Initiative and the commitment to search widely for talented students with potential mathematical interest dictate that the selection process should be very flexible. Experiments with near-qualifier selection criteria going beyond test scores has shown some promise. Thus, the definition of a near-qualifier will be examined in a broader context. Among the broader criteria are:

1. Teacher identification of students who may show potential but have not been particularly successful to date.
2. Parent identification, with additional evidence gathered to check recommendations.
3. Unusual circumstances indicating selection with very little standard academic evidence (e.g., newly arrived immigrant families, or identification by a community leader).

These special selection procedures will be carefully monitored for success in identifying potentially successful UMTYMP students.

Progress report on equity activities

The data collected since 1988 on the five goals for the Bush Intervention Program indicate some significant progress. In each of these years, the percentage of females testing for UMTYMP varied between 42% and 46%, exceeding the Programs's goal. During 1989–1991, the quality of the female applicant pool, measured by the percentage of females among the total qualifiers, improved substantially over the base year 1987–1988, and more modestly over the base year in the last 2 years. Finally, enrollment reached over 40% in 1989–1991, and is currently about 32%. Again, this has exceeded the Program's goal of 30% in each year. Table 2.4 indicates summary results for females.

The overall changes in the Program have also led to improvements in retention rates. The retention rate from Algebra I to Algebra II for girls is now slightly better than for boys. Prior to any interventions (the 1987–1988 school year), the corresponding retention rates were 85.7% for girls and

Table 2.4. *Female performance on UMTYMP qualifying examination*

	1986–7	1987–8	1988–9	1989–90	1990–1	1991–2	1992–3
% testing	43	42	44	45	46	42	44
% qualifying	23	29	30	43	42	36	33
% enrolling	21	22	32	40.3	40	37	32

Table 2.5. *Retention rates: Algebra, Geometry, and Mathematical Analysis*

	Bush Group I	Bush Group II	Bush Group III
Retention rates: (in %)	F88–S89	F89–S90	F90–S91
Algebra I to Algebra II			
Males	92.7	92.4	86.3
Females	93.4	98.1	90.2
Algebra II to Geometry			
Males	79.2	76.0	80.6
Females	70.6	80.0	71.4
Geometry to Math Analysis			
Males	98.3	79.7	
Females	100.0	83.3	71.4

Note: For Math Analysis to Calculus, see Table 2.6.

90.7% for boys. The retention rate from Algebra II to Geometry varies from year to year between boys and girls, and no clear pattern has emerged. On the other hand, retention rates from Geometry to Math Analysis again slightly favor females over males, as shown in Table 2.5.

Table 2.6 provides additional details. Most important, qualification and participation in calculus for females has dramatically improved. The preintervention participation of female students in Calculus I has risen from 17–20% to the current figure of between 28% and 36%. In the difficult 1992 Qualifying Examination, the top score, as well as 40% of the qualifying scores in the top quartile, were achieved by females. Table 2.6 gives detailed information through 1991–1992.

In examining female performance as measured by grade distribution, our expectation was that the additional female students recruited under the Bush Intervention Program would maintain and enhance the academic stature of UMTYMP. Table 2.7 indicates that female students overall are indeed achieving at a level equal to the male students. This level of achievement has been realized at the same time that the Program has strengthened its overall curriculum. It is thus clear that equity efforts of the UMTYMP Program have not diluted the integrity of the curriculum.

The data from the interventions for the near-qualifying females support their significance. One measure is the size of the pool of females who test, become near-qualifiers, and then subsequently qualify for UMTYMP. In 1990, 41 near-qualifiers retested in the spring and 13 (32%) qualified for UMTYMP. In the spring of 1991, 46 near-qualifier girls retested and 15 (37%) qualified. Over this same period, near-qualifying females consistently showed gains of between 6 and 11 points when retesting 1 year later. Moreover, many near-qualifying girls retook the test in the fall if they were unable to test in spring, or did not qualify in the spring. In fall 1990, 24 near-qualifying girls retested in the fall and 11 (46%) qualified. By comparison,

Table 2.6. *Retention from Mathematical Analysis to Calculus*

Calc I	Base #	Qual #	Qual %	Attend #	Attend %	Total %	Gender %
1988–89							
Male	62	43	69	35	81	91	95
Female	7	3	43	2	67	67	5
1989–90							
Male	50	38	76	32	84	89	78
Female	14	11	79	9	82	100	22
1990–91							
Male	51	38	75	33	87	95	80
Female	21	13	62	8	62	69	20
1991–92							
Male	43	36	84	30	83	92*	64
Female	35	26	74	17	65	88*	36

*These percentages are the maximum possible if all of the three male and six female students who deferred in 1991 continue in a later year.

Definitions:

Base #: The number of students who achieved at least a B− grade in UMTYMP Mathematical Analysis in the prior year

Qual #: The number of students from the Base group who qualified for UMTYMP Calculus by examination

Qual %: Qual # / Base # times 100

Attend #: The number of students from the Qual group who started UMTYMP Calculus

Attend %: Attend # / Qual # times 100

Total %: (Attend # + number of students who deferred to a later year) / Qual # times 100

Gender %: Percentage of males and females in the starting UMTYMP Calculus class

Table 2.7. *UMTYMP grade distributions*

Bush Group I	Algebra I Fall, 1988	Algebra II Spring, 1989	Geometry Fall, 1989	Math Analysis Spring, 1990
# of students	M = 81 F = 38	M = 76 F = 37	M = 59 F = 28	M = 58 F = 28
% obtaining A	M = 50.6	M = 44.7	M = 54.3	M = 48.3
	F = 39.5	F = 35.1	F = 60.7	F = 53.6
% obtaining B	M = 39.5	M = 40.8	M = 39	M = 38
	F = 55.2	F = 51.3	F = 35.8	F = 25.1
% obtaining C	M = 3.7	M = 6.5	M = 5.1	M = 5.1
	F = 2.6	F = 2.7	F = 3.6	F = 3.6
% obtaining W	M = 6.2	M = 7.9	M = 1.7	M = 8.6
(withdrawal)	F = 2.6	F = 8.1	F = 0.0	F = 17.9

Bush Group II	Algebra I Fall, 1989	Algebra II Spring, 1990
# of students	M = 79	M = 73
	F = 53	F = 52
% obtaining A	M = 41.8	M = 39.7
	F = 54.7	F = 40.4
% obtaining B	M = 44.3	M = 45.3
	F = 39.7	F = 46.1
% obtaining C	M = 6.4	M = 1.4
	F = 3.8	F = 5.7
% obtaining W	M = 7.6	M = 13.7
(withdrawal)	F = 1.9	F = 7.7

10% of all students testing in the fall, including females who have not been through the Program's intervention program, typically qualify for UMTYMP.

Since the Cray Alternative Course has just started, there is very little data on its outcomes. One preliminary measure is the return rate to the second-year 1992–1993 class from the initial 1991–1992 alternative course. From the original 20 who entered in 1991–1992, 17 returned for the second-year class. One student moved out of town, and another, who dropped the class in 1991–1992, has returned to the new 1992–1993 class. This impressive retention rate of 90% initially indicates that the Alternative Course is successful at increasing participation and retention for underrepresented groups.

Some outcomes are not easily quantified and are best expressed in anecdotal remarks. One such outcome is the overall aim of the Bush Intervention Program to create a supportive environment in UMTYMP, which encourages capable females to seriously involve themselves and develop genuine interests in mathematics. The success of these interventions in providing this atmosphere is best indicated by the following quotes:

I realize the importance of the early encouragement I got in UMTYMP; I will pass on that encouragement to other girls as a role model and through volunteer projects. (A UMTYMP graduate and former UMTYMP Teaching Assistant)

Last year was our daughter's first, and I saw the benefits in light of her growth and development and love of mathematics. (A UMTYMP parent)

She has never thought of herself as "very good" at mathematics, having been in a class with other equally good students. However, the reality of it is now dawning on her and it has really made a difference to her self-confidence. (A UMTYMP parent)

During the course of its equity efforts, the UMTYMP Program has developed initiatives to address the psychological and emotional needs of the talented student. Program personnel have worked hard to provide female students with a (totally justified) sense of self-confidence and an honest sense of accomplishment and self-worth. These are female students who are very aware of their abilities to succeed in demanding academic situations involving both males and females. The Program consistently emphasizes that with significant effort on their part, their achievements will rank among the best of any students. We hope to further support and strengthen the clear sense of self-direction that persists with the female graduates of UMTYMP. We are using the same strategies with students from other underrepresented groups, and fully expect to achieve the same effects.

Another respect in which outcomes are difficult to quantify concerns family support for the Program. The Program now heavily emphasizes the roles of supportive and proactive parents and works extensively with the families to help them provide a home environment conducive to success in UMTYMP. This support does not require knowledge of mathematics on the part of the parent(s), but simply involves providing a decent study environment, seeking assistance for those students who are struggling, and letting their sons and daughters know that participation in the Program is valued and encouraged. As previously noted, UMTYMP invites parents to a variety of academic-year activities such as orientation sessions, workshops on learning styles, and a mathematics fun fair to sustain parental involvement. As one indicator of parental commitment, the families played a crucial role in settling the current Minnesota budget crises for UMTYMP by generating many thoughtful letters to legislators, regents, and the governor attesting to the value of UMTYMP for their students. UMTYMP parents appear to be excellent advocates for its continuation and are very well informed about the importance of mathematics for the future of their students.

Future directions

A careful review of the recent trends of female participation in UMTYMP indicated some reasons for concern. Evidence from prior intervention programs and current national data suggest that in several areas, successful outcomes for females in mathematics and science majors and careers are being reversed after several years of success. UMTYMP appears to be experiencing its own mild reversal at this time. As an example, the percentage of females qualifying (see Table 2.4) has dropped from 42% in 1990–1991 to 33% in 1992–1993, and the percentage enrolling has also declined from 40% in 1990–1991 to 32% in 1992–1993. Also, the qualifying rate of the female testing pool nearly equaled the overall qualifying rate in 1989–1991, differing by only 2% and 4%; in the past two years, however, this gap has widened to 6% and 11%. Several factors may influence these changes. The budget crises in UMTYMP during 1991–1992 and the attending uncertainty in the schools about the Program's future seemed to affect females more heavily than males. The overall budgetary climate in schools, together with recent program cuts, have increased student interest in the Program, particularly among the male students. Overall, however, school support and encouragement for the Program seem to be ebbing. The Program clearly needs to avoid resting on its laurels and must continue to work intensely on institutionalizing successful activities and interventions in Program structures, especially within the schools. Over the next two years, UMTYMP will attempt to create greater public awareness of this issue. Attempts will be made to identify the most critical features of the interventions and to put greater effort and attention in these directions. An expanded near-qualifiers program will probably play a key role.

The complete 5-year UMTYMP Program includes a 3-year component of university honors-level calculus. In many ways, these special calculus courses, created specifically for UMTYMP students and taught by senior University of Minnesota mathematics faculty and outstanding graduate teaching assistants, are the most distinctive and influential courses in the UMTYMP Program. Although the study skills and curriculum of the high school component of UMTYMP are clearly very important for success in the Calculus component of UMTYMP, the calculus courses are the critical bridges that provide the UMTYMP students with both college-level content *and* college-level discipline and expectations. The historical data in Calculus prior to the introduction of the Bush Intervention Program indicates some impediments. Typically, about 17% to 20% of the Calculus I class and about 10% to 15% of the Calculus II class were female. Calculus III would have, at most, one or two female students (zero percent to 10%) and Calculus IV (a special-topics course for students who started UMTYMP at a young age) rarely had any female students. The 1992–1993 Calculus I class has about twice the historical percentage of female students, and the secondary impact of the Bush Intervention Program on Calculus II is already detectable. Based on this background, the next key step if the Program is to ensure full benefits for female students in UMTYMP is to increase participation and retention in the calculus component.

A major thrust for the current phase of the Bush Program will be to expand and develop activities and interventions for the calculus component that will enable female and male students to achieve similar levels of qualification, enrollment, performance, and retention in Calculus. One possible new approach will involve discussions and mentoring for students making the transition to college, graduate school, and career. As an example, a recent study conducted by the University of Michigan's Department of Mathematics (Shure, Lewis et al., 1992) documents some of the problems, such as a "chilly environment" and personal stress, that female graduate students frequently encounter. Program personnel believe that in order to ensure that female graduates are better prepared to deal with these concerns, it is important to start addressing such issues early in the process of creating a supportive environment for the UMTYMP calculus component. Thus, a series of seminars on graduate school environment, career, and work-environment issues will be considered. Additional activities will be developed for Geometry/Mathematical Analysis students and their families to make them more aware of the calculus component and the opportunities it represents for the students. The major goal will be to have the same percentage of females testing for and participating in Calculus I as have successfully finished Geometry/Mathematical Analysis.

Another issue to be addressed is performance within UMTYMP Calculus classes. Program data indicate that for Calculus I, the female and male performances over the period 1988–1992 are roughly similar. The major difference is the growth in the female student population from a few students in the first 2 years to about 15 in the 1990–1993 period. With one exception (second semester, 1989–1990), performance levels have been maintained over this period of growth. Since the growth in female enrollment in Calculus I coincides with the intervention of the Bush grant, it would appear that the overall atmosphere engendered by the Bush intervention activities has already had a positive effect. Additional studies will be conducted over the next 2 years to determine whether performance levels are similar for male and female students, and precisely what factors are having the most impact.

Based on historical data, the issue of female performance (and the related issue of persistence) in Calculus II seems to be in need of further analysis and potential intervention. The small number of female students for 1988–1991 makes any definitive statement suspect. Nevertheless, overall female performance appears essentially consistent, with the latest class indicating a slightly stronger performance. There is some indication that female students are more hesitant than males to participate in Calculus II directly after Calculus I and more likely to postpone enrollment for one or more years. The impact of heightened awareness about mathematics and its importance in career planning, as addressed by the current Bush activities, might have a positive effect on these enrollment patterns. However, it seems clear that some additional interventions will be necessary to ensure that female students who are successful in Calculus I will participate in Calculus II at the same rate as the male students. The female population beyond Calculus II has been too small historically to use as a basis for drawing any conclusions at this time. Nevertheless, this population is growing (21%, or 2 of 9, in 1991–1992) and will potentially continue to grow, based on the increased Calculus I female population. Thus, it appears necessary to develop retention activities and interventions that will appeal to the female students in the entire range of UMTYMP calculus courses. This will be reflected in future programs.

Final comments

UMTYMP has developed in its 15 years of operation as one of the most comprehensive and sophisticated long-term educational programs for mathematically talented students in the United States, or abroad for that matter. Its goals have been to provide a total mathematically oriented learning community in a supportive and positive environment. It has attempted to create a culture of mathematics for its students and, thus, has dealt with issues of educational philosophy, leadership, and environment. Its staff has learned that to appropriately address the educational needs of its talented students, the Program must also deal with their families, their schools, their communities, and their lives.

Through its efforts in core issues – equity and excellence – the Program staff learned a great deal and worked hard to address the central issues necessary to the creation of real improvements. In this chapter, we have indicated how we became more knowledgeable about the general issues of equity, how we identified specific problems regarding equity that we could address, how we designed and applied specific interventions that made sense for UMTYMP, and, finally, how we have continued to measure the outcomes.

Based on the experience gained in its efforts, the Program has increasingly refined its educational commitment to its students, as formulated in the statement:

UMTYMP provides, in addition to nationally recognized quality course work, a support system and network of students and faculty which enable students from any background to find companionship with other students in a success-oriented environment. It engages them in activities and interventions which help to boost their self-esteem and self-confidence, challenges them intellectually in a highly demanding and highly supportive culture of mathematics, and fosters an atmosphere for students and faculty that cultivates self-worth.

We will continue to use this litmus test as a guide for the development of future UMTYMP goals and directions. Moreover, UMTYMP principals have become acutely aware of the need to remain innovative, flexible, and responsive to the challenge of creating new curricula, procedures, and structures as we learn more about educating such extraordinary students. For UMTYMP, equity has strengthened excellence.

References

Chronicle of Higher Education. January 24, 1990. p. A33.
  June 5, 1992. p. A25.

Keynes, H. B. (1991). Equity and excellence in the University of Minnesota Talented Youth Mathematics Program (UMTYMP). AMS/CBMS *Issues in Mathematics Education, 2,* 85–96.

Lang, S., & Murrow, G. (1988). *Geometry, a high school course* (2d ed.). New York: Springer-Verlag.

National Council of Teachers of Mathematics. (1989). *Curriculum and evaluation standards for school mathematics.* Reston, VA: Author.

National Research Council. (1989). *Everybody counts: A report to the nation on the future of mathematics education.* Washington, DC: National Academy Press.

Shure, P., Lewis, D. et al., (1992). Summary of "Women in mathematics and physics: Inhibitors and enhancers," *AWM Newsletter* 22 (May–June).

Tobias, S. (1990). *They're not dumb, they're different – Stalking the second tier.* Tucson, AZ: Research Corporation.

Who's who among American high school students. (1991). Twenty-second Annual Survey of High Achievers. Lake Forest, IL: Educational Communications.

3   Equity and mathematics education

Deborah A. Carey, Elizabeth Fennema,
Thomas P. Carpenter, and Megan L. Franke

Two decades of intensive work have resulted in comprehensive knowledge
about the major inequities that exist in mathematics outcomes for females,
certain ethnic groups, speakers of English as a second language (ESL), and
those from lower socioeconomic groups. Among the most notable of these
inequities is the fact that people from these groups tend not to participate
in mathematics-related occupations (American Association of University
Women, 1992; Dossey, Mullis, Lindquist, & Chambers, 1988). The problems are easily identified, but their causation is complex and influenced by
multiple factors – many of which are outside the schools' control – that
differ by group. Intervention programs can alleviate the problem for some
students (Clewell, Anderson, & Thorpe, 1992). However, inequities in
mathematics achievement and personal belief systems about learning mathematics and its usefulness still exist among various ethnic groups, speakers
of diverse languages, and females and males. It is clearly documented that
inequities exist and that they can be alleviated. However, in most classrooms and to many mathematics educators, equity is seldom a concern. In
a recent review of literature related to equity issues, Secada (1992) noted
"its marginal status relative to mainstream mathematics research" (p. 654).
Meyer (1991) called equity the missing element in recent reform agendas
for mathematics education. While most documents that call for reform in
mathematics education include statements about the necessity for *all* students to learn mathematics, even casual reading of the documents provides
no information about the inequities that exist, or how equity for diverse
groups of currently disadvantaged students may be achieved. There are at
least two paths being suggested for achieving equity.

Paths to achieving equity

Diverse curricula for diverse groups?

Multicultural curricula have been suggested as one approach to developing
equitable mathematics programs. Those who advocate this approach suggest that instruction should reflect the multicultural or gender-related back-

93

ground of students and that it should be organized so that a variety of learning styles can be accommodated. Some curriculum projects, for example, are steeped in the cultural heritage of African American children and focus on expressive as well as receptive language skills (Hale-Benson, 1990).

Advocates of multicultural education suggest that diverse cultures must be represented in all curricula. (See, for example, Banks, 1991b; Grant, Sleeter, & Anderson, 1986.) They suggest that instructional activities must be organized around and embedded in multicultural contexts so that each learner can relate his or her own personal background to what is to be learned. It also is argued that rich multicultural contexts will help learners develop a strong sense of identity with the roots of their own culture, as well as develop knowledge and beliefs in the importance of a multicultural society. According to proponents, multiculturalism must be included in all classrooms so that learners can relate to the relevance of the curriculum and develop feelings of self-worth as a result of recognizing the importance of their culture. By learning about a variety of cultural viewpoints, learners come to appreciate and want to participate in a society composed of people from many cultural backgrounds. Thus, diversity of cultural contexts is a major consideration in the development of a multicultural curriculum.

Some scholars, however, believe that adding content on ethnic groups and women to existing mainstream curricula is compromising and does not address the academic performance of minorities (Ogbu, 1992). As Banks (1991a) states:

When the curriculum is revised using either an additive or an infusion approach, the basic assumptions, perspectives, paradigms, and values of the dominant curriculum remain unchallenged and substantially unchanged, despite the addition of ethnic content or content about women. (p. 130)

Existing multicultural mathematics programs tend to present a limited view of mathematics. For example, a typical multicultural activity is learning about non–Hindu-Arabic counting systems. This activity may give children an appreciation of the development of number, but it is limited in helping students understand place-value concepts, which are essential for learning more advanced mathematical concepts. Introducing children to games from their cultural heritage may increase their level of interest and participation, but such activities do not necessarily enable children to understand the mathematics. Nor can all mathematics be embedded in such activities.

Another justification for the development of diverse curricula for diverse groups has come from those concerned with learning styles. For example, some evidence suggests that males learn best in a competitive, individualistic environment (Fennema & Peterson, 1986). However, the evidence that confirms the existence of differential learning styles among groups is not convincing to most scholars. The argument for basing curriculum on diverse learning styles is more strongly supported on theoretical and philosophical grounds than on empirical grounds (Cheek, 1985; Gilbert & Gay, 1985; Hale-Benson, 1986). Measures of cognitive styles suggest that learning preferences do exist, but the literature does not support the idea that instruction that attempts to take learning styles into account results in improved learning (Tiedemann, 1989).

It is important to keep in mind that the norms under which we have described learning and academic success in the past are suspect (Secada, 1992). That is, the academic achievements of an individual have been recognized when they conform to traditionally held beliefs about what constitutes success in school. By many accounts, some of which are expressed in other chapters in this book, success has been defined from a white male–oriented perspective, to which all accomplishments are then compared. As a result, what is to be learned, and an individual's ways of knowing and behavior within the school environment, have been dictated by these established norms. For example, the literature on field-dependent and field-independent learners tends to characterize African American students as having considerable learning deficiencies. In examining a list of characteristics associated with specific cognitive or learning styles, those attributed to African American students may be interpreted as limitations in terms of current school practice (Hale-Benson, 1986, Tables 1 and 2, p. 33). As a group, their learning style is identified as field-dependent. However, it makes sense that children who have been unsuccessful with traditional school tasks either become dependent on the learning environment in order to succeed, or become disengaged from the learning process. Unfortunately, their dependency is perceived as a learning issue rather than a social issue. Classrooms that support a traditional value system encourage children to conform, causing conflict within students who are from populations other than the population who determines the norm. Children from minority groups continually struggle to make sense of the learning environment and its rules and regulations, and to adapt to the situation. At the same time, they are trying to maintain their sense of identity. Children may not always be successful in resolving these differences; for example, Soldier (1992) suggests that "Native American children may determine that it is easier to emulate only the values and behaviors of the non–Native American world" (p. 17) in order to be accepted and be successful in school.

In summary, up to this point in our efforts, developing mathematics curricula for diverse groups has not been a successful approach to the achievement of equity. The mathematics taught has been too narrowly defined, which limits the mathematics learning trajectory of these student populations. The justification for a curriculum based on learning styles has rested on weak scholarship and a negative view of learners from diverse cultural groups.

One curriculum for all?

Another approach to the development of equitable classrooms is to develop one curriculum that will be equally effective for all learners. This approach is advocated by most current calls for reform. The belief that one curriculum can be equally effective for all learners appears to have been held by many for a long time. However, this belief has not always proved valid.

Consider the case of gender differences in mathematics. It has been recognized for almost 50 years that males achieve at higher levels in mathematics than do females (Fennema, 1974). Even when these inequities in achievement have been recognized, in most cases no special efforts have been made to alleviate them. For example, throughout most of the reform movements of the 1960s, there were major attempts to change the mathematics curriculum to improve students' learning of mathematics. However, little or no attention was given to increasing the achievement of females, and the gender differences that existed prior to the introduction of those reforms exist today. Although overall learning of mathematics might have been improved, the development of new and better programs have simply enabled existing inequities to be perpetuated. Thus, if history is an accurate guide, such a monolithic effort to develop a mathematics curriculum does not achieve equity.

Even those mathematics curricula that have been developed for diverse groups have been too narrow in their mathematical content and have limited students' learning of mathematics; in fact, the development of a curriculum designed to serve all students has perpetuated inequities. One reason these programs have not been as successful as one might hope is that their developers have not considered what is known about how children learn mathematics with understanding. Unfortunately, there has been little communication between those in mainstream mathematics education research, which has not been concerned directly with equity issues, and those doing research on equity, which has not been concerned with critical mainstream research. Before truly equitable classrooms can be developed, there must be an integration of equity concerns and knowledge about children's learning.

Blending research on equity and children's learning

Knowledge gained using a cognitive science research paradigm is contributing to our understanding of learning in schools. Research on children's thinking and the pervasive qualities or factors in the way they develop mathematical concepts can help to inform instruction that addresses the needs of all students. Instead of considering groups as inherently different, with different needs, one looks for universals that can apply while taking into account cultural diversity. Instead of trying to develop an explicit curriculum for learners of all backgrounds, universals that enable diverse students to learn are identified. By helping teachers to understand these universals, they can develop equitable classrooms. This idealistic approach to curriculum development is potentially achievable because of increased knowledge we have about children's learning.

Research on children's learning: Some universals

A large body of research on the learning of mathematics suggests that all children, no matter what their cultural background, learn mathematics in similar ways. When classrooms are structured to take into account this knowledge about how children learn mathematics, learning is improved (Carpenter & Fennema, 1992). There are several common themes in current research on learning mathematics and multicultural curricula. An exploration of these common themes helps in understanding and making decisions about how to design equitable classrooms.

First, let us briefly consider what is known about learning mathematics. Hiebert and Carpenter (1992) suggest that one of the most widely held tenets about learning mathematics is that it should be learned with understanding. Mathematical ideas are understood if they are part of an internal network of representations. The degree of understanding "is determined by the number and the strength of the connections within the network" (p. 67). In order for a person to learn a new idea in mathematics, the learner must be able to relate it to previously acquired knowledge – that is, the connection between new ideas and old ideas must be evident *to the learner*.

Second, there are universals in how people come to understand certain basic arithmetic ideas. Counting and modeling strategies are universal and are developed intuitively in order to make sense of one's environment. There is increasing evidence that unschooled people successfully solve mathematical problems that confront them by using invented procedures that utilize resources they have, such as fingers, other body parts, or other counters such as stones (Saxe, 1981). Such problems are contextualized in reality, in a naturally familiar setting, and the solutions are found by using a familiar tool, such as fingers (Hiebert & Carpenter, 1992; Nunes, 1992). When young children in more schooled societies are given the opportunity to solve contextualized problems in any way they wish, although they use different tools, they also develop the same counting and modeling strategies used in societies where people are asked to solve contextualized problems to survive in their daily lives.

These universals cut across cultures. Carpenter and Moser (1984) describe how children in the United States use informal, intuitive strategies to solve problems; Secada (1991) describes the same strategies used by Hispanic children in the United States; Adetula (1989) describes how schooled and unschooled children use similar strategies in Nigeria; Jenkins (quoted in Fennema, Franke, Carpenter, & Carey, 1993) identified the same strategies in Sierra Leone; and Olivier, Murray, and Human (1990) describe similar strategies in young black and white children in South Africa.

There are a number of programs being developed in which formal instruction is predicated on the intuitive procedures that all children use, and there is increasing evidence that such programs enable children to grow in their knowledge and skills in mathematics (Carpenter & Fennema, 1992). When children are able to see connections between the intuitive, informal knowledge that they bring to school and the formal mathematics that they are asked to learn there, they are able to learn mathematics with understanding.

Building a mathematics program that enables each child to construct connections between his or her own informal knowledge and new knowledge requires that several things be taken into consideration: the background culture of the child, so that the context in which the mathematics is embedded is meaningful to the child; the kind of mathematical problems the child is able to solve informally so that he or she can see relationships between out-of-school knowledge and in-school requirements; and the tools the child intuitively uses to solve problems, such as fingers or other counters. Thus, the culture of each child is used to structure the learning environment so that he or she is able to construct relationships and learn mathematics with understanding.

Thus, we have a reasonably clear picture of how many basic mathematical ideas develop in children. This research has shown that all children enter school with well-developed informal or intuitive systems of mathematical knowledge that can be used as a basis for the further development of their understanding of mathematical concepts, symbols, and procedures. Even before children are introduced to formal notations of addition, subtraction, multiplication, and division, they can solve a variety of problems involving the actions of joining, separating, comparing, grouping, partitioning, and the like.

To understand children's intuitive problem-solving processes, it is necessary to understand the different problem situations that characterize these four operations. Some of the distinctions among subtraction problems and division problems are illustrated by the following:

1. Keisha had 12 beads. She gave 8 beads to Imani. How many beads does Keisha have now?
2. Keisha had 8 beads. Imani gave her some more beads and now she has 12. How many beads did Imani give her?
3. Keisha had some beads. Imani gave her 8 more beads and now she has 12. How many beads did Keisha have to start with?

4. Keisha has 12 beads. Imani has 8 beads. How many more beads does Keisha have than Imani?
5. Keisha had 12 beads. She put 4 beads in each braid. How many braids have beads?
6. Keisha had 12 beads. She made 4 braids with the same number of beads in each braid. How many beads are in each braid?

The distinctions among these problems are critical because they reflect the ways in which children think about and solve the problems. Initially, children model the action or relations in the problem directly. Children who use a direct modeling strategy solve the first problem by making a set of 12 counters (to represent the beads), then removing 8 of them. They solve the second problem by first making a set of 8 counters, then adding on more counters until they have 12. Many young children cannot solve the third problem because the initial quantity, the number of beads Keisha had to start with, is unknown and, therefore, makes the problem difficult to model directly. The fourth problem is often solved by matching, in a one-to-one correspondence, a set of 12 counters with a set of 8 counters. The fifth problem is solved by putting counters into groups of 4, then counting the number of groups. The last problem is solved first by dealing out 12 counters into four groups, then counting the number of objects in each group. With the possible exception of the third, all of these problems can be solved by children who are in kindergarten or first grade, if they are given the opportunity to model the problem situations (Carpenter, Ansell, Franke, Fennema, & Weisbeck, 1993).

Modeling strategies, which directly represent problems with concrete objects, provide the foundation for the development of more abstract ways of solving problems and thinking about numbers that involve counting. For example, children come to recognize that it is not necessary to make a set of objects initially to solve the second problem. They can find the answer just by counting from 8 to 12 and keeping track of the number of counts. Similarly, the first problem can be solved by counting back 4 from 12, and the fifth problem can be solved by counting by 4s (4, 8, 12). The sixth problem, on the other hand, is more difficult to solve by counting. Because the number of objects in each group is not known – that is, the number of beads in each braid – children do not have a specific multiple to count. This analysis of problems and children's strategies for solving them provides a principled basis for understanding differences in the difficulty of the problems and why children may have more difficulty in using particular strategies to solve certain problems.

In the process of solving problems, children learn number facts, not as isolated bits of information, but in a way that builds on the relationships between facts. Certain facts, like doubles (i.e., 6 + 6), are learned earlier than other facts. Children use this knowledge to solve problems and to learn other facts. For example, consider how one child figured out that 8 + 9 is 17:

Well, 8 and 8 is 16, so 8 and 9 will be one more because 9 is 1 more than 8. It's 17.

Knowledge of place value and computational algorithms also can be developed through problem solving. The counting and modeling solutions that children use with smaller numbers are extended naturally to problems with larger numbers. Rather than using individual counters and counting by 1s, children use physical representations for 10s and 100s to model two- and three-digit numbers. They learn to use symbols by inventing procedures for solving two- and three-digit problems without counters, as illustrated below. Symbols, then, are not learned as abstractions, but as ways of representing situations that children already understand. Rather than ex-pecting children to learn skills in isolation and then apply those skills to solve problems, the learning of computational procedures is facilitated by problem-solving experiences that permit children to invent ways to calcu-late answers to problems, as exemplified by the responses of the children to two problems:

Susan had 27 stickers. She bought 34 more stickers. How many stickers did she have then?

Megan: Mmmm 27, 37, 47, 57. Now I need 4 more. Well, 58, 59, 60, 61. [Megan mentally separated 34 into 30 and 4, counted on 30 by 10s, then counted on 4 more.]

Todd: Well, 20 and 30, that's 50; and the 4 and the 7, that's 11. So it's 61. [Todd combined the 10s to get 50, combined the 1s to get 11, then added the two sums.]

Sam had 41 candies. He ate 23 of them. How many candies did Sam have left?

Michael: Well, 40 take away 20 is 20. But it was 41, so that's 21 take away 3, that's 20, 19, 18. He had 18. [Michael changed the numbers to 40 and 20, then added the one he had taken away from 40. He then subtracted the 3 he had taken away from the 23.]

Janice: 40 take away 20 is 20, take away 3 more is 17, but we have to put one back, so it's 18. [Janice changed the numbers to 40 and 20. She then subtracted the 3 she had taken away from the 23 and added the one she had taken away from the 41.

In summary, children start school with a conception of basic mathematics that is much richer and more integrated than that presented in most tradi-tional mathematics programs. Children's understanding of number, the vari-ety of problems they can solve, and the informal algorithms they generate, indicate that they can successfully engage in meaningful mathematics.

Cognitively Guided Instruction

One program that has been developed to build on the knowledge that children bring to school is Cognitively Guided Instruction (CGI).[1] Currently in its tenth year of funding from the National Science Foundation, CGI was developed by Elizabeth Fennema, Thomas Carpenter, and Penelope Peterson as a research program to investigate the impact of research-based knowledge about children's thinking on teachers and their students. CGI was not designed with an explicit focus on any group of children, but with the belief that if teachers had research-based knowledge about children's thinking in general, they would be more able to focus on individual children. Such research-based knowledge would enable the teacher to assess accurately each individual child's knowledge. It was anticipated that having more accurate knowledge of each individual would enable the teacher to make decisions about instruction based on a child's mathematical thinking rather than on some expectation of a child's performance based on group membership such as race, gender, or ethnicity.

Indeed what happens in a CGI class is that as the teacher comes to understand each child's thinking, he or she designs a mathematics program on the basis of what each child knows and can do. Because the child has to be able to make connections between intuitive, informal knowledge and school-based knowledge, the curriculum includes components the child understands, which are derived from the child's experiences and culture. (See Fennema, Franke, Carpenter, & Carey, 1993, for a complete description of one CGI classroom.)

Cognitively Guided Instruction is not a traditional primary school mathematics program. Although the importance of ascertaining children's thinking is stressed, the scope and sequence of the mathematics to be taught is not explicitly prescribed. Instructional materials or activities for children are not provided and no suggestions about an optimal way to organize a class for instruction are included. Instead, knowledge about how children think in mathematics is shared with teachers. The learning environments of CGI workshops are structured so that teachers learn how the knowledge about children's mathematical thinking can help them learn about their own children. With CGI staff support, teachers decide how to use that knowledge to make instructional decisions.

Even though CGI does not prescribe instruction, CGI classrooms do show similarities (Carpenter & Fennema, 1992). Children in CGI classrooms spend most of their time solving problems. Usually, problems are related to a book the teacher has read to the children, a unit they may be studying outside of mathematics class, or something going on in their lives. Various physical materials are available to children to assist them in solving problems. Each child decides how to solve a problem, which may involve using materials, including fingers and paper and pencil, or doing so mentally. Children are not shown how to solve the problems. Instead, each child solves them in any way that he or she can (sometimes in more than one way), and shares how the problem was solved with peers and the teacher. The group listens and questions until members understand the strategy the child used, then another child shares his or her solution strategy. The entire process is repeated with another problem. Using information from each child's reporting of a problem solution, teachers make decisions about what each child knows and how instruction should be structured to enable that child to learn.

Starting at the kindergarten level, CGI teachers ask children to solve a large variety of problems involving addition, subtraction, multiplication, or division. Children learn place value as they invent procedures to solve problems that require grouping and counting by 10s. Little work is focused explicitly on the mastering of counting, basic facts, or computational algorithms. Instead, problems are selected carefully so that children (1) count by 1s, 10s, or 100s, depending on the child; (2) discuss relationships between basic number facts; and (3) invent procedures to solve problems involving two- and three-digit numbers.

The climate in a CGI classroom is one in which each person's thinking is important and respected by the group. Children approach problem solving willingly and recognize that their thinking is critical. Each child is perceived by the teacher to be in charge of his or her own learning, as individual knowledge of mathematics is used to solve problems that are relevant and understood.

What research has shown about CGI

Previous studies have investigated whether the CGI knowledge shared in the workshops had an impact on teachers and on students; the results have been reported in a variety of publications (see Carpenter & Fennema, 1992). The studies have used various methodologies, including precise observations of teaching, paper-and-pencil assessments, individual interviews, and in-depth case studies. To assess children's thinking, standardized tests, project-developed paper-and-pencil tests, and individual interviews have been used. The findings from a number of studies that have been conducted over the past 8 years are synthesized here.

Becoming a CGI teacher is not accomplished overnight, nor is it achieved by the end of an in-service teacher workshop. It takes time and interaction with children to learn the content knowledge as it relates to children's thinking, and to incorporate it into the classroom. The more this knowledge is used to gain an understanding of individual children's thinking and ability, the more important it becomes to teachers. They increasingly ask questions that elicit children's thinking, listen to what children report, and build their instruction on what is heard. Teachers increasingly come to believe in the importance of children's thinking as they see what children are able to do and what they are able to learn when given the opportunity to engage in problem solving appropriate to their ability.

Children and CGI

The learning and beliefs of children who spent one year in a classroom taught by teachers who had attended a CGI workshop have been compared with children of teachers who had no CGI education. Children in the CGI teachers' classrooms spent more time solving problems and less time working on computational procedures and talking about mathematics with their peers and teacher than did children in non-CGI teachers' classrooms. They reported more confidence in their ability to do mathematics and a higher level of understanding than did non-CGI students. When compared to non-CGI students, children in CGI classrooms were better problem solvers. In spite of the fact that they spent only about half as much time explicitly practicing number facts, they actually recalled number facts more readily than did non-CGI students.

CGI children became more flexible in their choice of solution strategies and increased their fluency in reporting their mathematical thinking. Children in CGI classrooms learned much more than has been typically expected of children in traditional classrooms. They learned to solve a variety of addition/subtraction and multiplication/division problems; their understanding of place value increased; and they learned to be flexible in their use of invented strategies to solve multidigit problems.

CGI in an urban environment

Academic success for the majority of African American students has not been achieved (Lomotey, 1990). Although there have been attempts to account for the disparity among students, it remains clear that the "under-achievement of African American students in public schools has been persistent, pervasive, and disproportionate" (p. 2). In terms of mathematics education, standardized achievement data suggest that minority students have made increasing gains in mathematics performance; however, these gains are limited to basic skills (Dossey et al., 1988; Matthews, Carpenter, Lindquist, & Silver, 1984). The CGI studies just reported were conducted in classrooms with predominantly white student populations. In order to see whether CGI holds the promise for providing a context in which African American children could succeed, it was implemented in some schools that serve predominately African American children from lower socioeconomic groups.

During the 1990–1991 school year, 22 first-grade teachers from 11 schools in Prince George's County, Maryland, an urban school district bordering Washington, D.C., participated in a study designed to examine the efficacy of CGI with African American students. The student population of the classrooms in this study was greater than 70% African American. Seven of the 11 schools were participating in Chapter 1, a federally funded program of Title 1 of the Elementary and Secondary Education Act, "which funds supplementary services for 'educationally deprived' students in schools with concentrations of children from low-income backgrounds" (Knapp, Shields, & Turnbull, 1992, p. 1).

The teachers, who volunteered to participate in the study, attended a 2-week summer in-service program that was followed with five full-day in-services conducted during the school year. The in-service program focused on the content knowledge of addition and subtraction and children's solution strategies. The purpose of the in-service program was to provide the teachers with knowledge about children's thinking, not to prescribe a program of instruction. During the in-service meetings, the teachers used this knowledge of problem types and solution strategies as a framework for discussing instructional decisions and assessment issues. As the school year progressed, the in-service meetings provided a forum for the teachers to discuss implementation issues. As part of each meeting's agenda, the teachers came with specific information about how individual children in their classes solved problems, and they solicited feedback from their colleagues regarding appropriate instruction.

One of the major assumptions of CGI is that teachers and children "interpret and make sense of new knowledge in light of their existing knowledge and beliefs" (Peterson, Fennema, & Carpenter, 1991, p. 74). This assumption is also fundamental to addressing the needs of minority students (Boateng, 1990; Sleeter, 1991). As this assumption was put into practice in classrooms, the content of the mathematics curriculum, the context within which mathematics was learned, and the role of the teachers and the students was redefined, while traditionally held beliefs about the teaching and learning of mathematics were challenged. The following descriptions of first-grade teachers and students in CGI classrooms with a predominantly African American population are offered as evidence that a CGI approach to the teaching and learning of mathematics can contribute to the emergence of equitable classrooms. Data sources are classroom observations, teachers' interviews, and students' work gathered during the study.

The content of CGI mathematics in Prince George's County

There is a critical need to redefine what is good mathematics for minority populations. Traditionally, mathematics for at-risk students has focused on basic skills, primarily low-level computation skills, and mathematics has been perceived as a hierarchy of skills that are learned in a particular sequence. It has been believed that students must complete the computational algorithms for addition, subtraction, multiplication, and division with speed and accuracy before they can successfully solve problems that require reasoning with mathematics (Means & Knapp, 1991). Suggestions gleaned from process–product research for helping low-SES or low-achieving students improve their performance in mathematics included "more active instruction and feedback, more redundancy, and smaller steps with higher success rates. This will mean more review, drill, and practice, and thus more lower level questions" (Brophy & Good, 1986, p. 365). This perspective of mathematics instruction precludes children's involvement with a problem-solving approach to mathematics and limits the opportunity for them to engage in discussions about their mathematical thinking (Haberman, 1991).

Before the Prince George's County teachers learned about CGI, their mathematics instruction had many of the characteristics identified with traditional curricula. Most of the 22 teachers reported that word problems were introduced during the second half of the year. During the first half of the year, the content of the mathematics program was determined by the sequence of topics presented in the textbook and focused on specific procedures for solving problems and learning number facts that were assessed using timed tests. In most instances, teachers assessed children's learning by whether or not they produced correct answers. When word problems were presented to the children, they typically involved joining and separating situations with the resulting quantity unknown (i.e., typical textbook addition and subtraction problems).

The use of the textbook as a source of word problems presents two difficulties. First, the problems offer little relevant context for children. The lack of context limits children's ability to use their informal knowledge of the problem situation to help them generate a solution strategy. Lack of context also limits the potential for engaging children in problem solving. Problems posed by an individual or the class, which naturally emerge from some investigation or situation relevant to the lives of the children, tend to be more motivating and present a real-world aspect to problem solving. Second, because textbook problems generally are limited to joining and separating situations, children seldom have the opportunity to reflect upon and solve a variety of problems. For example, textbook exercises often require children to categorize a word problem by the operation of addition or subtraction, which is determined by the numbers given in the problem; that is, when the numbers in the problem represent two parts, they are added to find the total, and when the numbers in the problem represent a part and a total, the numbers are subtracted to find the missing part. Determining the part–whole relationship of numbers is a sophisticated strategy, and young children's understanding of this concept develops over time. Requiring children to use this strategy in this way is premature and ignores the range of strategies they can use to solve problems.

Prior to the CGI study, most of the teachers taught strategies for solving word problems that included a focus on key words. The key words were to help the children decide whether they should solve a problem by adding (joining) or subtracting (separating) the numbers given in a problem. For example, in describing how she would work with word problems with her students, Ms. Ashe initially responded, "I would give them key words like 'take away,' 'how many left,' for subtraction. They would have to listen to key words in the sentences to decide if it would be addition or subtraction. That would mean something."[2] In response to the kinds of word problems that children should learn in first grade, another teacher, Ms. Coyne, used key words to classify problems, commenting, "And I think by the time they [students] get out of first grade they should know those two terms, how many in all and how many are left." The key-word approach was an effective strategy for children to use when they were assessed on the criterion-referenced test that was administered to all first graders in the county in the spring of the school year. This assessment test included five word problems, three addition problems with the words "in all," and two subtraction problems with the word "left." In an effort to help the children succeed, the teachers encouraged this strategy and had the children solve these two problem types. However, a key-word approach is often misleading because problems that include the same key words or phrases may require different solution strategies (e.g., a word problem written with the word "altogether" is not always solved by adding the two numbers given). If children are encouraged to use this superficial analysis of problems, they eventually may abandon their own powerful problem-solving strategies.

The CGI workshops helped the Prince George's County teachers to redefine their mathematics curriculum. Children in the CGI classes were engaged in problem solving from the beginning of the school year. The content knowledge of addition and subtraction word problems that was made available to teachers during the in-service program expanded their repertoire of word problems, which in turn enriched the mathematics curriculum. During the first year of implementing CGI, the children were successfully solving many problems that were not typical of the first-grade curriculum. Teachers' perceptions of appropriate problems for children to solve were different after implementing CGI. For example, a critical problem type used to assess children's thinking is the join-change-unknown problem. This problem provides teachers with information about children's level of problem solving, particularly their ability to begin to understand the part–whole relationship of quantities, a fundamental mathematical concept. The following illustrates several teachers' responses about whether they would have their children solve a join-change-unknown problem.

Teacher interview question:
Would you have children in your classroom solve a problem like: "Ann had 7 toy cars. Her brother gave her some more. Now she has 12 toy cars. How many toy cars did her brother give her?" Why would/wouldn't you include this join-change-unknown problem?

Teachers' responses:
Ms. Brook:

Spring 1990	No. I haven't. I didn't. I just never did. It's hard. I can see that it would be harder for them. It's just really something I never got to or because I was not aware of that particular format myself.
Spring 1991	Yes. It makes them look at the numbers in a different way. It's not always, "I'm going to put these two numbers together," or "I can subtract." Even though they might still add or subtract, the whole format of it is so different it requires them to think through about what would make sense here.

Ms. Girard:

Spring 1990	I do think there is a place for it in first grade but I think some of the children would be much better off if you didn't frustrate them with something of that type.
Spring 1991	Yes. I'd probably choose it to see how well the children did and notice what I need to do to continue and see where further difficulties lie, that I could pick up on that and then go from there.

Ms. Haley:

Spring 1990	My experience in the first grade up to this point is we haven't done anything quite that way. I would say then I wouldn't give them one of those. I think they would try all kinds of different things with that problem and come out way wrong.
Spring 1991	Sure. They would try that. We could act that one out. Some children would be able to do that on their own, and others we could act that out, just to give them another relationship, to put numbers in instead of the traditional one-plus-one-equals-two format. It makes them better thinkers. They have to think more about what's going on.

Ms. South:

Spring 1990	I have not done that with my first graders. However, I don't see why they couldn't be taught to do a problem like that. Maybe some of them wouldn't pick it up but I'm sure the majority would. It's more than what's introduced in the mathematics program this year.
Spring 1991	Yes. I think that they are able to work with those numbers, and I think that by working with problems like that and listening to the

children's explanations of how to solve them, I feel confident that most of them are able to solve that type of problem now, that they understand it.

Ms. Winne:

Spring 1990 That's a hard one because she has some more. I know it is understanding what it is that you are doing, but with that word more I think that would throw them. I don't think I would word it that way. She would have seven toy cars and then you wouldn't say about the more. You would phrase it a different way so that it was a little more specific.

Spring 1991 Yes, we've done that. They solve those pretty well. They need to find the unknown and it's not always at the beginning or the end. They need to understand that it could be in the middle. They need to learn how to figure out how to solve the problem.

Ms. Wilde:

Spring 1990 At this point in time, no. We have had an algebra strand here but we haven't really gotten to a lot of word problems in that algebra strand. The wording would be confusing. They would be able to do the computation but the wording would confuse them I think at this point in time.

Spring 1991 Yes. Because it lets me see if they are keying on key words or numbers, or putting things together just by seeing numbers, or if they really have an understanding that you can start at one number and count up. It shows me what level they're on, and that's why I would give it to them.

Initially, only five teachers in the study said they would have their children solve this type of problem. After implementing CGI, all 22 of the teachers said they would have their students solve this problem type. Generally, the teachers believed that children should solve a variety of word problems because children were capable of problem solving; the opportunity to solve a variety of problem types made the children better problem solvers, and it was a way to assess children's thinking.

By the end of the school year the children were able to articulate their thinking, using very precise descriptions of a problem and its solution. As part of one set of interviews, the children were asked to solve a join-change-unknown problem, then asked what they would tell their teacher about how they solved the problem. The following is an excerpt from a student interview that reflects a typical response:

I: Angela has 8 stickers. How many more stickers does she need to collect to have 15 stickers altogether?

S: [pause.] 7.

I: Mrs. B [the teacher] wants to know what you did in solving that problem. What would you tell her?

S: I would tell her that I did adding. I started with the number 8, then I said, "9, 10, 11, 12, 13, 14, 15."

In responding to the same question, another child said:

S: I got 7 more. I would tell her that I put out 8 first, 1, 2, 3, 4, 5, 6, 7, 8 [modeling a set of 8 objects], and then I would tell her that I counted on, 9, 10, 11, 12, 13, 14, 15 [adding on 7 more objects]. And I added on.

These two children clearly understood the problem, and their solution strategies reflected the action in the problem. The language that each child used was typical of the language that other children in CGI classes used to share their thinking. The richness of the children's problem-solving experiences depended, in part, on their teachers' knowledge of problem types. The teachers' knowledge of the range of solution strategies also helped them understand what the children were thinking and enabled them to consider appropriate instruction.

The adopted mathematics curriculum indicated that first-grade children work with numbers from zero to 99, and add and subtract two-digit numbers without regrouping. However, children often generated problems with sums exceeding 100 that involved regrouping concepts. Children generated solutions to their problems by using a variety of strategies that included modeling, counting, and grouping numbers. In some instances the children were given story frames – for example, "Ana had __ pennies in the jar. She puts in __ more pennies. Now how many pennies does she have in the jar?" – and several sets of numbers that could be used in the story, for example, (a) 8 and 7, (b) 16 and 5, and (c) 28 and 14. Each child could select the numbers he or she wanted to work with and then solve the problem. One teacher indicated that this problem format offered flexibility because if "maybe you want to do something new or you want to evaluate where somebody is, you can adjust those numbers easily."

As the year progressed, the teachers became more confident that the county mathematics objectives were being addressed when the children were engaged in problem solving. During the in-service meetings held throughout the school year, the teachers often discussed how the children were learning the mathematics outlined in the curriculum through a variety of problem-solving tasks. The teachers shared and discussed activities they used with their students that they felt supported the objectives. As part of the sharing, the teachers analyzed the activities and enumerated the objectives they thought the activities addressed. They were often surprised to discover the range of possibilities associated with one activity. For example, solving a word problem with two-digit numbers could emphasize different objectives, such as reading, writing, and ordering two-digit numbers, representing two-digit numbers with models, skip-counting by 10s, exploring number patterns, and so on. The teachers realized that each of them interpreted and analyzed the activity in terms of using it with their own students. The needs of the students were influencing how each teacher viewed the task and, therefore, the potential for the task was determined by the teacher's knowledge of her students. The teachers began to see problem solving as a continuous theme within the mathematics curriculum. This changing perspective of problem solving was reflected in this comment:

I'd say the biggest difference is that I'd never used problem solving throughout the curriculum, from day one to the end. And now it's interspersed with all our skill and activities and concepts. So that, as a teacher, that's the big difference for me. When I think of introducing a new concept, I think about how to put it into a word-problem setting. So it's a different way of thinking for myself, also.

The use of informal algorithms.

Understanding place value and working with the concept of 10s and 1s is a focus of the first-grade curriculum. The teachers often presented children with problems that provided opportunities for them to engage informally with these concepts. Before children were taught computational algorithms, the specific rules or procedures for solving problems, they were developing and using their own informal algorithms. For example, during one observation in Ms. Brook's class, the children exhibited a great deal of understanding of place value and grouping. Prior to this lesson, the children had experience representing numbers with unifix cubes and grouping numbers by 10; for example, 36 unifix cubes can be grouped into three rods of 10 unifix cubes and 6 single unifix cubes. In this lesson, the children were graphing the colors of valentine candy hearts. In each group, the four children had counted their hearts the previous day and had made a graph representing their collection. During this lesson, the children had to figure out the class totals for each color. The following was the list of numbers that Ms. Brook recorded on the board:

White
19
11
10
15
16
15

Each child had a plastic container of unifix cubes grouped by 10s and a Ziploc bag of single "loose" unifix cubes. The children decided that they had to figure out how many white hearts there were by adding up the number from each group. Ms. Brook drew a ring around the numbers in the 1s column. She suggested that they might want to start by putting together the "loose" cubes first, then adding up all the 10s. As the children began to figure out the total, Ms. Brook reminded them several times that they might want to start with the 1s.

Many of the children began to solve the problem using strategies other than representing each number with the manipulatives. They were using their fingers, paper and pencil, or counting mentally. Many children did not pay attention to Ms. Brook's suggested solution strategy to the problem. The class then discussed their solutions. One child explained:

Well, 15 and 15 is 30, and 16 more is 46. Then 10 more is . . . 47, 48, 49 [he started to count on by ones, then adjusted by counting a unit of 10], . . . no, 46, 56. Then 66, 67 [for the 11, as 10 plus 1]. Then 19 more, 67, 68, 69, 70 [again he started counting by ones, then changed his mind]. . . . no, 67, 77, 78, 79, 80, 81, 82, 83, 84, 85, 86 [keeping track with his fingers as he counted on 9, as part of the 19].

After the class had determined that there were 86 white hearts, they tallied the purple hearts. Ms. Brook elicited the number of purple hearts from each group. On the board, next to the list of the number of white hearts, was the following:

Purple
12
11
12
16
15
14

During the previous day's lesson, each child had predicted the color he or she thought there would be more of in the bag of candies. Many of them predicted purple, because that seemed to be their favorite color. Once these numbers were on the board and before the children added them up, Ms. Brook asked them what they thought about the number of purples in relation to the number of whites. "Do you think there will be more or less purples?" Since many of them had predicted more purples, they were not ready to agree that the numbers listed might contradict their predictions. She then let them total the column. Again she reminded them to deal with the "loose" ones first. During a discussion of the various solutions, one child explained:

Well, I knew that 5 plus 5 is 10 [pointing to the 5 and 6 in the 1s column] and 1 to the 4 is another 5, so that is 15. Then the 2 and 1 and 2 make another 5, so that would be 20. Then I counted these [pointing to the 10s], 1, 2, 3, 4, 5, 6, that's 60 and 70, 80.

At the end of the lesson, Ms. Brook commented that she was doing this a little fast and the children didn't have any formal instruction with the regrouping process, particularly in terms of dealing with the representation. She was not quite sure how appropriate the task was for them; however, she was confident that all the children had some strategy for solving the problems, and she wanted to see what they would do. She was hoping that a few of them might begin to develop some type of algorithm they could share with the rest of the group.

As the children shared their strategies, it was clear that there were many different ways the set of numbers could be grouped to find the solution. Regardless of how each set of numbers was grouped, the total was the same. After the children offered their solutions, Ms. Brook asked them about the similarities and differences in the various strategies. Not only did the children have a chance to explain their thinking, but they had an opportunity to hear how other children grouped the numbers. During this discussion the teacher was able to assess the children's thinking. For example, there were children who used unifix cubes to model the problems directly; some of the children counted only by 1s, whereas others who modeled the problems counted by 10s and 1s. Some children in the class solved the problems with an informal algorithm, using their knowledge of grouping, and counting by 10s and 1s. The sophistication of the solutions was determined by the child. In this lesson, all the children could successfully participate in solving problems by using solution strategies based on their own mathematical knowledge.

The context of CGI mathematics in Prince George's County

Children's shared experiences within the classroom can be appropriate and powerful contexts from which to develop meaningful mathematics. All of the teachers used children's literature during the year to provide contexts for problem solving. Often, the stories reflected African American culture, which children were learning about while the stories were shared, and mathematical problems emerged from the context of the stories. The following problems were generated from the book *Imani's Gift at Kwanzaa* (Burden-Patmon, 1992). Kwanzaa is an African American celebration that takes place the last week in December.

1. Ma'Dear braided Imani's hair. There were 3 beads in each braid and Imani had 7 braids. How many beads did Imani have in her hair?
2. Imani and Enna counted 24 people at the *karamu* or feast. If they put 4 people at a table, how many tables will they need?
3. Imani was giving *zawadi* or gifts to the guests. There were 8 guests. She gave 4 gifts to each guest. How many gifts did Imani give?
4. Imani has 28 candles. There are 7 candles for each *kinara*. How many *kinaras* does Imani need for all the candles?

Literature also provided the context for integrated units. For example, *The Patchwork Quilt* by Valerie Flournoy (1985), a Coretta Scott King Award–winning book, was used as the theme for a unit that involved language arts, mathematics, and art. The story is about a little girl, Tanya, who loved to listen to her grandmother talk about the patchwork quilt she was making, using colorful scraps of material from clothing of different members of the family. The children became involved in problems about the numbers of squares in the quilt and the shape and design of the quilt. They generated their own word problems and wrote descriptions of the squares they designed for a class quilt.

Use of the textbook

Most of the teachers had relied on the textbook to determine the content and context of the curriculum prior to CGI. As one teacher, Ms. Riley, stated, "I would say that during the year we try to pace ourselves to complete the book. We do basically what the book has." However, as the teachers began to incorporate more word problems into their curriculum and adjust their instruction to their children, they found their textbook less useful. As the year progressed, the teachers had a continuing conversation about how the textbook could be used to support their teaching goals. Although a couple of schools required the teachers to use the textbook as part of their daily lesson planning, many of the teachers did not rely on the textbook because they felt it did not meet the needs of the students, particularly in terms of providing a context for problem solving. The teachers often looked to the students as a resource for determining lesson content. In explaining how she decided on the content, Ms. David remarked:

I would use the children as the basis for our learning. With a book, you can't do that. You know, when you're on page such and such, you just can't do that. And what I did, I took the objectives, Prince George's County objectives, saw what I had to teach, and then I applied it to the children. And with the children writing story problems, giving their different experiences, it was just much easier. And they felt more comfortable and they had ownership of math, then.

By the end of the first year of implementing CGI, the teachers generally used the text for homework assignments, to assign pages for the children to complete as seat work during small-group work, or they did not use the textbook at all. The shift in focus from the textbook to the children, as a way to determine the content, enriched the mathematics instruction because the teachers built on the experiences of the children. By listening to children and being sensitive to what they were saying, the teachers were able to situate the mathematics within a context that needed no introduction for them. Ms. Brook talked about the opportunities the children presented to her and how she used them:

Sometimes we would start a lesson and they [the students] would say something and that would start us right off on some new skill, or something that you were going to cover next week. And here it was, all ready for you. And it always was a nice surprise how the kids kept it going. The kids will keep it going all by themselves, with the problems and sharing. It's really been amazing to me how that happened. So I feel very good about CGI.

The role of the teacher

Creating an environment. As part of the initial summer in-service program, the teachers viewed videotapes of children solving word problems, read and discussed classroom vignettes of problem-solving lessons, and read articles about children's strategies. They were intrigued, yet cautious, about embracing these ideas, and seriously questioned the feasibility of engaging their students in the types of activities they were seeing on videotape and reading about in the articles. The existing examples of CGI classrooms had little demographic resemblance to the classrooms in Prince George's County. The teachers naturally raised questions about differences in student population, the structure of the curriculum, accountability, the testing program, and so forth, which they felt could impact the implementation of CGI. To some degree, each teacher addressed these questions in her own classroom through the support of her colleagues and her willingness to experiment and redefine her role as a teacher.

In September the teachers found their students quite capable of solving word problems, although there were differences in ability. Communication, then, was important:

CGI made me want to set up my classroom so that I was free to talk to kids. And I never felt the need for that before. You know, I could walk around and see what someone else was doing, and maybe ask a few questions, but now I want to talk some more. I want to say, "What were you thinking?" "How did you get that?" And it takes time. So that desire made me create an environment in the classroom that allowed me to do that. Maybe that's what happened first. (Ms. Morris)

A major concern then was how to encourage the children to share their ideas. Because the teachers previously had instructed children on how to solve problems, there had been limited discussion about alternative strategies. Each teacher needed to develop her own procedures for facilitating discussion among students. Two aspects of classroom communication initially addressed were (1) helping children to express their thoughts, and (2) encouraging them to listen to one another.

At the beginning of the year it was common to hear a teacher ask, "Did anyone solve the problem another way?" Providing an answer to a problem was just the beginning of the discussion, and it became clear to the students that the teacher expected more than just an answer. In an effort to encourage children to express their strategies, teachers were accepting of all responses. In the beginning they would ask specific questions about how the problem was solved when a child had difficulty articulating the strategy. For example, teachers would comment: "I saw you use your cubes. What did you do with your cubes to help you solve the problem? What did you do first with your cubes? What numbers did you count?" and, "Tell us what numbers you counted." These direct questions were intended to focus on the specific aspects of a child's strategy. A teacher usually had observed a child solving a problem and was able to help him or her reconstruct the solution. Because the children had become better at describing their thinking, the teachers asked them fewer questions.

This pattern of communication did not require children to listen to one another because they were all able to share their strategies. As the year went on, teachers would have children talk about the similarities and differences of what each child had to offer. When a child described a strategy that was similar to one that had already been presented, the teacher would ask the child how his or her way of solving the problem compared with the one that had been shared. In order for a child to contribute to the class discussion, it then became important to know what had already been presented and discussed.

The teachers had the children use the overhead projector as a medium for sharing strategies. This worked particularly well for children who used direct modeling strategies. When individuals or pairs of children were explaining their strategy at the overhead projector, they sometimes forgot the numbers they were working with or miscounted. The other children in the class were able to offer assistance when this occurred, which increased the level of participation among the students.

Throughout the year the teachers struggled with their traditional ideas about teaching and learning mathematics. The emphasis on the role of the teacher had been that "the teacher should be a good model. She should explain it in several ways . . . give a lot of teaching experiences so that they will learn the concepts." As the teachers began to look to the children for direction, they felt less compelled to present the mathematics and control the situation. In reflecting back on the first year of CGI, Ms. Gold commented:

Math is so nonstructured now, I think. It's structured to a point but then you just, you kind of let it go. [The students] are kind of on their own to solve their problems, and then you bring them all back together, to go over it and see the solutions, you know. Whereas last year it was, no, "We're going to do this, and we're going to do this, and then *you're* [her emphasis] going to do it." And now it's kind of "Here's the problem, see what you can do. We'll meet back in two minutes." I'm mean it's structured, we have a definite routine.

The environment that the teachers created with the help of the students placed less responsibility on the teacher and more on the student. From a practical point of view, it first took teachers time to adjust to the level of conversation in the class and to be patient with students. From a pedagogical point of view, what distinguished teachers who allowed the children the freedom to direct their learning from those who imposed constraints on the learning environment was the ability to recognize what the children had to offer. All of the teachers moved in the direction of helping children express their ideas. Not all of the teachers were able to react to what they heard from children. It is heartening to know that the teachers took the first step in developing an equitable classroom by encouraging student dialogue. Nevertheless, it takes time and support for the teachers to hone their pedagogical skills and effectively respond to their students' thinking.

Teachers' interpretations of CGI. Content knowledge of addition and subtraction problem types and children's solution strategies are critical components of CGI. This knowledge was shared with the teachers and they decided how they would use it in their classrooms. Because CGI is not a prescribed program of instruction, it was important to ascertain what the teachers meant when they talked about implementing CGI. During the year, the teachers were asked several times to describe CGI. Their descriptions and interpretations were influenced by their experiences with children, particularly the quality of the interactions they had with children when they were solving problems.

At an in-service meeting during the year, one of the teachers, Ms. Gold, asked the group for suggestions about how she could organize and share information about CGI with colleagues at her school. Ms. Gold's principal had asked her to make a presentation to the faculty during one of their in-service days. Since several teachers in the project were asked to make similar presentations at their schools, the teachers felt it would be valuable to spend some time discussing how information about CGI could be shared. Before the teachers started the discussion, each made notes on what they would include in an in-service meeting. All of the teachers indicated that they would share information about problem types and strategies. However, the extent to which they related the information to student learning and its potential for influencing instructional decision making gave some insight into what they thought of as the essence of CGI. For example, 5 of the 22 first-grade teachers did not give consideration to how the content knowledge might affect student learning. It seemed that they viewed CGI as a static body of knowledge, as indicated by such statements as, "[I would] explain problem types used by CGI and illustrate each problem using manipulatives" and "I would attempt to explain the different kinds of story problems and that there is a variety of acceptable methods of solving each kind of problem." For these teachers, such knowledge was an end in and of itself and, as a result, had a limited influence on their interactions with children's ways of thinking. The critical information that they would share with other teachers focused on the academic aspects of CGI. They suggested giving teachers handouts of the content knowledge, similar to the material they had received in the initial summer in-service program. There was no attempt to situate students' prior knowledge, interests, and beliefs within the context. It seemed that they had taken little ownership of the knowledge and had little insight to offer colleagues about the implications of this information for teaching and learning.

All of the other teachers responded that, in addition to information about problem types and solution strategies, they would share students' work with their colleagues in an effort to help them understand CGI. For these teachers, the richness of CGI was inextricably linked to the teaching experiences they had had with it. The teachers suggested that the in-service should include such activities as sharing students' actual responses to problems, displaying students' journals, and/or viewing videotapes of their students discussing and solving problems (e.g., "I would share with the staff one or two word problems that my class has recently solved with the variety of solutions that were given"). Many of the teachers suggested that they would have their colleagues actually solve problems, then discuss the different strategies. Overall, they felt that sharing a few examples of students' work would generate more questions and discussion than a packet of material. After conducting workshops, the teachers reported that sharing evidence of first-graders' thinking certainly was provocative and, ultimately, their discussions raised several issues about how to support this type of problem solving as children progressed through the grades. The teachers did maintain that it was difficult to convey their enthusiasm for implementing CGI or to help others understand the potential for CGI unless they presented some evidence of how it affected student learning. This belief is reflected in Ms. Bond's comment:

It's hard to tell a teacher what it [CGI] is unless they can see it. You know, it's something that you have to see in action. I don't think just telling about it gives justice to the program. I mean it's so exciting to me to see children who were really nonverbal coming to my classroom and knowing that I was open, to listen to what they had to say.

The teachers in the project eventually developed a reference book for other teachers that would help them begin to implement CGI. Their primary goal, as stated in the introduction, was to encourage teachers to engage in conversations with their students about problem solving. They felt that the dynamics of interacting with children was critical in helping teachers understand what was meant by CGI. The following excerpt is part of the introduction the teachers wrote for their reference book:

We've learned a great deal about how children think and have made many adjustments in our teaching. This is an ongoing process – the more we learn about children's thinking, the more we adapt our instruction. We have found that math has become an exciting and successful experience for our children, as well as ourselves! Consider this . . .

The first week of school we gave our first-graders this problem:

Paul had 3 cookies in his lunch box. His friend gave him 4 cookies. How many cookies does he have now?

Then we:

1. Gave the children time to solve the problem.
2. Asked – "Who would like to share how they found out how many cookies Paul had?"
3. Listened beyond their answer. (Answers are just a small part of the discussion. We praised and accepted all responses.)
4. Listened to their comments and vocabulary.

By focusing on problem solving and emphasizing the children's thinking, we implemented a CGI approach to math, and so can you.

The first message the teachers wanted to convey was the importance of giving children the opportunity to solve problems and listening to what children had to offer as they shared their solutions. They believed that if teachers first gave children an opportunity to share their thinking before suggesting specific procedures for solving problems, they then could begin to appreciate the power of children's thinking. Once teachers were in a position to hear what children had to say, the content knowledge would become relevant because it could help them make sense of children's explanations and inform instruction. Suggesting to other first-grade teachers that this might be a way to begin their mathematics program was a definite departure from traditional practice. However, the project teachers felt strongly that this type of experience might encourage other teachers to seek additional information about a cognitively guided instruction approach to the teaching and learning of mathematics.

The role of the students

Unlike past practice, which assigned specific solutions to a given set of problems, the expanded repertoire of problems supported the idea that children think in different ways. The acceptance of alternative interpretations of problems and ways to solve them was a way to recognize and value diversity in the classroom. The children responded positively to this curriculum because they had a role in determining what problems to solve and how to solve them.

Willingness to engage in problem solving. Children were aware that their contributions to the class were considered by the teacher and the other students:

CGI gives them [students] an opportunity to talk about what they do. Talk about what they know. Talk about what they don't know. And to feel a real comfort level. To know that whatever they say is being respected. (Ms. Bond)

Although many children would solve a problem using a particular strategy, there was no need to conform to a given norm. The individual was held responsible for making clear how he or she solved a problem, but beyond that, there were no established expectations or standard procedures for solving a problem. This atmosphere had a positive influence on children's willingness to solve problems. A statement that resonated among the teachers was:

Many of these children don't have a good [self-]concept when it comes to school. They're not very positive, they don't want to come to school because it's a struggle. But math allows them to, number one, be themselves. And it was a comfort level that they truly enjoyed. . . . And you know, they just were very excited about math. And I had not seen that. I really had not seen that in the past. (Ms. Bond)

Taking responsibility for learning. Students who were in classrooms where the teachers had a strong commitment to implementing CGI generally recognized and respected the variety of solutions strategies that could be used to solve problems (Franke & Carey, in press). The children were also confident that if they solved the problem by using what they thought was an appropriate strategy, then the answer was correct. The measure of success was determined, in part, by how a child evaluated his or her strategy. Children also felt empowered by their ability to decide how to solve problems, as one child indicated:

And you can always use [unifix] cubes. . . . I get stuck I would always use my fingers or the cubes or the beans or something like that. And if that doesn't help, I would always think in my mind to get it.

During the in-service meetings throughout the year, the teachers reported that students were not fazed by any mathematics task presented to them. This was particularly true when the children were completing the county criterion-referenced test that was administered in the spring. Overall:

[The children were] always willing to tackle the problems regardless of my numbers. . . . Their attitude about math and about problem solving is very positive. Very seldom do they say, "I can't do it." And that would come only after they've tried. Then they realize something's wrong. Which is good, too. So they have a sense that "This isn't working." (Ms. Grant)

Beyond first grade

The content knowledge shared and discussed with teachers during the workshops focused on addition and subtraction concepts.[3] However, after the initial in-service program there were five instructors who were not first-grade teachers of mathematics. These teachers continued to participate in the ongoing in-service because they felt they were benefiting from the discussions and had another perspective of CGI to share with their colleagues. Although these teachers did not have specific content knowledge for their grade level, similar to the addition and subtraction literature, to guide their instructional decisions, they appreciated that children came to their class with prior knowledge and experience.

During one of the seminar days in the school year, the teachers were asked to respond to the question, "In describing my teaching of mathematics this year I would say . . ." One third-grade teacher responded:

I think I am a better math teacher this year. I encourage my students to think of different ways to solve a problem and share that information with others. I am more accepting of their individual approaches to solving problems . . . I don't use my text as much, yet I feel more confident about what my students know. (Ms. Bentz)

One teacher, who was no longer teaching mathematics, responded:

Before doing [a science] experiment or project I have begun to ask my kids what they know already and what they think will happen. Then they are involved in the experiment. They come up with their own conclusions. . . . The kids' ideas and answers are important for me to understand if they understand the concept being taught. (Ms. Bales)

It is not clear how much content knowledge is necessary to enable teachers to recognize and appreciate children's thinking. These teachers were aware that their students used different strategies to solve problems, but found it difficult to articulate what it would mean to implement CGI beyond suggesting that there should be an emphasis on problem solving. As one teacher wrote:

We concentrate on problem-solving strategies. For example, children are given daily problem-solving activities (word problems) to be completed in their journals with a written (or picture) explanation. When we go over the problems in class we stress the different types of strategies used. (Ms. Bentz)

To compensate for the lack of specific content knowledge, the teachers seemed to focus on having the children understand the concepts by modeling with pictures and manipulatives, then talking about their representations.

Children's expectations of teaching and learning mathematics presented a constant struggle for these teachers. They felt that it was difficult to implement CGI if children already had experienced more traditional mathematics instruction. For example, when the teachers were asked "How would you respond to other teachers, if they asked if CGI would be appropriate for other grade levels?" two teachers wrote:

CGI can be used in any grade level. In older children this might be difficult at first because of previous training. The students have to get out of the "Which operation to use" mode. The teacher needs to reinforce the idea "whatever strategy works for you," so to make the students feel comfortable. (Ms. Bentz)

CGI is appropriate for other grade levels. You can develop so much of your math program around what experiences they [students] had. My principal feels "CGI" is a primary program – but would certainly encourage and expect problem solving in general to continue at the 4–5–6 levels. (Ms. David)

Assessing children was an issue with the first-grade teachers because the content was more complex than that specified in the first-grade curriculum. The demands of giving students grades and communicating a child's progress to parents and principals were difficult to address. Assessment was a concern for all of the teachers in the project because they felt it was difficult to communicate accurately and efficiently the different dimensions of children's mathematical thinking, which included ability, progress, and achievement. Because the teachers had acquired more knowledge about the development of children's mathematical thinking and content, it made the job of assigning grades much more difficult. The teachers felt that the existing grading system was limited and did not provide a complete picture of a student's capabilities. As the teachers continued to work together after the initial implementation year, they began to develop and pilot alternative assessment-reporting forms, which they felt better reflected their program.

During the tenure of this project, the Maryland Department of Education (1990) introduced a comprehensive assessment program to be implemented across the state. As part of the program, a performance-based assessment instrument was administered to students in Grades 3, 5, 8, and 11. The assessment tasks integrated reading/writing, language usage, and mathematics. Tasks were presented in a contextual format, requiring children to work cooperatively and explain their work. All of the teachers in the CGI project felt that this type of assessment program would better recognize the achievements of their students, as opposed to the existing criterion-referenced tests that tended to focus on the computational aspects of mathematics. The new assessment tasks were similar to the types of activities the children were already doing successfully in their classes. The assessment program supported the teachers' efforts and helped alleviate the conflict they felt existed between what was learned and what was assessed. It is not always the case that the realities of schooling, such as testing, support mathematics reform in the classroom. Fortunately for these teachers, they believed that the assessment program offered additional support for the implementation of CGI.

Summary

The efficacy of a CGI approach to the teaching and learning of mathematics with an African American population was established by the successful implementation of CGI in Prince George's County. Students realized their potential for engaging in relevant, thoughtful problem-solving tasks. This challenged existing norms regarding what might be considered appropriate mathematics content for first-grade children in urban classrooms, who have traditionally been subjected to low-level drill-and-practice type activities. Although the degree of implementation varied across classrooms, there was recognition of the power of children's thinking in all of the classrooms. There was universal appreciation that the children in these classrooms, who were predominantly African American, could successfully engage in meaningful mathematics. Cognitively Guided Instruction facilitated a shift in beliefs and curriculum practice, and the content framework that was offered to teachers was a place to begin to explore the possibilities with their students. As one teacher defined CGI:

I think CGI is creative, generous, and inventive. Creative because it allows children to create whatever strategies they want in terms of solving a problem. Generous because it incorporates everybody. Everybody can do math. And inventive because it actually allows children to invent new ways. And they become better problem-solvers and better thinkers. (Ms. David)

The story of implementing CGI with teachers and students in Prince George's County, Maryland, is similar to implementation projects at other sites in terms of realizing students' potential in mathematics. The strength of the project in Prince George's County is an affirmation that all children, when provided with appropriate context and content, can develop their academic potential without compromising ideals, beliefs, or culture.

Conclusions

Classrooms must, and can be, structured so that all learners, regardless of gender, ethnicity, language, or disability will learn mathematics. This can be done when equity concerns that have been articulated by many are blended with knowledge-derived mainstream mathematics education research about children's learning. CGI is one example of how this blending can take place. Fortunately, there is little conflict between what is known about the learning of mathematics and the idea of a diverse curriculum for diverse learners. Teachers in CGI classrooms are able to use what is known about children's learning to develop classrooms in which cultural diversity is valued and used as a vehicle to enable all children to learn mathematics with understanding – classrooms in which children value themselves as learners of mathematics and believe that they have the power to learn mathematics.

Empowering children to make decisions about what is appropriate for them in terms of context and content of mathematics is a critical feature of equitable classrooms. The responsibility for learning needs to be placed with students if they are going to develop a sense of control over their environment. Therefore, supporting young children to make decisions in the mathematics classroom can be the beginning of their empowerment.

Cognitively Guided Instruction contributes to the development of equitable classrooms. Using CGI does not ensure that equity will be attained. Nor is it equally effective in all classrooms. Its success depends on teachers who are concerned about all children, and are willing to confront their own teaching practice and decide how it can be improved. CGI has been called a romantic approach to changing mathematics teaching and learning because so much is required of teachers. No instructional prescriptions are given; no instructional activities are provided; and overt control over what is learned is given to children. Teachers struggle with implementing CGI over several years before they are really comfortable with their classrooms. However, the struggle, and the outcomes, appear to be worthwhile to both teachers and students as classrooms approach equity.

Acknowledgments

The research reported in this chapter was supported in part by the National Science Foundation under grant numbers MDR-8550236 and MDR-8954629. The opinions expressed are those of the authors and do not necessarily reflect the views of the National Science Foundation.

Notes

1 For more information about Cognitively Guided Instruction, contact Elizabeth Fennema, Wisconsin Center for Education Research, 1025 W. Johnson St., Madison, WI 53706.
2 All teacher quotes are from interviews conducted during the year of the study. Interviews were audiotaped and transcribed as part of data collection.
3 Since the Prince George's County study, CGI workshops have been expanded to include multiplication, division, fractions, the numeration system, and geometry.

References

Adetula, L. O. (1989). Solutions of simple word problems by Nigerian children: Language and schooling factors. *Journal for Research in Mathematics Education, 20,* 489–497.

American Association of University Women. (1992). *How schools shortchange girls: A study of major findings on girls and education.* Washington, DC: American Association of University Women Educational Foundation.

Banks, J. A. (1991a). A curriculum for empowerment, action, and change. In C. E. Sleeter (Ed.), *Empowerment through multicultural education* (pp. 125–141). Albany, NY: SUNY Press.

(1991b). *Teaching strategies for ethnic studies.* Boston, MA: Allyn & Bacon.

Boateng, F. (1990). Combatting deculturalization of the African-American child in the public school system: A multicultural approach. In K. Lomotey (Ed.), *Going to school: The African-American experience* (pp. 73–85). Albany, NY: SUNY Press.

Brophy, J. E., & Good, T. L. (1986). Teacher behavior and student achievement. In M. C. Wittrock (Ed.), *Handbook of research on teaching* (pp. 328–375). New York: Macmillan.

Burden-Patmon, D. (1992). *Imani's gift at Kwanzaa.* The Children's Museum, Boston: Modern Curriculum Press.

Carpenter, T. P., Ansell, E., Franke, M. L., Fennema, E., & Weisbeck, L. (1993). Models of problem solving: A study of kindergarten children's problem-solving processes. *Journal for Research in Mathematics Education, 24,* 428–441.

Carpenter, T. P., & Fennema, E. (1992). Cognitively Guided Instruction: Building on the knowledge of students and teachers. In W. Secada (Ed.), *Curriculum reform: The case of mathematics in the United States.* Special issue of *International Journal of Research in Education* (pp. 457–470). Elmsford, NY: Pergamon.

Carpenter, T. P., & Moser, J. M. (1984). The acquisition of addition and subtraction concepts in grades one through three. *Journal for Research in Mathematics Education, 15,* 179–202.

Cheek, H. N. (1985). Increasing the participation of Native Americans in mathematics. *Journal for Research in Mathematics Education, 15,* 107–113.

Clewell, B. U., Anderson, B. T., & Thorpe, M. E. (1992). *Breaking the barriers: Helping female and minority students succeed in mathematics and science.* San Francisco: Jossey-Bass.

Dossey, J. A., Mullis, I. V. S., Lindquist, M. M., & Chambers, D. L. (1988). *The mathematics report card: Are we measuring up?* (Trends and achievement based on the 1986 National Assessment, Report No. 17-M-01). Princeton, NJ: National Assessment of Educational Progress, Educational Testing Service.

Fennema, E. (1974). What difference does it make? *Wisconsin Teacher of Mathematics, 25* (1), 5–6.

Fennema, E., Franke, M. L., Carpenter, T. P., & Carey, D. A. (1993). Using children's mathematical knowledge in instruction. *American Educational Research Journal, 30,* 555–583.

Fennema, E., & Peterson, P. L. (1986). Teacher–student interactions and sex-related differences in learning mathematics. *Teaching and Teacher Education, 2*(1), 19–42.

Flournoy, V. (1985). *The patchwork quilt.* New York: Dial.

Franke, M. L., & Carey, D. A. (in press). Young children's perceptions of mathematics in problem solving environments. *Journal for Research in Mathematics Education.*

Gilbert II, S. E., & Gay, G. (1985, October). Improving the success in school of poor black children. *Phi Delta Kappan,* 133–137.

Grant, C. A., Sleeter, C. E., & Anderson, J. E. (1986). The literature on multicultural education: Review and analysis. *Educational Studies, 12*(1), 47–71.

Haberman, M. (1991, December). The pedagogy of poverty versus good teaching. *Phi Delta Kappan,* 290–294.

Hale-Benson, J. (1986). *Black children: Their roots, culture, and learning styles.* Baltimore, MD: Johns Hopkins University Press.

(1990). Visions for children: Educating black children in the context of their culture. In K. Lomotey (Ed.), *Going to school: The African-American experience* (pp. 209–222). Albany, NY: SUNY Press.

Hiebert, J., & Carpenter, T. P. (1992). Learning and teaching with understanding. In D. A. Grouws (Ed.), *Handbook of research on mathematics teaching and learning* (pp. 65–97). New York: Macmillan.

Knapp, M. S., Shields, P. M., & Turnbull, B. J. (1992). *Academic challenge for the children of poverty: A summary report of the study of academic instruction for disadvantaged students.* Washington, DC: United States Department of Education.

Lomotey, K. (1990). Introduction. In K. Lomotey (Ed.), *Going to school: The African-American experience* (pp. 1–9). Albany, NY: SUNY Press.

Maryland Department of Education. (February, 1990). *The comprehensive plan for the Maryland school performance program.* Baltimore, MD: Author.

Matthews, W., Carpenter, T. P., Lindquist, M. M., & Silver, E. (1984). The Third National Assessment: Minorities and mathematics. *Journal for Research in Mathematics Education, 15,* 165–171.

Means, B., & Knapp, M. S. (1991). Introduction: Rethinking teaching for disadvantaged students. In B. Means, C. Chelemer, & M. S. Knapp (Eds.), *Teaching advanced skills to at-risk students: Views from research and practice* (pp. 1–26). San Francisco: Jossey-Bass.

Meyer, M. (1991). Equity: The missing element in recent agendas for mathematics education. *Peabody Journal of Education, 66*(2), 6–21.

Nunes, T. (1992). Ethnomathematics and everyday cognition. In D. A. Grouws (Ed.), *Handbook of research on mathematics teaching and learning* (pp. 557–574). New York: Macmillan.

Ogbu, J. U. (1992). Understanding cultural diversity and learning. *Educational Researcher, 21*(8), 5–14.

Olivier, A., Murray, H., & Human, P. (1990). Building on young children's mathematical knowledge. In G. Booker, P. Cobb, & T. N. Mendicuti (Eds.), *Proceedings of the Fourteenth International Conference for the Psychology of Mathematics Education* (Vol. 3, pp. 297–304). Oaxtepec, Mexico: Program Committee of the Fourteenth PME Conference.

Peterson, P. L., Fennema, E., & Carpenter, T. P. (1991). Teachers' knowledge of students' mathematics problem-solving knowledge. In J. Brophy (Ed.), *Advances in research on teaching: Teacher's knowledge of subject matter as it relates to their teaching practice* (pp. 49–86). Greenwich, CT: JAI.

Saxe, G. B. (1981). Body parts as numerals: A developmental analysis of numeration among the Oksapmin of Papua New Guinea. *Child Development, 52,* 306–316.

Secada, W. G. (1991). Degree of bilingualism and arithmetic problem solving in Hispanic first graders. *Elementary School Journal, 92,* 213–231.

(1992). Race, ethnicity, social class, language, and achievement in mathematics. In D. A. Grouws (Ed.), *Handbook of research on mathematics teaching and learning* (pp. 623–660). New York: Macmillan.

Sleeter, C. E. (Ed.). (1991). *Empowerment through multicultural education.* Albany, NY: SUNY Press.

Soldier, L. L. (1992). Working with Native American children. *Young Children, 47*(6), 15–21.

Tiedemann, J. (1989). Measures of cognitive styles: A critical review. *Educational Psychologist, 24,* 261–275.

4 Making mathematics meaningful in multicultural contexts

Gloria Ladson-Billings

> What do I need to hear about multicultural education for? . . . I teach math!
>
> Middle school math teacher

> And even in the certitude of science or mathematics it has been unfortunate that the approach to the Negro has been borrowed from a "foreign" method.
>
> Carter G. Woodson (1933)

Despite all of the recent attention it has received, multicultural education, or more specifically, its principles, are not new concepts. As far back as the 1930s, African American historian Carter G. Woodson identified special educational needs of African American children that were ignored by the nation's public schools (Woodson, 1933). Even though the late 1950s ushered in two decades of struggle for the desegregation of public schools, there is historical evidence to suggest that during the post–Civil War era there were African American proponents of separate schools for African American children (Lowe, 1988) because of the ways that these children were treated by white teachers and students. However, equal educational opportunity for racially and culturally diverse students is but one aspect of multicultural education.

James Banks (1989a) defined multicultural education as at least three things; an idea or concept, a process, and a reform movement. All three are concerned with change. The underlying assumption of multicultural education is that the nation's educational system promotes the status quo and that the status quo is rife with inequity along race, class, gender, and ability lines. Second, multicultural education assumes that students are social, political, and cultural actors and that through experiences with schoolwide change they can promote social change. Third, multicultural education assumes that this schoolwide change is important as a way to ensure not only that students of diverse race, social class, and gender groups experience equal educational opportunity, but also that all students,

126

including white, male, and middle-class students, receive accurate knowledge and understandings of, as well as appreciation for, the increasing human diversity of our democratic society.

An often-overlooked aspect of multicultural education is its benefit to dominant-group students. Along with promoting equal educational opportunity, multicultural education is designed to promote the public good. Studies of white teacher-education candidates indicate that their knowledge and understanding of those who are different from themselves is both limited and distorted (Gomez & Tabachnick, 1991; King, 1991; King & Ladson-Billings, 1990; Ladson-Billings, 1991a). Experiences in a well-developed, theoretically sound multicultural educational program can and should help *all* students develop the necessary critical and multiple perspectives that allow them to ask important questions about structural inequality, ideology, and their own miseducation (King, 1991).

The formal concept we have come to call "multicultural education" began to appear in the literature in the early 1970s (Sleeter & Grant, 1987). It is a direct descendant of the ethnic studies and earlier Black Studies movement (Harding, 1970). It is a further elaboration of the intergroup education movement that emerged in the late 1940s and early 1950s (see Taba, 1946; Taba, Brady, & Robinson, 1952). However, it differs from the intergroup education movement because intergroup education was an adaptive response to ethnic and racial tensions in the society and was designed primarily to reduce prejudice and stereotyping and permit marginalized groups to participate in the existing social framework. Black studies, ethnic studies, and multicultural education are all designed to promote systemic change for equity and to encourage the development of multiple perspectives.

Multicultural education was an outgrowth of earlier attempts toward a more inclusive curriculum. It took hold initially in social studies and history curricula. The civil rights and social change movements of the 1960s altered the United States in dramatic ways. Students of color, particularly African American students, began to demand that their history be included in the curriculum.

With the increasing shift in population demographics (Hodgkinson, 1989), the saliency of multicultural education has become more apparent. Gay (1992) suggests that the research and scholarship in multicultural education has been ongoing since the early 1970s, despite the shift in public and educational-practitioner interests. Thus, although scholars and researchers have continued a line of inquiry related to multicultural education, the development of multicultural practice has lagged significantly. School and classroom practices in multicultural education often fail to emulate the conceptual and theoretical work of scholars. What passes for multicultural education in many schools and classrooms is the equivalent of food, fiestas, and festivals. Instead of serious and systematic investigations of historical, political, economic, and cultural knowledge about diverse groups, students often experience multicultural education as an extracurricular, nonrigorous exercise that consists of eating ethnic foods and doing ethnic dances.

The schoolwide changes that proponents of multicultural education advocate include what Banks (1991) specifies as the dimensions of multicultural education. These dimensions include content integration, the knowledge-construction process, prejudice reduction, an equity pedagogy, and an empowering school culture and social structure. The limitations of time and space make it impossible to discuss fully each of these dimensions in this chapter. However, the concepts of content integration, knowledge construction, and an equity pedagogy are relevant and will receive further elaboration here.

Content integration

Content integration refers to the ways in which teachers, scholars, and researchers include and infuse data and examples from diverse cultural groups into their work. In the mathematics curriculum, that infusion might include statistical data that describe the disparity among the life chances of different cultural groups, or the differences between male and female test scores in mathematics achievement. At the school level, James Banks (1989b) suggests that there are at least four levels of content integration that guide us toward effective multicultural school programs.

At the first level, school programs take a contributions approach – that is, without changing the structure or content of their curriculum, they include information about "notable others." This looks very much like Vincent Harding's (1970) notion of "Negro history." At the second level, school programs take an additive approach. Here, histories and contributions of significant "others" are added to the curriculum. Thus, students may be exposed to Native American history, African American literature, or other such course offerings. The structure of the so-called regular curriculum remains unchanged and unchallenged. At the third level, school programs take a transformative approach. Here students experience a curriculum that is dramatically changed to incorporate the perspectives and understandings of others. Not only do they examine, for example, a historical event as presented in a textbook, but they search for alternative interpretations of it. For example, along with Columbus's perspective on his arrival in the Americas, students examine a Native American perspective on (or reaction to) this first contact with Europeans, perhaps through the writings of Bartholomew de las Casas. At the fourth level, school programs take on a social action approach. Here, not only do students experience a transformed school curriculum, but also they are expected to *do* something. The civic responsibility that schools claim to develop is an integral part of this fourth level. An example of this approach might be what happened in a New York City alternative program (Torres-Guzman, 1989). A group of Puerto Rican youngsters were studying about environmental hazards and toxic waste dumping. During the course of their study, the students discovered that one such waste site was in their own neighborhood. Instead of sitting idly by and accepting this as a consequence of being poor and Latino, the students designed a plan of action to bring about change. By carefully documenting the presence of the waste dump, which was illegal, the students were able to contact and inform the proper authorities and have the dump owner cited, fined, and ordered to clean up the site. Several mathematical connections were a part of the students' investigation. They had to estimate the number of illegal barrels of toxic waste that were being brought to the dump site each week. They had to estimate the number of people (based on the number of residences) affected by the site. They had to calculate the approximate cost of the cleanup. The contextualization of the mathematics helped to make it meaningful and useful to students who had previously experienced nothing but school failure.

Knowledge construction

In 1970, Thomas Kuhn broke new ground in mainstream scholarship by cogently describing the ways in which all scientists (social, behavioral, and natural) create knowledge and use implicit cultural assumptions, biases, perspectives, and frames of references in the creation of that knowledge (Kuhn, 1970). As important as Kuhn's work was, the challenge to Western empiricism had been made by African American scholars decades before (DuBois, 1935; Woodson, 1919). Unfortunately, the typical classroom rarely affords students the opportunity to understand or engage in the knowledge-construction process. Students are presented with knowledge as facts not to be questioned. They are not challenged to ask, "Whose knowledge?" in their quest to understand the world. The subject-matter fields they are required to study are established and codified. They do not understand their role as inquirers about the nature of that knowledge, much less their role as creators of knowledge.

Any attempt to challenge "established knowledge" meets with opposition. At the university level, the suggestion that the literary canons of Western Civilization be reexamined has sparked heated and vitriolic debate (Hughes, 1992). At Stanford University, the proposal that the Western Civilization course include the works of women and people of color provoked the wrath of none other than the U.S. Secretary of Education. Throughout the nation, scholars have become divided over what multiculturalism means in the classroom, on the campus, and in university hiring and promotion practices. Almost everything concerning affirmative action, equal employment opportunity, and equity has fallen under the rubric of multiculturalism – usually without attention to the principles of multicultural education.

An example of knowledge construction in mathematics might be seen in Claudia Zaslavsky's *Count on Your Fingers African Style* (1980). Through the story, young children learn that various African peoples arrange their fingers in different ways to express numbers. Thus, although the way students in this country use their fingers for counting may seem "normal" or "correct," they learn that even finger counting can be culturally mediated. Teachers can encourage their students to devise alternate ways to use their fingers for counting. Even at very early grade levels, the students can be involved in knowledge construction.

Equity pedagogy

The notion of an equity pedagogy refers to the opportunities that *all* children have to benefit from classroom instruction. A number of studies (Chunn, 1989; Comer & Haynes, 1991; Kozol, 1991; Oakes, 1985) have pointed to the lack of access and equity that students of color experience in the classroom. Some evidence suggests that inequitable teaching can occur within the same classroom (see Rist, 1970); that is, in a single classroom, a teacher can deny some students access to educational opportunities while providing special opportunities for others. Sorting, grouping, or tracking students into lower levels where they receive minimal or no instruction from the teacher, while the higher-track students are presented with challenging and intellectually stimulating curriculum and instruction, is an example of how such inequity is structured.

As an example of this inequity, Jonathan Kozol (1991) describes his visit to a New York City public school in the affluent Riverdale community. Here students were engaged in a curriculum that "emphasizes critical thinking, reasoning, and logic" (p. 96). The classrooms were almost exclusively white. However, in the school's special education class, Kozol found 12 children, 1 white, 11 African American. I ask, along with Kozol, "How could so many of these children be brain-damaged?" (p. 95).

Fortunately, the work of instructional theorists and developers who advocate more equitable pedagogical strategies is beginning to receive greater attention (Cohen, 1986; Gardner, 1983; Slavin, 1990). Thus, an increasing number of classrooms are taking advantage of cooperative and collaborative learning, where *all* students are expected to meet more rigorous educational challenges. Scholars who are interested in the impact of culture on cognition also are engaged in research that looks at how teaching can be structured to maximize students' interest in home and community culture (Au & Jordan, 1981; Cazden & Leggett, 1981; Cervantes, 1984; Erickson, 1987; Hale-Benson, 1986; Jordan, 1985).

Multicultural education and mathematics

How do these dimensions of multicultural education intersect mathematics? What are the connections? In an attempt to improve the school performance of students of color, competing ideological paradigms have arisen. One such paradigm, Afrocentricity (Asante, 1987, 1991), has been surrounded by controversy. According to Asante (1991), "Afrocentricity is a frame of reference wherein phenomena are viewed from the perspective of the African person" (p. 171). The perceived threat inherent in Afrocentricity is that it is divisive and "trashes" the Western tradition (Ravitch, 1990). However, a deeper reading of the perspective suggests that the backlash it engenders is a result of its insistence on uncovering the biases of the Eurocentric perspective (or even acknowledging the existence of the heretofore implicit Eurocentric perspective) and in suggesting that there are multiple ways to experience the world and construct knowledge about it. Although the multicultural perspective does not overprivilege the Afrocentric perspective, it does not deny or ignore its potential for including other voices in the educational dialogue. Perhaps the most useful understanding of Afrocentricity is one that helps us remember that learning becomes meaningful when it connects to the lives and understandings of the learner, and that the learner in many of our urban schools is African American.[1]

In a field such as mathematics, the curriculum has long been seen as neutral, objective, and immune to discussions concerning multicultural education. However, as Kuhn (1970) has shown us, paradigmatic shifts are capable of reshaping and redefining the way we understand everything. For too long we have assumed that success in mathematics is limited to certain students (Frankenstein, 1990). The presumption that mathematics is the purview of a select group affects both those who are successful and those who are not.[2] We rarely examined the ways in which mathematical curriculum and instruction disadvantage some students and advantage others. In a discussion with a colleague[3] I learned that a group of inner-city African American youngsters were grappling with a mathematics problem similar to the following:

It costs $1.50 to travel each way on the city bus. A transit system "fast pass" costs $65 a month. Which is the more economical way to get to work, the daily fare or the fast pass?

The white, middle-class, suburban youngsters who read this problem suggested that the daily fare was cheaper. At $1.50 each way, a worker would pay $3 a day on approximately 20 work days a month, for a total of $60, five dollars cheaper than the "fast pass." By contrast, many of the inner-city youngsters felt that there was not enough information provided for them to solve the problem. One of their questions was, "How many jobs are we talking about?" Their own experiences were that people often held several low-paying part-time or full-time jobs to make a living wage. Thus, it is conceivable that a worker would need to ride the bus several times a day (and pay several fares) to get to different jobs. The students further suggested that most people they know ride the bus because they do not own a car and would be using the bus for reasons other than commuting. Going to stores, church, visiting, and to the movies might all involve using the bus. The 20 days the nine-to-five suburban commuter might use the bus is not the same as the 30 or 31 days a month an inner-city person without a car might require public transportation. Finally, the inner-city students asked, "If the fast pass is not cheaper, why do they constantly advertise them on the TV as the best way to go?" Their question addressed the ethics of business and advertising to which they are subjected.

The scenario described above illustrates the importance of context to mathematical understanding (see also Carpenter & Fennema, 1992). And, as Fennema (1980) suggested in her work on mathematics and gender bias more than a decade ago, the amount of attention given to students, the type of rewards, the availability of remedial help, the kinds of questions that get asked, and who gets asked (or called upon in the classroom) are important determinants of academic success.

Discussion about mathematics and culture was affected by the success of Jaimé Escalante, a Los Angeles mathematics teacher, who teaches Latino students in an inner-city school. Escalante's ability to consistently produce high-achieving students in advanced mathematics classes focused national attention on his teaching methods. To motivate his students, Escalante suggested to them that they were "heirs" to a great mathematical tradition. Telling the students that their "ancestors, the Mayans, were the first to discover the concept of zero, something neither the Greeks nor the Romans had considered," was one of Escalante's ways of destroying the categories of exclusion that the students had been led to believe about the nature of knowledge.

Opponents of multicultural education have dismissed the recognition of these kinds of cultural connections as "ethnic cheerleading" (Ravitch, 1990) that does little to make students of color feel better or perform more successfully. What is missing on the part of these critics is an understanding of how the complete assimilation they advocate renders them incapable of developing informed empathy vis-à-vis students of color. The critics are so committed to the notion of "universality" they ascribe to the Western tradition that they develop an ideological blind spot that does not allow them to entertain alternate conceptualizations and motivations for learning. The Black Studies movement of the 1960s, initiated by students, was a call for curricular changes that included the contributions and perspectives of African Americans. Something about the kind of education African American students had received prior to this movement was an obstacle to their academic achievement. Perhaps what they experienced was best articulated by Carter G. Woodson in 1933:

The same educational process which inspires and stimulates the oppressor with thought that he is everything and has accomplished everything worth while, depresses and crushes at the same time the spark of genius in the Negro by making him feel that his race does not amount to much and never will measure up to the standards of other peoples. (p.xiii)

The case of Ms. Rossi

There is substantial empirical data documenting the gap between the performance of white and African American students in mathematics (Quality Education for Minorities in Mathematics, Sciences, and Engineering Network, 1992). There is considerable debate about the reasons for this discrepancy (see, for example, Frankenstein, 1990; Orr, 1987; Stiff & Harvey, 1988). However, what is more important to school administrators, curriculum specialists, classroom teachers, and parents is what happens in those classrooms where children of color are successful mathematics students.

Since 1988, I have been involved in an ethnographic study of successful teachers of African American students. The eight teachers in the study are engaged in what I have termed "culturally relevant teaching" (Ladson-Billings, 1991b, 1992). In brief, this notion of culturally relevant teaching is similar to that of critical pedagogy, which Giroux and Simon (1989) explain as

a deliberate attempt to influence how and what knowledge and identities are produced within and among particular sets of social relations. It can be understood as a practice through which people are incited to acquire a particular "moral character." As both a political and practical activity, it attempts to influence the occurrence and qualities of experiences. (p. 239)

Culturally relevant teaching differs from critical pedagogy in that it emphasizes the collective rather than the individual. It also differs from critical pedagogy in that the specific oppression of racism becomes a central unit of analysis. Teachers engaged in culturally relevant pedagogy work to help their students better understand what racism is, how it works, and what they can do to work against it. The decidedly political stance of culturally relevant teaching is important because of the real lives and circumstances of African Americans. Dramatic statistical evidence from organizations such as the Children's Defense Fund (Edelman, 1987) indicate that life chances for African American youngsters are much more limited than those of their white counterparts. If education maintains its social reproductive function, we will continue to experience these huge differences between haves and have-nots. Consequently, culturally relevant teaching begins to function as an intervention, to emancipate students from the bondage of education that fails to prepare them to think and act in a democratic and multicultural society. In this section, I attempt to describe what transpires in the classroom of a culturally relevant teacher as she teaches mathematics.

Ms. Rossi is an Italian American woman in her mid-40s. She began her teaching career in the late 1960s as a Dominican nun. She has taught students in both private and public schools from white, wealthy communities to low-income communities of color. At the time of the study, she was teaching sixth grade in a low-income, predominately African American school district. She was identified by a group of African American parents as a very effective teacher of their children. In an ethnographic interview (Spradley, 1979), Ms. Rossi revealed that she knew her students regarded her as "strict," but she believed that they respected her for being a demanding, yet caring teacher.

On one of the days I was scheduled to observe Ms. Rossi, I met her in the courtyard outside of her classroom before the morning bell. Although we exchanged pleasantries, it was apparent that her mind was on the lesson she intended to teach. Prior to the day's lesson, Ms. Rossi had talked to her students about the African origins of algebra. The students learned that the first definitive evidence of the use of algebra appeared in the writings of Ahmes, an Egyptian mathematician who lived about 1700 B.C., or earlier. They learned that much later the Greeks contributed to the early development of algebra. Ms. Rossi felt that the "setting of the context" was important for motivating her students to learn algebra. She attempted to make it clear to them that it was related to their own heritage. There was no reason for them to think of it as "foreign." As Ms. Rossi said to me, tongue-in-cheek, "It's not *Greek* to them!"

Ms. Rossi gave her room key to one of her students and asked her to go in and take care of some housekeeping chores. When the bell rang the students filed noisily into the classroom. They settled down as they entered the room and took their seats. At 8:35 Ms. Rossi greeted the students with a cheery "Good morning." The students responded in kind. What followed Ms. Rossi's good morning greeting was a whirlwind of activity, perhaps too complex to fully explain here. However, with apologies to both Ms. Rossi and her students, I will attempt to synthesize what transpired.

The entire time I observed her class that morning, Ms. Rossi and her students were involved in mathematics. Although they were engaged in problem solving using algebraic functions, no worksheets were handed out and no problem sets were assigned. The students, as well as Ms. Rossi, posed problems.

From a pedagogical standpoint, I saw Ms. Rossi make a point of getting every student involved in the mathematics lesson. She continually assured students that they were capable of mastering the problems. They cheered each other on and celebrated when they were able to explain how they arrived at their solutions. Ms. Rossi's time and energy were devoted to mathematics. Taking attendance, collecting lunch money, or other such tasks were handled by students in an unobtrusive, almost matter-of-fact manner that did not interfere with the group's mathematics discussion.

Ms. Rossi moved around the classroom as students posed questions and suggested solutions. She often asked, "How do you know?" to push the students' thinking. When students asked questions, Ms. Rossi was quick to say, "Who knows? Who can help him out here?" By recycling the questions (and consequently, the knowledge), Ms. Rossi helped her students understand that they were knowledgeable and capable of answering questions posed by themselves and others. However, Ms. Rossi did not shrink from her own responsibility as teacher. From time to time, she worked individually with students who seemed puzzled or confused about the discussion. By asking a series of probing questions, Ms. Rossi was able to help students organize their thinking about a problem and develop their own problem-solving strategies. The busy hum of activity in the classroom was directed toward mathematics. Every so often, Ms. Rossi would suggest a problem and the students would work frantically to solve it. Each time she did this, a new set of questions and possible solutions entered the discussion. I was amazed at how "comfortable" the students seemed as the discussion proceeded. No one student, or group of students, dominated the discussion. Responses and questions came from throughout the classroom.

As I sat taking notes, I heard a student exclaim, "This is easy!" while others nodded their heads in agreement. Never one to miss an opportunity to make mathematics accessible to her students, Ms. Rossi used the students' expression of how easy they found mathematics to make a comment reminding the members of her class how intelligent and capable they were.

At one point in the morning, Ms. Rossi directed the students to a page in the prealgebra textbook she had scrounged for the class. Rather than assign pages in the text, Ms. Rossi showed the students how the textbook representation of what they had been doing looked different. "Don't let this scare you," she urged. "You do know how to solve problems like these." From a very pragmatic position, Ms. Rossi was assuring her students that the good work they were doing in class would not be mitigated by the district and state assessments. She knew that her students would be required to perform on standardized tests, and that their performance might prove to be a significant factor in their mathematics placement the following year, when they went on to the departmentalized middle school.

On another level, Ms. Rossi may have been reassuring the students that what they were doing was "legitimate." Because so much of their work was not out of a textbook, students (and perhaps their parents) may have questioned whether they were really using "algebra" to solve mathematical problems.

By 9:59, it was time to prepare for recess. For almost an hour and a half Ms. Rossi and her students had been engaged in mathematical problem solving. She had not at any time needed to stop to discipline or reprimand a student. In the few instances during which students seemed to be off-task, Ms. Rossi or another student posed a problem that brought the attention of the class back to the mathematics discussion. Ms. Rossi told the students how proud she was of the way they had worked that morning. She also told them that they were doing work that some eighth graders could not do. At 10 A.M., 26 happy sixth graders marched out to recess. Ms. Rossi smiled but had a look of sadness in her eyes. She turned to me after the last student had left the room and said:

They're *so* smart but so few teachers really recognize it. I'm so afraid they will meet the same fate as last year's class. . . . We worked so hard to get them into algebra and then they go to the middle school where they're treated like they don't know anything. Last year's students were so bored with the math they had – it was actually *arithmetic* – that they started cutting math to come back over here for me to teach them. When I explained that I couldn't teach them they just stopped going to math class altogether and failed for nonattendance. (field notes, April 29, 1991)

As I sat in Ms. Rossi's class, I could not help but contrast what I saw with one of my student teachers who struggled to maintain order (and perhaps his sanity) in a sixth-grade classroom in an upper-middle-class community on the other side of town. Whereas Ms. Rossi was able to keep an entire classroom of low-income students of color actively engaged in higher mathematics, Aaron[4] could not get four middle-class white boys to pay attention long enough to learn how to change mixed numbers to improper fractions and vice versa. Each time Aaron attempted to "teach," he would direct the students to the textbook and try to get them to follow a problem-solving sequence outlined in the text. No sooner than one boy would begin, another would poke or tease him, and the entire quartet would erupt in laughter. Aaron grew exasperated and began to berate the boys for their failure to pay attention. He told them that they would never learn if they did not listen to him. In frustration, he told them to take their books, papers, and pencils to their desks where they would just have to do the work without his help.

At the "postobservation conference," I attempted to be sensitive to Aaron's frustration. I began by asking him to describe what he had taught. He spoke tentatively and fitfully, "Well . . . I planned to teach them how to change mixed numbers into improper fractions." At that point, I interjected. "You told me what you *planned,* but you didn't tell me what you taught."

Several times, Aaron began with what he had planned. Each time I reminded him that what he planned was different from what he taught. Finally, he shrugged his shoulders and suggested, "I guess I didn't teach them anything." I insisted that he had taught them *something;* however, it was not what he planned. As he reflected on what had transpired, Aaron told me that he taught the students implicitly that mathematics teaching (and perhaps teaching in general) was available only to students who were "well-behaved." He also felt that he taught the students that their needs and interests were secondary to his needs as a teacher. The contrast between Ms. Rossi's and Aaron's classes was striking and ironic. Typically, the kinds of students in Ms. Rossi's class would learn the "lessons" of Aaron's class. Fortunately, they were being taught by a teacher who knew those lessons rarely help students learn mathematics.

What we learn from teachers like Ms. Rossi

Although it may be obvious that Ms. Rossi is a special teacher, to dismiss what she does and how she does it merely as a function of her personality and/or idiosyncratic teaching style does her, and teachers like her, a disservice. Seven other equally talented teachers were a part of this study (Ladson-Billings, 1991b) and despite some obvious personality and teaching-style differences, they all have helped African American students produce impressive academic results. Also, it is important to look at Ms. Rossi's work at the classroom level because so much of effective educational practice is considered primarily at the school level (Edmonds, 1979; Stedman, 1987). Fortunately, more research literature is developing at the classroom level as we attempt to understand the role culture plays in cognition (see, for example, Au & Jordan, 1981; Cazden & Leggett, 1981; Macias, 1987; Moll, 1988; Torres-Guzman, 1989).

It is important to attempt to understand Ms. Rossi's pedagogy as a useful heuristic for solving the problem of poor mathematics performance of African American students. Using the vignette already described, we can extrapolate some tentative guidelines or principles about the successful teaching of students who have traditionally failed to perform well in mathematics – in this case, African American students.

Students treated as competent are likely to demonstrate competence. Although there has been an abundance of literature on the impact of teacher expectation on student achievement (for example, see Cooper, 1979; Crano & Mellon, 1987; Smith, 1980), Linda Winfield's (1986) work on teachers' beliefs about academically at-risk students in urban schools gives us some specific insights concerning how these expectations apply to inner-city – in this case, African American – students. Winfield suggests that teachers expect to either improve or maintain the at-risk performance of urban students and act in ways in which they assume or shift the responsibility for student achievement.

Another conception of teacher expectations and their impact on student performance is found in the literacy research. Gee (1987) suggests that the explanation for the wide differences in literacy achievement between African American working- and lower-class students, and white, middle-class students, is the way the two groups experience instruction. White, middle-class students are treated as if they already have knowledge, and experience instruction as *apprenticeship*. However, African American students often are treated as if they do not have knowledge and experience instruction as *teaching*. When students are apprenticed, they are afforded the opportunity to perform tasks that they have not fully learned. An example might be found in the way we "teach" our children to do household chores. Parents rarely write down step-by-step instructions for washing the dishes, mowing the lawn, or making the beds. Instead, they allow their children to begin working on a chore and encourage their success through assistance and coaching. In the classroom, this apprenticing is played out by teachers treating white, middle-class students as if they are competent in areas they are not. They are treated as if they come with knowledge (which they do). However, African American youngsters often are treated as if they have *no* knowledge. Thus, as "empty vessels" they must be filled. In a recent workshop with white teachers teaching in a desegregated school setting, one teacher wrote the following on a notecard: "These students generally lack that 'spark' for learning because all these environmental factors (e.g., poverty, neglect) are interfering. How do we try to correct all of these problems?"[5] This teacher has a conception of African American students that suggests they are not equipped to receive instruction. She cannot apprentice these students because she does not believe that they have anything on which to build.

Providing instructional scaffolding for students allows them to move from what they know to what they do not know. Rather than worry over what students do not know, Ms. Rossi demonstrated that it is possible to use the students' prior knowledge as a bridge to new learning. Her instructions to students to not allow the organization of the textbook to distract them was a key strategy for helping them use their prior knowledge in a new situation.[6] Too often, students of color find themselves in classrooms in which the teacher insists that certain prerequisites are necessary before any instruction can take place. If students lack these prerequisites, they are seen as "unworthy" of instruction. Again, note cards from the teacher in-service provide relevant examples:

Most of the black students who attend [school name] live in the . . . neighborhood. [This] neighborhood has a very poor reputation and a history of problems. What insights might you have about dealing with students from this neighborhood?

Parents can also be roadblocks to their child's education – mobility – lack of interest in child's education – no homework time – no supplies – not coming to conferences. What can I do? I don't have time to work on these issues with parents.

I find myself buying, giving, many more extras, even much more attention, to minority students. Doesn't this seem to be the reverse of acting discriminatory? I seem to go too far to the right to try to make the [minority] student succeed.

The first two teachers reflect an attitude that the children are somehow responsible for their personal economic and social situations. Rather than look for any intellectual potential in the children, the teachers are expressing a belief that the students cannot learn because they live in a neighborhood "with a poor reputation" or have parents with a "lack of interest" in their children's education. Neither sees the contradiction between their attitudes and the notion that education is supposed to help one rise above one's circumstances. They are allowing the students' circumstances to define their possibilities.

The third teacher suggests that the African American students are entitled to only so much of her time and resources. If she works harder to help them succeed, then she is somehow being unfair. Implicit in her comment is the attitude that the students are not worthy of any additional time or attention.

The major focus of the classroom must be instructional. The vignette of Ms. Rossi's teaching demonstrates her efficient use of instructional time. From the moment the students entered the classroom until they were dismissed for recess, they were engaged in mathematics. Additionally, Ms. Rossi was engaged in mathematics *instruction* the entire time. She did not attempt to occupy the students with "busy work." Instead, she was committed to the academic success of each of the students and accompanied them on the instructional journey. Knowing that she was right there with them provided the students with the assurance that their progress would be monitored and that they would not be allowed to stray too far off the instructional path. On the one occasion when a few students became restless, Ms. Rossi's response was to adjust instruction. Rather than take this restlessness as a student deficiency, Ms. Rossi accepted it as a pedagogical cue to fill an instructional void.

Contrast Ms. Rossi's concerns about instruction with the concerns of the teachers at the in-service:

Our minority students are all economically deprived. How do we "mix" the haves and have nots?

During whole-group instruction I regularly had to separate the black boys because they would not pay attention. Then they would continue to make faces to each

other across the room. Separating or sitting together, neither worked to have good classroom control. . . . How can we let these students sit by their friends and teach at the same time?
We need help accepting black children's differences which are so drastically different than the white upper class students who also attend this school. (Some staff aren't able to accept this).

Here, the teachers attending the in-service seem to be less concerned about instructing the students, regardless of their racial and cultural background, and more concerned about ways in which to have the students "fit in" and "behave." If the teachers maintain attitudes that suggest that the students have little academic potential, then what they want from the students ultimately is compliance around issues of discipline and deportment.

Real education is about extending students' thinking and ability beyond what they already know. Ms. Rossi's decision to teach the students prealgebra even when it was not mandated by her district's curriculum was a conscious decision to help her students discover their capacity to learn and perform at higher and more sophisticated levels than had been demanded of them previously. Instead of attempting to maintain the students at low levels of academic performance, Ms. Rossi provided challenging mathematics content for *all* of the students.

By contrast, one of the in-service teachers wrote, "So many minority (students) have a difficult time with math – do you have any information why this occurs?" The teacher's statement implies that there is something about the nature of mathematics or the capability of students of color (or both) that precludes their success in mathematics. Ms. Rossi's approach was just the opposite: *Everyone* can succeed in mathematics, even the "allegedly special education student."

Effective pedagogical practice involves in-depth knowledge of students as well as of subject matter. There is no disputing that effective teachers must be knowledgeable about content. Additionally, Shulman (1987) suggests that beyond knowledge of their various content areas, teachers must know how that knowledge is best taught; that is, they must have command of pedagogical content knowledge. Other research that looked at teacher success with diverse learners (Ladson-Billings, 1991b; Shulman & Mesa-Baines, 1990) indicates a third aspect of effective teaching: the ability to cultivate and maintain strong interpersonal relationships between teachers and students. These strong teacher–student relationships were apparent on the part of each of the teachers in my research (Ladson-Billings, 1991b, 1992). In contrast, the teachers attending the in-service expressed little or no real knowledge about their African American students:
I would like to know how to make different students feel like they belong in my class.

I have difficulty dealing with the amount of anger some African American students seem to bring to class with them.

In identifying "the bright ones" – what measures can one use other than standardized tests? [O]r how can one get past the poor achievement to see what potential is there?

Spindler (1982) reports that teachers, perhaps unconsciously, favor those students whom they perceive to be most like themselves. This takes the form of attending more to these students, valuing their responses more highly, and evaluating their performances more favorably. Effective teachers of African American students develop a positive identification with their students so that they do perceive the students to be like them (Ladson-Billings, 1991b). The teachers from the in-service do not see a connection between themselves and their African American students. The fact that they work in a desegregated school affords them the opportunity to develop connections and identification with the white, middle-class students in their classes. Other students are viewed as intruders in the orderly, academically oriented classrooms they envision. In their minds, the best that these students can do is to try to "fit in" to the established order.

Some concluding thoughts

The basic premise of this chapter is that all students can be successful in mathematics when their understanding of it is linked to meaningful cultural referents, and when the instruction assumes that all students are capable of mastering the subject matter. Suggested here is that one way to make those cultural linkages is by ensuring that students experience an education that is multicultural and social reconstructionist (Sleeter & Grant, 1987). This means that no area of the curriculum is exempt from the multicultural dimensions of content integration, knowledge construction, prejudice reduction, equity pedagogy, and an empowering school culture and social structure.

Mathematics has been widely touted as the subject-matter field that has made the greatest strides in the development of national standards (Romberg, 1991) and, consequently, is seen as the leader of the education reform movement. School reformers are optimistic about the potential for school renewal and excellence. The multicultural perspective holds that without excellence *and* equity, this reform is doomed to failure. Mathematics cannot be left out of the excellence-and-equity school reform equation. Teachers and researchers must search for ways to make mathematics meaningful and accessible to all students, not only to a select few. We as a nation must be committed to the idea that mathematics is important for every student if we are serious about educational reform. We must be committed to a multicultural education for all students if we are to survive as a diverse democratic society.

Notes

1 A handout that was distributed at a workshop during the National Council of Teachers of Mathematics annual meeting included a picture of Hypatia, a female Egyptian mathematician of the fourth century. The artistic rendering of Hypatia was reminiscent of European women of the era. However, more egregious than the illustration was a geographic error that appeared on the handout. Beneath Hypatia's picture were the words, "born, Alexandria, *Greece*" (my emphasis). The dominance of Ancient Greece (and Rome) in our thinking about important intellectual movements and personages stands in the way of our ability to conceive of "others" as knowledge creators.

2 Similar arguments can be made for Latino, Native American, Asian American, feminist, and working-class perspectives.

3 Thanks to William Tate, University of Wisconsin, Madison, for sharing this anecdote.

4 As with other names in this paper, this is a pseudonym.

5 At the beginning of teacher in-service workshops, I often ask teachers to write anonymously what they expect from the workshop. Unwittingly, teachers reveal much about their own attitudes and beliefs about children of color in their writings.

6 This may be seen as the application level of Bloom's *Taxonomy of Educational Objectives* (1956).

References

Asante, M. K. (1987). *The Afrocentric idea*. Philadelphia: Temple University Press.

(1991). The Afrocentric idea in education. *Journal of Negro Education, 60*(2), 170–180.

Au, K., & Jordan, C. (1981). Teaching reading to Hawaiian children: Finding a culturally appropriate solution. In H. Trueba, G. Guthrie, & K. Au (Eds.), *Culture and the bilingual classroom: Studies in classroom ethnography* (pp. 139–152). Rowley, MA: Newbury House.

Banks, J. A. (1989a). Multicultural education: Characteristics and goals. In J.A. Banks & C. M. Banks (Eds.), *Multicultural education: Issues and perspectives* (pp. 2–26). Boston: Allyn & Bacon.

(1989b). Integrating the curriculum with ethnic content: Approaches and guidelines. In J. A. Banks & C. M. Banks (Eds.), *Multicultural education: Issues and perspectives* (pp. 189–207). Boston: Allyn & Bacon.

(1991). The dimensions of multicultural education. *Multicultural Leader, 4,* 5–6.

Bloom, B. S. (Ed.). (1956). *Taxonomy of educational objectives: The classification of educational goals. Handbook I: Cognitive domain*. New York: McKay.

Carpenter, T. P., & Fennema, E. (1992). Cognitively Guided Instruction: Building on the knowledge of students and teachers. *International Journal of Educational Research, 17*(5), 457–470.

Cazden, C., & Leggett, E. (1981). Culturally responsive education: Recommendations for achieving Lau remedies II. In H. Trueba, G. Guthrie, & K. Au (Eds.), *Culture and the bilingual classroom: Studies in classroom ethnography* (pp. 69–86). Rowley, MA:

Cervantes, R. A. (1984). Ethnocentric pedagogy and minority student growth: Implications for the common school. *Education and Urban Society, 16*(3), 274–293.

Chunn, E. W. (1989). Sorting black students for success and failure: The inequity of ability grouping and tracking. In W. D. Smith & E. W. Chunn (Eds.), *Black education: A quest for equity and excellence* (pp. 93–106). New Brunswick, NJ: Transaction.

Cohen, E. (1986). *Designing groupwork: Strategies for the heterogeneous classroom.* New York: Teachers College Press.

Comer, J., & Haynes, N. (1991). Meeting the needs of black children in public schools: A school reform challenge. In C. V. Willie, A. Garibaldi, & W. Reed (Eds.), *The education of African Americans* (pp. 67–78). New York: Auburn House.

Cooper, H. (1979). Pygmalion grows up: A model for teacher expectation communication and performance influence. *Review of Educational Research, 49*(3), 389–410.

Crano, W., & Mellon, P. (1987). Causal influences of teachers' expectations on children's academic performance: A cross-lagged panel analysis. *Journal of Educational Psychology, 70*(1), 39–49.

DuBois, W. E. B. (1935). *Black reconstruction.* New York: Harcourt Brace.

Edelman, M. W. (1987). *Families in peril: An agenda for social change.* Cambridge, MA: Harvard University Press.

Edmonds, R. (1979). Effective schools for the urban poor. *Educational Leadership, 37,* 15–24.

Erickson, F. (1987). Transformation and school success: The politics and culture of educational achievement. *Anthropology and Education Quarterly, 18*(4), 335–356.

Fennema, E. (1980). Teachers and sex bias in mathematics. *Mathematics Teacher, 73,* 169–173.

Frankenstein, M. (1990). Incorporating race, class and gender issues into a critical math literacy curriculum. *Journal of Negro Education, 59*(3), 336–347.

Gardner, H. (1983). *Frames of mind: The theory of multiple intelligences.* New York: Basic.

Gay, G. (1992). The state of multicultural education in the United States. In K. Adam-Moodley (Ed.), *Education in plural societies: International perspectives* (pp. 47–66). Calgary: Detselig.

Gee, J. (1987). What is literacy? *Teaching and Learning, 2*(1), 3–11.

Giroux, H., & Simon, R. (1989). Popular culture and critical pedagogy: Everyday life as a basis for curriculum knowledge. In H. Giroux & P. McLaren (Eds.), *Critical pedagogy, the state and cultural struggle* (pp. 236–252). Albany, NY: SUNY Press.

Gomez, M. L., & Tabachnick, B. R. (1991). *"We are the answer": Preparing pre-service teachers to teach diverse learners.* Paper presented at the annual meeting of the American Educational Research Association, Chicago.

Hale-Benson, J. (1986). *Black children: Their roots, culture, and learning styles.* Baltimore: Johns Hopkins University Press.

Harding, V. (1970). *Beyond chaos: Black history and the search for the new land.* Black paper No. 2. Atlanta: Institute of the Black World.

Hodgkinson, H. (1989, May). *The schools we need for the kids we've got.* Paper distributed at the Tenth Anniversary Colloquium of the Council on Academic Affairs. New York: College Entrance Examination Board.

Hughes, R. (1992, February 3). The fraying of America. *Time* (pp. 44–49).

Jordan, C. (1985). Translating culture: From ethnographic information to educational program. *Anthropology and Education Quarterly, 16*(2), 105–123.

King, J. (1991). Dysconscious racism: Ideology, identity, and the miseducation of teachers. *Journal of Negro Education, 60*(2), 133–146.

King, J., & Ladson-Billings, G. (1990). The teacher education challenge in elite university settings: Developing critical perspectives for teaching in democratic and multicultural societies. *European Journal of Intercultural Education, 1*(2), 15–30.

Kozol, J. (1991). *Savage inequalities.* New York: Crown.

Kuhn, T. S. (1970). *The structure of scientific revolutions* (2d ed., enlarged). University of Chicago Press.

Ladson-Billings, G. (1991a). Beyond multicultural illiteracy. *Journal of Negro Education,* *60*(2), 147–157.

——— (1991b). Returning to the source: Implications for educating teachers of black students. In M. Foster (Ed.), *Readings on equal education* (Vol. 11, pp. 227–244). New York: AMS.

——— (1992). Liberatory consequences of literacy: A case of culturally relevant instruction for African American students. *Journal of Negro Education, 61*(3), 378–391.

Lowe, R. (1988, December/January). The struggle for equal education: An historical note. *Rethinking schools, 2*(2), 5.

Macias, J. (1987). The hidden curriculum of Papago teachers: American Indian strategies for mitigating cultural discontinuity in early schooling. In G. Spindler & L. Spindler (Eds.), *Interpretive ethnography at home and abroad* (pp. 363–380). Hillsdale, NJ: Erlbaum.

Moll, L. (1988). Some key issues in teaching Latino students. *Language Arts, 65*(5), 465–472.

Oakes, J. (1985). *Keeping track: How schools structure inequality.* New Haven, CT: Yale University Press.

Orr, E. (1987). *Twice as less: Black English and the performance of Black students in mathematics and science.* New York: Norton.

Quality Education for Minorities in Mathematics, Science, and Engineering Network. (1992). *Together we can make it work: A national agenda for minorities in mathematics, science, and engineering.* Washington, DC: QEM Network.

Ravitch, D. (1990, Summer). Multiculturalism: E pluribus plures. *American Scholar,* 337–354.

Rist, R. (1970). Student social class and teacher expectations: The self-fulfilling prophecy in ghetto education. *Harvard Educational Review, 40,* 620–635.

Romberg, T. (1991, December). *The NCTM Standards as a model for discipline-based school reform.* Paper presented at the Conference on Telecommunications as a Tool for Educational Reform, Aspen Institute, Aspen, CO.

Shulman, J., & Mesa-Bains, A. (1990). *Teaching diverse students: Cases and commentaries.* San Francisco: Far West Laboratory for Educational Research and Development.

Shulman, L. (1987). Knowledge and teaching: Foundations of the new reform. *Harvard Educational Review, 57*(1), 1–22.

Slavin, R. (1990). *Cooperative learning: Theory, research and practice.* Englewood Cliffs, NJ: Prentice-Hall.

Sleeter, C., & Grant, C. (1987). An analysis of multicultural education in the United States. *Harvard Educational Review, 57*(4), 421–444.

Smith, M. (1980). Meta-analyses of research on teacher expectation. *Evaluation in Education, 4,* 53–55.

Spindler, G. (1982). Roger Harker and Schonhausen: From the familiar to the strange and back again. In G. Spindler (Ed.), *Doing the ethnography of schooling* (pp. 20–46). Prospect Heights, IL: Waveland.

Spradley, J. (1979). *The ethnographic interview.* New York: Holt, Rinehart & Winston.

Stedman, L. (1987). It's time we changed the effective schools formula. *Phi Delta Kappan, 69*(3), 215–224.

Stiff, L. V., & Harvey, W. B. (1988). On the education of black children in mathematics. *Journal of Black Studies, 19,* 190–203.

Taba, H. (1946). Intergroup education through the school curriculum. *Annals of the American Academy of Political and Social Science, 244,* 19–25.

Taba, H., Brady, E. H., & Robinson, J. T. (1952). *Intergroup education in public schools.* Washington, DC: American Council on Education.

Torres-Guzman, M. (1989, May). *Stories of hope in the midst of despair: Culturally responsive education for Latino students in an alternative high school in New York City.* Paper presented at the colloquium in conjunction with the tenth anniversary meeting of the College Board Council on Academic Affairs, New York.

Winfield, L. (1986). Teacher beliefs toward at-risk students in inner urban schools. *Urban Review, 18*(4), 253–267.

Woodson, C. G. (1933). *The mis-education of the Negro*. Washington, DC: Associated Publishers.

(1919). *The education of the Negro prior to 1861*. New York: Arno.

Zavslavsky, C. (1980). *Count on your fingers African style*. New York: Crowell.

5   Social and critical dimensions for equity in mathematics education

Walter G. Secada

A recent exchange between Thomas Romberg (1992a) and Michael Apple (1992a,b) illustrates how tensions come into view when efforts to enhance the teaching of mathematics are assessed vis-à-vis the social contexts within which those efforts are played out. Apple argued that the National Council of Teachers of Mathematics (NCTM) *Standards* (1989, 1991) should be read not only for their substantive and technical points (many of which he saw as meritorious), but also as a set of carefully crafted slogan systems whose vision and vagueness can rally people to take action that is both substantive and symbolic. Granting that many substantive efforts to reform school mathematics are being undertaken by individuals and professional organizations, one can still see convocations and other actions that seem valued as much for their symbolism as for any other reason. This is not to argue that substance and symbolism cannot mix, but it is to note that they mix with varying degrees of effect. Meetings held by the NCTM contain both substance and symbolism due to their focus on the *Standards* (for example, Garrett, 1992), whereas many other meetings, at which the same documents are celebrated by state governors and others who have not even read them (let alone understood what they are trying to accomplish), stress symbolism over substance.

On the substantive side, Apple also argued that these documents did not go far enough in that they did not take into account "the realities of differential power, the economic crisis, and the social construction of what counts as mathematical literacy and of the problems it [school mathematics] should focus on" (1992a, p. 428). Rather, the two *Standards* documents – by their appeals to the economic crises of the late 1980s – accepted and granted legitimacy to a particular view of society much as the New Math movement of the late 1950s and 1960s accepted and extended (into the domain of school mathematics) the cold-war rhetoric of the post-Sputnik era (see Pitman, 1989).

Romberg's response called attention to what the *Standards* did try to accomplish: Lay out a vision for changes in school mathematics that would take account of newly developing understandings of how people learn, of

146

economic and social needs for democratic citizenship, and of the costs of those changes. Hence, although not disagreeing with Apple's assessment of the *Standards'* symbolic nature, Romberg argued that rationality and substance could be found in the *Standards* and that these played major roles in their development. In a recent article, Romberg (1993) weaves together the substantive and symbolic concerns of the *Curriculum Standards* (NCTM, 1989), which he calls "a rallying flag for mathematics teachers."

This is not the first time that writers have noted that school mathematics is a social artifact combining symbolism with substance and technique, nor is it likely to be the last. Cornbleth (1987) and Popkewitz (1987, 1988) called attention to the ways in which the school mathematics curriculum is subject to forces that simultaneously (a) treat the discipline of mathematics as a symbol, (b) argue for a transcendent, cross-cultural universality and neutrality of mathematics, (c) maintain that the translation of mathematics into a school subject is directly tied to the nature of the discipline itself, and (d) argue consequently that school mathematics has a similar, privileged status. Cornbleth (1987) argued that both the value of mathematics as a school subject and the difficulty that any reform efforts will have can be related to the persistence of myths and mythmaking that draw on deeply held beliefs about student learning, our society, and how schools both sort and prepare students for life in that society.

Popkewitz's (1987, 1988) analysis was cast in terms of public discourse and the shared assumptions that support and make possible such discourse. Popkewitz outlined three functions that school mathematics can play in society: giving a symbolic reference to the scientific and technological base of that society, providing higher status to experts who have mastered the subject, and obscuring the socially constructed nature of many phenomena that are studied via mathematics (for some examples of the latter, see Chapter 6 in this volume). These functions, according to Popkewitz, create and support social forces that help shape school mathematics and that enable reform to operate on both symbolic and technical levels.

Likewise in mathematics education research, there is a developing body of inquiry that seeks to place that research within the social contexts in which it gets carried out. For example, in an earlier paper (Secada, 1991), I scrutinized scholarly research that is based on cognitivist models of learning and knowing, from the standpoint of how such work addresses issues of student diversity and, ultimately, of equity. I argued that such work constrains our interpretations of what are essentially public and social states of affairs (for example, school performance) as being private, psychological, and individual (for example, personality traits, cognitive processes, or beliefs). Moreover, I argued that scholarly inquiry that tries to investigate equity group-based differences is seen as derivative (it replicates someone else's studies), or is limited to searching for group-based differences. In either case, the results are that the group being studied is compared to a dominant norm (much as Suzanne Damarin, Chapter 10 in this volume, writes about "othering") and that the individual scholar's work is in danger of being seen as unoriginal.

Claims of basic science, by which people who engage in cognition-based research seek to ensure a privileged position for their work, are used to justify cognitive science's failure to directly address issues of student diversity or, what may be equivalent, generalizability. Claims to a privileged status are based on basic research's pursuit of universally applicable psychological phenomena without addressing the confounding effects of social context, affect, and the like. In my earlier paper, I argued that there are other ways of beginning scholarly inquiry than by concentrating on the individual, and that the beliefs and ideological claims on which basic research rests should themselves be subject to scrutiny vis-à-vis social concerns and claims of equity.

My intent in this chapter is to continue in the line of inquiry that occurs when technical – and indeed, quite substantive – efforts to improve school mathematics are placed in the social and political context of equity. I argue that efforts to include equity in current reform and research tend to be scrutinized according to criteria that result from certain social, political, and symbolic processes and beliefs. Though these beliefs and associated processes help to create and sustain the community of mathematics educators, they also can become barriers to equity. Thus, this critique is not intended to diminish the importance nor the substance of efforts for reform; nor is it meant to question the good intentions of people who engage in those efforts. Rather, it is intended to make explicit and articulate the problèmatique of some of the community's shared beliefs and assumptions about reform and research from the perspective of equity.

In this chapter, I also depart from the practice of relying solely on either research or events that are distanced from the observer. Rather, much as Marilyn Frankenstein has done in Chapter 6 of this volume, as Lampert (1986, 1990) has done in her own work on teaching, and in an approach consistent with developing conceptions of feminist scholarship (Collins, 1991), as well as action research by teachers (Delpit, 1986; Lewis & Simon, 1986; McDonald, 1986; Zeichner, in press), I will rely on personal experiences as data for my analyses. In sharing these experiences with colleagues in the mathematics education community, I have found that many who work in equity have had similar experiences. Hence, this chapter can be thought of as an essay that gives voice to some common concerns about equity as a component of contemporary research on reform.

Some social events

As someone who works in equity, I am called upon – with increasing regularity – to serve on advisory panels and commissions and to present at conferences and meetings. Repeatedly, I have encountered very concerned people who ask the same questions and engage in the same behaviors when it comes to including equity in their efforts. They are deeply concerned about "the equity problem." But also, they want answers that are immediately and easily applicable, are elaborated and fit into current research paradigms and preexisting belief systems, focus exclusively on differences, and can meet standards of evidence and scrutiny beyond those that are applied to their other beliefs.

Immediate answers

There clearly is a felt urgency involving issues of equity, a welcome change from the recent past when equity was perceived to be opposed to excellence (Tomlinson, 1986). Unfortunately, that urgency is often translated into a rush for answers and solutions, not only among policymakers and the larger community of practitioners, but also among researchers and others who usually take the time to carefully define issues and concerns in all areas of scholarly inquiry.

This rush for solutions finds symbolic expression in terms like "the equity issue" or "the equity problem," which have become codes for referring to a wide range of often competing notions. "The equity issue" glosses over the complexity of student diversity and of the notions and traditions under which people work in this area; indeed, one might just as easily write about "the problem-solving issue." This term signals the belief that there is a single, monolithic issue to be addressed, and that what applies to one equity group can transfer to other groups, a position that is not shared by many equity advocates (Secada, 1992a).

I have observed this push to a quick solution on many advisory committees on which I have served. Those committees take seriously the charge to reform school mathematics; indeed, many of them have been constituted to promote a specific facet of the reform agenda. They consciously adopt an active role in targeting their efforts toward the vision of mathematics as articulated in the *Standards* (National Council of Teachers of Mathematics, 1989, 1991), *Everybody Counts* (National Research Council, 1989), and other reform documents (e.g., Quality Education for Minorities Project, 1990). The rush to reform means that when an issue of equity gets raised it must be solved almost immediately.

For example, during work on a recent research project, I participated in a meeting of language minority scholars who had been asked to review recent efforts to create authentic assessments on a national scale. Many of these individuals are highly respected for their substantive contributions to policy development, school improvement, testing and measurement, and the study of teaching and learning. One of the meeting participants asked if the group was important or marginal, and if it had been convened only to ratify decisions that already had been made elsewhere. The response was revealing: Insofar as we solved problems, we were told, our input would be highly valued and central; but insofar as we raised problems and asked more unsolvable questions, our contributions would be marginal – this in spite of the fact that many of our questions had not been considered in the project's efforts to that point.

Such situations pose serious challenges to equity advocates since many of them are also active in the research community. Those raising an equity concern must agree to help modify an evolving effort without sending everything back to the drawing board, or they risk being seen as obstructionists who are not really committed to reform. Unfortunately, the results are often superficial – symbolic changes that fail to address the real issues at hand. Sometimes, it is easier to be silent.

Elaboration and fit

It is not enough to raise an issue of equity or even to provide the beginnings of an answer. Rather, that solution must be elaborated so that it fits into the dominant discourse; that is, solutions must fit mainstream agendas for reform and research. Without that fit, proffered solutions are discarded, issues become unsolvable problems, and they are put aside in order that the original effort may proceed.

An example of this misfit comes from my work in school-based efforts to enhance a mathematics program (Secada & Byrd, 1993). Some mathematics education reform advocates have argued that the schools attended by many lower socioeconomic-status (SES) children experience high staff turnover, unstable leadership, and other problems that "fall outside of the domain of mathematics education." Since, they argue, we should focus attention on those things that we "can do something about," we should put aside concerns about the school and instead attend to curriculum and teaching (in other words, solve a simpler problem à la Polya, 1957) – as if mathematics educators could really affect a school's curriculum and teaching without taking into account the entire school. That this overly narrow view of school mathematics and its reform is highly value laden; that it results not just in a decoupling of equity from reform, but also in the subordination of equity to the imperatives of reform; and, finally, that it is likely to result in the restratification of opportunity or in the complete failure of the reform effort are never considered.

Mathematics for communication. Another example of this issue of fit and elaboration concerns the use of mathematics for communication. Multicultural educators recommend that teachers know and understand the norms of communication in diverse social and cultural groups (see, for example, Damen, 1987; Grant & Sleeter, 1989; Heath, 1986; Nieto, 1992; Sleeter & Grant, 1988). Yet, because cross-cultural communication has a more general focus than mathematics, it is relegated to general classroom management. In the process, cross-cultural communication gets removed from the domain of how one teaches mathematics per se. This occurs in spite of the fact that mathematical communication (one of the five major NCTM curriculum standards) is itself derived from the larger universe of communication.

What is more, the norms inherent in the claim that mathematics should be used for communication (e.g., the creation of discourse communities à la Lampert, 1990) are not scrutinized in terms of the norms for cross-cultural communication; rather, the reverse is true. Thus, the person who suggests that mathematics teachers should know about cross-cultural communication must provide an elaborate explanation of how such knowledge will enable someone to teach mathematics. I have never seen anyone ask how using mathematical language for communication or creating discourse communities helps teachers teach diverse student populations. What little evidence I have suggests that the creation of a "discourse community" may result in the exclusion of children of limited English proficiency (Secada, 1992b). Barbara Merino (personal communication) has expressed similar concerns about current reforms in the teaching of science.

The tacit assumption is, of course, that we can adapt mathematics for communication to the case for diverse student populations, or that mathematics used for communication is itself cross-cultural. The result of such assumptions is a narrow view of mathematics qua discipline without recognizing that, absent shared norms for communication (that is, cross-cultural communication), mathematics itself cannot be used for communication.

Good teaching. In various efforts to reform the teaching of mathematics, what has become highly valued are a set of teacher behaviors (Grouws, Cooney, & Jones, 1988; Koehler & Grouws, 1992; National Council of Teachers of Mathematics, 1991), beliefs and knowledge (Fennema & Franke, 1992; Thompson, 1992), and characteristics (for example, "the reflective practitioner," Zeichner, in press) that are themselves culturally bound and narrowly construed. In *Professional Standards for Teaching Mathematics* (National Council of Teachers of Mathematics, 1991), one sees scant mention of the many things that teachers of diverse student populations must do inside and outside of the classroom. Instead, the recommendations for good teaching are focused on a very narrow conception of teaching as what takes place inside the classroom, and as linked to notions of content and pedagogical-content knowledge (for example, *Educational Evaluation and Policy Analysis,* 1990; *Elementary School Journal,* 1992). But there are broader conceptions of teaching, especially when teaching is viewed from the perspectives of group affiliation (Ladson-Billings, Chapter 4 in this volume), access to more-advanced courses (Oakes, 1990; Silver, Smith, & Nelson, Chapter 3 in this volume), and ultimately access to opportunity in the larger society itself (Chipman & Thomas, 1987; Delpit, 1986; National Research Council, 1989). These broader concerns are crucial for success in teaching that includes diverse populations.

Under this broader conception, good teaching includes ensuring student access to opportunity. Indicators of accomplished practice would include diverse student access to advanced mathematics, perseverance in course taking, and, ultimately, diverse student access to postsecondary mathematics-related degrees and careers. In other words, good teaching should help keep students in the mathematics pipeline. According to that standard, for example, teachers whose minority students pass the advanced placement examination in calculus must be considered accomplished teachers.

Yet, this broader definition of craft practice and knowledge is not acknowledged by documents like *Professional Standards for Teaching Mathematics* (National Council of Teachers of Mathematics, 1991). Things that occur outside the classroom or that seem at odds with evolving conceptions of classroom practice are not considered as being mathematics instruction per se. Rather, they are excluded from consideration as good teaching in mathematics, and they are tacitly – if not explicitly – devalued. For example, I have participated in meetings where others have claimed that many teachers of minority students focus on basic-skills development, dominate discussions, and supplement their lectures with demonstrations. Hence, the judgment follows that these teachers' practices do not meet the standards for teaching articulated by NCTM (1991). When I have raised the issue of access and inquired about how we would measure success against that criterion, I have been told that students' placement in advanced courses like calculus is not the only (or the most important) criterion for successful teaching, or that, Yes, these teachers are highly successful, not in terms of their classroom practices but for other (and by implication, nonteaching) reasons.

What concerns me is how readily these tensions and contradictions are dismissed. Rather, it would seem that tensions like these should raise issues about the validity of the various reform documents themselves. That teaching has been so narrowly construed to acknowledge only what takes place within the confines of the classroom, and that criteria for success do not take account of the fact that student access to courses and opportunity remain pressing equity concerns, are major shortcomings of the reform effort. To put it bluntly, while we are reforming school mathematics, we still must ensure that equity groups have access to the system in place, regardless of how flawed it may seem to the reformers.

Focus on differences

Repeatedly, issues of equity are changed into questions of group differences. This is understandable, since a driving force for equity has been the persistence of group-based disparities along a range of academic and career-related indicators (Secada, 1992a). However, this focus on differences has also meant that equity issues tend to be legitimated only in reference to group differences (Campbell, 1989).

The focus on group differences is part of a larger pattern of research and practice (Campbell, 1989) wherein differences represent real results and their absence do not. As a consequence, the search for group differences grants legitimacy to the view that diverse student populations are somehow deficient, exotic, or primitive when measured against the dominant norm. However, if all one can write or speak about is how a specific group is different from the norm, then the results are an impoverished view of that group and the validation of the belief that equity groups are somehow inferior.

Feminist teaching. Suzanne Damarin (1990, and Chapter 10, this volume) has included not just the avoidance of sexist behaviors and the proactive linking of mathematics to later-life opportunity, but also the use of cooperative groups, focus on reasoning, and the provision of a safe, noncompetitive classroom climate as central tenets in feminist conceptions of teaching. One question I have heard asked of Damarin is whether the latter are "just good teaching." People might well ask whether the richly textured characterizations of QUASAR and CGI classrooms in urban settings (Silver & Nelson, Chapter 1, this volume; Carey et al., Chapter 3, this volume) are also simply examples of good teaching.

Culturally sensitive teaching. Within the dominant research traditions of mathematics education, cooperative groups are thought of as good teaching, and cross-cultural communication as an instructional strategy linked to cultural diversity. From the perspective of culturally sensitive teaching as well as one of equity, the inclusion of cooperative groups in recommendations for classroom practice should serve as a reminder that *access* to good teaching is a constant issue where culturally diverse populations are concerned. From the same perspectives, cross-cultural communication increases the general efficacy of any classroom's discourse features, be it individualized, in a small group, or in the whole class. In other words, the use of cooperative groups, which are regarded by the mathematics education community as indicative of good teaching, can be construed as an equity issue; and cross-cultural communication can also be thought of as good teaching.

The intersection of multiple principles. People who are interested in feminist conceptions of teaching, in culturally sensitive teaching, and in equity would argue that practice should proceed at the *intersection* of cooperative groups and cross-cultural communication; that is, classrooms organized to use cooperative groups should try to use cross-cultural communication, and classrooms in which the norms of communication are cross-cultural should incorporate cooperative groupings. Moreover, research is needed in classrooms that blend cross-cultural communication and cooperative groupings in order to understand how such a merger is possible; the conditions under which one is subordinated to the other; and how both cooperative groups and cross-cultural communication, acting in concert, might help enhance student learning. In other words, is the whole greater than the sum of its parts?

Impoverished discourse. What is possible – in both research and practice – becomes impoverished within a discourse that is predicated solely on group differences. Notions of access to quality instruction and of the greater texture of possibilities at the intersection of cooperative groups and cross-cultural communication, and even of how diversity itself is thought of, become constrained if all that can be referred to is a single dimension – for example, cross-cultural communication.

The focus on group differences gets played out in a context in which what is central to mathematics education has already been constrained (see my points on how reform advocates would avoid certain kinds of schools or how they would relegate cross-cultural communication to the periphery in discussions on mathematics teaching). Hence, a not-uncommon scenario is one in which an equity advocate suggests something like cooperative groups and cross-cultural communication as worthwhile features for a mathematics classroom that contains diverse student populations. Due to the focus on group differences, cooperative groups are removed from the equity agenda because they are "simply good teaching"; and, due to the focus on mathematical communication, cross-cultural communication gets removed from the reform agenda, or is consigned to general classroom management as not being sufficiently mathematical in nature. What began as a thoughtful recommendation ends up as yet another example of an equity issue being stifled.

Differential standards of evidence

Another interesting phenomenon is that equity concerns are often subject to a level of scrutiny that, to equity advocates, suggests that reform advocates are making only nominal commitments to equity. For example, one can go to a meeting or a conference where the shared assumptions about teaching or constructivism are so widespread that no need is felt to create elaborate arguments for specific conclusions and recommendations. These require little or no justification, since they follow from a shared belief system whose evidence is already well known and accepted as normative; hence, conclusions and recommendations are agreed upon almost without comment. In contrast, equity considerations undergo scrutiny as to how they fit into the discourse, as does the evidence that supports or falsifies their conclusions.

Complicating matters is the fact that equity advocates often agree with the shared assumptions of the mathematics education community on issues like teaching and constructivism. Hence, equity advocates find themselves agreeing with the dominant group on those issues, isolated on others, and under pressure to explain and justify not only specific conclusions but even why certain issues have been framed as they are.

Concluding comments

These considerations need not form an exhaustive list of the hidden criteria that are applied to equity concerns. There are likely to be additional or other ways of characterizing the issues and events I am referring to. But the important point is that the dynamics just described are a part of the shared beliefs of the mathematics education community. The characterization I have developed, then, focuses on four interrelated dimensions: a search for immediate answers, the demand for elaborated answers that fit a preset agenda, an exclusive focus on group differences, and differential standards of scrutiny for equity concerns.

When equity advocates participate in actions that bind the mathematics education community (meetings and conferences whose nominal purposes are reform or research), they find themselves participants in these dynamics. Since many equity advocates are members of the larger mathematics education community and have been socialized accordingly, they share and accept many of the larger community's core beliefs. Hence, equity advocates may unwittingly participate in the co-construction of the events that I refer to.

If this treatment of equity results from widely shared, albeit unexamined beliefs, then my effort to expose them to scrutiny should be regarded as a first step in understanding and, hopefully, modifying them. However, these sorts of events also occur in a larger social-historical context. The narrative now turns to a macroanalysis of some of the processes within that context.

Underlying social processes

Events like those already described are not accidental. They occur due to social processes that serve to create and maintain the boundaries of the community (for example, the mathematics education community) and that support differential power relationships in that community (see Bourdieu, 1991; Giroux, 1983; Popkewitz, 1992). They represent specific instances of three general phenomena – silencing, the expropriation of constructs, and marginalizing.

Silencing

Recent scholarship involving teachers, women, and people of color has begun to focus on the notion of voice (Delpit, 1986; Ladson-Billings & Tate, 1993; Lewis & Simon, 1986; McDonald, 1986; Trueba, 1989), which is a theoretical elaboration of the commonsense belief that people should speak for themselves. Voice refers to the discourse that is created when people define their own issues in their own ways, from their own perspectives, using their own terms – in a word, speak for themselves. Voice represents a contrast with the case in which others speak on behalf of individuals and groups, telling them what their problems "really" are, and transforming the way in which personal and group issues are construed.

Implicit in the idea of voice is that not just anyone can speak on behalf of a group. Beyond a person's technical knowledge and skills, which *do* remain criteria for that person's right to speak on behalf of a group, voice is an issue of that individual's membership in the group, of his or her understanding of how that particular group negotiates and maintains its membership boundaries, and of his or her ability to articulate issues in ways the group would validate as being representative. A person may speak with an individual voice, but not just anyone can speak authentically on behalf of a group, and no single individual can capture the complexity of a group's voices. What is more, within groups, there are ways of negotiating that indicate whose voices will be given greater or lesser weight.[1]

Voice also stands in opposition to silencing. By silencing, I am referring to social settings and processes that do more than simply make it difficult for someone to fully articulate a position; everyone confronts such settings. Rather, silencing refers to the processes that make it seem as if it is simply not worth the effort of speaking. The terms of discourse used by the dominant group, and the unspoken assumptions supporting that discourse, make it virtually impossible for someone to raise and define issues according to a nondominant group's perceptions – in a word, to object. To do so would seem irrational in the eyes of those operating from within the dominant discourse.

Silencing applies to multiple groups and their respective constituencies. For example, teachers find themselves silenced at meetings that ostensibly are seeking their input on the creation of national standards for teaching. They find their opinions discounted and voices ignored in the face of expert opinions about what "really" constitutes good teaching.

In the experience of equity advocates, silencing occurs in many ways. For example, equity concerns about student learning are met with assurances that reform agendas will address equity, but the evidence to support such assurances cannot be seen except under the slogans that equity and excellence are compatible goals and that reform will help all students. How can anyone object to something that helps all students, without seeming irrational or biased?

The struggle for voice should not be construed as a call for political correctness. Nor does voice mean an automatic acceptance of how issues get framed simply because a person of color has spoken. Rather, the struggle for voice should be seen as an effort to increase the likelihood that we really listen to how diverse groups perceive their educational status in general and their mathematics education in particular. How students of diverse backgrounds recount the experiences, beliefs, and values embedded in their stories should be regarded as an important, and hitherto ignored, source of information.

For example, successful mathematics teachers of minority students may encounter a dilemma in the reform movement's calls for deemphasis on computational-skills instruction (Ladson-Billings, 1993). There is a powerful folklore among minorities to the effect that failure to master such skills has differential consequences. Deficiency in computational skills results in greater social sanctions for students who are stereotyped as lacking mathematical ability than it does for students who are not stereotyped in this manner. For students who are stereotyped as lacking mathematics ability (African Americans, Hispanics, girls, students of low socioeconomic status), a deemphasis on computational skills is more than something to be compensated for by providing pocket calculators. Such a deemphasis represents a profound potential impact on later-life opportunities, since lack of computational skills will be interpreted as resulting from a basic lack of mathematical ability, rather than as the result of instructional emphases that were in keeping with some reform recommendations. This risk is profound. Reformers' impatience with this dilemma – that it is not taken seriously and is relegated to being a social issue that either cannot be addressed or that will be addressed through the promissory note of students' enhanced problem-solving skills – transform the issue into another discourse. What is more, they miss the point: Minority students will *not* be given the opportunity to demonstrate their problem-solving skills without first demonstrating basic-skills mastery. Unfortunately, in the rush to reform, such concerns are made to seem irrational, and people who would express them are silenced.

Expropriation of constructs

Elsewhere in this volume, Warren and Rosebery (Chapter 13) write about people who appropriate ways of speaking by imbuing language with their own personal intentions. Likewise, groups of people appropriate the forms of knowledge, patterns of discourse, and cultural artifacts that were originally developed by others outside the group. One can think of examples from adolescent culture in which different groups appropriate language, modes of dress, and other artifacts across racial, ethnic, social class, and age boundaries. Likewise, mathematics education has appropriated constructs and discourse patterns from other disciplines; for example, even a cursory reading of the *Handbook of Research on Mathematics Teaching and Learning* (Grouws, 1992) reveals ideas taken from psychology commingled with those from mathematics.

A key part of appropriation lies in the ways in which groups that appropriate particular forms of knowledge and language modify and transform this material to fit their particular needs, values, and cultural norms. In the *Handbook,* Kilpatrick (1992) describes how mathematics education has used the disciplines of mathematics and psychology for its own ends.

Beyond appropriation lies "expropriation." By expropriation, I mean those settings and processes in which those who have appropriated constructs, artifacts, or language deny others – even the people who contributed in the development of those constructs – the right to what has been appropriated. This denial can be symbolic or economic, or it can take some other form. The spread of Montessori schools in the United States provides a potent historical example of symbolic and economic expropriation. Maria Montessori (1912) developed her methods among poor children living in the slums of Milan, Italy. In the United States, Montessori schools are reserved for the wealthy, and poor children's access to them is severely limited. Indeed, it seems almost extravagant to recommend Montessori schools for poor children.

Mathematics education has appropriated many ideas in its own research under the rubric of reform. One such idea is the use of cooperative groups. The study of groups and group processes goes back some years and includes the study of intergroup (i.e., race) relations and counseling (Anderson, 1969; Kagan, 1966). During the 1960s and 1970s, cooperative groups were used to promote school desegregation and to study its impact on intergroup race relations (Cohen, 1986; Sharon, 1980; Slavin, 1980). The study of cooperative groups for academic purposes – for example, mathematics (Good, Mulryan, & McCaslin, 1992) – finds its roots in these other uses of group work.

The appropriation of the use of cooperative groups in the mathematics education community has resulted in cooperative groups no longer being seen in terms of their rich and varied purposes; that is, cooperative groups have been expropriated by the mathematics education community. When equity advocates promote cooperative learning, they must justify their recommendation on the basis that it serves other purposes than that of good teaching. The expropriation of cooperative groups in mathematics settings has made it difficult for equity advocates to promote such groups in ways that encompass noncognitive, nonmathematical, or nonclassroom concerns.

Marginalizing

Every discipline must regulate what is central and what is peripheral to its concerns; that regulation is part of how the field constitutes itself. Traditionally, the central concerns for mathematics education have been derived from mathematics and psychology (Kilpatrick, 1992; Stanic & Kilpatrick, 1992). The field has had difficulty addressing issues that cannot easily be related to those traditions; typically, questions regarded as incidental to this core get transformed, or are consigned to the periphery.

In a recent review of research on the mathematics education of diverse student populations, I observed that public events like student performance on achievement tests get transformed into private states of mind like ability, cognitive structures, or beliefs; issues of diversity become individual differences; and prior achievement becomes a proxy for ability, while achievement at a later time becomes evidence of program impact (Secada, 1992a). When people try to resist these transformations and address equity concerns as socially constructed, their efforts are seen as peripheral to the mainstream.

What makes these transformations problematic is that race, ethnicity, language, social class, and even gender have socially constructed dimensions. Membership in any of these groups is complexly and symbolically negotiated between an individual who claims (or rejects) membership, the group itself (which monitors its own membership), and people outside the group (who ascribe their own meanings to the original group). To understand fully how mathematics education is presented to students who belong to culturally diverse groups, we must resist the temptation to transform group membership into psychological terms of discourse and to place social concerns at the margins of the field.

Equally problematic are the dual expectations of scholars who are members of equity groups. On the one hand, there is a tacit assumption that they should be concerned about issues involving these groups; on the other, there is the assumption that many of these individuals lack the capabilities for engaging in mainstream research. Hence, in the regulation of the field, what is not central becomes peripheral, resulting in the marginalization not just of whole bodies of work but also of individuals who may choose to do this work.

Developing a critical dimension

At their core, silencing, expropriation, and marginalization are factors in the way any field is constituted as an area of study; further, they determine the way relations among the community that studies that field are tied to differential power and status. There must be viable ways of building consensus, of appropriating ideas and elaborating them, and of negotiating what is central; and, what is more, there must be ways of enforcing those norms. But when we forget or ignore the socially constructed nature of any field of inquiry or practice and, instead, accept the premises and the historical agreements that created that field as if they were unquestioned givens, then consensus building becomes silencing, appropriation becomes expropriation, and concern for what is central becomes marginalizing.

Each of these three macroprocesses is related to my experiences in the research community and on advisory groups. The search for immediate answers, the insistence on solutions that fit into existing discourses, the focus on group differences, and the differential standards of evidence work together to silence people who would object to too facile an acceptance of certain norms, beliefs, research, and reform activities. Equity advocates have learned they must resort to a discourse that, through its technical and psychological references, constrains their voices. Simultaneously, they must defend their right to use terms and constructs (like teaching, communication, and cooperative groups) that have been appropriated by the mathematics education community for very narrow purposes. Moreover, they must struggle to move equity from the margins of the community's concern. In such a context, equity must develop a critical dimension. Equity advocates must name the events that support and constrain their efforts. They need to understand the social processes that give rise to those events.

My intent here has been to highlight some problematic features in how mathematics education research and reform are constituted. This critique and others like it are not ends in themselves, since there is much of worth in the mathematics community's efforts. Nor should such a critique result in the belief that nothing can be done.

Rather, the development of critical dimensions in equity should help to create a discourse and a community that operates at the intersection of multiple domains. I am *not* calling for abandoning equity-based work that relies on disciplinary or on psychological constructs (e.g., see Secada, 1993). Rather, equity-based analyses should draw on multiple disciplines and voices, appropriate ideas as needed, and remain tentative in what is counted as central to the field. In other words, what is needed is to create ways of talking about research and reform that allow for more textured analyses of phenomena.

On a more practical level, the community of mathematics educators needs to become less rushed and a bit more patient with people who work in equity. Haste may shortchange equity concerns. The good news, as evidenced by the work in this volume, is that we are beginning to make inroads in these efforts.

Acknowledgments

The preparation of this document was supported in part by the National Center for Research in Mathematical Sciences Education (NCRMSE), by the U.S. Department of Education, Office of Educational Research and Improvement (OERI, grant number R117G10002), and the Wisconsin Center for Education Research (WCER), School of Education, University of Wisconsin, Madison. Findings and opinions are the author's and do not necessarily have the endorsement of NCRMSE, OERI, or WCER.

Note

1 For example, Richard Rodriguez's (1982) *Hunger of Memory* is one individual's retelling of succeeding in the American educational system. No one would deny Rodriguez's right to his voice in framing how he recounted his deeply personal experiences. Yet very few Hispanic educators would endorse *Hunger of Memory* as providing a basis for educational policy involving Hispanic children, since its proposals are very particularistic, and within the Hispanic community there are other no-less-authentic ways of interpreting similar experiences.

References

Anderson, A. R. (1969). Group counseling. *Review of Educational Research, 39*(2), 209–226.
Apple, M. W. (1992a). Do the *Standards* go far enough? Power, policy, and practice in mathematics education. *Journal for Research in Mathematics Education, 23*(5), 412–431.
(1992b). Thinking more politically about the challenges before us: A response to Romberg. *Journal for Research in Mathematics Education, 23*(5), 438–440.
Bourdieu, P. (1991). *Language and symbolic power.* Cambridge, MA: Harvard University Press.
Campbell, P. (1989). Educational equity and research paradigms. In W. G. Secada (Ed.), *Equity in education* (pp. 26–42). New York: Falmer.
Chipman, S. F., & Thomas, V. G. (1987). The participation of women and minorities in mathematical, scientific, and technical fields. In E. Z. Rothkopf (Ed.), *Review of research*

in education (Vol. 14, pp. 387–430). Washington, DC: American Educational Research Association.

Cohen, E. G. (1986). *Designing groupwork: Strategies for the heterogeneous classroom*. New York: Teachers College Press.

Collins, P. H. (1991). *Black feminist thought*. New York: Routledge.

Cornbleth, C. A. (1987, March). The persistence of myth in curriculum discourse. In T. A. Romberg & D. M. Stewart (Eds.), *The monitoring of school mathematics: Background papers* (Vol. 3, pp. 27–58. Program report 87-3). Madison: Wisconsin Center for Education Research, School of Education, University of Wisconsin.

Damarin, S. K. (1990). Teaching mathematics: A feminist perspective. In T. J. Cooney & C. R. Hirsch (Eds.), *Teaching and learning mathematics in the 1990s* (1990 *Yearbook,* pp. 144–151). Reston, VA: National Council of Teachers of Mathematics.

Damen, L. (1987). *Culture learning: The fifth dimension*. Reading, MA: Addison-Wesley.

Delpit, L. D. (1986). Skills and other dilemmas of a progressive black educator. *Harvard Educational Review, 56*(4), 379–385.

Educational Evaluation and Policy Analysis, 12(3) (1990), 233–353.

Elementary School Journal, 93(2) (1992), 145–228.

Fennema, E., & Franke, M. L. (1992). Teachers' knowledge and its impact. In D. A. Grouws (Ed.), *Handbook of research on mathematics teaching and learning* (pp. 147–164). New York: Macmillan.

Garrett, D. G. (1992, April 4). Alexander applauds efforts of math group to reform study. *Tennessean,* 5B.

Giroux, H. A. (1983). *Theory and resistance in education*. South Hadley, MA: Bergin & Garvey.

Good, T. L., Mulryan, C., & McCaslin, M. (1992). Grouping for instruction: A call for programmatic research on small-group processes. In D. A. Grouws (Ed.), *Handbook of research on mathematics teaching and learning* (pp. 165–196). New York: Macmillan.

Grant, C. A., & Sleeter, C. E. (1989). *Turning on learning*. New York: Merrill.

Grouws, D. A. (Ed.). (1992). *Handbook of research on mathematics teaching and learning*. New York: Macmillan.

Grouws, D. A., Cooney, T. J., & Jones, D. (Eds.). (1988). *Effective mathematics teaching*. Hillsdale, NJ: Erlbaum.

Heath, S. B. (1986). Sociocultural contexts of language development. In Bilingual Education Office, California State Department of Education (Eds.), *Beyond language: Social and cultural factors in schooling language minority students* (pp. 143–186). Los Angeles: Evaluation, Dissemination, and Assessment Center (EDAC), California State University.

Kagan, N. (1966). Group procedures. *Review of Educational Research, 36*(2), 274–287.

Kilpatrick, J. (1992). A history of research in mathematics education. In D. A. Grouws (Ed.), *Handbook of research on mathematics teaching and learning* (pp. 3–38). New York: Macmillan.

Koehler, M., & Grouws, D. A. (1992). Mathematics teaching practices and their effects. In D. A. Grouws (Ed.), *Handbook of research on mathematics teaching and learning* (pp. 115–126). New York: Macmillan.

Ladson-Billings, G. (1993, March). *Skills and other dilemmas revisited: Mathematics and cultural diversity*. Paper presented at the research presession of the 71st Annual Meeting of the National Council of Teachers of Mathematics, Seattle, WA.

Ladson-Billings, G., & Tate, W. (1993). *Toward a critical race theory of education*. (Unpublished manuscript). Madison, WI.

Lampert, M. (1986). Knowing, doing, and teaching multiplication. *Cognition and Instruction, 3,* 305–342.

Lampert, M. (1990). When the problem is not the question and the solution is not the answer: Mathematical knowing and teaching. *American Educational Research Journal, 27,* 29–63.

Lewis, M., & Simon, R. I. (1986). A discourse not intended for her: Learning and teaching within a patriarchy. *Harvard Educational Review, 56*(4), 457–472.

McDonald, J. P. (1986). Raising the teacher's voice and the ironic role of theory. *Harvard Educational Review, 56*(4), 355–378.

Montessori, M. (1912). *The Montessori method: Scientific pedagogy as applied to children's homes.* New York: Stokes.

National Council of Teachers of Mathematics. (1989). *Curriculum and evaluation standards for school mathematics.* Reston, VA: Author.

(1991). *Professional standards for teaching mathematics.* Reston, VA: Author.

National Research Council. (1989). *Everybody counts.* Washington, DC: National Academy Press.

Nieto, S. (1992). *Affirming diversity: The sociopolitical context of multicultural education.* New York: Longman.

Oakes, J. (1990). Opportunities, achievement, and choice: Women and minority students in science and mathematics. In C. B. Cazden (Ed.), *Review of research in education* (Vol. 16, pp. 153–222). Washington, DC: American Educational Research Association.

Pitman, A. (1989). Mathematics education reform in its social, political and economic contexts. In N. F. Ellerton & M. A. Clements (Eds.), *School mathematics: The challenge to change* (pp. 101–119). Geelong, Australia: Deakin University.

Polya, G. (1957). *How to solve it* (2d ed.). New York: Doubleday.

Popkewitz, T. S. (1987). Institutional issues in the monitoring of school mathematics. In T. A. Romberg & D. M. Stewart (Eds.), *The monitoring of school mathematics: Background papers* (Vol. 3, pp. 3–26. Program report 87–3). Madison: Wisconsin Center for Education Research, School of Education, University of Wisconsin.

(1988). Institutional issues in the study of school mathematics: Curriculum research. *Educational Studies in Mathematics, 19,* 221–249.

(1992). Review of *Handbook of research on teacher education,* by W. R. Houston (Ed.). *Journal of Teacher Education, 43*(1), 63–75.

Quality Education for Minorities Project (1990). *Education that works: An action plan for the education of minorities.* Cambridge, MA: Author, MIT Press.

Rodriguez, R. (1982). *Hunger of memory.* New York: Bantam.

Romberg, T. A. (1992). Further thoughts on the *Standards:* A reaction to Apple. *Journal for Research in Mathematics Education, 23*(5), 432–437.

(1993). NCTM's standards: A rallying flag for mathematics teachers. *Educational Leadership, 50*(5), 36–41.

Secada, W. G. (1991). Diversity, equity, and cognitivist research. In T. P. Carpenter, E. Fennema, & S. Lamon (Eds.), *Teaching and learning mathematics* (pp. 17–53). Albany, NY: SUNY Press.

(1992a). Race, ethnicity, social class, language, and achievement in mathematics. In D. Grouws (Ed.), *Handbook of research on mathematics teaching and learning* (pp. 623–660). New York: Macmillan.

(1992b). Evaluating the mathematics education of LEP students in a time of educational change. *Proceedings of the second National Research Symposium on Limited English Proficient Student Issues: Focus on evaluation and measurement* (Vol. 2, pp. 209–256). Washington, DC: Office of Bilingual Education and Minority Languages Affairs (OBE-MLA), U.S. Department of Education.

(1993, October). Equity and a social psychology of mathematics education. In J. R. Rossi & B. J. Pence, *Proceedings of the 15th annual meeting, North American chapter of the International Group for the Psychology of Mathematics Education* (pp. 17–30). San Jose, CA: San Jose State University.

Secada, W. G., & Byrd, L. (1993). *School level reform in the teaching of mathematics. Working paper no. 1: The selection of schools from the first year's survey.* Paper presented at the annual meeting of the American Educational Research Association, Atlanta.

Sharon, S. (1980). Cooperative learning in small groups: Recent methods and effects on achievement, attitudes, and ethnic relations. *Review of Educational Research, 50*(2), 241–272.

Slavin, R. E. (1980). Cooperative learning. *Review of Educational Research, 50*(2), 315–342.

Sleeter, C. E., & Grant, C. A. (1988). *Making choices for multicultural education.* New York: Merrill.

Stanic, G. M. A., & Kilpatrick, J. (1992). Mathematics curriculum reform in the United States: An historical perspective. *International Journal of Educational Research, 17*, 407–417.

Thompson, A. (1992). Teachers' beliefs and conceptions: A synthesis of the research. In D. Grouws (Ed.), *Handbook of research on mathematics teaching and learning* (pp. 127–146). New York: Macmillan.

Tomlinson, T. M. (1986). *A nation at risk:* Background for a working paper. In T. M. Tomlinson & H. J. Walberg (Eds.), *Academic work and educational excellence: Raising student productivity* (pp. 3–28). Berkeley, CA: McCutchan.

Trueba, H. (1989). *Raising silent voices.* New York: Harper Collins.

Zeichner, K. M. (in press). Conceptions of reflective practice in teaching and teacher education. In G. Harvard & P. Hodgkinson (Eds.), *Action and reflection in teacher education.* Norwood, NJ: Ablex.

6   Equity in mathematics education: Class in the world outside the class

Marilyn Frankenstein

Why is the development of socioeconomic class consciousness part of ensuring equity in mathematics education? How can a business and consumer mathematics curriculum grapple with socioeconomic class issues, and therefore, be part of the struggle for equity in mathematics education?

This chapter focuses on the second question – a curriculum I have been creating to integrate business/consumer mathematics and socioeconomic class issues. I discuss the first question in order to clarify my rationale for this curriculum. To properly do that, I need to situate the answer in a particular context, starting with the perspective that there are serious class inequities in our society[1] and that most people's lack of knowledge of class structure is a part of why these class inequities persist. Further, these social class inequities create and perpetuate inequities in schools: Kozol (1991) documents the vast and growing material differences among school districts and their impact on education; Braverman (1974) and Noble (1984) show how employers' needs for reserves of unemployed people who blame themselves for their economic plight indirectly control the curriculum by increasing the credentials required for various jobs, contrary to the actual knowledge needed; and Weis (1990) finds that the working-class parents in her ethnographic research did not have the prior learning experience to demand more than the *form* of education, nor did they realize that the form, without substance, provided by the school would not lead their children to upward social mobility, or in many cases, even to college.

So, I argue that mathematics education in general, and mathematics in particular, will become more equitable as the class structure in society becomes more equitable. Since I also contend that working-class consciousness[2] is an important component in changing class inequities, developing that consciousness during teaching could contribute to the goal of ensuring equity in mathematics education. Finally, I believe that teaching about socioeconomic class issues is appropriate for a business and consumer mathematics curriculum because I think that mathematical disempowerment impedes an understanding of how our society is structured with respect to class interests. In other words, to fully understand business and

165

consumer mathematics means to understand the larger context in which those mathematical calculations take place.

In the next section of this chapter, I look briefly at a number of explanations for why so many people in the United States lack class consciousness. I then develop in more detail the role mathematical disempowerment plays in people's clouded ideas about class structure. In the following section, I discuss the institutional context in which I work and summarize the underlying methodologies of my teaching activities. I then present a detailed outline of my curriculum, focusing on the new material I have added to the traditional business/consumer mathematics syllabus, and on how that material tries to raise students' class consciousness. In the final section, I include student reactions to the curriculum, concentrating on their ideas about class structure in our society. I conclude with reflections about how I can improve the curriculum.

Class unconsciousness

When discussing a friend's research with my mother, I gained firsthand insight into how so many people in the United States think they are middle class. My friend was involved in a large project that studied women and mental health, interviewing low-income mothers of young children. In one of the many interviews, the mothers were asked to define their social class. Almost everyone answered "middle class."[3/4] My mother, who has always had a strong sense of the injustices and inequities of the capitalist system, found it fascinating that these women did not see their societal disempowerment. As our discussion continued, I tried to point out that I was glad, especially given my educational and political activities, that I had not had a typical middle-class upbringing. But before I could expand upon this thought, the moment I uttered the phrase "not brought up in a typical middle class–" my mother freaked out, screaming, "What do you mean, we weren't middle class!"

After much more screaming and arguing, I realized that my mother heard my comment as a strong insult – that my parents had not provided for me what the parents of the middle-class kids with whom I was tracked at school had provided for their kids. My mother, in spite of her insight into the unfairness of the economic *system,* would feel like a *personal* failure if she and my father had not provided me with a middle-class upbringing. My anticapitalist mother felt she was responsible for her class position! Sennet and Cobb (1972), analyzing the consciousness of working-class people, refer to Sartre's contention that people "need to make sense of social life in terms of intimate experience." They conclude that abstract analysis of class positions is not helpful to people as they try to construct meaning in their lives: "The constrictions of freedom in their lives can be made sense of only by assigning a measure of inadequate coping, insufficient ability at work, to themselves" (pp. 95–96). Or, in my mother's case, by denying that there were any "constrictions of freedom."

So one reason for the absence of a strong working-class consciousness in the United States is that what we know intellectually is different from what we must feel in order to create meaning in our daily lives. In addition, people struggling to get by do not usually have the time to reflect, to analyze why they are barely surviving economically – they are too busy and tired trying to make ends meet (Steele, personal communication). The murkiness of class consciousness is also explained by the history of working-class formation in the United States (Hogan, 1982; Zinn, 1980) and by the other structural divisions in our society, such as sexism and racism,[5] which divert attention from class stratification (Boggs, 1970; MacLeod, 1987; Reich, 1978; Zinn, 1980). The common interests of workers have more recently been clouded by the international division of labor between poorer and richer countries (Hymer, 1978) and the growing gap between high- and low-paid workers (Tilly, 1990). Further, the mass media atomize these divisions in the working class by bombarding the public with images of how "every-body's really the same," so all one needs is motivation and persistence to make it to the top (DeMott, 1991), or luck (e.g., legalized gambling in state lotteries).

All of these structural and ideological impediments to class awareness are reinforced by the process and content of schooling. Because schools are ostensibly organized according to merit, students who do not do well internalize blame and take individual responsibility for their failure, lower their aspirations, and "accept their eventual placement in low-status jobs as the natural outcome of their own shortcomings" (MacLeod, 1987, p. 113). The reality, as Bowles and Gintis (1976) so convincingly documented, is that socioeconomic background is the major predictor of educational attainment, and that regardless of the latter, socioeconomic background is the major predictor of future economic success. In addition, various ethnographies have shown that educational tasks and social relations are much more mechanical and formulaic in working-class schools, so these students are tracked out of higher schooling and jobs (Anyon, 1980; Weis, 1990). Also, the curricula taught in schools virtually ignore working-class history[6] and present particular views of that history as the only perspective.[7]

Moreover, at the heart of my curriculum-development work is my contention that the applications of mathematical knowledge taught in schools impart an image of neutrality and naturalness to particular societal arrangements that obscure the class structure of our society. This kind of mathematical disempowerment works by presenting mathematics applications that support a particular interpretation and organization of society (Frankenstein, 1987, 1989);[8] by omitting information that shows the usefulness of statistical data in understanding economic, political, and social issues; and by ignoring data that present alternative explanations and visions about the structure of society (Frankenstein, 1987, 1989).[9/10]

A mathematically disempowered person, someone who "avoids" numbers, someone who does not regard statistical data as a part of understanding economic, political, and social issues, will not delve deeply enough into school mathematics problems to reflect on the picture they present of our society. For a mathematically disempowered person, solving problems is an exercise in finding some key-word clue that indicates what operations or formula should be used to transform the given numbers into the answer. The content of the applications is simply absorbed semiconsciously as material that confuses what to do with the numbers. This content sends very powerful messages. Gill (1988), for example, shows how "profit" is defined as "the difference between the selling price and the cost price" in a widely used text in England. She contrasts this "antiseptic" definition with Marx's concept of "profit as ultimately unpaid labour" (p. 123). Maxwell (1988) gives mathematics examples from other cultures involving guerilla fighters helping peasants or landlords demanding compound interest from poor tenants, which "strike most of us as blatantly political, a part of the indoctrination of the young into the currently dominant values in these societies" (p. 118) to argue that all maths examples are political. I have argued that

even trivial maths applications, like finding the total from a grocery bill, carry the non-neutral hidden message that it's natural to distribute food according to individual payment. Even traditional maths courses which provide no real-life data carry the non-neutral hidden message that learning maths is separate from helping people understand and control the world. (Frankenstein, 1989, p. 5)

Using ethnographic data of U.S. adults' use of mathematics in the supermarket, Lave (1988) found that during shopping, choices are first made qualitatively – that is, an item may be the best buy mathematically, but is rejected because the package is too big to fit on the pantry shelf. However, people fall back on arithmetic calculations when there are no other criteria for choice. This then provides a basis for believing that their decision is rational and objective: "Price arithmetic contributes more to constructing the incorrigibility of 'rationality' than to the instrumental elaboration of preference structures" (p. 158). School mathematics, Lave contends, is filled with shopping applications so that money becomes a value-free, "natural" term, just a form of neutral school arithmetic. Borba (1991), discussing the politics intrinsic to academic mathematics, theorizes that the use of mathematics in everyday life not only makes our choices seem more "rational," but also serves to end all discussion. Once we use mathematics to justify a decision, no one can question it – after all, it is now "scientifically proved."

In addition to absorbing a picture of society that presents current arrangements as natural and eternal, a mathematically disempowered person does not have the kind of real access to data that explodes many of the widely held myths about class structure in the United States. That is, even when news stories appear with this data, people who are mathematically disempowered skip over the numbers or ignore the entire article. For example, if after-tax income is any marker of class stratification, government statistics show a deeply divided country: "The richest two and a half million Americans now have nearly as much income each year as the 100 million Americans with the lowest incomes" (Jackson, in the *Boston Globe,* 1991). This inequality is supported by a tax system in which, during the 1980s, "the average federal tax burden of the poorest fifth of households increased 16 percent, while that of the top one percent *fell* 14 percent" (Herman, 1991). This financial redistribution was so marked that even Richard Gephardt, the House majority leader, accused Reagan and Bush of waging "a class war" (Frisby, 1991). However, Herman (1991) points out that the *New York Times,* in an article about Reaganomics' "10th birthday," lists as losers people who had invested heavily in tax shelters, and as the biggest winners, wage earners with few deductions, credits, or exclusions under the old tax law. "The beneficiaries of the capital gains tax changes, the drop of the top rate from 70 to 28 percent . . . – the constituency of the top one percent – are not the big winners in this account, only a subclass of wage earners" (p. 18). Would a careful analysis of the data ignore these income and tax inequities? For another example, a step toward overcoming the racial divisions splitting workers might be taken if white workers were familiar with and understood statistical analyses that counter the belief that racial discrimination against blacks benefits whites because of reduced competition for jobs. Reich (1978) uses correlation coefficients between various measures of racism and white incomes to show that racism results in lower wages for white as well as black workers, and in higher profits for the capitalist class.

So, overcoming these forms of mathematical disempowerment can contribute to clarifying people's understanding of the class structure of our society. In the next section, I will detail how my business and consumer mathematics curriculum attempts to raise working-class students' class consciousness.

Class consciousness in the curriculum

I teach at the College of Public and Community Service (University of Massachusetts, Boston). My students are mainly working-class, urban adults in their 30s, 40s, 50s, and older who have not been "tracked" for college; many of them were labeled as "failures" in secondary school; most have internalized negative self-images about their knowledge and ability in mathematics. Approximately 60% are women, 30% people of color. Most work (or are looking for work) full-time, have families, and attend school full-time. They work in various public and community service jobs; many have been involved in organizing for social change. The students in our business and consumer mathematics class (which we call "Public Service Mathematics") are somewhat atypical. We have two "exit level" mathematics requirements–the course just referred to and statistics for the social sciences. The Public Service Mathematics students are usually disproportionately younger white males who are police workers. On the basis of informal interviews, it seems apparent that this is because they see no need to use mathematics in their work, and think Public Service Mathematics is the easier requirement.

Much of the curriculum in the college is interdisciplinary and/or project-oriented. Students can work toward their degree using prior learning from work or community organizing, or new learning from classes or from community service (e.g., students lobbied the legislature and organized for welfare rights, forming the Massachusetts Coalition for Basic Human Needs; students, asked by the community, worked with faculty to serve as consultants for the Roxbury Technical Assistance Project to help that community participate in planning its own development). The faculty are activists as well as intellectuals; approximately 50% are women, 30% people of color. Teachers have less institutional power over students than in most universities because we do not give grades, and students can choose another faculty member to evaluate their work if they are dissatisfied with their initial faculty evaluation. We cannot require attendance or any other work that is not clearly discussed in the competency statement that details the criteria and standards for demonstrating knowledge of the topic the students are studying.

Through the Public Service Mathematics curriculum, I try to raise students' consciousness about class in a number of ways: Through empowering learning activities; through challenges to widely held conceptions about how one learns mathematics and about what counts as mathematical knowledge; and through statistical data that reveal the actual class structure and inequities in the United States. Activities such as working in groups, exploring feelings and learning processes through journal writing, and evaluating ones' own learning[11] empower people to realize that they already understand more mathematics than test results have led them to believe. This is important in developing the self-confidence that enables them to participate in dialogue about the structure of our society, which focuses on the statistical picture.

Moreover, these activities and others that I will discuss in the curriculum outline are based on Paulo Freire's theory that liberatory education does not dichotomize the activity of teachers and students.[12] People are not "cognitive" – only learning – at one point, and then they "know it all," so at the next point, they own the knowledge that has been stuffed into their heads by the teacher. Rather, each of us constantly reforms our knowledge, based on our own and others' reflections. Students and teachers are "critical co-investigators" in the process of learning–teaching (Freire, 1970, pp. 67–68).[13] As students create and re-create mathematical knowledge for themselves, and as they revise their conception of what counts for mathematical knowledge, they begin to see mathematical aspects "in the midst" of other knowledge they have, or to ask mathematics-related questions about their knowledge. When they participate in the dialogue about the structure of our society, they can probe behind the data, interrogating, for example, which categories are created to sort the data,[14] who was counted in each of those categories, and what information has been obscured by mathematically transforming the data. Thus, students can interact actively with the content of the course – statistical content that explodes the myths of classlessness.

In the curriculum outline that follows, I concentrate on the content I have added to the traditional business/consumer mathematics syllabus.[15] The discussion is organized according to the major curriculum units: Budgets, investments, loans, insurance, and taxes. In particular, I want to detail the kinds of information about our class structure that can be integrated into that traditional syllabus. The methodology, or how the material is presented and how the lessons unfold, conforms to the ideas and philosophy just sketched and fully developed in the cited references. The underlying philosophy of both the content and methodology of the curriculum is that the students' intellectual work is respected. Too often, students have internalized the views of the dominant classes in which "the intellectual activity of those without power is always labeled non-intellectual" (Freire & Macedo, 1987, p. 122). The academic content, the interconnections among mathematics and other disciplines, and the theory building and other intellectual work are designed to change this self-perception.

Curriculum overview

The syllabus covers the mathematics of personal consumer finance – budgets, bank savings and other investments, loans, insurance, taxes – and the citizen context in which those personal financial situations unfold. For example, when we study loans, we do not limit this to the calculations needed to discover the most favorable interest, but also consider in whose interests banks are calculating, and why it is so difficult for some persons to get loans. Each unit includes data about some of the injustices that exist related to that business/consumer mathematics topic; counter-information that challenges the commonly held assumptions about that topic; and information that suggests alternative structures that may effect greater justice in the economic area covered by the unit.

The introduction to the course challenges a traditional assumption about the value of learning mathematics for use in the real world. I ask the students to think about a problem discussed in Lave's (1988) ethnographic study of arithmetic activity in grocery shopping. One shopper found an unusually high-priced package of cheese in a bin. Weight, price per pound, and total price were printed on each package. He suspected an error. How could he determine if that were the case?[16] Most students say he should multiply or divide to check, some say he should have it reweighed. In Lave's study, the shopper searched through the bin for a package weighing the same amount and inferred from the discrepancy between their prices that his suspicions were correct. We then discuss Lave's analysis that calculation is not a disconnected cognitive function that is transferred from situation to situation, but that the situation actually influences the calculation: "Activity-in-setting, seamlessly stretched across persons-acting and setting often turns the latter into a calculating device" (p. 154). Lave goes on to describe the process of transforming information through mathematical operations as "dissolving problems," where problems "disappear into solution with ongoing activity" (p. 120). I use this example to start the first class for a number of reasons: to have students think about when and how they use basic mathematics in their lives as consumers; to begin to present a different view of learning and of mathematics (Why learn calculations if we can solve problems in other ways? Was the shopper's solution mathematical?); and to break the teaching/learning dichotomy by having students discuss the implications of mathematics education research for math education as they are learning mathematics. Then, after reviewing the syllabus, we explore the connections between consumer and citizen mathematics through discussing the meaning of political cartoons like those shown in Figure 6.1.

We end the introductory lesson by working on an example that illustrates that, indeed, mathematical knowledge can be important in shopping. Recently, I have used a news note from *Nutrition Action* that shows how a product can be "95% fat free" and also get 40% of its calories from fat (Food porn, 1990).[17]

Budgets

The larger context of this topic includes wealth and welfare in the United States. The information about injustices ranges from Ivana Trump flying Paris couturiers to New York because she saves money shopping that way: "I could buy five more dresses for the $100,000 it costs me to bring my

Figure 6.1a and b. Exploring the connections between consumer and citizen mathematics. ("The Education Prez!" cartoon: *Auth* © 1990. *The Philadelphia Inquirer*. Reprinted with permission of Universal Press Syndicate. All rights reserved. "The industrial economists are sluggish . . ." cartoon: Dan Wasserman, copyright 1987. *Boston Globe*. Distributed by the Los Angeles Times Syndicate. Reprinted by permission.)

SYLVIA   by Nicole Hollander

Figure 6.2. Income distribution in the United States. ("Harry, did you know" cartoon: © 1990 by Nicole Hollander. All rights reserved.)

plane to Paris" (Lives of the rich, 1989), to the fact that the number of children living in poverty in the United States "would constitute the fourth most populous city on Earth, behind Mexico City, Cairo, and Shanghai" (Jackson, 1991). Information that reveals the actual class structure of our society includes the fact that since the Civil War, through all the major changes society has undergone, the richest 1% of the population continues to own 25% of the net worth of all adults (Knoll, 1990); and that from 1969 to 1989, the median income of the wealthiest 5% of U.S. families has risen from $72,633 to $92,663, whereas the median income of the poorest 20% has fallen from $9,920 to $9,431 (Jackson, 1991). The cartoon in Figure 6.2 captures the point.

Information that challenges commonly held beliefs about wealth and welfare includes data indicating that, contrary to the "lazy underclass" stereotype, "more than 85% of the poor in the U.S. is either under 18 or over 65, disabled or working" (Poor characteristics, 1991); that most people do not stay on welfare for very long periods – 70% of all people on AFDC between the mid-1960s and late 1970s were on for 7 years or less; 30% were on for 2 years or less – and only 20% of girls from families that have been "heavily" dependent on AFDC "had become dependent themselves by the time they had reached their mid-twenties" (Welfare's worth, 1988). Information about alternatives includes the Children's Defense Fund calculations that every poor U.S. family could be lifted to the poverty line for $28 billion, whereas in 1990, the top 1% of U.S. taxpayers received tax breaks amounting to $39 billion (Jackson, 1991); that most major industrialized capitalist countries spend a much greater percentage of their Gross Domestic Product on social programs than does the United States, and that when the regressive U.S. tax system, which pays for our social programs, is considered, "labor in the U.S. pays at least three quarters of the taxes that go to finance the welfare state" (Comparing social paychecks, 1989).

Of course, in class we discuss what is traditionally considered "mathematics" too – we read matrix charts about the percentage income share of each fifth of the population, discussing what "constant dollars" mean, and we practice understanding algebraic demonstrations through investigating recreational problems such as the counterintuitive result that sometimes it is to one's financial benefit to choose a $200 salary raise every 6 months rather than a $1,000 raise every year (Somers, 1989).

Investments

The larger context of this topic includes "redlining" – where banks disinvest in particular neighborhoods – ostensibly because the people in that area are high-risk in terms of defaulting on their loans, and the savings and loan crisis. Studies have countered this myth: "Atlanta's Citizens Trust Bank, a black-owned bank which made nearly all of its housing loans in minority neighborhoods, had the lowest default rate on real estate loans of any bank in the nation in 1986" (Mortgage lending in black and white, 1990). Further studies support the contention that racism, not ability to pay, is the explanation of redlining: Figure 6.3, prepared by the Greater Roxbury Neighborhood Authority (1989), shows that "the difference in volume of mortgage lending in black and white areas of [Boston] are staggering, even when income and other demographic factors except for race are held constant." In 85 of the 100 largest metropolitan areas in the country, the mortgage rejection rates for high-income blacks are greater than those for low-income whites (Mortgage lending, 1990). A recent (1991) Federal Reserve report

Comparison of Black Middle-Income Roxbury Tracts with White Middle-Income Tracts in Roxbury, South Boston, and East Boston			
	Roxbury Garrison Trotter	South Boston City Point	East Boston Jefferies Point
Total Amount Home Mortgage Loans (in Millions)	$2.59	$21.33	$14.62
Total Number Home Mortgage Loans	39	237	331
Total Population	3,450	3,526	3,282
Total Units	3,235	1,575	1,389
Median Household Income	$10,914	$12,241	$10,897
Percent of Owner Occupied Units	26%	36%	35%
Median Value	$28,000	$29,200	$25,000

Figure 6.3. A comparison of home mortgage loan distribution in three communities in the Boston area. (Used with permission of the Greater Roxbury Neighborhood Authority.)

shows that "blacks are rejected three times more often than whites for mortgages in Greater Boston . . . even when blacks classified as 'higher income' seek homes outside Boston's minority neighborhoods, they are refused mortgages far more often than whites who live on the same streets and who earn similar incomes" (Zuckoff, 1991).

We also examine the excesses that typify the continuing banking crisis, outrages that explode the myth that welfare benefits to poor people are what is draining our economy. For example, before Reagan's election, the largest number of federally insured savings banks to fail in a single year (1941) was 13; during the first 3 years of his presidency, 435 thrifts failed. In 1984, Continental Illinois failed: "If you added together all the deposits of all 10,000 banks that failed during the Great Depression, you would have a bank only one-quarter the size of Continental Illinois in 1984" (Sherill, 1990, p. 607). The government was afraid that if it let Continental go under, the entire banking system would collapse, so it pumped $9.5 billion of our tax money (i.e., welfare) into it and the FDIC guaranteed all deposits, including those exceeding the $100,000 limit, at the 12 largest banks in the country, at a cost to the taxpayers of $1 trillion, to restore confidence in the banking system. "The nation's eighth largest bank had, in effect, been nationalized by the most conservative administration in 50 years" (Woodruff, quoted in Sherill, 1990, p. 607). As Sherill concludes, this represents "capitalism for profits, socialism for losses" (p. 607).

Further, during the 1980s, regulators delayed an average of 2 years in closing bankrupt thrifts, costing taxpayers billions of dollars (Sherill, 1990, p. 593); a key reason for this was that accounts over $100,000 constituted nearly 20% of deposits at the failed banks; at seven of the bailed-out thrifts, the average jumbo account contained more than $1 million. However, the average savings account is only about $8,000 – since the cost of the cleanup to taxpayers is estimated to be as high as $14,000 per family, the signed-number mathematics of the bailout shows a transfer of money from the poor to the wealthy (Financial Democracy Campaign, 1990). Moreover, all banks' jumbo accounts were not treated equally. Harlem's Freedom National Bank, the only black-owned commercial bank in New York City, was swiftly closed as it began to fail, in spite of the fact that a group of New York businessmen had pulled together about $6 million to try to help the bank. The dozens of charities and nonprofits that had jumbo accounts there, after announcing that their losses would lead to drastic cuts in day care, foster care, and so on, were covered by the taxpayers at only 50 cents to the dollar. As the *Nation*'s editorial headline summarized (Redlining a black bank, 1991), this black bank was redlined.

We then discuss alternative plans like the Financial Democracy Campaign's struggle to jail the real crooks,[18] confiscate the money they stole, reregulate the financial industry, and work toward establishing financial consumer associations to give citizens more say in monetary policy-making.[19]

Of course, we also solve typical textbook problems using the compound interest formula (and show for a few particular cases how it is derived from the simple interest formula), reading the relevant banking tables, using the present-value and annuity formulas, and showing how mathematical analysis reveals problems with certain kinds of investments. For example, the ads that say $2,000-a-year IRAs will make you a millionaire in 35 years are based on underlying assumptions of continuing inflation. Such inflation would result in $1 million having the buying power of around $34,000 in the year you opened the account (Brom, 1982). For another example, the exponential growth in the number of persons needed to make "pyramid" schemes, like chain letters, work makes it realistically certain that they will break down.

This unit also contains information about other kinds of investments. There are examples of the way our current capitalist economic system supports problematic ventures. For example, in a "No Comment" column in the *Progressive* (1986), editors quoting *Fortune* noted that "investors looking for a double scoop of capital gains have been finding it in doubly troubled nuclear utilities – companies that not only own nuclear power plants, but also have had severe enough problems with them to reduce or eliminate some dividends. Even General Public Utilities, owner of Three Mile Island, the granddaddy of nuclear nightmares, has seen its stock shoot up nearly 150% over the past two years" (Invest in America, 1986, 13). Finally, information about alternative, ethical investments is discussed (Domini & Kinder, 1985; McAlister, 1990), including the difficulties that can arise in those choices, such as "what if a company has a woman on its board of directors while simultaneously acting to prevent its largely female workforce from unionizing?" (Strom, 1990). Another example is that of IBM in 1985, when that company strongly supported inner-city development and paid its employees well, had had no layoffs in 40 years, and had provided an open system for complaints, but was a top defense contractor and had automated South Africa's apartheid bureaucracy (Domini & Kinder, 1985, p. 17).

This topic ends by looking more creatively at what happens to investments. Student interpretations of Figure 6.4 are generally quite critical of banks:

· You deposit money and get very little in return.
· The money the average person puts in the bank is like throwing it in the garbage.
· Your deposits are used for "garbage" or worthless investments.
· Making money is more important than using money to keep our world clean – we finance the pollution of our world.

Figure 6.4. Speculating about investments. (© Joseph Blough. Used with permission.)

Nevertheless, as I discuss below, the students' critical insights in specific instances do not seem to come together into a consciousness of the entire class structure. In spite of all the information in the curriculum, most students continue to regard each injustice as isolated, not systemic.

Loans, insurance, and taxes

The larger context of these topics fits the theme of "welfare for the rich," or government transfer of public monies from the poor to the rich. For example, when Neil Bush's Silverado Savings and Loan was approached by a developer for a loan of $10 million, he was allegedly told that Silverado would loan him $15 million if he used the extra $5 million to buy some of its stock. Silverado would then show an infusion of "new capital"! When Silverado failed, taxpayers, who fund the FDIC, picked up the tab. In another example, Mario Renda laundered $6 billion through 3,500 thrifts, before his 1987 arrest, by allegedly approaching the S&L with an offer that if it made loans to certain borrowers that he would send, he would supply the money to lend to them (Sherill, 1990, pp. 597, 599). Perhaps one of the more "creative" uses of loans comes from the art world, which does not appear to be intimately tied to financial institutions. In 1987, Sotheby's art auctioneers sold Van Gogh's "Irises" for $53.9 million; they immediately loaned $27 million of this to the "buyer," and as of 1990, Sotheby's "has retained possession of the painting for all but six months since the sale and has it now" (Bob, 1990, p. 33). This practice inflates the prices of paintings sold at future auctions – the "buyer" of "Irises" sold another painting he had bought through Sotheby's at 276% more than he paid for it, and used his profit to reduce his debt on "Irises" (Bob, 1990, p. 36).

The class also looks at ways insurance is used creatively by capitalists. In 1980, after the MGM Grand Hotel fire in Las Vegas, "faced with damage claims far exceeding its $30 million in coverage, MGM Grand bought, for about $37 million, an extra $170 million of insurance – fully one month after the night that 84 people died" (How to write off major disasters, September 2–8, 1991). Imagine working-class people being allowed to buy retroactive health insurance, after getting cancer or some other serious and costly illness! And because liability claims paid by an insurance company are tax deductible (i.e., subsidized by public monies), but those paid directly by the hotel are not, the hotel could wind up doing reasonably well financially, as do the insurers who charge highly for such after-the-fact coverage. Consumers, of course, do not do so well: Insurers have an interest in dragging out court claims so they can pile up interest on their premiums, and hotels have "no direct financial interest in safeguarding their buildings: Why pay for prevention when you can deduct the cost of the cure from your taxes?" (How to write off, September 2–8, 1991). Further, in 1986, the insurance industry cried "liability crisis," but gave out no figures to back this up, no information about how much they were paying out in malpractice verdicts and settlements, and "earned after-tax profits of $19 billion, more than double the average annual profits during the previous ten years" (Stagnation and the nation, sidebar, June 1987).

In addition, the class examines how corporations that make giant profits often pay very little in taxes: In 1987, Bank of Boston paid no state taxes while declaring $19 million in profits; in 1978, Digital Equipment Corporation paid $2.1 million in state taxes on Massachusetts income of $24.5 million; in 1979, they paid $288,000 in taxes on $15.6 million of Massachusetts income (Mohl, 1989). Because Massachusetts does not have a graduated income tax and because sales, excise, and property taxes take a larger portion of middle- and low-income families' income, "middle income Massachusetts families pay 10.5 percent of their income in state and local taxes, and low income families pay 13.4 percent. But the wealthy pay only 6.8 percent" (McIntyre, 1991). However, when politicians such as President Bush called for tax cuts, they meant the cuts, like those on capital gains, to benefit the rich:

In 1980, the richest one percent of American households had an average income from all sources of $313,206. That will increase 75 percent to $548,969 this year, according to the Washington-based Center on Budget and Policy Priorities. Of the $313,206 income in 1980, the average household received $83,000 in capital gains. But in 1990, the average capital gains for this group are projected at more than $175,000 – double the 1980 amount. Some people argue that a capital gains tax cut will help everyone. But while capital gains will account for 32 percent of the income of the richest one percent of households in 1990, it will account for only one percent of the income of the bottom 90 percent." (To George Bush, 1990)

Moreover, the unfairness of a tax system that transfers money from the poor to the rich is masked by the way we label various categories. For example, in 1981, the housing subsidy for homeowners' real estate taxes and mortgage interest (usually called a "tax deduction") was greater than the money HUD had spent in all of its housing programs for low-income families since 1937 (Reagan condemns public housing, 1983).

Finally, the class discusses alternatives to the various state and local fiscal crises such as taxing land used for commercial purposes (a tax with the additional advantage of lowering land prices because capitalists cannot decide to "produce less of it and charge more for it," as they do with other taxed goods). "It's no coincidence . . . that the one large city in the country with such a tax, Pittsburgh (cited in 1989 by the Rand McNally *Almanac* as America's second most liveable city), has the lowest housing prices of any major city in America" (Fitch, 1990, p. 481); taxing the elite nonprofits – "In New York City alone, tax-exempt assets of private educational institutions (temporarily ignoring the churches, the private hospitals, the foundations, etc.) could generate nearly $100 million in property taxes, or enough to bring the city's welfare grants [to the poor] up to the federal poverty level" (Fitch, 1990, p. 481); and taking away developers' exemptions – "Welfare for developers is very different from welfare for the poor and destitute: There is no humiliating application process . . . once you're on, you're on, and there's no reexamination of your case to see if you still qualify. In New York City, three tax abatement programs waste nearly $500 million a year – two and a half times as much as a controversial home-relief program that doles out meager grants to 150,000 people annually" (Fitch, 1990, p. 482).

Curriculum summary

During the last two or three lessons, I focus on what I have tried to bring out through all the examples of inequities and through all the alternatives to these conditions.[20] The injustices in our society are not isolated exceptions: They are logical consequences of the institutional structures of our society, and it does not have to be that way – there are other choices we can make to reorganize our institutions. We reflect on this theme through two fables about a little red hen, which illustrate the capitalist versus a leftist, working-class perspective. In one, the capitalist hen got rich on her own initiative, finding wealth "scratching around the barnyard" and laboring by herself, since the workers would not help her without all sorts of guarantees and union protection. Then the government forced the hen to share with the lazy workers, so the capitalist hen stopped producing. In the counter to this, the capitalist hen[21] got rich through theft and inheritance, aided by bribes and government help to get favorable tax laws, and by poorly paid workers. The hen had much more than she needed, but hoarded it instead of sharing it with the workers who built her business (Riddell, Shackelford, & Stamos, 1982). We also examine this summary theme of capitalism world-wide, using Alexander Cockburn's (1989) "Scenes from the Inferno" in the course of which the author indicates, for example, that there are 25 million underfed children in Latin America – the biggest food exporter next to the United States – children who eat cakes made from wet newspapers. These scenes in 1989 included Chile,

laboratory of "free market" policy, [where] the Pinochet regime takes a creative approach to the statistics of hunger. Instead of measuring malnutrition in relation to a person's weight and age, as is usual, it looks at weight and height. So a stunted child is not counted as malnourished, and thus is not eligible for food supplements because her weight falls within an acceptable range for her height.

In some Santiago neighborhoods, the diet of about "80 percent of the people does not have sufficient calories and proteins, by internationally established standards, to sustain life" (p. 510). The Cockburn report also included Peru, where in 1981, the "former president of the Peruvian Senate declared that 'it was healthier to eat less, that thin women were far more attractive than fat ones, and that Jewish children who had gone hungry in concentration camps had not become stupider as a result' " (p. 510). These scenes involve an average of $20 billion dollars a year exported from the Third World to the First over the past decade ($43 billion in 1988), with the capitalist class explanation that the trouble is that these countries are not truly capitalist. "But these countries have private ownership and operate under the aegis of the IMF; any state intervention is of the capitalist variety" (Cockburn, 1989, p. 511). Moreover, the capitalist class says "free market" strategies have worked: "They extol Chile, where the minimum wage, which in 1971 could buy 313 kilograms of bread each month, now buys only 85 kilograms a month, and where 46 to 48 percent of the population lives in poverty" (Cockburn, 1989, p. 511). Similar stories from Africa and Asia and "the bodies bundled in niches on New York's streets and lodged amid the bushes under the Los Angeles freeways" (Cockburn, 1989, p. 511) are evidence that must be factored into any conclusion about the triumph of capitalism, with the collapse of central Europe and other such events from the so-called socialist countries.

Finally, we discuss the connections illustrated in the political cartoon in Figure 6.5.

Investment Strategies

EDWARD SOREL

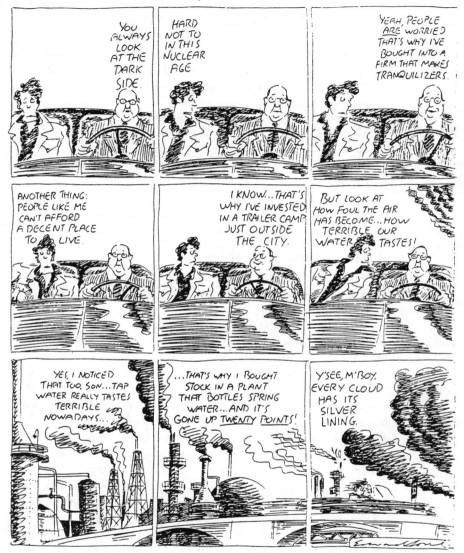

Figure 6.5. Investment strategies. (Cartoon strip by Edward Sorel. From *The Nation*. Used with permission of E. Sorel.)

Class consciousness raised?

Although some students feel what they have learned in the class is useful and talk about a general kind of raised consciousness, this awareness usually centers around specific issues and does not move toward a more overarching class analysis:

- The most useful thing I learned was that I need to try and understand (or at least be aware) of the issues around me. My awareness of issues that I have a tendency to not key in on was sparked. I realized that I need to know the relationship I share with my environment. I think these things are important because too often I take the easy way out and dissociate myself from these issues.
- I never really knew about the bailout facts – one of the things I skipped all the time in the paper because it involved financial information I didn't grasp. Maybe this class will change my attitude on this. It now seems very shocking to me, now that I understand it.
- I think that it is outrageous and even a *sin* that the government can stipulate such a low minimum wage and feel that they have given the poor working man something by giving him a $.90 hike in pay. . . . All those believing that $4.25 an hour is an adequate income . . . should receive that income and forfeit the excess to those now receiving minimum wage and it should be equally distributed so that all salaries are raised.

Many students are very defensive about the wealthy. From their writing, and class and office discussions, I think this is because in spite of the fact that they are middle-aged and nowhere near wealthy, with probable futures that make it highly unlikely they will ever be wealthy, they cling tenaciously to the "American Dream," to the belief that they too will "make it." Their arguments do not take into account all the readings, all of the data, all of the discussions from the course about how our tax money is redistributed to the rich; how the purpose of a progressive, graduated income tax is to redistribute more money from the wealthy than from the middle and lower classes into social programs that will benefit all; or the unethical, unjust ways in which most wealth is accumulated – as their statements indicate:

- Thomas Michl believes that the inequality of ownership of Treasury Bonds, bills and notes, causes a negative distribution of income . . . because 98.8% of these instruments are owned by the wealthiest 10% of families. He believes it is analogous to an entitlement like Social Security. I am in awe of his reasoning. How can he possibly see interest on an investment as welfare for the rich? Does he see anyone who puts money in a bank and thus receives interest as a welfare recipient? This is a capitalist company [sic] country. It is neither illegal or unethical to gain interest on an investment. It is available to anyone. Savings bonds are available in small denominations to all workers. The government needs people to buy these instruments. They are a benefit to us all. Maybe the government shouldn't spend what it doesn't have, but that is not part of Michl's argument. As long as Bonds, Bills, and Notes are available, people will buy them and benefit.

- Personally, I would not like to be governed in just how much I can make. A salary cap or maximum wage would only deter me and prevent me from trying and doing my best. A maximum wage would also have the same effect on society and strengthen our already class system. People in society would be more predestined and prevented from bettering their life. Part of the American dream is to do better than the ones before us. How can we, as a society, reach for the stars when being limited in our income. To impose a maximum wage would only serve to shatter the American dream and stifle society.

Even more striking is the extent of their mixed consciousness: Don't touch the wealthy, but, sure, there should be more equity:

- The main point of the article is to criticize the wealthy for being wealthy, and to criticize Ronald Reagan. Why do the rich get slammed for being rich? Doesn't someone who pays 28% personal income tax on say $2,000,000 paying more than someone paying 33% on $50,000 ($560,000 vs. $16,500). What about the people that the person making $2,000,000 employs? And the taxes that his/her corporation or company pays? There is no doubt that there should be more equity, but should we vilify the people who make it rich? Wouldn't you like to make $2,000,000 a year some day so you can pay $560,000 in taxes?
- My opinion is that we shouldn't have a maximum wage because it would destroy the American dream. I do, however, think that the rich should be taxed more, much more, than the poor and middle class. [And in response to another assignment:] I think it's sad, I do not understand why, for example, a country cannot find food for its people if it exports a large quantity.
- If management is making huge sums of money out of someone else's talent (an athlete, for example), then I don't think a maximum should be placed on the person with the talent. If there could be some way of getting the money from the ones at the top and redistributing it all the way down to the people at the bottom, I would be all for that; but it seems in every country in the world, no matter what kind of government they have, there is always a group of people who manage to live well off the labor of the majority. If I knew the answer on how to solve the problem, I would be rich myself and then I probably wouldn't care if it didn't get solved. [And in response to another assignment:] It is my opinion that they should cut defense spending and put that money back into the programs to help the middle and lower classes, especially the homeless.

So the avalanche of statistics, the myriad data that examine microscopically the myths supporting the American Dream and explode their substance, the scenes of heart-rending devastation from capitalism's inferno, do not seem to instill a sense of class consciousness, do not instill a sense that there is a class struggle that needs to be engaged in order to create a just world. The first section of this paper discussed major impediments to the development of class consciousness in the United States. The experience of teaching this course underlines for me how deep a struggle must be waged to cut through the mythology that has covered the constructs underlying the structure of our society.

The mixed consciousness of so many student comments is a source of hope. I need to discover how to encourage the students to learn about numbers in ways that make this new information a more significant part of their worldview than the dataless myths that have such a strong emotional hold. First, in the future, I think it would help to include more experience for students in analyzing the arguments of the capitalist class.[22] Possibly, discussing these arguments presented in the capitalists' own words, along with data challenging their assertions, will raise more questions for my students about how our society works. Second, I also would like to develop more effective ways of tying all the separate instances together, ways of having the students develop a range of explanatory theories about how our economic, political, and social systems function.[23] Maybe I should present the little red hen fables early in the term and have students write their own versions, revising them as they study the larger context of the various topics in the syllabus. Finally, although we discuss alternatives, that clearly is not enough to instill in people the idea that the structure of our society can change, that it is not a fixed, permanent object, but instead, a set of contingent relations.[24] Perhaps we could pick a small project, some consumer/citizen concern we can all agree to pursue throughout the term, setting a realistic goal for change. I question the efficacy of this: In the absence of a unifying liberation struggle, small victories become isolated instances that may support, rather than challenge, the system. How to help students feel, at a deep enough level to challenge the American Dream, that things can be different, is the most unclear to me, especially in the light of the changes I did help make in one student's life. He was one of my younger (mid-20s) white male policemen. At one point during the term, a statement he made showed both acute insight and cynical acceptance:

The whole capitalist system is based on people getting rich off others and some people have to suffer for others to excel. It may not be right, but that's the way our government works.

He told many people how much he loved the class, how much it had helped him make various consumer decisions, and he wrote me the following note at the beginning of the next term:

Comrad [*sic*],

Thanks to you and your class, I am now buying a 1-family house with an extra 4400 sq. ft. lot that I can hopefully build on. This is in addition to the condo I bought while in your class.

If you can't beat these Capitalist Pigs, join them!

Thanks.

Notes

1 For example, McClain (1992) reports on a recently released study that details that "US wealth concentration in 1989 was more extreme than that of any time since 1929."

2 I define this loosely as a sense that collectively, workers have common interests, and share common daily material conditions that will not allow more than a small percentage of individuals to cross class boundaries, and that workers can change these conditions only through a collective struggle whose goal is to reorganize the socioeconomic structure of society.

3 Emilie Steele was a core staff member of the "Stress and Families" project, which is written up in Belle (1982).

4 Secada's (1992) comprehensive review of research in mathematics education that relates to race, ethnicity, social class, and language issues indicates that students "seemed not to have well-articulated conceptions of social class. For example, students who lived just above poverty seemed to think that they were just like everyone else" (p. 626).

5 As Frank (1992) points out, "David Duke's candidacy symbolized . . . the failure of class politics in this country. One anecdote in the *New York Times* summed it up perfectly. Sharon Duhe, 22-year-old white, single mother, explained her vehement support for Duke all in terms of race: 'They just have those babies and go on welfare,' she complained to a reporter. She herself, though, was unemployed and on welfare. Yes [she replied], but the 'blacks get more.' "

6 Anyon's (1979) review of the treatment of economic and labor history between the Civil War and World War I in 17 widely used secondary school United States history textbooks revealed that, "The average length of the section in the texts on labor history is six pages. Most strikes are not even mentioned, and although there were more than 30,000 during the period, the texts only describe a few of them. Fourteen of the 17 books choose from among the same three strikes, ones that were especially violent and were failures from labor's point of view." (p. 393).

7 Anyon (1979) also found an absence even of the concept of, or label for, "the working class," and a clear underlying theme that "the methods appropriate for solving economic and labor problems and the view of consensual and orderly social change inherent in them are actions that maintain the balance of power in society; confrontation between contending groups which could increase the likelihood of changes in the power structure are not implied" (p. 383). The mass media reinforce this perspective; in "What's good for GM," (1992), the *Boston Globe,* a newspaper with a relatively liberal editorial policy, states that "the interests of GM [General Motors] and those of the country are closely intertwined."

8 Secada (1992) points out that for the mathematics education research community, "social class differences are not as problematic in the literature as are racial, ethnic, or other disparities. For example, while the research literature and mathematics education reform documents (for example, National Council of Teachers of Mathematics, 1989; National Research Council, 1989) at least mention women and minorities, issues of poverty and social class are absent from their discussions. Frankly, the literature does not bristle with the same sense of outrage that the poor do not do as well in mathematics as their middle-class peers as it does with similar findings along other groupings. . . . It is as if social class differences were inevitable or that, if we find them, the results are somehow explained" (p. 640). This is not the focus of this chapter, but I wanted to note it here because it is certainly instructive to see that research in mathematics education is yet another area in which the "naturalness" of current societal groupings is taken for granted.

9 Secada (1992) pointed out that this kind of disempowerment actively socializes people to see mathematics as not at all relevant for purposes of social analysis.

10 I have discussed how schools mathematically disempower people by perpetuating myths about who can learn math and about how one goes about learning math (Frankenstein, 1984). This results in students being shut out of college-preparation tracks in high school and/or out of many areas of study in college. So this kind of mathematical disempowerment also clearly contributes to class inequities in society.

11 For many examples of learning mathematics through these methods, see my adult literacy text, *Relearning Mathematics* (1989); for a more extensive, developed approach to using writing in learning mathematics, see Powell and Lopez (1989).

12 I have written a much more extensive manuscript about the reasons, and many methods, for breaking down the dichotomy between teaching and learning (Frankenstein, 1991).

13 A significant example of coinvestigation in mathematics education is in Powell, Jeffries, & Selby (1990).

14 The U.S. government, for example, rarely collects health data broken down by social class. In 1986, they did this for heart and cerebrovascular disease, and found enormous gaps: "The death rate from heart disease, for example, was 2.3 times higher among unskilled blue-collar operators than among managers and professionals. By contrast, the mortality rate from heart disease in 1986 for blacks was 1.3 times higher than for whites." Navarro (1991) goes on to remark that "the way in which statistics are kept does not help to make white and black workers aware of the commonality of their predicament" (p. 436).

15 The traditional text I use is Bittinger and Rudolph (1984).

16 I want to make clear that I do not lecture this at the students. In this case, they first discuss this question in groups and report back to the entire class. Usually someone asks me what happened in the real situation. I present the findings and analysis of Lave (1988), which leads to further class discussion centered around the questions in the description just given. For example, I do not merely tell the students why I use Lave's example; I ask them why they think I started the class with that example.

17 Throughout this chapter, I will not detail the more obvious mathematical learning that the curriculum contains. In this case, for example, students review that

when analyzing a percentage, one needs to ask "95% of what?" and to realize that weight is a different measure than calories. We also review formulas by looking at the one that relates grams of fat to percentage of calories from fat: percent of calories from fat = (9 x grams of fat in one serving) ÷ (total calories in one serving) because 1 gram of fat = 9 calories.

18 As of 1990, the average sentence for S & L criminals was 1.9 years; the average sentence for bank robbers was 9.4 years. Of the $2.5 million ordered in restitution by Texas courts that year, only $50 has been paid (Sherill, 1990, p. 618).

19 One of the actions they are taking is to supply paper bags printed with "I won't be left holding the bag" to all who support their plan for mailing to congresspeople. They can be contacted at 739 8th Street SE, Washington, DC 20003, (202) 547-9292, or at 329 Rensselaer Avenue, Charlotte, NC 28203, (704) 372-7073.

20 Of course, we also review all the formulas, tables, and charts related to the traditional mathematical aspects of the curriculum.

21 The counterfable does not, but should – to be accurate – make the hen a man, and white.

22 We do a bit of this. We discuss the misleading arguments in a Tiffany ad about how investments by the rich support about 100 people in part and full-time jobs. Recently, a student brought in an article that argues it makes no sense to "soak the rich" because even if they were taxed at 100%, the government could run for only about 25 days on that revenue (Cuniff, 1989). We discuss the fallacies of these arguments.

23 Marcuse (1964) argues that without an overarching theory, which the individual events illuminate or challenge, the organizing structures of society will be clouded, and the sense that people control those structures disappears. "The trouble is that the statistics, measurements, and field studies of empirical sociology and political science are not rational enough. They become mystifying to the extent to which they are isolated from the truly concrete context which makes the facts and determines their functions. This context is larger and older than that of the plants and shops investigated, of the towns and cities studied, of the areas and groups whose public opinion is polled or whose chance of survival is calculated. . . . This real context in which the particular subjects obtain their real significance is definable only within a *theory* of society" (p. 190).

24 The media often reinforce this view. For example, Schaap (1991) quotes an op-ed article in the *Wall Street Journal*, which supports a view of inevitability in the economic inequalities in our society: "During periods of economic expansion, those who are in the top one-third of the income distribution will *always* benefit disproportionately, as compared with those below." For another example, an anonymous voter in the Boston area said he's voting for Bush "because in the day and age we live, we need a president who is going to choose life over death. The economy is the economy. No one is going to have the answer to that" (One voter speaks, 1992). An alternative view – that laws and policies of the government "aggressively . . . distribute income upward" (p. 15) – is not even hinted at.

References

Anyon, J. (1979). Ideology and United States history textbooks. *Harvard Educational Review, 49*(3), 361–386.

(1980). Social class and the hidden curriculum of work. *Journal of Education, 162*(1), 67–92.

Belle, D. (Ed.). (1982). *Lives in stress: Women and depression.* Beverly Hills, CA: Sage.

Bittinger, M. L., & Rudolph, W. B. (1984). *Business mathematics.* Reading, MA: Addison-Wesley.

Bob, M. L. (1990). Artful dealing. *Monthly Review, 41*(10), 33–37.

Boggs, J. (1970). *Racism and the class struggle: Further pages from a black worker's notebook.* New York: Monthly Review Press.

Borba, M. C. (1991, January). *Intrinsic political aspects of mathematics in education.* Paper presented at the Joint Mathematical Association of American Mathematical Society Meetings.

Bowles, S., & Gintis, H. (1976). *Schooling in capitalist America.* New York: Basic.

Braverman, H. (1974). Labor and monopoly capital. *Monthly Review, 26*(3), 1–134.

Brom, T. (1982, February 10–16). IRAs, the unfairest pension plan of all. *In These Times,* 7, 9.

Cockburn, A. (1989, April 17). Scenes from the inferno. *Nation,* 510–511.

Comparing social paychecks. (1989, October). *Dollars & Sense,* 23.

Cuniff, J. (1989, September 22). *Why not just soak the rich?* Associated Press release.

DeMott, B. (1991, January 20). In Hollywood, class doesn't put up much of a struggle. *New York Times,* section 2, 1.

Domini, A. L., & Kinder, P. D. (1985, July/August). Your money or your ethics. *Environmental Action,* 16–20.

Financial Democracy Campaign. (1990). *Fact sheet: What your bailout dollars are paying for.*

Fitch, R. (1990, October 29). Money's there – 5 ways to get it. *Nation,* 480–482.

Food porn. (1990, December). *Nutrition Action,* 16.

Frank, D. (1992, February 17). A couple of white chicks. *Nation,* 209–211.

Frankenstein, M. (1984). Overcoming math anxiety by learning about learning. *Mathematics and Computer Education, 18*(3), 169–180.

(1987). Critical mathematics education: An application of Paulo Freire's epistemology. In I. Shor (Ed.), *Freire for the classroom* (pp. 180–210). Portsmouth, NH: Boynton/Cook.

(1989). *Relearning mathematics: A different third R – Radical maths.* London: Free Association.

(1991). *Breaking down the dichotomy between learning and teaching mathematics.* Unpublished manuscript.

Freire, P. (1970). *Pedagogy of the oppressed.* New York: Seabury.

Freire, P., & Macedo, D. (1987). *Literacy: Reading the word and the world.* South Hadley, MA: Bergin & Garvey.

Frisby, M. K. (1991, September 13). Rich got richer, poor poorer, another study on taxes finds. *Boston Globe,* 79.

Gill, D. (1988). Politics of percent. In D. Pimm (Ed.), *Mathematics teaching and children* (pp. 122–125). Milton Keynes, England: Open University.

Greater Roxbury Neighborhood Authority. (1989, September/October). Redlining bleeds local economy. *Labor Page,* (40), 1, 6–7.

Herman, E. (1991, September). Wage earners "big winners." *Lies of Our Times,* 18.

Hogan, D. (1982). Education and class formation: The peculiarities of the Americans. In M. Apple (Ed.), *Cultural and economic reproduction in education: Essays on class, ideology and the state* (pp. 32–78). London: Routledge & Kegan Paul.

How to write off major disasters. (1991, September 2–8). *In These Times.*

Hymer, S. (1978). The multinational corporate capitalist economy. In R. C. Edwards, M. Reich, & T. E. Weisskopf (Eds.), *The capitalist system* (pp. 492–499). Englewood Cliffs, NJ: Prentice-Hall.

Invest in America: No Comment section. (1986). *Progressive, 50*(6), 13.

Jackson, D. Z. (1991, June 16). Young, hungry, and poor. *Boston Globe,* A-33.

Knoll, I. (1990). Same old gang. *Progressive, 54*(9), 4.

Kozol, J. (1991). *Savage inequalities: Children in America's schools.* New York: Crown.

Lave, J. (1988). *Cognition in practice.* New York: Cambridge University Press.

Lives of the rich and famous: No Comment section. (1989). *Progressive, 53*(10), 11.

MacLeod, J. (1987). *Ain't no makin' it: Leveled aspirations in a low-income neighborhood.* Boulder, CO: Westview.

Marcuse, H. (1964). *One-dimensional man.* Boston: Beacon.

Maxwell, J. (1988). Hidden messages. In D. Pimm (Ed.), *Mathematics teaching and children* (pp. 118–121). Milton Keynes, England: Open University.

McAlister, M. (1990, October). The movement for progressive funding alternatives. *Z,* 63–69.

McClain, J. D. (1992, October 30). Study shows rich got richer in the 1980s – Much richer. *Boston Globe,* 67.

McIntyre, R. (1991, September 23). Massachusetts tax structure favors the wealthy. *Boston Globe:* Letter to the editor, 10.

Mohl, B. (1989, October 25). Tax activists say two firms failed to pay fair share. *Boston Globe,* 75.

Mortgage lending in black and white. (1990, April). *Dollars & Sense,* 23.

National Council of Teachers of Mathematics. (1989). *Curriculum and evaluation standards for school mathematics.* Reston, VA: Author.

National Research Council. (1989). *Everybody counts.* Washington, DC: Author.

Navarro, V. (1991, April 8). The class gap. *Nation,* 436–437.

Noble, D. (1984, spring). The underside of computer literacy. *Ravitan,* 37–64.

Note on p. 9. (1987). *Progressive, 51*(6).

One voter speaks. (1992, October 5). *Boston Globe.*

Powell, A. B., Jeffries, D. A., & Selby, A. E. (1990). An empowering participatory research model for humanistic mathematics pedagogy. *Humanistic Mathematics Network Journal, 4,* 29–38.

Powell, A. B., & Lopez, J. A. (1989). Writing as a vehicle to learn mathematics: A case study. In P. Connolly, & T. Vilardi (Eds.), *The role of writing in learning mathematics and science* (pp. 157–177). New York: Teachers College.

Reagan condemns public housing. (1983, April). *Dollars & Sense,* 12–14.

Redlining a black bank. (1991, January 7/14). *Nation,* editorial, 1.

Reich, M. (1978). The economics of racism. In R. C. Edwards, M. Reich, & T. E. Weisskopf (Eds.), *The capitalist system* (pp. 381–388). Englewood Cliffs, NJ: Prentice-Hall.

Riddell, T., Shakelford, J., & Stamos, S. (1982). *Economics: A tool for understanding society.* Reading, MA: Addison-Wesley.

Schaap, W. H. (1991, October). Eternal verities. *Lies of our times,* 15.

Secada, W. (1992). Race, ethnicity, social class, language, and achievement in mathematics. In D. A. Grouws (Ed.), *Handbook of research on mathematics teaching and learning* (pp. 623–660). New York: Macmillan.

Selective prosperity. (1991, August 30). *Boston Globe.*

Sennet, R., & Cobb, P. (1972). *The hidden injuries of class.* New York: Vintage.

Sherill, R. (1990, November 19). The looting decade: S&L's, big banks, and other triumphs of capitalism. *Nation,* 589–624.

Somers, K. B. (1989, October). When less means more. *Mathematics Teacher,* 556–558.

Stagnation and the nation (sidebar). (1987). *Progressive, 51*(6), 9.

Strom, A. (1990, April 25–May 1). Socially irresponsible. *In These Times,* Letter to the editor, 15.

Tilly, C. (1990). The politics of the "new inequality." *Socialist Review, 20*(1), 103–120.

To George Bush, politics is taking care of friends. (1990, October 17–23). *In These Times,* editorial, 14.

Weis, L. (1990). *Working class without work; high school students in a de-industrializing society.* New York: Routledge.

Welfare's worth: Does it act more as a trap than a safety net? (1988, April). *Scientific American,* 30–32.

What's good for GM . . . (1992, November 6). *Boston Globe,* editorial, 14.

Zinn, H. (1980). *A people's history of the United States.* New York: Harper.

Zuckoff, M. (1991, October 27). Federal study suggests broader loan bias. *Boston Globe,* 1.

7 Economics, equity, and the national mathematics assessment: Are we creating a national toll road?

William Tate

> Comparing them by their faculties of memory, reason, and imagination, it appears to me, that in memory they [blacks] are equal to the whites; in reason, much inferior, as I think one could scarcely be found capable of tracing and comprehending the investigations of Euclid; and that in imagination, they are dull, tasteless, and anomalous. It would be unfair to follow them to Africa for this investigation. We will consider them here, on the same stage with the whites, and where the facts are not apocryphal on which a judgment is to be formed.
>
> Thomas Jefferson (1954, p. 139)

> We have started down a promising path. We have entered into a . . . Jeffersonian compact to enlighten our children and the children of generations to come.
>
> (*America 2000*, United States Department of Education, 1991, p. 80)

> Although the past may not repeat itself, it does rhyme.
>
> Mark Twain

Educational policy brings together the resources of government – money, rules, and authority – to achieve political objectives (McDonnell & Elmore, 1987). The way a policymaker frames a problem, in some respects, dictates how the resources of government are to be used. However, very few policymakers have the autonomy to choose a policy without constraints that limit their options. McDonnell and Elmore (1987) stated:

> The selection of a policy instrument depends on the constraints a policymaker faces and the resources available either to diminish the force of those constraints or to enhance the effectiveness of a given instrument. In simplest terms, identifying resources and constraints is how policymakers assess what is feasible, given how they define a policy problem. (p. 146)

Politicians and educational policymakers not only define policy problems, but they must "sell" potential solutions to the public. This often requires the politician to associate a potential solution with a slogan, that is, a symbol or metaphor that is widely accepted by a constituent group (Apple, 1992; Appleby, 1992). Indeed, choosing an acceptable slogan can be as

191

important as the policy formulation and its implementation. This is especially true given that many people associate more with a slogan than with the merit and potential impact of a policy.

In *America 2000* (United States Department of Education, 1991), the federal government under then-president Bush proposed a series of educational policy reforms and goals. In the introduction to *America 2000,* the Bush administration described its commitment to the achievement of the stated education goals as part of a new "Jeffersonian compact." Thus, the Bush administration formulated a set of policy recommendations and framed them by its appeal to a powerful symbol of American democracy – the man who crafted the Declaration of Independence, Thomas Jefferson. *America 2000* proposed a voluntary national assessment in mathematics as one of its recommendations for revamping the U.S. educational system. That recommendation will be the focus of my discussion.

Scholarship in mathematics education has made little effort to explore and critique public policy in the field (Apple, 1992; Davis, 1992). There are few published works focused on mathematics education policy that analyze the interrelationships among the policy problems being addressed, the basic design features of a policy, and the potential equity problems that a policy may help to resolve or exacerbate. The purpose of this chapter is to provide such an analysis of the voluntary national mathematics assessment proposed in *America 2000*. More specifically, I will examine the policy in terms of its potential impact on African American students in urban centers of the United States.

National mathematics standards and assessment

Many mathematics educators associate national assessment with the National Assessment of Educational Progress (NAEP) or with a widely administered standardized testing program (e.g., California Achievement Test [CAT] or Iowa Test of Basic Skills [ITBS]). Norm-referenced standardized tests are an annual ritual in most schools in the United States. These tests are designed to rank students on the basis of narrowly defined mental abilities. The scores are used in program selection and placement decisions. Berlak (1992) argued that the only major difference between the NAEP and standardized tests is that standardized tests are normed. NAEP is a criterion-referenced test on the basis of which a panel of experts judge what percentage of responses constitutes minimal competence. Both types of tests have a major impact on the lives of students – both in school and after completing K–12 education. However, neither type of test is *directly* linked to postsecondary-school employment opportunities. In contrast to standardized tests and the NAEP, the voluntary national mathematics assessment proposed in *America 2000* is intended to have a direct impact on students' postsecondary employment. Also, the voluntary national assessment has a history that is somewhat different from that of the NAEP.

Adam Smith

The idea of a national assessment in mathematics similar to that found in *America 2000* can be traced to the economic writings of Adam Smith (1937):

The public can impose upon almost the whole body of the people the necessity of acquiring those most essential parts of education [e.g., mathematics], by obliging every man to undergo an examination or probation in them before he can obtain the freedom in any corporation or be allowed to set up any trade either in a village or town corporate. (p. 738)

Smith also argued that the government should support the development of standards in mathematics education:

But though the common people cannot, in any civilized society, be so well instructed as people of some rank and fortune, the most essential parts of education, however, to read, write, and account, can be acquired at so early a period of life, that the greater part even of those who are bred to the lowest occupations, have time to acquire them before they can be employed in those occupations. (p. 737)

Adam Smith called for the United States to establish academic standards and a national examination to gauge whether the citizenry was meeting them. However, his standards and examinations were for the purpose of sorting people in terms of their later-life employment and economic opportunities.

The current context

Similarly, today the mathematics education community in the United States has called for new academic standards. The *Curriculum and Evaluation Standards for School Mathematics* (National Council of Teachers of Mathematics, 1989) propose a new set of standards to be established in mathematics education. As an "isolated" policy instrument, however, these standards lack the incentive and accountability mechanisms required for systemic change (O'Day & Smith, 1993). How should students, schools, school systems, and states be held accountable for achieving the new mathematics standards? O'Day and Smith (1993) provide some insight into recent thinking on this question:

The approach most often suggested in current policy proposals is a performance-based accountability model with clearly defined outcome standards for schools. The standards would be based on average levels of student performance and would specify a satisfactory gain over time or an absolute level of achievement. There are two conceptions of how performance-based accountability would work. One would operate on the fuel of good intentions and self-correction, assuming that schools and school systems will respond quickly and productively when they receive evidence of problems from outcome assessments. (p. 270)

The first performance-based accountability model is designed to provide corrective feedback to schools and school systems. The purpose of this model is to serve as a diagnostic tool. The second model of performance-based accountability is more consistent with the voluntary national assessment proposed in *America 2000*. O'Day and Smith (1993) describe the second model of performance-based assessment:

An alternative performance-based model would hold students and schools, and presumably school systems and even states, accountable for their respective performances. If they failed to meet a preestablished performance standard, some corrective action would be required. Conversely, if they met or surpassed their goals, they would receive a reward. Unlike the first model, this strategy would provide stimulating mechanisms for both continued improvement and corrective action, possibly including penalties. Judiciously used, it might be an important stimulus for equity, though it also would close the barn door too late. (p. 271)

The *New Standards Project* (Learning Research and Development Center [LRDC] and National Center for Education and the Economy [NCEE], 1992) combines both models in its attempt to develop "an examination system in which effort clearly pays off. Students passing a final examination in high school and completing all their *merit badges* [my emphasis] will receive a certificate that will signify true accomplishment, and not just time in the seat" (Learning Research and Development Center & National Center for Education and the Economy, 1992, p. 2). Within the same document, the authors argue that "students, for the first time, would not bear the whole burden of meeting the standard, because the professionals would be held accountable for student progress" (p. 5).

Yet, what do O'Day and Smith (1993) mean by "it would close the barn door too late"? What problem could lead to the policy choice of a voluntary national assessment in mathematics and for which the barn door may be closing too late? What problems are the analysts concerned about when they note that that assessment model may in fact indicate we are closing the barn door too late?

The problem

Any policy problem has both analytical and normative components (McDonnell & Elmore, 1987). For example, research and indicator systems (National Science Board, 1991) are analytic tools that help to frame the nature of a problem and its probable causes since they tell us how the educational system is functioning. However, those indicators acquire meaning based on normative assumptions about how the educational system *should* function (McDonnell & Elmore, 1987). Likewise, the policy problem in mathematics education for African American students in urban schools has analytic and normative components.

Analytic component. In theory, the voluntary national assessment was recommended as a mean of improving the mathematics performance of African American students (United States Department of Education, 1991). Recent NAEP mathematics assessments indicate that African American children are less likely to take college preparatory mathematics courses than white children (Dossey, Mullis, Lindquist, & Chambers, 1988). Further, African American children as a group are consistently outperformed by white children on national assessments of mathematics achievement (Anick, Carpenter, & Smith, 1981; Dossey et al., 1988; Johnson, 1984). This relationship between exposure to higher-level courses and mathematics achievement should not be shocking. In fact, one of the most powerful predictors of mathematics achievement is course taking (Dossey et al., 1988; Welch, Anderson, & Harris, 1982). For example, the National Assessment of Education Progress reveals the substantial increase in mathematical performance that is associated with students completing higher-level mathematics courses.

Lack of opportunity to engage in higher-level school mathematics is one of many obstacles facing the African American student. The African American student in a disadvantaged urban community is more likely to attend a school that is staffed with less-qualified mathematics teachers and that has fewer resources than a student attending a school serving a middle-class community (Irvine, 1990; National Science Board, 1991; Oakes, 1990).[1]

Recent reform documents (National Council of Teachers of Mathematics, 1989, 1991) call for a radically different vision of mathematics education and, subsequently, of mathematics assessment (Berlak, 1992; Romberg, 1992). This vision will require urban schools to reallocate current funds and/or seek additional funding to incorporate a new assessment policy; to improve teachers' mathematics qualifications; possibly to decrease class sizes; to update instructional materials (such as textbooks, science laboratories, and computer capabilities); and to enhance the quality of many other resource inputs. Each of these inputs will require a funding source. This implies that preparing students for tests instituted under a new policy (i.e., national assessment) has important connections to issues of fiscal equity for urban schools.

Fiscal equity for urban schools is one of the United States's most critical dilemmas. The Council of Great City Schools (1992) indicates that 76.1% of large urban centers are financially independent; that is, they have their own taxing authority. All of these school systems use property taxes as the main source of locally generated revenue; 46.2% use tuition or fees (in states where it is legal), 34.6% use sales taxes; 11.5% use personal income tax; 7.7% use auto taxes, and 3.8% use some form of value-added tax (Council of Great City Schools, 1992). None of the urban districts used a corporate income tax or commuter tax to generate revenue for the schools.

When the needs and conditions of urban schools are taken into consideration, along with the capacity of these systems to generate revenue, a clearer picture develops of the lack of fiscal support provided urban school districts (see, generally, Kozol, 1991). For example, urban schools spend more on health care and nutrition than their suburban counterparts. The average per-pupil expenditure in large urban school districts was $5,200 in 1990–1991 compared to $6,073 in suburban public school systems (Council of Great City Schools, 1992). Hence, though urban schools allocated the same percentage of their budget (62%) to classroom instruction as did suburban schools, they spent about $506 less per child (1992).

Current methods of generating funding in urban public schools – largely a combination of local property taxes and state revenue – are not adequately serving the needs of African American children (Strickland & Ascher, 1992). The additional resources required by a policy decision to participate in the national mathematics assessment will increase the burden on the already fiscally stressed systems of urban education. Thus, mathematics assessment, local property assessment (i.e., property taxes), and state funding become linked in the struggle to achieve social and educational equity.

Normative component. The normative component in a policy problem consists of the policymakers' convictions regarding how the system ought to work (McDonnell & Elmore, 1987). This includes those values typically associated with the education policymaker's ideology or political philosophy. McDonnell and Elmore (1987) stated:

Regardless of what indicator data may suggest about a particular policy problem, policymakers prefer policy instruments consistent with their own values. So, for example, we would argue that those believing in a strong governmental role are likely to look to mandates; those who believe in the preeminence of market mechanisms are likely to prefer inducements or system-changing instruments. (p. 145)

The slogan associated with America 2000 – "the Jeffersonian compact" – provides some insight into the normative component of the policy problem (United States Department of Education, 1991). It is quite possible that the Bush administration's policymakers used this slogan both to win support for the policy proposal and to disclose their viewpoint on how the education system ought to work. Brick (1993) provides some insight into the educational ideology associated with a Jeffersonian approach to education:

In Jefferson's scheme, schools functioned to compensate for lack of opportunity, not for lack of readiness. The individual student was responsible for proving what he could do based on what Jefferson termed his "innate ability." Because of his belief in natural law and natural endowments, he did not believe education would equalize society. (p. 3)

Peters (1982) suggests that Jefferson's beliefs about African Americans took on moral overtones. Humanity and the attributes associated with humanity, such as intellectual ability (to Jefferson) were white, and any deviation from this premise was either not true or not plausible. Peters further argues that the Jeffersonian view of African Americans helped lay the groundwork for segregation in America. For example, in his *Notes on the State of Virginia* (1954), Jefferson expanded on these themes:

Why not retain and incorporate the blacks into the state, and thus save the expense of supplying, by importation of white settlers, the vacancies they will leave? Deep-rooted prejudices entertained by the whites; ten thousand recollections, by the blacks, of the injuries they have sustained; new provocations; the real distinctions which nature has made . . . will divide us into parties, and produce convulsions which will probably never end but in the extermination of the one or the other race. To these objections, which are political, may be added others, which are physical and moral. . . . their existence appears to participate more of sensation than reflection. To this must be ascribed their disposition to sleep when abstracted from their diversions, and unemployed in labor. An animal whose body is at rest, and who does not reflect, must be disposed to sleep of course. (Jefferson, 1954, pp. 138–139)

Jefferson's comments typify a policy mind-set that resulted in the formation of a racial state (see, e.g., Bell, 1980, 1987, 1992; Crenshaw, 1988; Marable, 1983). According to Omi and Winant (1986), the United States was conceptualized on the basis of racial politics. Every state institution is a racial institution, but not every institution approaches racial politics in the same way. In fact, the various state institutions may work at cross-purposes. Thus, racial politics must be understood as representing a variety of positions within different state institutions and at different historical moments. The philosophical tenets of the Bush administration that influenced the normative component of this policy problem at the time the national mathematics assessment policy was being created illustrate this point.

Apple (1993) contends that the Reagan–Bush era can be described as a period of American history greatly influenced by a right-wing conservative coalition of neoliberals and neoconservatives. Neoliberals envision a society based on the "invisible hand" of the free market. This group seeks to free individuals of "unnecessary" mandates and laws (i.e., it advocates a weak state). In contrast, neoconservatives are guided by a vision of the strong state in certain areas – particularly with respect to gender and racial politics, social standards, values, and the knowledge that should be passed on to future generations.

The neoliberal and neoconservative philosophical positions represent an epistemological conflict. The impact of this conflict is the development of policy compromises that combine weak and strong state recommendations where the former concerns are market-driven and the latter are standards-driven. Apple (1993) describes the possible ramifications of education policy built on the neoliberal and neoconservative compromise:

There will be a relatively less regulated and increasingly privatized sector for the children of the better off. For the rest – and the economic status and racial composition in, say, our urban areas of the people who attend these minimum schools will be thoroughly predictable – the schools will be tightly controlled and policed and will continue to be underfunded and unlinked to decent paid employment. (p. 11)

The voluntary national mathematics assessment policy proposed in *America 2000* represents a similar policy compromise between the neoliberal and the neoconservative factions. Apple's analysis suggests that the proposal of a voluntary national assessment requires closer scrutiny, especially with respect to the question, "Whose children will be benefited by this compact?"

National assessment as toll road

The use of a voluntary national assessment to "drive" the development of new assessment standards in mathematics flows directly from two objectives of the Bush administration's federal tax policy – tax neutrality and equity. Woo (1982) provides insight into the tax neutrality objective within the Reagan–Bush economic model:

The driving force behind supply-side economics is the ideal that the tax code ought not to influence economic decision making. The desirable tax system keeps the distortions of economic decisions to a minimum, and thereby improves the prospect for economic efficiency and growth. . . . The most important criterion is tax neutrality. A neutral tax system would result in economic decisions that are made without reference to that system. (p. 148)

This notion of neutrality is at odds with classical ideas of taxation, wherein tax policy is purposefully crafted to effect certain social and economic benefits. For instance, people receive tax deductions for interest on home-ownership loans because the government encourages the buying of homes; industries seek and receive tax breaks as an inducement to build in specific locales.

A second objective of the Reagan–Bush tax system was to give the appearance of being fair and equitable, one tenet for fairness being that those who benefited from a service should pay for it. Wonnacott and Wonnacott (1982) dubbed this the benefit principle:

This principle recognizes that the purpose of taxation is to pay for government services. Therefore, let those who gain the most from government services pay the most. If this principle is adopted, then a question arises: Why not simply set prices for government services which people can *voluntarily* [emphasis added] pay if they want services? In other words, why not charge a price for a government service, just as General Motors charges for cars? This approach may work, for example, for a toll road from which drivers can be excluded if they do not pay. (p. 86)

Again, the notion that people should pay for government services is at odds with classical ideas about the purposes of government and taxation. According to these ideas, a primary purpose of government is to promote the common good. Those who have more should pay more as their fair share.

The voluntary national mathematics assessment is a direct product of the dual objectives of federal tax neutrality and equity (in the form of the benefit principle). It facilitates the shifting of funding responsibility from federal to local education agencies. The federal government does not have to assume fiscal responsibility for helping local school districts meet the new mathematics standards created by a policy instrument such as a voluntary assessment (Verstegen, 1990). This translates into limited, if any, new federal taxes to support this particular initiative. Hence, the voluntary mathematics assessment can then be construed as tax neutral with respect to federal taxes. The funding responsibility, however, has been shifted to local and state entities. This shift occurs during a period when state revenues targeted for urban schools are declining and local property tax is a less viable method of urban school finance (Council of Great City Schools, 1992).

Recall that taxes must give the appearance of being fair. This is where the benefit principle – that is, those who benefit should pay – comes into play. That is, those local school districts that want to implement the voluntary national mathematics assessment and who would benefit from the new mathematical standards associated with it should pay the implementation costs. Like the toll road, those who cannot pay are excluded from receiving the service; in this case, they are excluded from receiving the benefits of new mathematics teaching standards that would be reflected in the voluntary national assessment. According to the benefit principle, moreover, the voluntary national mathematics assessment would be equitable.

Unfortunately, this policy will create further educational inequities for African American students, who are overrepresented in school districts with inadequate local tax bases. Many urban districts, hampered by fiscal constraints, are unable to build the capacity required to meet the new mathematics standards, for example, by improving teachers' mathematics qualifications, decreasing class sizes, and introducing appropriate instructional materials, including technological capabilities.

Suburban control

The voluntary national assessment policy will also create an opportunity for affluent school districts to control the mathematics reform movement.

Those school systems that can afford to implement the voluntary policy will control how mathematics gets defined and taught within the reform movement. Apple (1992) warns of this danger:

Without giving much further thought to the realities of differential power, the economic crisis, and the social construction both of what counts as mathematical literacy and of the problems it should focus on, it will be all too easy for leadership to be exerted by the most conservative elements in the ideological coalition that is organized under the *Standards'* umbrella. Its lasting impact may be to give support to the formation of a national curriculum, guided by a national test and largely organized around rightist idelogical [*sic*] and educational policies. (p. 428)

Assessment is the glue that holds together the various components of the learning process (Graue & Smith, in press). Assessment is also a part of the neoliberal and neoconservative compromise that will ensure that the more affluent, conservative groups within the society will maintain control of school knowledge. As a by-product of this control, African American students will continue to receive the following:

What is considered right for children at DuSable [Chicago Public School] and their counterparts in other inner-city schools becomes self-evident to anyone who sees the course of study in such schools. Many urban high school students do not study math, but "business math" – essentially a very elemental level of bookkeeping. Job-specific courses such as "cosmetology" (hairdressing, manicures), which would be viewed as insults by suburban parents, are a common item in the segregated high schools and are seen as a realistic preparation for the adult roles that 16-year-old black girls expect to fill. (Kozol, 1991, p. 76)

Advocates of the voluntary national assessment suggest that inequities like those described by Kozol can be eliminated by setting standards with the national assessment policy (see, for example, Ravitch, 1991). This argument positions the voluntary national policy within the debate involving forms of equality articulated by Crenshaw in 1988.

Restrictive access

Crenshaw (1988) argues there are two distinct rhetorical visions of equality – expansive and restrictive. The expansive view stresses equality as a result. This interpretation of equality seeks to eliminate conditions of African American subordination and utilizes the power of the system to eradicate racial inequalities. The second interpretation is a restrictive view that may coexist with the expansive view. The restrictive interpretation defines equality as a process and minimizes the results of the system's actions. The Jeffersonian view of equality is restrictive: Its goal is *not* to eliminate racial inequalities. Likewise, the voluntary national mathematics assessment, which is heralded as part of a new Jeffersonian compact, is also restrictive since it is focused on a process (the institution of new standards and assessment) without concern for the real danger that inequalities will be exacerbated. The national assessment policy is built on the assumption that the process of defining and obtaining consensus on a set of testing standards (i.e., educational outcomes) in mathematics is the appropriate approach to achieving equity. For example, Ravitch (1991) stated:

As a democracy, our challenge is to provide equity and excellence in education: Not only education for all, but also high-quality education for every child. . . . We do not need a national curriculum to stimulate high achievement. What we do need is clear consensus – standards – in the different subject fields about what all children should know and be able to do. Standards *define* [emphasis added] outcomes: For example, children of certain ages should understand the historical causes of major events, should be able to use mathematics to solve problems, and should understand basic scientific concepts. The states themselves must decide the curriculum and policies that will produce those outcomes. (p. 2)

Ravitch has defined equity in terms of the creation of mathematical standards. Her argument implies that no school mathematics standards exist when, in fact, at least two sets of school mathematics standards already exist in the United States – college preparatory and remedial. Educational systems have created few opportunities for inner-city African American children in college preparatory mathematics coursework (Cohen, 1982; Kamens & Benavot, 1991; Oakes, 1990; Useem, 1992). African American students are twice as likely as white children to be placed in courses designed for the remedial standard (National Science Board, 1991). This reality appears to confirm the inability of school systems to provide African American students a mathematics education principled on the "college preparatory standard."

How will changing the mathematics standard via a voluntary national assessment policy alter the philosophical, instructional, and/or financial capacity of urban school systems to educate African American students? It will not. This is a limitation of policies based on the restrictive, Jeffersonian vision of equality. The voluntary national mathematics assessment policy articulated in *America 2000* (United States Department of Education, 1991) lacks a capacity-building component. It is not a mechanism that will promote the advancement of new mathematics standards for all students.

The need for capacity building

To change the current conditions of mathematics education for African American students in urban schools will require policy decisions that build long-term capacity. The philosophical basis of the Jeffersonian concept of equality coupled with its failure to provide for capacity building limit the voluntary national assessment from an equity perspective. Changing capacity is very different from providing a school system with inducements in the form of a temporary influx of additional money and then waiting for African American mathematics achievement to increase. The use of inducements suggests that the institutional capacity exists to create an equitable mathematics education for African American students, or that such an education can be created with monetary incentives. However, although capacity-building involves the transfer of money to an institution, its function is to support the development of future benefits – material, intellectual, or human resources (McDonnell & Elmore, 1987).

The selection of capacity-building policy instruments in support of the reform of urban mathematics education will require two policy initiatives. First, policymakers must decide that an equitable mathematics education for African American students is desirable in its own right (Secada, 1989). Second, policymakers must determine that a particular urban school system requires a restructuring and/or increase of resources to achieve the goal of an equitable mathematics education for African American students.

McDonnell and Elmore (1987) pointed out that policymakers often confuse short-term inducements with long-term capacity building:

A federal program to produce greater competence in mathematics and science, as a response to competition from abroad, can only produce limited results in the short-term because it is calling on the limited capacity of elementary and secondary schools to teach mathematics and science. By the time investments in capacity reach maturity, in the form of more highly qualified, better trained teachers, policymakers may or may not still be worried about the nation's competitive edge. The only way to assure a short-term response, in other words, is to call upon existing capacity. (p. 143)

While space limitations make it impossible to delineate all of the possible capacity-building options available to policymakers, it is important to discuss first steps for the teachers, administrators, and mathematics educators who would be involved in this activity in urban school districts. These first steps are based on the assumption that all students should be provided a high-quality mathematics education and that many of our urban school systems require additional resources and commitment to achieve this goal.

If the recently developed mathematics *Standards* (National Council of Teachers of Mathematics, 1989, 1991, in draft) are to be taken seriously, states and urban school districts will need to develop finance systems that enable them to meet the mathematics performance goals (Odden, 1992). The implementation of new mathematics standards will involve teaching college-bound students on the basis of principles very different from those that inform current college preparatory standards. Thus, urban school districts and specific schools within these districts that are not performing well in terms of prevailing mathematics standards will require greater effort and more resources than will districts and schools currently meeting the college-preparation levels of performance.

The development of new school finance formulas will be technically complex. This process will require mathematics educators with program expertise who can identify strategies that work in producing high levels of mathematics understanding by African American students (see Chapters 1, 3, and 4 in this volume. Also see Anderson, 1990; D'Ambrosio, 1985; Frankenstein, 1990; and Tate, in press) and financial analysts to develop strategies that will support the new programs. Mathematics educators need to think seriously about the financial structures that will be needed to implement the *Standards* (National Council of Teachers of Mathematics, 1989, 1991, in draft) equitably. Failure to do so will only result in policy proposals like that of the voluntary national mathematics assessment, which avoid the fiscal-equity issues inherent in school mathematics reform.

Concluding remarks

The citizenry of the United States shares a common historical and cultural heritage in which race and racism have played a central role (Lawrence, 1987). The mathematics education community is embedded within this social, cultural, and economic matrix. We must recognize that policies exist to distribute and allocate goods and services. Given the combination of demand for mathematics education and scarcity of resources to meet this demand, no mathematics education policy – including the voluntary national assessment – is neutral in its distribution process.

I have attempted to outline the problematic nature of the neoliberal and neoconservative compromise of the new Jeffersonian compact. More specifically, I contend that the voluntary national mathematics assessment as presented in *America 2000* will serve as a national toll road for the African American child in inner-city schools. The design and philosophy of this policy suggest that fiscal considerations will determine which students will be empowered mathematically. Thus, the debate about funding to urban schools must move to the foreground of discussion in mathematics education. Failure to do so can only result in the maintenance and/or further deterioration of our urban school systems' mathematics education programs. As a community, mathematics education must move beyond the Jeffersonian compact.

Ironically, Thomas Jefferson (1954) provided an appropriate ending for this analysis and a new beginning for researchers and policymakers in mathematics education.

History by apprising them of the past will enable them to judge of the future; it will avail them of the experiences of other times and other nations; it will qualify them as judges of the actions and designs of men; it will enable them to know ambition under every disguise it may assume; and knowing it, to defeat its views. In every government on earth is some trace of human weakness, some germ of corruption and degeneracy, which cunning will discover. (p. 148)

I challenge the mathematics education community to move the issue of fiscal equity to the forefront as the nation implements the new mandates of mathematics education reform. History awaits us.

Acknowledgment

I would like to thank Michael Apple, Carl Grant, Gloria Ladson-Billings, Walter Secada, Richard Kitchen, and Kimberly Tate for their comments on various versions of this chapter.

Note

1 The National Center for Education Statistics (1984) defined disadvantaged urban communities as "cities having a population greater than 200,000 where a high proportion of residents are on welfare or are not regularly employed" (p. 54).

References

Anderson, S. E. (1990). Worldmath curriculum: Fighting Eurocentrism in mathematics. *Journal of Negro Education, 59*(3), 348–359.

Anick, C. M., Carpenter, T. P., & Smith, C. (1981). Minorities and mathematics: Results from the National Assessment of Educational Progress. *Mathematics Teacher, 74*, 560–566.

Apple, M. W. (1992). Do the *Standards* go far enough? Power, policy, and practice in mathematics education. *Journal for Research in Mathematics Education, 23*, 412–431.

   (1993). The politics of official knowledge: Does a National Curriculum make sense? *Teachers College Record, 95*(2), 222–241.

Appleby, J. (1992). Rediscovering America's historic diversity: Beyond exceptionalism. *Journal of American History, 79*(2), 419–431.

Bell, D. A. (1980). Brown and the interest-convergence dilemma. In D. A. Bell (Ed.), *New perspectives on school desegregation* (pp. 90–107). New York: Teachers College Press.

   (1987). *And we are not saved: The elusive quest for racial justice.* New York: Basic.

   (1992). *Faces at the bottom of the well: The permanence of racism.* New York: Basic.

Berlak, H. (1992). The need for a new source of assessment. In H. Berlak (Ed.), *Toward a new science of educational testing and assessment* (pp. 1–22). Albany, NY: SUNY Press.

Brick, B. (1993). Changing concepts of equal educational opportunity: A comparison of the views of Thomas Jefferson, Horace Mann and John Dewey. *Thresholds in Education, 19*(2), 2–8.

Cohen, P. C. (1982). *A calculating people: The spread of numeracy in early America.* University of Chicago Press.

The Council of the Great City Schools (1992). *National urban education goals: Baseline indicators, 1990–91.* Washington DC: Author.

Crenshaw, K. W. (1988). Race, reform, and retrenchment: Transformation and legitimation in anti-discrimination law. *Harvard Law Review, 101*, 1331–1387.

D'Ambrosio, U. (1985). Ethnomathematics and its place in the history and pedagogy of mathematics. *For the Learning of Mathematics, 5*, 44–48.

Davis, R. B. (1992). Reflections on where mathematics education now stands and on where it may be going. In D. A. Grouws (Ed.), *Handbook of research on mathematics teaching and learning* (pp. 724–734). New York: Macmillan.

Dossey, J. A., Mullis, I. V. S., Lindquist, M. M., & Chambers, D. L. (1988). *The mathematics report card: Are we measuring up?* Princeton, NJ: Educational Testing Service.

Frankenstein, M. (1990). Incorporating race, gender, and class issues into a critical mathematical literacy curriculum, *Journal of Negro Education, 59,* 336–351.

Graue, M. E., & Smith, S. Z. (in press). A conceptual framework for instructional assessment. *Educational Assessment.*

Irvine, J. (1990). *Black students and school failure.* Westport, CT: Greenwood.

Jefferson, T. (1954). *Notes on the State of Virginia.* New York: Norton.

Johnson, M. (1984). Blacks in mathematics: A status report. *Journal for Research in Mathematics Education, 15,* 145–153.

Kamens, D. H., & Benavot, A. (1991). Elite knowledge for the masses: The origins and spread of mathematics and science education in national curricula. *American Journal of Education, 99*(2), 137–180.

Kozol, J. (1991). *Savage inequalities: Children in America's schools.* New York: Crown.

Lawrence, C. R. (1987). The id, the ego, and equal protection: Reckoning with unconscious racism. *Stanford Law Review, 39,* 317–388.

Learning Research and Development Center & National Center on Education and the Economy. (1992). *The new standards project: An overview.* Unpublished manuscript, University of Pittsburgh.

Marable, M. (1983). *How capitalism underdeveloped Black America.* Boston: South End.

McDonnell, L. M., & Elmore, R. F. (1987). Getting the job done: Alternative policy instruments. *Educational Evaluation and Policy Analysis. 9*(2), 133–152.

National Center for Education Statistics. (1984). *Condition of education.* Washington, DC: United States Government Printing Office.

National Council of Teachers of Mathematics. (1989). *Curriculum and evaluation standards for school mathematics.* Reston, VA: Author.

 (1991). *Professional standards for teaching mathematics.* Reston, VA: Author.

 (in draft). *Assessment standards for school mathematics* (Working Draft). Reston, VA: Author.

National Science Board (1991). *Science & engineering indicators* (NSB 91–1). Washington DC: United States Government Printing Office.

Oakes, J. (1990). Opportunities, achievement, and choice: Women and minority students in science and mathematics. *Review of Research in Education, 16,* 153–222.

O'Day, J. A., & Smith, M. S. (1993). Systemic reform and educational opportunity. In S. H. Fuhrman (Ed.), *Designing coherent education policy: Improving the system* (pp. 250–312). San Francisco: Jossey-Bass.

Odden, A. R. (1992). School finance and education reform: An overview. In A. R. Odden (Ed.), *Rethinking school finance: An agenda for the 1990s* (pp. 1–40). San Francisco: Jossey-Bass.

Omi, M., & Winant, H. (1986). *Racial formation in the United States.* New York: Routledge.

Peters, E. (1982). *Ethnic notions: Black images in the white mind.* Berkeley, CA: Exhibition catalog, Berkeley Art Center.

Ravitch, D. (1991, Winter). Message from the assistant secretary, Diane Ravitch. *Office of Educational Research and Improvement Bulletin,* p. 2.

Romberg, T. A. (1992). Assessing mathematics competence and achievement. In H. Berlak (Ed.), *Toward a new science of educational testing and assessment* (pp. 23–52). Albany, NY: SUNY Press.

Secada, W. G. (1989). Agenda setting, enlightened self-interest, and equity in mathematics education. *Peabody Journal of Education, 66,* 22–56.

Smith, A. (1937). *An inquiry into the nature and causes of the wealth of nations.* New York: Modern Library.

Strickland, D. S., & Ascher, C. (1992). Low income African-American children and public schooling. In P. W. Jackson (Ed.), *Handbook of research on curriculum* (pp. 609–625). New York: Macmillan.

Tate, W. F. (in press). From inner-city to ivory tower: Does my voice matter in the academy? *Urban Education.*

United States Department of Education. (1991). *America 2000: An education strategy.* Washington, DC: United States Government Printing Office.

Useem, E. C. (1992). Getting on the fast track in mathematics: School organizational influences on math track assignment. *American Journal of Education, 100*(3), 325–353.

Verstegen, D. A. (1990). Education fiscal policy in the Reagan administration. *Education Evaluation and Policy Analysis, 12,* 355–373.

Welch, W. W., Anderson, R. E., & Harris, L. J. (1982). The effects of schooling on mathematics achievement. *American Educational Research Journal, 19,* 145–153.

Wonnacott, P., & Wonnacott, R. (1982). *Economics* (revised ed.). New York: McGraw-Hill.

Woo, M. N. (1982). Taxation, savings, and labor supply: Theory and evidence of distortions. In D. A. Raboy (Ed.), *Essays in supply-side economics* (pp. 119–150). Washington, DC: Institute for Research on the Economics of Taxation.

Part II

8   Equity inside the mathematics classroom: Fact or artifact?

Gilah C. Leder

Much attention has been focused in recent decades on the status of women, and on the life and educational opportunities available to them. Equity in mathematics education, a subset of these issues, is addressed in this chapter. The extent that societal beliefs and traditions shape and influence educational practices and contribute to recorded and perceived gender differences is depicted in a number of ways – by drawing on historical data, by reviewing contemporary research paradigms and the broad findings they have harvested, and, finally, by examining in some depth the nature of teacher–student and between-student interactions in a contemporary mathematics classroom. Collectively, the data illustrate that gender differences in mathematics learning are often a reflection of prevailing circumstances rather than an indication of absolute and unchangeable differences between females and males.

The assertion that females deserve the same educational opportunities as males is not solely a modern phenomenon. In Book 5 of *The Republic,* Plato argued that individuals, both females and males, should be educated in the same way – to prepare them as effectively as possible for the occupation for which they were best suited:

"There is therefore no function in society which is peculiar to woman as woman or man as man; natural abilities are similarly distributed in each sex, and it is natural for women to share all occupations with men, though in all women will be the weaker partners."
"Agreed."
"Are we therefore to confine all occupations to men only?"
"How can we?"
"Obviously we can't; for we are agreed, I think, that one woman may have a natural ability for medicine or music, and another not."
"Yes."
"And one may be athletic, another not; one be good at soldiering, another not."
(Plato, 1955, p. 209)

Even though this plea for equal opportunity prompted McGrath (1976) to describe Plato as the first recorded feminist, the advice, it seems, went

209

largely unheeded. More than 2,000 years later, Defoe (1697) still called for a reassessment of society's attitudes to the education of women.

> I have often thought of it as one of the most barbarous customs in the world that we deny the advantages of learning to women. . . . If knowledge and understanding had been useless additions to the sex, God Almighty would never have given them capacity; for he made nothing needless. (Defoe, 1697, pp. 283–284)

Another three centuries have passed since then, and, undeniably, much has changed in the intervening years. Contemporary statistics (e.g., United States Bureau of the Census, 1990) indicate that in the United States, as well as in many other Western countries, a greater number of females than males continue in full-time education beyond the compulsory years. Yet, many of those concerned with the planning and delivery of education recognize that complacency about gender-equity issues is premature. A comparison of females' and males' participation in the educational process today with that of two to three centuries ago illustrates the enormous progress that has been made and illuminates the issues that still need to be addressed. Because of the considerable influence exerted by English traditions on colonial America, it is appropriate to consider the educational climate of the former first.

Historical overview

England

At the time Defoe wrote his essay, illiteracy was still widespread in England. Fifty years after the essay appeared, in the 1750s, it is estimated that only 64% of adult males and less than 40% of adult females were literate (Lawson & Silver, 1973). Since "writing was taught only to those who could read 'competently well,' and figures were taught only after the art of writing had been mastered" (Schofield, 1968, p. 316), levels of numeracy would have been considerably lower still. The prevailing attitude was that only the leisured classes should have leisure pursuits, and that anything that distracted the laboring classes from their labors was dangerous (Adburgham, 1972). This helps to explain the patterns of access to formal education, and why schools that provided elementary education were few and grossly inadequate. Defoe's comments were typical of the widespread condemnation of schools and universities in the first half of the 18th century, when he wrote of his

> deep sorrow for the present decay of learning among us and the manifest corruption of education. Our young gentlemen are sent to universities 'tis true, but not under restraint of correction as formerly; not to study, but to drink. (Quoted in Earle, 1976, p. 246)

The educational picture was even more dismal for girls. Girls born into aristocratic families were usually educated by a governess in their own homes. Daughters of successful tradesmen and merchants were more likely to be sent to boarding school. At best, they might be taught French, reading, writing, and sufficient arithmetic to enable them to keep household accounts. The main emphasis was, however, on accomplishments such as singing, dancing, painting, and needlework. The end product of these educational endeavors was rather depressing:

Any lady of ton in the last century [i.e., the 18th century] who could read tolerably well, and who could write her own name, was set down by all whose opinion was worth having as a learned woman. If she was further equal to the feat of inditing an occasional vivacious epistle to her friends and acquaintances without outrageously violating the ordinary rules of English syntax, the consensus of opinion proclaimed her nothing short of brilliant. (Sydney, 1892, pp. 94–95)

The generality of the poor educational diet available to females is confirmed by the experiences of Mary Somerville, still recognized as a successful mathematician. During her lifetime, Somerville was honored by being elected, with Caroline Herschel, as the first female members of the Royal Astronomical Society. Today, Somerville is probably best remembered for her translation and popularization of important scientific works. Her first such venture, *Celestial Mechanics* (adapted from Pierre Laplace's *Mécanique céleste*), was particularly well received. A useful account of other aspects of her work can be found in Perl (1978).

Mary Somerville was born in Scotland in 1780. Her own writings (Somerville, 1873) reveal that her parents attached considerably more importance to the education of their sons than of their daughter. Initially, it was thought sufficient for her to be taught to read the Bible by her mother, but at the age of 10 she was sent for a year to a fashionable boarding school. She emerged from there "with a taste for reading, some notion of simple arithmetic, a smattering of grammar and French, poor hand writing and abominable spelling" (Patterson, 1974, p. 270). Some years later, quite fortuitously, she came across an algebra problem that aroused her curiosity. In Somerville's own words:

At the end of the magazine, I read what appeared to me to be simply an arithmetical question, but on turning the page I was surprised to see strange-looking lines mixed with letters, chiefly Xs and Ys, and asked "what is that?" "Oh," said the friend, "it's a kind of arithmetic; they call it algebra; but I can tell you nothing about it.". . . On going home I thought I would look if any of our books could tell me what is meant by algebra. (Tabor, 1933, p. 98)

She continued studying mathematics against her father's wishes. There was support from other sources, however. Financial independence to pursue her studies came through a modestly comfortable inheritance with the early death of her first husband. William Wallace, then editor of an English mathematics journal, was an effective friend and mentor. Her second husband accepted and encouraged her mathematical endeavors.

The United States

As in England, literacy rates for males in colonial America were considerably higher than for females. By the middle of the 18th century, approximately 80% of males in some regions (e.g., New England) were deemed literate. Even optimistic assessments put the literacy rate for females at only 45% (Lockridge, 1974). Again, as in England, arithmetic was considered more suitable for students who had already mastered reading and writing. Since girls, when they attended school, typically did so for only a few years, the discrepancy between female and male numeracy rates was even greater than that in literacy rates. Generally, "there was no attempt to teach girls written arithmetic, simply because it was assumed that women had no need of it in adult life" (Cohen, 1982, p. 140). In this social climate, arguments about females' facility for number skills and arithmetic were clearly irrelevant. Such assertions came later, with improved schooling and levels of participation in education.

In the 1820s, with the spread of the common-school system and the insertion of arithmetic into the elementary curriculum, female pupils for the first time encountered arithmetic, and educators, also for the first time, were forced to articulate the reasons why arithmetic beyond the Rule of Three was inappropriate for girls to learn. A whole corpus of books and articles asserted that it was useless or even impossible to teach girls to reason logically about mathematics. . . . It seems supremely ironic that at the precise moment when arithmetic was finally within the reach of the female half of the population, because it was now decently taught in local schools, the stereotype of the nonmathematical feminine mind became dogma. (Cohen, 1982, p. 139)

This brief historical sketch provides an important context against which the contemporary educational climate in Western countries can be assessed. Today, in these generally affluent societies, we take for granted the formal rights of all citizens to have full access to education. Yet, despite apparent universal educational opportunity, subtle differences persist in the degree to which females and males participate in certain aspects of education.

Contemporary perspectives

As already indicated at the outset of this chapter, contemporary statistics confirm that much progress has been made toward educational equity. Yet, as implied by Bingham's (1982) colorful description of the current social climate, a number of small but consistent discrepancies remain.

Let us have "sweet girl graduates" by all means. They will be none the less sweet for a little wisdom, and the "golden hair" will not curl less gracefully outside the head by reason of there being brains within. Nay, if obvious practical difficulties can be overcome, let those women who feel inclined to do so descend into the gladiatorial arena of life. Let them, if they so please, become merchants, barristers, politicians. Let them have a fair field, but let them understand, as the necessary correlative, that they are to have no favour. (Bingham, 1982, p. 179)

Turning to mathematics, it is clear that there is now much overlap in the participation patterns of males and females in mathematics courses, though differences in favor of male enrollments continue to be reported for higher-level and more intensive mathematics courses, related applied fields, and occupations that require mathematical sophistication (see Leder, 1992, for a more detailed discussion). For example, in Australia – a country that prides itself on providing ready access to education for all its citizens – statistics indicate that among those with postschool qualifications in science, computing, mathematics, and agricultural and veterinary sciences, males outnumber females more than 2:1. Females compose less than a quarter of managers and administrators, less than 10% of tradespersons, but more than three-quarters of clerks, and more than 60% of salespersons and personal-service workers (Department of Employment, Education and Training, 1990).

Formal statistics also reveal that there is much overlap in the mathematics achievement of females and males. Yet some performance differences, typically in favor of males, continue to be reported – in particular, differences on selected mathematical tasks assessed through standardized and large-scale testing. Inspection of cross-cultural data confirms the generality of these findings (see, e.g., Leder, 1992).

Whether differences such as those just described occur in "a fair field," to use Bingham's phrase (1982), is addressed in the remainder of this chapter. In the first instance, relevant research is summarized. Emphasis is placed on teacher and student variables. Next, the strengths and weaknesses of the work reviewed are discussed. Finally, an alternative way of monitoring important correlates of the process of learning mathematics is described.

Current research: The broader context

It has been argued (Romberg & Carpenter, 1986) that two broad approaches dominate current research on formal mathematics learning: Research on classrooms and research on students' ideas and intuitive learning strategies. The former has tended to focus on group performance; the latter, on that of individual students.

Two further major strands can be identified in the research on classrooms: Work within the process–product research paradigm, and studies particularly concerned with teachers' cognitive processes. The former has added much to our understanding of the mechanics of teaching. Certain teacher behaviors affect how the intended curriculum is delivered and realized as achievement gains by learners on standardized tests. The research on teachers' thought processes and decisions during teaching has revealed that teachers are indeed thoughtful professionals, sensitive to changing classroom circumstances, and able to modify their intended plans when this seems appropriate to them. During interactive teaching, for example, they frequently make decisions at a rate of once every 2 minutes. Rich insights into other aspects of decision making have been provided by teachers highly knowledgeable about mathematics (Lampert, 1984; Schoenfeld, 1985). Comprehensive summaries of the two broad fields of classroom research are found in Brophy and Good (1986) and Clark and Peterson (1986), respectively.

Those interested in gender differences have tended to focus on teacher behaviors, less explicitly on teachers' cognitive thought processes. An overview of the relevant work in this area is provided in the next section.

Teachers

Classroom observations have revealed marked similarities in the way the mathematics curriculum is delivered in schools (Brophy & Good, 1986; Leder, 1990a; Leinhardt & Putnam, 1987; Stodolsky, 1988). Most frequently, teacher exposition is followed by students' attempts at the work discussed. In lower primary grades, practice with manipulative materials may precede the paper-and-pencil work. This apparent uniformity of procedure has shaped attempts to describe in-class activities.

A great variety of observation schedules has been used to describe teachers' in-class behaviors. The bulk of this work has used low-inference observation schedules of classroom events, rather than the more qualitative and interpretive data-gathering techniques. The methodology employed generally relies on data collected by observers seated, as unobtrusively as possible, in the back of classrooms. Observations are typically recorded for part of the lessons (segments of predetermined length, alternated with periods of rest, also of predetermined length) and for specified target students rather than the total class.

Particular attention has been focused on the ways in which teachers interact with the female and male students in their classes, and the effects of these behaviors on the learning of their students. Early findings of this work have been discussed by Brophy and Good (1974). On average, they reported, males tended to receive somewhat more criticism, be praised more frequently for correct answers, have their work monitored more frequently, and have a greater number of contacts with their teachers. More recent work set in the mathematics classroom has largely replicated these findings (Becker, 1981; Grieb & Easley, 1984; Hart, 1989; Koehler, 1990; Leder, 1990b).

How aspects of the time spent by teachers with their students in mathematics classes differ for females and males has also been investigated. Gore and Roumagoux (1983) found that teacher wait times were longer for males than for females; in other words, they found that on average teachers gave male students slightly longer to respond than female students – without interrupting or prompting – to questions posed. Leder (1987a, 1990b) reported no significant differences in wait times, but observed that above Grade 3, females tended to receive more time than males on routine, low-cognitive questions; males slightly more time on the more difficult and challenging high-cognitive questions, which serve as preparation for more advanced mathematics courses. Collectively, these data suggest that the field is not as fair as might be suggested by formal documents or publicly espoused values.

Student variables

Two distinct yet overlapping strands of research can also be identified in the work on children's own mathematical ideas, which was reviewed by Romberg and Carpenter (1986): The authors provide detailed analyses of mathematical content and research that document student strategies for solving a range of problems. As a result, researchers have developed taxonomies of problem types and models of major levels in the development of children's concepts and skills in various content areas. Useful reviews of students' thought processes in the broader context are found in Wittrock (1986), and of research on students' mathematics cognitions in Carpenter and Fennema (1988) and Romberg and Carpenter (1986).

Student behaviors and thought processes have been studied by those concerned with gender differences in mathematics learning. Interest has most frequently been focused on affective components of learning, less frequently on cognitive aspects other than spatial skills. The small but recurring differences between females and males in personal-belief variables, such as confidence, risk-taking behavior, motivation, and related characteristics – including fear of success, attributional style, learned helplessness, mastery orientation, anxiety, and persistence – continue to attract research attention (Fennema & Leder, 1990; Leder, 1992). Space constraints prevent a detailed overview of further relevant literature.

There is a risk that excessive attention to small differences between groups of males and groups of females, ignoring the much larger within-group differences, may be counterproductive and lead to the perpetuation rather than redress of gender inequities. Nevertheless, some common findings should be cited. The weight of evidence suggests that, on average, females are somewhat less confident and more anxious than males about their ability to do mathematics and, for example, less likely to persist on the most challenging tasks. They are also more ambivalent about the value to them of mathematics as a field of study and occupational prerequisite. Students' beliefs about their own performance and long-term expectations are likely to be reflected in and reinforced by the values held by members of their peer group. More comprehensive discussions of these issues can be found in Fennema and Leder (1990) and in Leder (1992).

Initiatives to increase females' participation in mathematics are sometimes overtaken by events that occur in the wider context. In Australia, government initiatives have led to increased retention rates at school and increased participation rates in postschool education among both males and females. Females' participation rates in nonintensive postcompulsory mathematics courses have also increased. Unfortunately, these initiatives have occurred at a time of increased unemployment and decreased opportunities for participation in apprenticeship programs. Many disillusioned youth are skeptical about arguments that taking mathematics will lead to increased employment opportunities. They are generally able to supply much anecdotal evidence to support their doubts. Given the similarities between the economic climates in America and Australia, it is likely that this trend is also apparent in the United States. Once again, educational matters are influenced, if not overshadowed, by the prevailing economic and environmental climate.

Reflections on contemporary perspectives

It is arguable whether gender-equity issues continue to be investigated most effectively through research involving large samples and the application of statistical techniques that are so often used to describe and analyze data thus gathered. By concentrating on group differences rather than similarities, this approach tends to confirm and perpetuate popular stereotypes and beliefs about gender differences in mathematics learning.

Elsewhere (Leder, 1992), I have argued that the limitations of attempting to capture and describe the complex classroom environment through any one classroom observation schedule are increasingly being recognized. Studies that have focused on small-group instruction, on student–student interactions, or on detailed and intensive observations of a small number of students, have yielded much useful and additional information, not readily captured by work carried out within the more systematic teacher–student interaction framework. The rich and sometimes unexpected results yielded by alternate methodologies are well illustrated by the approach used by Rogers (1990).

A different perspective on classroom interactions

Instead of concentrating on disadvantaged females, Rogers (1990) sought to describe the characteristics and distinguishing features of an educational setting in which females fared particularly well. Extensive data were gathered for a relatively small sample. The setting selected for intensive investigation was a North American university with an outstanding record in attracting and retaining students, including a large percentage of females, to its undergraduate mathematics program. Interviews with students and staff, as well as observations of selected classrooms, yielded unexpected information. Particular attention was focused on one teacher who had students flocking to his courses, yet was described as being intimidating.

As one female student explained:

Sure you hate him while you're going through it, but, in retrospect you look back and "Wow! What a great teacher. I learned so much. I want to get him again!" And so when the class schedule comes out for the next semester, many students will look to see what he is teaching, then take it. (Rogers, 1990, p. 38)

This teacher, like others at the institution, made no special efforts to attract female students nor any special adaptations to make the course more attractive to them. He genuinely considered success in mathematics, however, to be within the reach of all students prepared to work for it, and not merely attainable by a small number of exceptionally talented individuals. His methods are worth noting:

In this teacher's class there is almost no lecturing. Most of the time, students are working together informally in small groups, discussing problems, arguing, negotiating meaning. The teacher walks around, looking over shoulders, asking questions. From time to time he sends a student to the board to write up her solution. Then there is some discussion with the student-teacher taking a leading role. The class may end with a brief lecture on some new material or an assignment of new problems to be taken up at the next meeting. (Rogers, 1990, p. 43)

Significantly, success in attracting females to mathematics courses well beyond the compulsory level was achieved, not by making special allowances or provisions for females, nor by dwelling on gender issues, but by creating a classroom environment open and supportive for all students – an environment in which the teaching style mirrored the nature of mathematical inquiry.

Much can be learned through in-depth small-sample research. An example taken from my own work (Leder, 1990c) with student and adult samples illustrates the benefits of such an approach. Only the latter is discussed here.

The study

The study involved 21 experienced and competent tertiary educators. Most were without special expertise in mathematics. (All but three were, in fact, my colleagues in the Faculty of Education at Monash University.) The participants attended four sessions, spread over two mornings, on content.

Participation was on a voluntary basis. Two mathematicians who were also experienced tertiary teachers and were members of a pure and applied mathematics department, respectively, acted as instructors. They were each asked to select a topic that could be taught in two 1-hour sessions to mature, educationally sophisticated but rather naive learners of mathematics. The Pythagorean theorem and practical applications of graph theory were chosen. As part of the latter, matrices were introduced as a way of representing information contained in a graph. Each session was videotaped and subsequently transcribed.

All participants, learners as well as instructors, were told that the purpose of the study was to increase our understanding of the learning process and to identify teaching strategies that seemed to exacerbate or minimize difficulties experienced in the learning of mathematics. The instructors were encouraged to present their material as clearly, logically, and meaningfully as possible. The learners were to attend carefully to the material as it was presented, by taking notes in specially provided notebooks, discussing the work at hand – both orally and in a margin left on each page specially for this purpose – by asking questions whenever something was not clear, and by reflecting in writing, in their notebooks, on their experiences after each session and at the conclusion of the teaching experiment. The learners were also asked to comment in their notebooks, as the lessons progressed, on the twin questions: "What could I, or the instructor, do to make it come clear?" As experienced educators, they were well placed to respond. The same prompt questions had been used by Tobias (1986) in her investigation of peer evaluation of the teaching of science. Where appropriate, participants were asked to expand on their written reflections and comments in individual interviews that were held after the four sessions had been completed.

Selected excerpts from the video transcripts and the students' notebooks are presented here. Further details can be found in Leder (1987b) and Leder, Jones, Paget, and Stillwell (1987).

Notebook extracts

The notebooks contained a wealth of information. Observations included comments on the anxieties associated with doing mathematics, the nature and structure of the experiment, reactions to classmates' behavior, reflections on the learning process, the relative effectiveness of various teaching strategies, and the difficulty of the technical terminology used. Some examples of the first category are given below.

I learnt a lot about myself these last two days. Where is my confidence? When [the instructor] asked, "did I have it" I said yes, even though I didn't mean it. Later I did get it . . . thanks to someone else's similar questions. . . . I feel panic when a classmate who earlier didn't understand now does.

Why was there no attempt to allay my anxieties right at the beginning?

Why does mathematics have to be more fun for the teacher than the students?

I like the simple calculations. They gave me a sense of success. . . . I like rote laws. (I know they are frowned on but I'm very prepared to accept rote rules, especially in the subject area where I'm uncertain.)

But people become self-conscious if they think their questions are holding up other people.

Even among this professionally and educationally highly qualified sample there was notable anxiety about doing mathematics, a lack of confidence about achieving success, and a reluctance by some to admit to the difficulties being experienced. Is it unreasonable to draw a parallel between the fears expressed by this mature sample and those likely to be felt by students in a typical classroom?

Transcript extracts

Inspection of the transcripts was also very informative and revealed a number of difficulties experienced by this group of learners. The annotated excerpts reproduced below highlight a number of these: The difficulties encountered in going from the familiar to the unfamiliar, the confusion created by the use of examples and illustrations, by terminology, by the speed at which the lesson developed, and the lack of opportunity to verbalize and/or talk about new concepts. All entries in the comments/thoughts column are, of course, hypothetical. They are my summaries of the classroom dialogue, participants' comments and reflections written during or after the sessions, from material obtained in the interviews, or from the informal discussions initiated with me by the participants themselves in the days that followed the study.

The transcript excerpt reproduced here begins just after the instructor moved from a discussion of matrix addition to the multiplication of two 2-by-2 matrices. His explanation is interrupted by Helen:

Transcript	*Researcher's comments/thoughts*
Helen: Could you do it the other way? From the second one in the rows multiplied by . . .	Asking for clarification (I'm competent. Surely I can master this.)
Instructor (In): No, no!	Gives no reason

In: It just happens to be that way.
There is no rule for multiplying matrices.
Graham: Could you say what multiplication actually means?

Relying on rote learning

In: I'll show you in a moment.

A further appeal for meaning
(Helen admitted she did not understand. Neither do I.)

Mark: Hang on. If you want us to
understand what is going on, then
we'll need to know. I don't accept
you just saying that we multiply rows
by columns.

Take this on trust.

Uncomfortable with rote learning.
Makes another attempt to achieve
understanding
(I can think for myself. Why not in
the mathematics class?)

In: I knew I'd have trouble here!

But usually I get away with it.

Mark: Are you saying there are a number of ways of possibly multiplying this
together – but one of them happens to
be useful for other purposes?

Surely there is a reason for the rule?
(If I am persistent we'll get there!)

In: Yes, that's basically what it is.

Helen: Why is B less than A? That's
what I don't understand. You have a
matrix B and you say you cannot take
the data from that in rows and multiply
it by columns in A. Therefore B must
be less than A.

A negotiated meaning – at one
level – at last
(That makes sense.)

Searching for meaning. Confused by
terminology
(I won't be put off. I'm going to understand this.)

In: No, no.
Linda: So which column by which column?

Barry: Why is it A × B and not B × A?

We obviously lack common ground.
Just give me the rule.
(I'm used to not understanding mathematics.)

In: Because in matrix multiplication it
matters in which order we multiply. AB
does not equal BA.

I'd like to understand.
It really does all make sense.

Mary: I can handle rules. I don't mind
if you tell me how to do it. I'm prepared
to accept rules.

I learned long ago that I could survive best by relying on rote learning.
(I'm too dumb to do mathematics
any other way.)

[The instructor continues with his explanation]

Mark: Hang on, you're going too quick.

I want to understand this.
(With persistence, I'll master this.)

David: I'm also losing it.
I can't see . . .

I also need to understand this.
(I'm going to master this.)

Helen: So you're actually multiplying?

What is the rule?
(If I can't understand, I'll settle for a
rule.)

Linda: And adding?

The rule is more complicated.
(But it has to be the right rule.)

[The instructor repeats the multiplication procedure. Various students comment on the procedure and ask questions. He sets an example for the students to try.]

In: David, what did you get?

David: 1, 3, 6, 8.

In: Yes, 1, 3, 6, 8.

Mark: I didn't get any of those numbers.

Help!
(I still haven't got it.)

In: None of them?

But I explained it so many times.

Mark: I'm completely wrong.

I knew this would happen!
(Perhaps I *am* beaten.)

In: Well, I'll do it quickly for those . . .

Mark: No, don't do it quickly. I need absorption time
. . . . Could we do it, with me telling you what I'm doing. I want you to hear it in my words.

We have to construct a shared meaning. This takes time. I've tried listening to you. How about listening to me?
(What happens if we follow my strategy and not yours?)

Among other things, this excerpt illustrates the active involvement of the participants in the lesson, their determined efforts to assign meaning to the new material to which they were exposed, their persistent attempts to assimilate it into their existing frameworks, and their attitudes and emotions as they grappled with the work. Encouraging the participants to "think aloud" as the lesson progressed provided valuable information about individual students. Even in this short excerpt, hints of subtle differences emerged in the way in which Helen and Mark seemed to be reacting. Further, careful analysis of the transcript should confirm or challenge the emerging hypothesis and suggest more constructive ways in which the students and teacher could interact.

There is considerable overlap between the research methodology just illustrated and that advocated by a growing number of mathematics educators working within the constructivist paradigm – with its emphasis on the importance of personally constructed conceptions, attitudes, and abilities on the learning of formal mathematics. By stressing individual differences, within-group as well as between-group differences can ultimately be traced.

Conclusion

In this chapter I have argued that it is important to consider gender differences in context. Until relatively recently, education was available only to a privileged minority. Few females were included in that group. Thus, through lack of opportunity, gender differences in mathematics learning were both a fact and an artifact of the prevailing circumstances.

As education became more readily available to a broader segment of society, the expected adult roles assigned to the two genders influenced the educational diet that was considered most suitable for them. In particular, proficiency in mathematics was considered relevant for males, but a luxury rather than a necessity for females. These expectations continued to be self-fulfilling. Without adequate mathematical qualifications, many careers and occupations were beyond the reach of those females engaged in work outside the home. Minimal levels of mathematics were considered sufficient for traditional homemakers.

The dominant cultural climate also left its impact inside the classroom. Teachers' as well as students' behaviors were shaped by it. Quantifying differences in mathematics – in engagement in the lessons, or in long-term intentions and expectations likely to influence in-class behaviors – was most readily accomplished with instruments administered to large-scale samples or through observation schedules with predetermined categories. The focus and quality of the instruments used determined the nature and quality of the data gathered. Reporting of results frequently emphasized gender differences at the expense of gender similarities. It could be argued that at least some of the differences identified were artifacts created by the content, structure, and approach of the instruments used to gather the data.

In recent years, the social climate has become more accepting of behaviors once considered inappropriate. Sex-determined boundaries have softened. Areas once closed to females have become accessible. But the traditions of many centuries continue to leave their mark in many subtle ways, both outside and inside the classroom. Research methodologies now used to describe and explain gender differences must take account of the changing ethos and be sufficiently flexible to concentrate on remaining inequities, and not those created as an artifact of the measurement or observation schedules used.

The quality and wealth of nuances in a data source collected through intensive observations of a small group of students has been illustrated in this chapter. Students' strengths as well as weaknesses were identified and interpreted against the changing demands of the lesson. The strategy used not only illuminated the multifaceted interactions among such factors as teacher behaviors, classroom practices, and student learning, but also pointed to constructive ways of redressing inequitable practices.

References

Adburgham, A. (1972). *Women in print*. London: Allen & Unwin.

Becker, J. (1981). Differential treatment of females and males in mathematics class. *Journal for Research in Mathematics Education, 12,* 40–53.

Bingham, C. (Ed.). (1982). *Wit and wisdom: A public affairs miscellany*. Melbourne University Press.

Brophy, J., & Good, T. L. (1974). *Teacher–student relationships: Causes and consequences*. New York: Holt, Rinehart & Winston.

——— (1986). Teacher behavior and student achievement. In M. C. Wittrock (Ed.), *Third handbook of research on teaching* (pp. 328–375). New York: Macmillan.

Carpenter, T. P., & Fennema, E. (1988). Research and cognitively guided instruction. In E. Fennema, T. P. Carpenter, & S. J. Lamon (Eds.), *Integrating research on teaching and learning mathematics* (pp. 2–17). Madison: Wisconsin Center for Education Research.

Clark, C. M., & Peterson, P. L. (1986). Teachers' thought processes. In M. C. Wittrock (Ed.), *Third handbook of research on teaching* (pp. 255–296). New York: Macmillan.

Cohen, P. C. (1982). *A calculating people: The spread of numeracy in early America*. University of Chicago Press.

Defoe, D. (1697/1969). *An essay upon projects*. (A Scholar facsimile.) Menston, England: Scholar Press.

Department of Employment, Education and Training. (1990). *Women and work, 12*(3). Canberra, Australia: Author.

Earle, P. (1976). *The world of Defoe*. London: Weidenfeld & Nicolson.

Fennema, E., & Leder, G. C. (Eds.). (1990). *Mathematics and gender*. New York: Teachers College Press.

Gore, D. A., & Roumagoux, D. V. (1983). Wait time as a variable in sex-related differences during fourth grade mathematics instruction. *Journal of Educational Research, 26,* 273–275.

Grieb, A., & Easley, J. (1984). A primary school impediment to mathematical equity: Case studies in rule and dependent socialization. In M. W. Steinkamp & M. Maehr (Eds.), *Advances in motivation and achievement, Vol. 2: Women in science* (pp. 317–362). Greenwich, CT: JAI.

Hart, L. H. (1989). Classroom processes, sex of student, and confidence in learning mathematics. *Journal for Research in Mathematics Education, 30,* 242–260.

Koehler, M. S. (1990). Classrooms, teachers and gender differences in mathematics. In E. Fennema & G. C. Leder (Eds.), *Mathematics and gender* (pp. 128–146). New York: Teachers College Press.

Lampert, M. (1984). Teaching about thinking and thinking about teaching. *Journal of Curriculum Studies, 16*(1), 1–18.

Lawson, J., & Silver, H. (1973). *A social history of education in England*. London: Methuen.

Leder, G. C. (1987a). Teacher–student interaction: A case study. *Educational Studies in Mathematics, 18,* 255–271.

——— (1987b). The mathematics classroom: Mature reflections. *For the Learning of Mathematics, 7*(2), 11–17.

——— (1990a). Talking about mathematics. *Australian Researcher, 17*(2), 17–27.

——— (1990b). Teacher–student interactions in the mathematics classroom: A different perspective. In E. Fennema & G. C. Leder (Eds.), *Mathematics and gender* (pp. 149–168). New York: Teachers College Press.

——— (1990c, July). *Does teaching equal learning?* Keynote address to the 13th Biennial Conference of the Australian Association of Mathematics Teachers, Hobart, Australia.

——— (1991). Television and school mathematics. *Australian Mathematics Teacher, 47*(1), 18–19.

——— (1992). Mathematics and gender: Changing perspectives. In D. A. Grouws (Ed.), *Handbook of research on mathematics teaching and learning* (pp. 597–622). Reston, VA: National Council of Teachers of Mathematics and New York: Macmillan.

Leder, G. C., Jones, P. L., Paget, N. S., & Stillwell, J. C. (1987). Peer perspectives on teaching: A case study in mathematics. *Higher Education Research and Development, 6,* 185–196.

Leinhardt, G., & Putnam, R. T. (1987). The skill of learning from classroom lessons. *American Educational Research Journal, 24,* 557–587.

Lockridge, K. (1974). *Literacy in colonial England: An enquiry into the social context of literacy in the early modern west.* New York: Norton.

McGrath, P. L. (1976). *The unfinished assignment: Equal education for women.* (Worldwatch Paper 7.) Washington, DC: Worldwatch Institute.

Patterson, E. C. (1974). The case of Mary Somerville: An aspect of nineteenth century science. *Proceedings of the American Philosophical Society, 118,* 269–275.

Perl, T. (1978). *Math equals: Biographies of women mathematicians and related activities.* Menlo Park, CA: Addison-Wesley.

Plato. (1955). *The republic* (H. D. P. Lee, Trans.). New York: Penguin.

Rogers, P. (1990). Thoughts on power and pedagogy. In L. Burton (Ed.), *Gender and mathematics: An international perspective* (pp. 38–46). London: Cassell.

Romberg, T. A., & Carpenter, T. P. (1986). Research on teaching and learning mathematics: Two disciplines of scientific inquiry. In M. C. Wittrock (Ed.), *Third handbook of research on teaching* (pp. 850–873). New York: Macmillan.

Schoenfeld, A. H. (1985). *Mathematical problem solving.* Orlando, FL: Academic.

Schofield, R. S. (1968/1975). The measurement of literacy in pre-industrial England. In J. Goody (Ed.), *Literacy in traditional societies.* Cambridge University Press.

Somerville, M. (1873). *Personal recollections from early life to old age of Mary Somerville.* London: John Murray.

Stodolsky, S. S. (1988). *The subject matters.* University of Chicago Press.

Sydney, W. C. (1892). *England and the English in the eighteenth century.* Vol. 2. London: Ward & Downey.

Tabor, M. E. (1933). *Pioneer women.* London: Sheldon.

Tobias, S. (1986). Perspectives on the teaching of science. *Change, 18*(2), 36–41.

United States Bureau of the Census. (1990). *Statistical abstract of the United States: 1990 (110th edition).* Washington, DC: Author.

Wittrock, M. C. (1986). Students' thought processes. In M. C. Wittrock (Ed.), *Third handbook of research on teaching* (pp. 297–314). New York: MacMillan.

9 Redefining the "girl problem in mathematics"

Patricia B. Campbell

A first step in determining new directions for equity in mathematics education is to examine the old directions and assess their successes and failures. An analysis of what worked and what didn't helps in the development of new and ideally improved ideas and models. Such a process needs to be applied to gender issues in mathematics, or to what has been defined as the "girl problem in mathematics." In this chapter, I will:

- Assess areas of success and failure of current efforts for dealing with the underrepresentation of women and girls in mathematics.
- Look at the characteristics of in- and out-of-school programs that have "worked" with girls.
- Explore how mathematics classrooms can be restructured to reduce, if not eliminate, overall gender differences.

Gender differences in mathematics achievement and course taking have decreased; this is a success, but we have had much less effect on girls' choice of mathematics-related college majors and careers. Our efforts need to shift away from changing girls toward changing how mathematics is taught, and how girls are treated when it is. In general, we need to redefine and expand the population for whom mathematics is "appropriate."

The "girl problem"

The underrepresentation of girls and women in mathematics and math-related careers has been seen primarily as a "girl problem." This label uncritically assumes that there is a problem between girls and mathematics. It is as if the problem were caused by girls, by something they do, or more often, by something they lack. To solve a problem defined in this way, one works either to change girls so they are more compatible with mathematics, or, more radically, to change mathematics so that it is more compatible with girls.[1]

Most efforts have focused on changing girls; that is, girls have been encouraged to use mathematics, to like mathematics, and to become the kinds of learners who do well in mathematics. At the same time, efforts to change mathematics, with very rare exceptions, have focused not on changing mathematics but on changing girls' perceptions of mathematics – another version of changing girls.

This definition of the problem and the resulting solutions minimize or ignore the role that teachers, schools, and the larger society play in who we are, how we learn, and what we learn. Putting aside for a moment the ethical issue of whether girls should be changed, this emphasis on girls and not on society works for only so long. As successful change agents in business have found, changing one component of a system can cause short-term but not long-term change. If you change a girl so that she "loves math," but then you put her back into the same environment and situations that caused her to hate mathematics in the first place, she will revert to hating mathematics.

Causes and effects

The educational system affects how girls view mathematics. As girls and boys go through school, gender differences in their perceptions regarding being good in mathematics increase even when there are no differences in achievement (Educational Testing Service, 1988). Girls in the upper grades report liking mathematics less than do girls in the lower grades, and feel less confident doing it (Greenberg-Lakes, 1990). In general, girls are more apt than boys to doubt their competence in mathematics and to be less confident in their mathematics ability (Hyde, Fennema, Ryan, Frost, & Hopp, 1990; Levine, 1991). As Fennema and Sherman (1978) found, girls in early adolescence experience a drop in their self-confidence in mathematics *before* they experience any academic decline.

This decrease in interest and confidence may be related to the differential treatment girls and boys receive in school. Although there is an assumption that females and males receive an equal education when they are in the same classrooms, with the same teachers using the same books (Benbow & Stanley, 1983), the assumption is false. Patterns of mathematics classroom interaction differ for girls and boys, with boys interacting more with teachers and vice versa. Classroom activities are chosen more often to appeal to boys than to girls (Fennema & Peterson, 1987; Stallings, 1985). Boys receive more praise, a greater number of disciplinary contacts, and more general teacher-initiated contacts. Teachers respond more frequently to boys' requests for help and criticize girls more frequently for the academic quality of their work. Even when overall sex differences are not found in patterns of interaction, a few male students often dominate teacher attention in mathematics classes (Eccles, 1989).

This differential treatment can contribute to faulty perceptions of who "does math" and to the identification of mathematics as masculine, feminine, or neutral. Perceptions remain, especially among males, that mathematics and science are male domains (Hyde et al., 1990; Linn, 1990). Indeed, men's-movement guru Robert Bly believes that the "genetic difference between women and men in mathematics is 3% . . . I think that for this century and this moment it is important to emphasize the 3% difference that makes a man masculine" (quoted in Goodman, 1991, p. 71).

Perceptions make a difference. The emphasis on girls' problems with mathematics may actually be counterproductive, by supporting the concept that mathematics is a male domain, that is, something that boys and men do and that girls and women do not do (or, at least, do not do well). Seeing mathematics as something that people of your gender do is related to persistence in taking mathematics courses and to achievement. Girls' view of mathematics as a male domain is negatively correlated with mathematics achievement (Tartre & Fennema, 1991) and with taking advanced mathematics courses (Armstrong, 1985; Hyde et al., 1990). Girls who are not accepting of traditional gender roles have higher mathematics achievement than girls who have more sex-stereotyped ideas (Armstrong, 1985).

At the college level, Hewitt and Seymour (1991) found that many women in mathematics, science, and engineering "expressed their feeling of being outsiders in a male-dominated culture" (p. 98).

Nearly all complained about the daily irritation of dealing with open (or thinly veiled) sexist remarks from their male peers, and with the inner stresses of feeling unwelcome and pressured. (p. 98)

It is not surprising that even girls with exceptional academic preparation in mathematics and science are choosing careers in these areas in disproportionately low numbers (National Science Foundation, 1990). In one statewide study, more than three times as many young men as young women who had taken physics and calculus were planning college majors in science or engineering (Dick & Rallis, 1991).

It is ironic that there are no gender differences in the percentage of high school seniors wanting to go into mathematics; basically nobody does. Five-tenths of 1% of high school senior girls and 0.6% of high school boys plan to major in mathematics according to a recent National Science Foundation study (1990).

To differing degrees, we have convinced middle-class young women and men that they need mathematics. For the first 3 years of high school mathematics courses, gender differences are either minimal or nonexistent among those choosing to take mathematics courses (Kolstad & Thorne, 1989; National Science Board, 1989). Efforts to convince girls of the value of mathematics in future career choices have been successful in convincing middle-class girls (and, perhaps more important, their parents and guidance counselors) that it is essential that they take enough mathematics to "get into a good college" (Gross, 1988).

Gender differences in mathematics course taking do not appear until precalculus and calculus (National Science Foundation, 1990) – courses needed in preparation for mathematics-related college majors, such as the physical sciences and engineering. A similar pattern occurs in mathematics achievement, where gender differences are declining to such a point that they are minimal or nonexistent. However, gender differences still occur in areas like complex problem solving and among students at the highest academic levels (Friedman, 1989; Hyde et al., 1990).

It is important to note that these data are class- and race-specific. Meta-analytic studies have found that gender differences in mathematics achievement among minority-group members are smaller than those found in whites (Friedman, 1989). If studies based on the SAT are excluded from consideration, gender differences among minority group members disappear (Hyde et al., 1990). Individual studies have found that African American elementary school girls scored higher than African American elementary school boys in mathematics (Hare, 1985), that nonwhite girls in Hawaii outperformed nonwhite boys in mathematics achievement, and that girls outnumbered boys in the highest-achieving groups (Brandon, Newton, & Hammond, 1987). Although on the surface this looks positive, it is not. With the exception of Asian Americans, minority groups score significantly lower than white students on a variety of mathematics achievement measures (Dossey et al., 1988; National Science Foundation, 1990). Girls and boys scoring equally poorly does not represent an advance.

Solutions: Pieces of the larger picture

The closing of the achievement gap and of differential course taking between females and males cannot be attributed solely to the fact that girls have changed in the past 20 years; so has the educational and social environment around them. In 1974, when Lucy Sells first argued that mathematics was a critical filter in career choice, it was a revolutionary idea. Now, the importance of mathematics is widely accepted. Federal and state laws such as Title IX and the Civil Rights Restoration Act have opened courses and programs to previously excluded populations and have conveyed the message that federal legislation protects the rights of girls to do mathematics. Further, girls are automatically included in the rhetoric of reform, namely, National Education Goal No. 4, that by the year 2000, "U.S. students will be first in the world in science and mathematics achievement" (United States Department of Education, 1991). Presumably, that rhetoric will translate into action.

The "successful" programs and the techniques and tips devised to involve girls with mathematics and to keep them involved that I describe here must be seen as part of this larger picture. Programs and techniques are needed, but they alone are not adequate. What is needed is institutional change (Personal notes, National Research Council's Conference on Women in Science and Engineering, 1991).

Also needed is attention to boys' perceptions of who can and should do mathematics and science. Since most adolescent females are very interested in males, what boys think can have an effect on girls. The effect can be negative:

Sometimes I act like I'm not as intelligent as I really am. I feel that if guys knew that I have a 4.0 average they would be intimidated – I have found this to be true. (Fresh Voices, 1991 p. 20)

The effect can also be positive:

During one summer at Douglass Science Institute a very attractive man taught the environment science sessions. Unlike other summers when there was little change in girls' specific career choice, that summer about 33% of the girls decided they wanted to be environmental scientists. (Campbell, 1991)

Unless boys as well as girls are convinced that "real women do math," efforts toward gender equity in mathematics will encounter obstacles based on stereotyped social roles.

Special programs: What works

My years of evaluation and follow-up of programs that encourage girls in mathematics, science, and engineering have provided some important clues regarding what works to encourage girls. The following is an overview of some of my findings.[2]

EUREKA!

EUREKA! is a 4-week nonresidential summer program run by the Women's Center of Brooklyn College. Participants are predominately minority junior-high girls from Brooklyn who are in neither gifted nor special education programs. EUREKA! focuses on junior-high girls because these are the years when major mathematics decisions are made. In eighth grade, most students decide whether they are going to take algebra – a necessary step for continuation in mathematics.

Seventh graders attend Math EUREKA!, a program of mathematics and sports, whereas returning eighth graders focus on science, engineering, and sports in Science EUREKA! Some students also return for a third year as interns. In addition, there is a series of winter Saturday follow-up sessions for EUREKA! students.

Students who participated in EUREKA! during its first 4 years increased the number of mathematics courses they were planning to take by 45%.

Follow-up 1 and 2½ years later found the girls' commitment to mathematics course taking remained high and that they were continuing to take mathematics courses. In addition, whereas originally 40% of the 1987 EUREKA! students who were in the follow-up program planned to take calculus, 2½ years later that figure had increased to 90%. With the institution of Science EUREKA! in 1989 came an increase in girls' science course-taking plans that reached an average of 60% even among the Math EUREKA! students.

To enable researchers to understand why EUREKA! has been successful, students were asked what they felt were major differences between EUREKA! and school mathematics. Students felt that EUREKA! teachers explained more, answered questions, and "made sure you understood," whereas school mathematics teachers were seen as less helpful and less inclined to use class time to answer questions. One girl explained that

girls went into EUREKA! thinking math was not for them. At EUREKA! they learned how to solve programs and thought, "This was good."

Students saw EUREKA! mathematics as fun and more relaxed, with an emphasis on thinking and problem solving. School mathematics was seen as more competitive and dependent on the quality of the teacher. During one summer session, the mathematics component of EUREKA! was conducted in a more competitive, less group-oriented problem-solving environment and, although the girls liked the teacher and the program, their mathematics course-taking plans did not increase. After a second summer of EUREKA!, mathematics course-taking plans did increase among those who returned.

Douglass Science Institute

The Douglass Science Institute (DSI) is a 2-week residential summer program for high school girls entering their junior year, who are already interested in and good at mathematics and science. The program is sponsored by the Douglass Project at Douglass College, Rutgers University, and about half of those attending are minority-group members. DSI features "hands-on" science, network building, role models, field trips, and fun. Like EUREKA!, DSI was designed for girls at a "math decision-making time," the summer between the sophomore and junior years. Most girls decide whether they are going to continue to take mathematics beyond that necessary to get into a good college during their junior year. Along with the summer program, DSI has a school year follow-up session that students and interested parents and teachers attend on campus for a "reunion."

DSI has not had an impact on girls' mathematics and science course-taking plans, since most of the young women entered the program planning to take as many mathematics and science courses as they could. It has, however, had an impact on their commitment to mathematics and science careers. About 25% of the participating girls felt that attending DSI made them more committed to careers in these areas. Thirty-nine percent felt that the major effect of DSI was that they learned more about math- and science-related careers.

Nine to 21 months after participating in DSI, about 30% of the students felt that DSI had increased their interest in math- and science-related careers, causing them to become "more focused on science as a career," to "definitely consider a career in science," and to "include science in my career plans." In addition, about 40% of the parents attending follow-up sessions felt DSI had guided their daughters toward a math- or science-related career. Sixty-five percent of DSI students who are now in college are majoring in mathematics, science, or engineering.

DSI has had an effect on girls' stereotypes regarding those who do mathematics and sciences. Prior to attending DSI, at least half of the girls (who are themselves very good in these courses) had negative stereotypes about people who are good in mathematics and science; they were seen as "nerds," "very serious," "nonsocial with no sense of humor," and "not caring about their appearance." In follow-up, 9 to 21 months after attending the program, over 50 percent of the participants felt their impressions of people who were good in mathematics and science had changed; in all but one case, the change was positive. Interacting with scientists and graduate students in informal settings helped reduce the "nerd" factor in their perceptions as the girls saw that those who are good in these fields can be "actually human." As one student explained: ·

I previously had a stereotyped vision of what a math or science whiz would look like and now I realize that they are no different from me or my friends from DSI and our common denominators are curiosity and the willingness to experiment.

Expanding Your Horizons

One-day career exposure programs for girls such as Expanding Your Horizons, sponsored by the Math Science Network of Oakland, California, have had an impact on participants' career interests. In these 1-day sessions, girls hear from, interact with, and work with women in different science and mathematics-related careers. A 6-month follow-up of girls attending Expanding Your Horizons found that they had increased their interest in careers in mathematics and science as compared to a presession measure (Anton & Humphreys, 1982).

Operation SMART

Girls Incorporated's Operation SMART (Science, Math and Relevant Technology) is a philosophy program with related hands-on activities that encourages girls in exploration, questioning, inquiry, and risk-taking. Infused into the curriculum at most Girls Incorporated (formerly Girls Clubs of America) sites, Operation SMART is the largest program designed specifically to encourage girls in mathematics and science. There is some indication that Operation SMART increases girls' interest and participation in mathematics and science activities. For example, one study found that

> girls eagerly participated in the stuff of math, science and technology, in the form of inviting demonstrations and hands-on puzzles and projects. Girls rarely sought out such opportunities, but thoroughly appreciated them when presented. (Frederick & Nicholson, 1991, p. viii)

Participating in a coed version of Operation SMART increased the number of hands-on mathematics and science-related activities of girls and boys in four urban after-school centers. In two of the four centers, teachers reported that when they labeled an activity as SMART, girls were more apt to participate than when girls thought it was a "science activity." Teachers in all four centers reported an increase in girls' participation. Specifically, they felt that

- After doing science hands-on with SMART, more girls were getting involved and asking to do more hands-on activities.
- Mostly boys were interested in science/hands-on; however, more girls were getting involved.
- Children still fell into traditional roles, but there had been some changes.
- SMART was effective in helping to erode gender barriers.

Similarities

There are a number of similarities among these programs. The programs:

- use many hands-on activities
- are fun
- are relaxed, with little or no emphasis on individual competition
- build girls' confidence
- provide girls with many opportunities to see that mathematics and science are as readily "girl" fields as boys'
- provide time for questions and an environment that encourages the asking of questions. The girls know that, as one EUREKA! student explained, "Someone is there who will keep working with me until I can say, 'I've got it!' "

Making changes

Increasing teacher awareness

A "necessary but not sufficient" component for change is to raise teacher awareness. Teachers are part of the cause of the differential gender practices that exist. If presented properly, this knowledge should be empowering; if teachers are part of the cause, then they have the power to contribute to helping to eliminate those practices (Fennema, personal communication, 1991).

Yet teachers are often not aware of differences in the ways they treat girls and boys (Karp, 1988). Indeed, teachers who have consciously tried to give girls equal amounts of attention have felt that they were being unfair to boys (Whyte, 1984). Teachers seldom deliberately treat boys and girls differently; instead, their behavior is unconscious and unexamined (Fennema & Meyer, 1989).

These behaviors can and should be made conscious in teachers. A number of materials have been developed for this purpose.[3] Training is also available through such national programs as EQUALS[4] and GESA (Gender Ethnic Expectations/Student Achievement).[5]

Although in-service staff development can help, teachers need to understand what is happening in their own classrooms. Teachers can use students as data collectors; they can audiotape, videotape, or involve other teachers in collecting information on the proportion of teacher attention that goes to girls and to boys. Specific things that teachers can look for include:

- the proportion of time they spend calling on girls or boys
- differences in the types of questions they ask girls and boys ("What is the correct answer?" versus "How did you get that answer?")
- differences in the kind of praise they offer girls and boys (praising work for being neat or on time versus praise for the academic content)
- the proportion of questions asked by girls versus those asked by boys

Once teachers realize that in spite of all their good intentions, they are part of the problem, there are a number of things they can do; this is where empowerment comes in. First and most immediately, teachers can make a conscious effort to equalize the amount and the type of attention they give girls and boys. Since change is hard to maintain, teachers will need to periodically check the success of their efforts. Again, they might use student data collectors, videotape, or audiotape to see how they are doing.

Changing classroom structures

There are ways of changing classroom structures that will enable girls to close the gap with boys in achievement. If students need to know it, teachers should teach it. Teachers should not assume that students have learned something outside of class. They should provide opportunities to students to equalize their information and experience base.

Girls still tend to have fewer out-of-school science- and mathematics-related experiences than do boys (Kahle, 1990; Kahle & Lakes, 1983). When mathematics teachers assume that students know something as a result of practical experience, scouting, or other out-of-school experiences, girls often suffer. As teachers operate on the assumption that "if it hasn't been taught, they don't know it," classrooms become more equal. One study of geometry classrooms found that when test items covered material that had been taught and learned almost exclusively in the classroom, there was no discernible pattern of gender differences (Senk & Usiskin, 1983). The extent to which measurement instruments include items that have not been explicitly taught, to that extent, gender differences will be found (Fennema, Carpenter, & Lubinski, 1990).

Teachers should structure the class such that homework on new materials, including reading and problem solving, is previewed prior to classroom lecture and discussion. Introducing new material in the classroom by having students read and try problems first and then having classroom lecture, discussion, and questions can improve both girls' performance and participation (Flores, 1990; Jorde & Lea, 1987). In an extensive multistate study, Flores (1990) found that in geometry classes in which students read the book and did problems first, and then had classroom discussion of the topic, girls outperformed boys in two of five geometric measures and scored equally in the other three. In traditional classes, where topics were introduced by lecture first and then students read the book and did the problems, small gender differences favoring boys were found on the measures.

Jorde and Lea (1987) found that using a similar process had an impact in science. If pupils began the activity at once with little introduction from the teacher, everyone had access to the experience. Discussion after everyone had done an activity resulted in greater participation by girls.

My daughter, Kathryn, set up such a situation for herself with the help of a student in a similar mathematics class that met earlier in the day. She would get and do the next day's homework prior to the class because she felt doing it first gave her a better idea of what the teacher was talking about.

Teachers may want to begin by trying this process for a unit or two and looking for effects on girls and boys in terms of achievement and participation.

Teachers should increase the focus on questions, particularly the asking and answering of "why questions." The EUREKA! students described earlier stressed the importance of having teachers who explained more, answered questions, and "made sure you understood." Their biggest complaint about school mathematics was that teachers were less helpful and were not willing to take the time to answer questions. One student spoke for the others when she explained, "School mathematics is sitting in a chair and listening to the teacher, not understanding what they are talking about."

"No time for questions in class" was also a major complaint of college women, but not men, about their mathematics, science, and engineering courses. Reflecting the comments of the EUREKA! students, these young women described the qualities of their favorite professors as: "interested in how you respond," "are around all the time so you can ask them to explain the material and they won't take your head off," and "calm you down and say, 'Don't worry if you don't get it, I can show you how' " (Hewitt & Seymour, 1991).

Teachers can encourage questions, but not by just asking if there are "any questions," which will elicit questions from the more aggressive students. Teachers should ask a mix of individual girls and boys (good, average, and below-average students) by name if they have questions. This individual attention will expand the pool of students who ask questions. Teachers should have students write down their questions at the end of class and answer those questions the following day. Teachers can schedule class time for individual and small-group work; while students are working, teachers can make sure that individual students have their questions answered so that they understand. As programs like EUREKA! have shown, in an atmosphere where all students are expected to ask questions, most students will.

Finding the time is hard. As one girl explained, "Teachers feel a lot of time pressure – kids sense it from teachers. 'We have got to get through this. I can't answer any more questions. We have to get on to the next topic' " (Campbell-Kibler & Campbell, 1991). The pressure of the syllabus is great. However, the National Council of Teachers of Mathematics, the Coalition of Essential Schools, and increasing numbers of educators are recommending in-depth coverage over "more is better." Teachers should not be rewarded for making it through the syllabus at the expense of student understanding. The time spent encouraging and answering questions to develop such understanding will be well spent.

Use hands-on activities within a structure that ensures that everyone is involved in the activities. Increasing the amount of hands-on activities in class may have a specific impact on girls' learning. Hands-on, active involvement in learning and doing mathematics helps students to gain confidence in it (Fennema & Sherman, 1977, 1978). An overuse of lecture/ discussion, seat work, homework, and tests has been associated with young white and minority women dropping out of or not continuing mathematics (Fey, 1979). Baker (1986) found that, in science laboratory classes with a hands-on orientation, girls initiated and received a greater number of academic interactions with teachers than they did in lecture classes.

There are many sources of hands-on activities based on the age of the students and the course of study. For elementary students, equity-based activities include *Family Math* (Stenmark, Thompson, & Cossey, 1986), *The Power Project* (Girls Incorporated, 1990), and increasing numbers of mathematics textbooks. Fewer sources have been available for high school students; this deficiency is being remedied by mathematics-curriculum development projects like those at the Education Development Center, and user networks for materials like the *Geometric Supposer*.

Simply utilizing hands-on activities is not enough. Unless specific structures are established to ensure that all students participate, the use of hands-on activities can become one more example of "Them that has, gets." Cooperative learning techniques that assign the members of small groups different tasks, and then rotate those tasks, is one possible structure for involving girls in the hands-on activities (Slavin, 1991). Cooperative learning principles and strategies also can help to reduce individual competition. Activities that stress competition over cooperation tend to favor boys over girls in the learning of mathematics (Fennema & Peterson, 1987). "Girl friendly" classrooms, that is, classrooms in which there are no gender differences in mathematics, are those with less social comparison and competition, and with an atmosphere that students regard as warmer and more fair (Eccles, 1989).

Teachers should make mathematics a gender-neutral activity. As indicated earlier, viewing mathematics in terms of its gender "appropriateness" can affect achievement and participation. There are a number of things that teachers can do to make mathematics a "gender neutral" activity. The first and perhaps most obvious is not to target a few students, usually male, for particular attention, or not to become preoccupied with those students, again usually male, who make the most noise, but instead to run an orderly class and call on everyone. Teacher interaction with students irrespective of their gender, and the maintenance of order, are characteristics of equitable mathematics classes (Eccles, 1989).

Stressing the importance and value of mathematics to all students is another characteristic of equitable mathematics classes (Eccles, 1989), and it is something that teachers can address. Teachers can make sure that girls participate equally in classroom leadership tasks and, when appropriate, are nominated for mathematics awards or invited to join the mathematics team. A general announcement, "Anyone who wants to sign up for the math team, let me know," is not enough. Specific requests to specific students suggesting that they might be interested increases the pool of girls.

Encouragement is important. Young female engineering students were most apt to list mathematics and science teachers as the people who, after their parents, encouraged them to go into engineering. The type of encouragement that they reported receiving was often something so basic as being told that they were good enough and to "go for it" (Metz & Campbell, 1987).

Classroom visits by people from the work world can give students opportunities to see that persons in mathematics-related fields need not fit the stereotypes of being "nerdy" and not fully human, or of being only white, only male, wearing broken glasses, and having no social life. Working with scientists and engineers can have an impact on girls' career interests, since it may lead them to consider similar careers, or to increase an already existing commitment (Campbell, 1990, 1991).

Teachers should not be sexist in language, in the materials they use, or in their humor. The use of generic terminology has a negative impact, since when most students hear "man" or "he," they do not think of people, they think of men (Miller & Swift, 1977). If the language and the materials in mathematics classes are predominately male, it is hard not to see mathematics as a male domain.

Teachers who want to assure that mathematics is a gender-neutral activity not only should avoid using sexist humor or making sexist comments themselves, but also they should not permit these practices in their classes. Teachers need to examine their own stereotypes about who is good at mathematics. For example, Fennema et al. (1990) found that first-grade teachers tended to rate boys' mathematics success to ability, but girls' success to effort. When they compared their best boy students to their best girl students, these teachers felt that their boys were more competitive, logical, adventurous, independent, volunteered answers more often, and enjoyed mathematics more than did their girls. And of course, teachers should be aware that there is no proven genetic or biological basis for gender differences in mathematics.

Teachers can discuss with their students societal issues related to girls and mathematics; however, they should be careful. One Douglass Science Institute study revealed that sessions for girls that stressed barriers to women in mathematics and science, without an emphasis on ways to overcome those barriers, increased girls' concerns about the difficulty of combining a career in mathematics/science with a family, and caused them to see being a woman in a math/science career as a problem. However, when the emphasis was placed on helping young women find ways to deal with stereotypes and overcome barriers, young women saw being a woman in mathematics/science as a plus (Campbell, 1991).

The larger context

A more general recommendation that should include not just teachers is to broaden the definition of the "girl problem in mathematics": education plays a key role in this problem. Education does not simply reproduce the inequality existing outside itself; it plays an active part in reinforcing the differences and inequalities that already exist. Educational processes contribute to the creation of girls' mathematics learning styles and to their attitudes toward mathematics. Not only does education tend to socialize girls to become pupils with a "feminine style," but it also helps determine the meaning of "feminine cognitive style" (Volman, 1990). Any real change, for other than small numbers of individual girls, must include changes in education in general, as well as in individual classrooms.

The research questions we ask need to change. Research must reflect the broader definition of the problem – the role that education and society play in perpetuating the problem and in any solutions. Less effort should go into studying the extent of gender differences and more should be spent asking, for example, "Why are gender differences in mathematics- and science-related majors and careers so much greater than achievement differences?"

Rather than continuing research emphasis on possible biological causes of gender differences in mathematics, increased emphasis should be placed on looking for educational causes and, more important, on developing solutions. More radically, rather than asking further questions about the existence of a mathematics gene, one might ask, "Why, in spite of all the refutations, does the unsupported concept of a mathematics gene generate such attention?" With the change in questions, there must be a change of language to reflect the gender diversity of girls and of boys, and to acknowledge that when we speak of the ways girls tend to be, or the way boys tend to be we are not speaking of all girls or all boys. Our language needs to reflect our knowledge that in any mathematics area, differences between similar groups of girls and boys are always smaller than differences within groups of girls and within groups of boys. We, girls and boys, women and men are, in mathematics, more similar than we are different.

We need to bring equity issues, research, and results into the mainstream of mathematics education. Stereotyping and discrimination should be addressed directly, as well as indirectly, via the suggestions already made for effecting change in mathematics classrooms. Teachers should consider involving girls in discussions of gender discrimination and barriers in mathematics as well as other areas. These discussions can include stories on how women have successfully dealt with barriers, stereotypes, and discrimination, and can provide opportunities for girls to develop their own strategies. Similarly, boys' perceptions of mathematics as a male domain and their stereotyped behavior need to be addressed, both in class and in separate sessions. If the role education plays in the "girl problem" in mathematics is acknowledged and incorporated in the development of solutions, the next steps will be to find ways to disseminate what we already know works to large numbers of teachers and to help them make changes in their classes.

But we must also continue to work on the development of strategies that will prevent the "girl problem" from happening in the first place.

Notes

1 This exploration of the "girl problem" in mathematics draws on Monique Volman's work on computer education as a gender relationship by deconstructing the dilemma of girl-friendly computer education (Volman, 1990).
2 The results of EUREKA! and the Douglass Science Institute, on which this section is based, are from a series of evaluation reports that are available from Dr. Campbell. The Operation SMART results are based on evaluation reports that are available from Dr. Campbell and from Girls Incorporated.
3 These materials are available from WEEAP Publishing Center, 55 Chapel Street, Newton, MA 02160.
4 Write to EQUALS at Lawrence Hall of Science, University of California, Berkeley, CA 94705.
5 Write to GESA, Graymill Foundation, Rt. 1, Box 45, Earlham, IA 50072.

References

Anton, K., & Humphreys, S. (1982). *Expanding your horizons: 1982 evaluation report.* Berkeley, CA: Math Science Network.

Armstrong J. (1985). A national assessment of participation and achievement of women in mathematics. In S. Chipman, L. Brush, & D. Wilson (Eds.), *Women and mathematics: Balancing the equation* (pp. 59–94). Hillsdale, NJ: Erlbaum.

Baker, D. R. (1986). Sex differences in classroom interactions in secondary science. *Journal of Classroom Interaction, 22*(2), 6–12.

Benbow, C., & Stanley, J. (1983). Differential course-taking hypotheses revisited. *American Educational Research Journal, 20,* 469–473.

Brandon, P. R., Newton, B. J., & Hammond, O. W. (1987). Children's mathematics achievement in Hawaii: Sex differences favoring girls. *American Educational Research Journal, 24*(3), 437–461.

Campbell, P. B. (1990). *EUREKA! participant follow-up analysis.* Groton, MA: Campbell-Kibler.

   (1991). *Douglass Science Institute: Three years of encouraging young women in mathematics, science and engineering.* Groton, MA: Campbell-Kibler.

Campbell-Kibler, K., & Campbell, P. (1991). *You, your daughter and math – You, your parents and math.* Unpublished manuscript.

Dick, T. P., & Rallis, S. (1991). Factors and influences on high school students' career choices. *Journal for Research In Mathematics Education, 22,* 281–292.

Dossey, J. A., Mullis, I. V. S., Lindquist, M. M., & Chambers, D. L. (1988). *The mathematics report card.* (Report no: 17-M-01.) Princeton, NJ: Educational Testing Service.

Eccles, J. (1989). Bringing young women to mathematics and science. In M. Crawford & M. Gentry (Eds.), *Gender and thought: Psychological perspectives* (pp. 36–58). New York: Springer-Verlag.

Educational Testing Service. (1988). *Profiles of SAT and achievement test takers.* Princeton, NJ: Educational Testing Service.

Fennema, E., & Meyer, M. R. (1989). Gender, equity and mathematics. In W. Secada (Ed.), *Equity in education* (pp. 146–157). London: Falmer.

Fennema, E., & Peterson, P. (1987). Effective teaching for girls and boys: The same or different? In D. Berliner & B. Rosenshine (Eds.), *Talks to teachers* (pp. 111–25). New York: Random House.

Fennema, E., Peterson, P. L., Carpenter, T. P., & Lubinski, C. (1990). Teacher attributes and beliefs about girls, boys and mathematics. *Educational Studies in Mathematics, 21,* 55–69.

Fennema, E., & Sherman, J. (1977). Sex-related differences in mathematics achievement, spatial visualization and sociocultural factors. *American Educational Research Journal, 14*(1), 51–71.

(1978). Sex-related differences in mathematics achievement and related factors: A further study. *Journal for Research in Mathematics Education, 9*(3), 189–203.

Fey, J. (1979). Mathematics teaching today: Perspectives from three national surveys. *Mathematics Teacher, 72,* 490–504.

Flores, P. (1990). *How Dick and Jane perform differently in geometry: Test results on reasoning, visualization, transformation, applications and coordinates.* Paper presented to the annual meeting of the American Educational Research Association, Boston, MA.

Frederick, J., & Nicholson, H. N. (1991). *The explorer's pass: A report on case studies of girls and math, science and technology.* Indianapolis, IN: Girls Incorporated.

Fresh Voices. (1991, February 10). *Parade Magazine,* 20.

Friedman, L. (1989). Mathematics and the gender gap: A meta-analysis of recent studies on sex differences in mathematical tasks. *Review of Educational Research, 59*(2), 185–213.

Girls Incorporated. (1990). *The Power Project.* New York: Girls Incorporated.

Goodman, E. (1991, February 3). The 3 percent gender gap. *Boston Globe,* p. 71.

Greenberg-Lakes Analysis Group. (1990). *Shortchanging girls, shortchanging America.* Washington, DC: American Association of University Women.

Gross, S. (1988). *Participation and performance of women and minorities in mathematics* (Vol. 1). Rockville, MD: Montgomery Public Schools, Carver Education Services Center.

Hare, B. (1985). Reexamining the achievement central tendency: Sex differences within race and race differences within sex. In H. P. McAdoo & J. L. McAdoo (Eds.), *Black children: Social, educational and parental environments* (pp. 139–55). Beverly Hills, CA: Sage.

Hewitt, N. M., & Seymour, E. (1991). *Factors contributing to high attrition rates among science and engineering undergraduate majors.* A report to the Alfred P. Sloan Foundation.

Hyde, J., Fennema, E., Ryan, M., Frost, L., & Hopp, C. (1990). Gender comparisons of mathematics attitudes and affect: A meta-analysis. *Psychology of Women Quarterly, 14*(3), 299–324.

Jorde, D., & Lea, A. (1987). The primary science project in Norway. In J. Kahle, J. Daniels, & J. Harding (Eds.), *Proceedings of Fourth GSAT Conference* (pp. 66–172). West Lafayette, IN: Purdue University Press.

Kahle, J. (1990). Why girls don't know. In M. Rowe (Ed.), *What research says to the science teacher: The process of knowing* (Vol. 6, pp. 55–67). Washington, DC: National Science Teachers Association.

Kahle, J., & Lakes, M. (1983). The myth of equality in science classrooms. *Journal of Research in Science Teaching, 20,* 131–40.

Karp, K. (1988). *Elementary school teacher's attitudes toward mathematics: Impact on students' autonomous learning skills.* Paper presented to the annual meeting of the American Educational Research Association Special Interest Group, Research on Women in Education, Hempstead, NY.

Kolstad, A., & Thorne, J. (1989). *Changes in high school course work from 1982 to 1987, evidence from two national surveys.* Paper presented to the annual meeting of the American Educational Research Association, San Francisco.

Levine, G. (1991). *Grade level differences between females and males in mathematics computation and motivation factors.* Paper presented at the annual meeting of the American Educational Research Association, Chicago.

Linn, M. C. (1990). *Gender, mathematics and science: Trends and recommendations.* Paper prepared for the summer institute for the Council of Chief State School Officers, Mystic, CT.

Metz, S. S., & Campbell, P. B. (1987). What does it take to increase the number of women majoring in engineering? In *ASEE Annual Conference Proceedings* (pp. 882–887). Washington, DC: American Society for Engineering Education.

Miller, C., & Swift, K. (1977). *Words and women: New language in new times.* Garden City, NY: Anchor.

National Science Board. (1989). *Science and engineering indicators, 1989.* Washington, DC: National Science Foundation.

National Science Foundation. (1990). *Women and minorities in science and engineering.* Washington, DC: Author.

Senk, S., & Usiskin, Z. (1983). Geometry proof writing: A new view of sex differences in mathematics ability. *American Journal of Education, 91,* 187–201.

Slavin, R. (1991). Synthesis of research on cooperative learning. *Educational Leadership, 48*(5), 71–81.

Stallings, J. (1985). School classroom and home influences on women's decisions to enroll in advanced mathematics courses. In S. Chipman, L. Brush, & D. Wilson (Eds.), *Women and mathematics: Balancing the equation.* Hillsdale, NJ: Erlbaum.

Stenmark, J. K., Thompson, V., & Cossey, R. (1986). *Family math.* Berkeley, CA: Lawrence Hall of Science.

Tartre, L. A., & Fennema, E. (1991). *Mathematics achievement and gender: A longitudinal study of selected cognitive and affective factors (Grades 6 to 12).* Presentation at the annual meeting of the American Educational Research Association, Chicago.

United States Department of Education. (1991). *American 2000: An education strategy.* Washington, DC: Author.

Volman, M. (1990). *Computer education as a gender relationship.* Paper presented at the Fourth International Interdisciplinary Congress on Women, New York.

Whyte, J. (1984). Observing sex stereotypes and interactions in the school lab and workshop. *Educational Review, 36*(1), 75–86.

10   Gender and mathematics from a feminist standpoint

Suzanne K. Damarin

This chapter attempts to begin a radical reorganization of the familiar ways of thinking about and interpreting issues and studies of gender and mathematics, and, by so doing, to shed a different light on this area. My method for achieving this reorganization is one of careful application of recent work by feminist epistemologists and philosophers of science to the specialized study of gender and mathematics within the science of mathematics education. To put it another way, within feminist scholarship there has developed a cogent critique of science; this critique has led to the framing of questions such as "Can there be a feminist science?" and "If so, what would it be like?" Feminist philosophers and scientists have made various responses to these questions. In this chapter, I entertain some of these responses as givens and, using them as guides, critique a particular branch of the science of mathematics education – namely, that branch which deals with gender and mathematics. This critique provides a vehicle both for reexamining findings within and outside that science, and for suggesting questions and methods for a more radically feminist scientific approach to the issues we associate with gender and mathematics: equity, sex differences, affective variables, the treatment of women in the classroom, and so on.

On the assumption that many readers will not be familiar with feminist science and epistemology, I begin by summarizing (and, of necessity, simplifying) some of the issues raised within these lines of thought, and then turn to compelling features of two resultant approaches to the conduct of science: (1) feminist empiricism, and (2) feminist-standpoint epistemology.[1] After a discussion of the intersection of feminist empiricism with existing studies in gender and mathematics, I turn to the question of the potential of feminist-standpoint epistemologies for understanding and further study of questions of gender, mathematics, and mathematics education. This articulation of feminist standpoints with mathematics education is the goal and the heart of the chapter.

A brief overview of feminism and science

The current feminist critique of science had its beginnings in those areas of science that attempt to describe and explain the origin and development of differences between the sexes – notably anthropology, biology, primatology, and psychology. Typical of the early findings of masculine bias in these sciences are the discussion and rejection of biologists' descriptions of prenatal development of the primary female characteristics as the failure of male characteristics to develop; see Fausto-Sterling (1985), and Ruth Hubbard's (1979) paper "Have Only Men Evolved?" in which she criticizes the theorizing of human evolution as selection and adaptation of traits favorable and facilitative to activities (e.g., hunting) that were ascribed solely to males. Almost simultaneously, similar criticisms arose in the social sciences, which focused on methodological biases (Sherif, 1979; Weisstein, 1971). In addition to critiques of particular lines of scientific study, writers such as mathematical biologist and philosopher Evelyn Fox Keller (1985) have focused feminist critiques on the historical foundations of science; Keller's work reveals the prevalence of (male) sexual imagery and misogynist metaphors in the description of and directives for the conduct of scientific inquiry.

These and related critical analyses and rejections of methods and findings of science clearly emerge from and with the more general feminist analysis of all fields of knowledge and academic discipline, and are a part of the interdisciplinary field of Women's Studies. It is important to note, however, that feminism is not the only current source of critiques that have challenged the authority of science during the last three decades. Kuhn's (1970) work on the structure of scientific revolutions, together with other studies of the history of science, challenge the notion of a unified single science progressing toward a fuller description of "reality." Postpositivist philosophers challenge the very notions of objectivity, reality, and truth that are at the root of traditional conceptions of science. The idea that "reality" is socially constructed has become widely discussed and often accepted even by philosophers of mathematics education (see Ernest, 1991). In the context of social constructivism, science (as we know it) is not considered to be "Truth"; rather, it is a socially meaningful and useful way of understanding the world. Feminist critique of science is an important component of the more general movement to redefine science; at the same time, the existence of the more general movement lends a type of legitimacy and support to the continuing development of feminist theories and critiques.[2]

Despite all these critiques and philosophical turns, for many women, and especially for many feminist women who are also scientists or philosophers, science remains a powerful way of knowing, and a system of knowledge and investigation that should not be cast aside. However, many of these women find certain "scientific findings" unacceptable, and are concerned that biased findings will continue to emerge from the conduct of "science as usual." In the attempt to resolve all of these mutually contradictory beliefs, the questions of whether there can be a feminist science, what it would be like, what principles might guide a feminist scientist, and related queries emerge as issues for analysis by feminist philosophers who study the origins and nature of knowledge, and for consideration by scientists themselves.

Several different constellations of answers to these questions have emerged; the two that will be considered in this chapter are labeled "feminist empiricism" and "feminist standpoints" (Harding, 1986, 1991).[3] Other responses, which will not be discussed explicitly here, include ecofeminism (Diamond & Quinby, 1988; Merchant, 1980), feminist postmodernism (Nicholson, 1990; Weedon, 1987), and radical rejection of (certain) scientific study (see, for example, Klein, 1991).

Feminist empiricism

As described by Harding (1986, 1991, 1993), feminist empiricism begins with the position that science and its global methods are basically sound, but that some practices, procedures, assumptions, and, therefore, findings of scientists are biased against women. Because these practices, or abuses, are detrimental both to women and to science, they must be identified and curtailed. The underlying ideas of feminist empiricism are popular with many women scientists, whether they identify personally with feminism or not, and have contributed to the problematizing of certain practices within virtually every field of scientific investigation. Within the fields of educational and psychological research, this position has led to detailed analyses of ways in which sexism influences research (e.g., Eichler, 1988, Squire, 1989). These analyses make evident the potential for gender bias to affect studies at all levels: in the framing of research problems, in the methods of gathering information, in the coding and analysis of data, and in the interpretation of results. For example, Corinne Squire (1989) argues that constructs that have prior associations with the masculine (e.g., aggression) tend to be studied with high-prestige experimental methods, whereas constructs initially thought to be feminine (e.g., anxiety) are studied through the "softer" method of questionnaires. Other familiar examples of bias include the drawing of conclusions about the general population based upon studies of males and the interpretation of research findings in relation to male norms. Feminist empiricists strive to eliminate all such biases from science. Further, feminist empiricists argue that the elimination of these biases allows the emergence within science of new constructs that can provide alternate descriptions and explanations of "the world."

Feminist empiricism, gender, and mathematics. Much of the research that has contributed to the study of gender and mathematics can be seen as belonging to the tradition of feminist empiricism. Early writings on gender and mathematics by Fox, Fennema, and Sherman (1977) begin by addressing problems in the (then-) current scientific literature and outline research issues and agendas for future, less sexist, study. Although a review of the extensive subsequent literature is well beyond the scope of this chapter, it is important to note not only the coherence of most of these studies of mathematics and gender with the ideas of feminist empiricism, but also the substantial and continuing contribution of this work on mathematics to the larger body of feminist empirical work related to the global study of gender.

In particular, educational researchers studying gender and mathematics have framed questions and designed studies in ways that avoid many of the problems identified by Eichler and Squire. In so doing, they have introduced many new constructs that have advanced the study of gender: critical filter (Sells, 1974), mathematics as a male domain (Fennema & Sherman, 1979), math anxiety (Tobias 1978, but see related terms in Fennema 1977). More recently, Fennema and Peterson (1985) have introduced "autonomous learning behaviors," whereas, in related work, Turkle (1984) has identified "hard" and "soft" forms of mastery; and in continuing work on gender and mathematics, Fennema (1990) has refined and elaborated the concept of equity. Other researchers have studied the relations of numerous affective variables with mathematics learning (see, e.g., Reyes, 1984; Reyes & Stanic, 1988) and developed complex psychological models that map the sex differences in the salience and interrelatedness of social and psychological predictors of mathematical achievement (e.g., Eccles et al., 1985; Ethington, 1992). Other researchers have challenged sex bias in mathematics testing with some success, and today, when tests are used appropriately, there are few sex differences in the measured mathematical performance of the sexes (Linn & Hyde, 1989). All in all, in fewer than 20 years, empirical research on gender and mathematics has in many ways reframed the scientific study of women and mathematics; this is a record to be proud of. Despite the major advances of feminist empiricism, however, this work is not complete and must continue, not only in order to produce new scientific knowledge, but also as a practice of the vigilant critique of "malestream" science.[4]

These successes notwithstanding, examination of feminist literature on bias in science raises several challenges for the continuation of feminist empiricist studies in mathematics education. Jaggar (1987), in her discussion of studies of sex differences across many areas, points out that by accepting the tradition of designing studies to test null hypotheses of no sex difference, and accepting findings as significant only when the null is rejected, "a literature of differences" is created. That is to say, the scientific literature positions gender as relevant only when a hypothesis of no sex differences is rejected at the 5% level. By accepting this framing of research methodology, any question of gender is reduced to framing in measurable terms. Considering Jagger's insight in relation to the study of gender and mathematics education, it is not difficult to think of questions whose complexity does not admit this framing. For example, when studies of the effects of the sex of the teacher on student mathematics learning are reduced to null hypotheses, they cast out some important gender-related factors, notably that male first-grade teachers have elected to enter a feminized profession and to adopt many practices that were first constructed by females, whereas female trigonometry teachers have made analogous accommodations to male-dominant classes during their collegiate study of mathematics. Clearly, in relation to teachers and to many other phenomena of gender and mathematics, the issues are far more complex than a "literature of differences" will allow.

The framing of questions as null hypotheses is not the only way in which bias occurs in the statement of problems for empirical investigation. Throughout the current literature on gender and mathematics, there is a persistent finding that girls excel at lower-level computational skills, whereas boys excel at higher-level problem solving. Framing what girls do well as "lower-level computational skills" (rather than as, say, "concern with, attention to, and appreciation of numerical detail," or "competence in handling numerical systems and their operators"), invites the belief that girls' mathematical behavior is fully understood through lower-level studies using lower-level tests. Moreover, this framing is consistent with the general tendency to describe all female behavior as less competent than male behavior; this trend, identified by many feminists, pervades the sex-differences literature and has multiple effects. In particular, attention is drawn to the question of what the boys are doing, and the study of "gender" is shaped (once again) toward the study of what is regarded as the dominant group. The intention of such study is to identify mathematical behaviors of the achieving males that might be taught to females. What is left unstudied, and even unrecognized, is the nature and meaning of the behavior of women in situations laden with mathematical content. The responses of women to such situations are among the interests of feminist-standpoint theorists.

Feminist-standpoint epistemology

Feminist-standpoint epistemology is a complex approach to the definition and description of a self-consciously feminist way of constructing and conducting science. The idea of a "feminist standpoint" was first introduced by Nancy Hartsock (1983) and had its conceptual roots in ideas borrowed from Marxist epistemology, particularly the Marxian notion of the proletarian standpoint. The conceptual bases of feminist-standpoint theory also include psychoanalytic theory as extended and reworked by feminist theorists, as well as the radical feminism of the 1970s. The following are important features and components of feminist standpoints as theorized by various feminists:

1. As theoretical positions for knowledge building, " 'subjugated' standpoints are preferred because they seem to promise more adequate, sustained, objective, transforming accounts of the world" (Haraway, 1991, p. 191). Women can know the world in valid ways that are not available to their oppressors; because they have less to lose in changing the status quo, they are less bound to it and better able to examine it (Harding, 1991, and others).

2. A feminist standpoint is "an achievement, not a birthright" (Haraway, 1991). That is to say, women do not automatically or "naturally" look at or come to know the world in a particular (feminine) way. Moreover, a standpoint is different from a perspective, which can be obtained simply by opening one's eyes (Harding, 1991). A feminist standpoint must be actively pursued and constructed as a way of knowing, which begins with the lives of (particular) women in the world.

3. Multiplicity is implicit in feminist-standpoint theory; there is not one "correct" feminist standpoint, but multiple feminist standpoints. For example, African American feminists (e.g., Collins, 1990) and Third World women (e.g., Spivak, 1990) construct feminist standpoints that are different, but not necessarily disjoint, from standpoints constructed by middle-class white women.

4. The "god-trick of seeing everything from nowhere" (Haraway, 1991, p. 189), which has been the goal of controlled experimentation in science, is simply impossible. Scientists do not stand outside the systems they study; scientists and all knowers understand the world from some position, and that position is material to the "truth" constructed.

5. Knowledge is always situated by the standpoint of the knower; from a feminist standpoint, knowledge begins with women's lives. The feminist standpoint is an imperative for women to construct knowledge beginning with their own lives and experiences.

6. Knowledge is always political and never value-free.

7. The idea that all aspects of the world or reality are socially constructed is rejected. It has been strategic for women to work from a social constructivist point of view in order to counter prior constructions such as "essential feminine virtue" and "biology is destiny." However, the view that everything is socially constructed implies that our bodies are simply blank slates on which society

writes its messages. This view is rejected by standpoint theorists because it leaves women (and men) without agency. Unless women have agency, they cannot construct and act upon a standpoint.

8. The feminist standpoint entails a "radical objectivity" (Haraway's term) or "strong objectivity" (Harding's term) in which *there are real objects for study and understanding that exist outside the knower*. Knowledge is achieved through the reciprocal relationship between the knower and the object of knowledge; the knower and the objects of study lie in the same "critical plane" (Harding, 1986). However, the objects of knowledge are not static and passive, but are actors; knowledge is constructed dialectically through interactions between object and knower (Haraway, 1991).

9. The nature/nurture dichotomy is rejected, as are other dualisms such as mind/body. Moreover, the traditional view of nature as fixed and unchanging is rejected. "The world" and "nature" are conceived not as givens, but as actors that operate over time and space.

Summarizing these points, feminist-standpoint theory is not a kind of relativism, but rather acknowledges that "the world" exists and is knowable through the study of our relations with it. Interrogating our own position in relation to the objects of study is a critical part of that study. Unless we begin with that interrogation, we cannot understand the value-laden aspects of our own perspectives. Because women (and other "marked" groups) bring to their study less investment in continuing current theories, conceptions, and practices, their relations to the objects of study are less bound to the acceptance of present understandings as "true" or "natural." Indeed, the idea of the "natural" is rejected. Thus, the feminist-standpoint idea allows for a multiplicity of truths, none of them complete, and finds most valuable those investigations that begin with the lives of women. For research on mathematics education, this implies a radical shift in underlying assumptions and standards; in particular, it requires a willingness to abandon beliefs about the nature of mathematics and how it must be taught and learned in order to be open to the "nature" of mathematics as it is experienced.

With respect to mathematics education, there are clearly many standpoints from which particular women view the issues facing them as they do, or do not do, mathematics. Some of the disparity of these views is discussed by Longino and Hammonds (1991) as they contrapose the views of women within the professional domains of mathematics, science, and engineering to the views of academic feminists who address these questions from outside mathematically oriented professions. The position of some women within mathematics denies any validity to the claims of feminist theorists. Hammonds (Longino & Hammonds, 1991) and others see mathematics as a practice and profession, not as a political force. On the other hand, feminist political scientists (Tobias, 1978) and historians (Cohen, 1982) join many educators concerned with equity in the perception that mathematical knowledge is deeply political (Frankenstein, 1987; Mellin-Olsen, 1987). As will be evident in the next section, there are also many other domains of variation in perspective.

Interrogating the author's position. In keeping with the intention to explore issues in the study of mathematics and gender from a feminist standpoint, it is essential to examine (publicly) my own position as I engage in this study. This position has undoubtedly been formed by many factors that mitigate both for and against the acceptance of scientific findings as the full "truth." These factors include: the anti-Darwinian messages of my parsonage childhood; my study of mathematics through doctoral course work, my consequent knowledge of mathematics, and various concomitant experiences at the social nexus of being female and doing mathematics in the early 1960s; my internalization of and dedication to the scientific view of the learning of mathematics as I worked at the Educational Testing Service (ETS), my training in and use of quasi-experimental methods in the study of mathematics education, and my experiences as a woman teaching mathematics to students who struggled with it at various levels and with various degrees of success. In my view, these experiences, while uniquely my own, are probably illustrative of the diversity of background influences that women bring to any field, and from which they construct their positionalities within that field.

With respect to the study of gender and mathematics, I have been an interested and appreciative student for about 15 years. Although I have not conducted an experimental study of psychological or instructional variables in relation to gender and mathematics, I have adapted my own teaching in response to such studies and have taught (and even "preached") their findings to students. From the beginning of my engagement with this work, my bias has been to do my own gender-related work at the level of curriculum development. Initially, I believed that "competence was the cure for anxiety," and turned my own efforts toward the development of texts that would, at every stage, honor the current levels of student competence over the traditional sequence of mathematics instruction (Damarin, 1983; Damarin & Leitzel, 1984). Although my theories and beliefs in this regard have grown in complexity over the past ten years, I retain the biases according to which instructional research and practice related to the improvement of the mathematical conditions of women must at every level honor the individual gendered student, believing that some of the answers to "the problem of women and mathematics" will be found at the level of the global structure of curriculum.

Through the study of feminist theory, postmodern philosophy, and particularly postmodern feminism, I have come to accept and even to enjoy the idea that all knowledge building is deeply ironic. No longer do I see all scientific understanding as a linear progression of findings, with each new result either building upon or displacing its predecessors. Instead, I have come to the postmodern view that "powerful statements of truth contain the seeds of their own untruth." What this means to me in the context at hand is that because researchers have constructed a powerful scientific discourse of mathematics and gender, we can seek in it the seeds of other ways of understanding.

Discourses of distance and feminist standpoints

To arrive at a feminist standpoint with respect to mathematics and mathematics education, the primary question to be addressed is "How do women experience mathematics?" A major part of this experience for many women is indirect; that is, the experience of mathematics does not take place within a community of creators or users of advanced mathematics, but rather in the general society. This experience is primarily discursive, not active, which is to say that the relation of most women to mathematics is constructed by the receipt of messages about mathematics. Thus, it is the content of these messages that creates the experience.

To begin, women (including young girls) experience mathematics as an area of competing discourses. Simultaneously told that it is important to learn mathematics, and that it is not important (for girls and women) to learn mathematics, women are subject to a multitude of other mixed messages about the importance of mathematics to their lives. In the following paragraphs I will examine some of these messages through the lenses of various feminist works and writings.

The maleness of mathematics. The effects of the idea that "math is a male domain" on the mathematical achievement of girls and women have been investigated empirically for more than 15 years. By and large, empirical study has posited that the equation of mathematics with maleness is an individual attitude measured in individual females; as such, it is subject to individual remediation through instruction in the affective domain. However, the "maleness of mathematics" is a message that permeates our society; regardless of how mathematically competent a woman becomes, she can never escape discursive practices that reify the idea that mathematics is, indeed, a male domain.[5] Thus, for a woman to continue to learn and to do mathematics, she must continually reject the messages that connote her "natural" position.

The message that math is a male domain links the present to a past in which a double argument insured the maleness of mathematics: the primary argument asserted that women *could not* do mathematics, whereas the back-up argument asserted that they *should not*. Both arguments linked mathematical and reproductive capacities in a relation of logical exclusion. This historical construction of mathematics lies outside the domain of women in the social and discursive construction of women's roles. Sociological explanations for women's separation from the study of mathematics speak to a need for adolescent women to choose among the demands of preparing for roles of wife, mother, and career (Maines, in Fennema, 1985). Moreover, in many ways the curricular and extracurricular teachings of schools speak to this bifurcation. Sex education programs, for example, although they do not speak directly to mathematics, do speak to the sex-bound differences in the sequelae and obligations of unplanned (and un-aborted) pregnancies. For young men, these are behaviors of financial responsibility associated with study for future employment, whereas for young women they entail an interruption (and possible termination) of schooling and longer-term study. Thus, it is not only the messages of career-guidance counselors and other "ill-informed" adults that suggest to women a trade-off between reproductive roles and mathematical/scientific schooling; it is the total curriculum of the schools in which they study.

The "othering" of women from mathematics extends beyond school and home. As Nelkin (1987) points out, the popular press describes scientists generally as male and remote from the realities of everyday life; women scientists, by contrast, are portrayed as homebodies who bake brownies and excel at all: career, wife, and mother. Through these messages, the press creates for women a confusing picture. Science and mathematics demand a remoteness from the mundane; but, even if a woman becomes a Nobel laureate, what will be noteworthy about her is her kitchen skills.

What counts as mathematics and mathematical ability seems to change over time. As historian Patricia Cohen (1982) documents, in the 19th century, calculation and computation were thought to be mathematics and outside the domain of acceptable female activity. With the industrial revolution, there arose a need for cheap labor to keep books and perform routine calculations; suddenly, arithmetical competence was no longer beyond the abilities of women, nor dangerous for them! Today, this same competence is associated with females and is a "lower-level skill." Cohen also cites other areas, such as that of spatial abilities, in which the recognition of women's competence has shifted in a negative direction as the abilities themselves have become more prestigious–that is, more mathematical.

Thus, within these contexts of history, society, the press, and schools, the message is alive and prevalent that mathematics is a male domain. Beyond the examples already given, even the continued study of women and mathematics (and the publicity that surrounds it) reminds women that their mathematical ability is a question worthy of scientific study. In this context, feminist researchers and theorists have responded with a variety of questions ranging from "Well, is mathematics essentially male?" to "How is the maleness of mathematics socially constructed and reproduced in schools?" I now consider some of these questions, beginning with the first.

The female mind-body and mathematics. The importance of combined physical and mental activity to the construction of mathematical knowledge is a theme that runs throughout the pedagogical and philosophical literatures of mathematics. Generally speaking, however, the question of what constitutes meaningful experience has not been addressed, at least not from a sex/gender point of view. The many uses of building blocks as manipulative materials might have differential meanings in terms of the sex/gender-linked differences in a male's or female's prior experience with building materials (Damarin, 1990). Similarly, the relations of meaning making in block building itself to prior experiences of sexuality and gender construction are basically unexamined.

In the context of the importance that mathematics educators attach to physical experience in relation to mathematics learning, feminist researchers might query sex-specific experience of the body in relation to the construction of mathematics. In her work, feminist philosopher Evelyn Fox Keller (1985) uncovers metaphorical relations between the biology and practices of male sexuality and descriptions of the purposes and procedures of science, including the mathematical sciences. Similarly, feminist philosopher-psychoanalyst Luce Irigaray (1987) queries the nature of mathematics itself in relation to the sexed bodies of women:

The mathematical sciences, in the theory of wholes, concern themselves with closed and open spaces, with the infinitely big and the infinitely small. They concern themselves very little with questions of the partially open, with wholes that are not clearly delineated, with any analysis of the problem of borders, of the passage between, of fluctuations occurring between the thresholds of specific wholes. (pp. 76–77)

In this and other examples, Irigaray argues that logic, mathematics, and science encode principles that reflect and honor male, but not female, biological and psychological development.

Working from Irigaray's perspective, we can return to the findings of the empirical study of women and mathematics with new questions. We might ask again, for example, why adolescence marks the increased separation of women from mathematics. In the context provided by Irigaray we can see an opposition between the linear time of mathematics problems of related rates, distance formulas, and linear acceleration versus the dominant experiential cyclical time of the menstrual body. Is it obvious to the female mind-body that intervals have endpoints, that parabolas neatly divide the plane, and, indeed, that the linear mathematics of schooling describes the world of experience in intuitively obvious ways?

A multiplicity of questions. If Irigaray's work leads us to question the assumptions concerning what is "obvious" that underlie the mathematics curriculum, other social scientists suggest different ways in which we might examine curriculum and instruction from a feminist standpoint. Based upon their study of "Women's Ways of Knowing," Mary Belenky and colleagues (1986) speak to women's relations to abstract knowledge:

Most of these women were not opposed to abstraction as such. They found concepts useful in making sense of their experiences, but they balked when the abstractions preceded the experiences or pushed them out entirely. Even the women who were extraordinarily adept at abstract reasoning preferred to start from personal experience. (pp. 201–202)

These findings suggest that more attention in the teaching of mathematics be given both to the provision of opportunities to accumulate observations and to the acknowledgment of experiences with diverse ideas before these ideas are treated as obvious and formalized in definitions. How this might be achieved within the current structures of schooling and curriculum is unclear.

It is well known that women often lack confidence in their mathematical knowledge and abilities. But how confident can women be if they lack an intuitive grounding for mathematical ideas, and if the value of their knowledge is continually undermined? Several researchers (Walkerdine, 1989; Willis, 1992) have uncovered evidence indicating that teachers attribute female success in mathematics to hard work, whereas they attribute comparable male success to ability. At the same time, there is an apparent arbitrariness to the sequence of mathematics instruction; the knowledge obtained as "prerequisite" for a course or topic is often not applicable in the subsequent context (Damarin, 1988) and often leaves students confused about their own mathematical power (Willis, 1992). We might ask, then, what can be the source or grounding of women's confidence in their own mathematical ability? In the absence of societal messages affirming that mathematics is a female domain, of personal intuitions and the opportunity to build on them, of teacher recognition for ability as evidenced in accomplishment, and of the opportunity to apply knowledge in subsequent courses, on what base might a woman build a sense of confidence in herself as a mathematician? Again, we have an enigma and a challenge for mathematics education.

Conclusion

The purposes of feminist research and theory are to understand better the condition of women and to decrease the power of patriarchy over the lives of women (and other marginalized groups). The status of mathematical and scientific knowledge within a society that values technological progress and the mastery of nature, together with the ascription of mathematical ability to men (as opposed to women), have meant that the "problem of women and mathematics" is an important aspect of feminist work. In the current "high tech" era, which is marked by continually emerging technologies, rapid scientific development, and the ascendancy of information as "the new capital," the ability to understand mathematics, and even to mathematize, is an important aspect of social power.

Within the broad field of feminist research, there are several lines of scholarly endeavor, each with its own theoretical underpinnings and methodologies. To date, the vast majority of studies and understandings regarding women and mathematics are based in one of these, namely, feminist empiricism, which has its roots at the intersection of the broader traditions of liberal feminism and mainstream social science. Other branches and literatures of feminism offer different ways of conceptualizing the experiences and problems of women in relation to mathematics; that is, they offer different standpoints from which to view these problems and, thus, different ideas of the nature of the problems. In this chapter, I have offered a sampling of some of these feminisms and associated views; I have offered these not as new or replacement "truth" but, rather, as ideas and questions that might enrich the study of gender and mathematics and, possibly, make it more responsive to the needs of women.

It is against all the messages and realities already described that individual women and their teachers must struggle if they are to learn and teach mathematics. Because these messages count group membership (i.e., belonging to the female sex) as definitive of individual mathematical worth, it is appropriate that this struggle be a group effort. Just as women as a group have claimed the right to vote and the right to control their own money, they might claim the rights both to learn mathematics and to have the mathematic knowledge they have constructed recognized as valuable, and acknowledged in curriculum and instruction.

Notes

1 For a brief introduction to feminist epistemologies, see Jaggar (1983); for more recent discussions, see the collection of essays in Alcoff and Potter (1993).
2 It might be noted that the general philosophical critique of science is mirrored in several significant turns in the study of mathematics education – notably, the rise of theories of situated cognition, the adoption of radical constructivist theories of learning, the development and use of "authentic assessment" techniques, and the adoption of qualitative research methodologies.
3 Except where otherwise noted, the discussions of feminist empiricism and the feminist standpoint in the remainder of this paper are derived from Haraway (1991), Harding (1986, 1987, 1991, 1993), and the papers in two special issues of *Hypatia: A Journal of Feminist Philosophy*, 2(3) (Fall 1987), and 3(1) (Spring 1988) on feminism and science; the latter papers are reprinted in Tuana (1990).
4 See, for example, the papers by Feingold (1992a,b) and Noddings (1992). Here, Feingold uses scientific data to "prove" that among females there is less variation

in mathematical (and other) abilities than among males; Noddings argues that his work fails to consider sociocultural factors in women's development of (their) mathematical ability; Feingold responds by arguing that his work is scientific, whereas Noddings's paper is political. Thus, in 1992, we see the emergence of another classic case of the scientific struggle; here, as often, the feminist interpretations of findings are dismissed as "political," and data are argued to speak for themselves.

5 The reader who doubts this statement is invited to read the messages on WISENET, a computer network on which women in science discuss issues they face in their work worlds. Problems of acceptance and employment are recurrent topics of discussion.

References

Alcoff, L., & Potter, E. (Eds.). (1993). *Feminist epistemologies.* New York: Routledge.

Belenky, M. F., Clinchy, B. M., Goldberger, N. R., & Tarule, J. M. (1985). *Women's ways of knowing: The development of self, voice, and mind.* New York: Basic.

Cohen, P. C. (1982). *A calculating people.* University of Chicago Press.

Collins, P. H. (1990). *Black feminist thought.* Boston: Unwin Hyman.

Damarin, S. K. (1983). Teaching algebra to adult students. Columbus, OH: Mathematics Department, Ohio State University, mimeo.

(1988). *The "women and math problem" in a computer age: Working toward feminist solutions.* Working Paper No. 33, Center for the Study of Women and Society. Eugene: University of Oregon.

(1990, April). *Gender and the learning of fractions.* Paper presented to the American Educational Research Association, Boston.

Damarin, S. K., & Leitzel, J. R. (1984). *Algebra: A book for adults.* New York: Wiley. (Reissued as *Algebra: An approach for success.* Minneapolis: Burgess, 1988.)

Diamond, I., & Quinby, L. (1988). American feminism and the language of control. In I. Diamond & L. Quinby (Eds.), *Feminism and Foucault: Reflections on resistance* (pp. 193–206). Boston: Northeastern University Press.

Eccles, J., Adler, T. F., Futterman, R., Goff, S. B., Kaczala, C. M., Meece, J. L., & Midgley, C. (1985). Self-perception, task perceptions, socializing influences, and the decision to enroll in mathematics. In S. F. Chipman, L. R. Brush, & D. M. Wilson (Eds.), *Women and mathematics: Balancing the equation* (pp. 95–121). Hillsdale, NJ: Erlbaum.

Eichler, M. (1988). *Nonsexist research methods.* Boston: Unwin Hyman.

Ernest, P. (1991). *The philosophy of mathematics education.* London: Falmer.

Ethington, C. A. (1992). Gender differences in a psychological model of mathematics achievement. *Journal for Research in Mathematics Education, 23*(2), 166–181.

Fausto-Sterling, A. (1985). *Myths of gender: Biological theories about women and men.* New York: Basic.

Feingold, A. (1992a). Sex differences in variability in intellectual abilities: A new look at an old controversy. *Review of Educational Research, 62*(1), 61–84.

(1992b). The greater male variability controversy: Science versus politics. *Review of Educational Research, 62*(1), 89–90.

Fennema, E. (1977). Influences of selected cognitive, affective, and educational variables on sex-related differences in mathematics learning and studying. In L. H. Fox, E. Fennema, & J. Sherman (Eds.), *Women and mathematics: Research perspectives for change* (pp. 79–135). NIE Papers in Education and Work, No. 8. Washington, DC: United States Department of Health, Education, and Welfare.

(1990). Justice, equity, and mathematics education. In E. Fennema & G. C. Leder (Eds.), *Mathematics and gender* (pp. 188–199). New York: Teachers College Press.

Fennema, E. (Ed.). (1985). Explaining sex-related differences in mathematics: Theoretical models. *Educational Studies in Mathematics, 16,* 303–320.

Fennema, E., & Peterson, P. L. (1985). Autonomous learning behavior: A possible explanation of gender-related differences in classroom interactions. In L. C. Wilkerson & C. B. Marrett (Eds.), *Gender-related differences in classroom interaction* (pp. 17–35). New York: Academic.

Fennema, E., & Sherman, J. C. (1979). Sex-related differences in mathematics achievement, spatial-visualization, and affective factors. *American Educational Research Journal, 14,* 51–71.

Fox, L. H., Fennema, E., & Sherman, J. (Eds.). (1977). *Women and mathematics: Research perspectives for change.* NIE Papers in Education and Work, No. 8. Washington, DC: United States Department of Health, Education, and Welfare.

Frankenstein, M. (1987). Critical mathematics education: An application of Paolo Freire's epistemology. In I. Shor (Ed.), *Freire in the classroom* (pp. 180–210). Portsmouth, NH: Heinemann.

Haraway, D. (1991). *Simians, cyborgs, and women: The reinvention of nature.* New York: Routledge.

Harding, S. (1986). *The science question in feminism.* Ithaca, NY: Cornell University Press.

(1987). *Feminism and methodology.* Bloomington: Indiana University Press.

(1991). *Whose science? Whose knowledge?* Ithaca, NY: Cornell University Press.

(1993). Rethinking standpoint epistemology: What is "strong objectivity?" In L. Alcoff & E. Potter (Eds.), *Feminist epistemologies* (pp. 40–82). New York: Routledge.

Hartsock, N. (1983). The feminist standpoint: Developing the ground for a specifically feminist historical materialism. In S. Harding & M. Hintikka (Eds.), *Discovering reality: Feminist perspectives on epistemology, metaphysics, methodology, and philosophy of science* (pp. 283–310). Dordrecht, Holland: Reidel.

Hubbard, R. (1979). Have only men evolved? In R. Hubbard, M. S. Henifin, & B. Fried (Eds.), *Women look at biology looking at women* (pp. 7–36). Cambridge, MA: Schenkman.

Irigaray, L. (1987). Is the subject of science sexed? *Hypatia: A Journal of Feminist Philosophy, 2,* 65–88.

Jaggar, A. M. (1983). *Feminist politics and human nature.* Totowa, NJ: Rowman & Allanheld.

(1987). Sex inequality and bias in sex differences research. *Canadian Journal of Philosophy* (supplementary volume) *13,* 24–40.

Keller, E. F. (1985). *Reflections on gender and science.* New Haven, CT: Yale University Press.

Klein, R. D. (1991). Passion and politics in Women's Studies in the nineties. *Women's Studies International Forum, 14*(3), 125–134.

Kuhn, T. S. (1970). *The structure of scientific revolutions* (2d ed.). University of Chicago Press.

Linn, M. C., & Hyde, J. S. (1989). Gender, mathematics, and science. *Educational Researcher, 18,* 22–27.

Longino, H. E., & Hammonds, E. (1990). Conflicts and tensions in the feminist study of gender and science. In M. Hirsch & E. F. Keller (Eds.), *Conflicts in feminism* (pp. 164–183). New York: Routledge.

Mellin-Olsen, S. (1987). *The politics of mathematics education.* Dordrecht, Holland: Reidel.

Merchant, C. (1980). *The death of nature: Women, ecology and the scientific revolution.* San Francisco: Harper & Row.

Nelkin, D. (1987). *Selling science.* San Francisco: Freeman.

Nicholson, L. (Ed.). (1990). *Feminism/postmodernism.* New York: Routledge.

Noddings, N. (1992). Variability: A pernicious hypothesis. *Review of Educational Research, 62*(1), 85–88.

Reyes, L. H. (1984). Affective variables and mathematics education. *Elementary School Journal, 18*(2), 207–218.

Reyes, L. H., & Stanic, G. M. A. (1988). Race, sex, socieoeconomic status and mathematics. *Journal for Research on Mathematics Education, 9*(1), 26–43.

Sells, L. W. (1974/1992). Mathematics: A critical filter. In M. Wilson (Ed.), *Options for girls. A door to the future: An anthology on science and math education* (pp. 79–82). Austin, TX: Foundation for Women's Resources.

Sherif, C. W. (1979). Bias in psychology. In J. A. Sherman & E. T. Beck (Eds.), *The prism of sex: Essays in the sociology of knowledge* (pp. 93–133). Madison: University of Wisconsin Press.

Spivak, G. C. (1990). *The post-colonial critic: Interviews, strategies, dialogues.* New York: Routledge.

Squire, C. (1989) *Significant differences: Feminism in psychology.* New York: Routledge.

Tobias, S. (1978). *Overcoming math anxiety.* Boston: Houghton Mifflin.

Tuana, N. (Ed.). (1989). *Feminism and science.* Bloomington: Indiana University Press.

Turkle, S. (1984). *The second self: Computers and the human spirit.* New York: Simon & Schuster.

Walkerdine, V. (1989). *Counting girls out.* London: Virago.

Weedon, C. (1987). *Feminist practice and poststructuralist theory.* London: Blackwell.

Weisstein, N. (1971). Psychology constructs the female, or the fantasy life of the male psychologist. In M. H. Garskoff (Ed.), *Roles women play.* Belmont, CA: Brooks/Cole.

Willis, S. (1992). The power of mathematics: For whom? In J. Kenway & S. Willis (Eds.), *Hearts and minds: Self-esteem and the schooling of girls* (pp. 191–212). London: Falmer.

11 Attitudes, persistence, and mathematics achievement: Qualifying race and sex differences

George M. A. Stanic and Laurie E. Hart

Knowledge of mathematics is essential for all members of society. In order to participate fully in democratic processes and to be unrestricted in career choice and advancement, individuals must be able to understand and apply mathematical ideas. Unfortunately, in the United States, certain groups are underrepresented in mathematics courses and do not achieve up to their potential. African American students and female students are prominent among these groups.

The main points we wish to make in this chapter have to do with the role of persistence in learning mathematics and with the way in which an individual student's attitudes about mathematics interact with each other. We will use the results of a case study of a seventh-grade mathematics classroom to make our argument. Underlying our conclusions about persistence and attitudes is an important assumption: Findings of race differences and sex differences in mathematics should not be overgeneralized. At the very least, it is crucial to look at the interaction of the categories of race and gender. Ultimately, the goal of research on equity in mathematics education should be to look beyond race, sex, and other convenient but problematic demographic categories toward the identification of what we refer to as *archetypes* of mathematics students. An archetype consists of a complex matrix of achievement, attitudes, and achievement-related behaviors within a particular context. Although a certain archetype may predominate for a race-sex group in a given context, we believe groups are characterized by multiple archetypes and that archetypes cut across groups. Archetypes are more appropriate descriptors than demographic characteristics because they explain rather than simply label differences. We will not describe or provide a comprehensive list of archetypes in this chapter; however, the students we describe in presenting the context of the classroom we studied, and in reaching our conclusions about persistence and attitudes, may provide the basis for the identification of archetypes in future work.

258

Conclusions from previous research

In our case study, we focused on mathematics achievement; the attitudes of confidence, usefulness, and enjoyment; and the achievement-related behavior of persistence. A number of reviews discuss previous research in these areas (e.g., Leder, 1992; Reyes & Stanic, 1988; Secada, 1992). These reviews illustrate almost exclusive attention to general sex and race differences, with little focus on differences among race-sex groups.

Gender differences in mathematics achievement in favor of males and race differences in favor of whites have been documented. The achievement difference favoring males over females is smaller, appears later, and is evident on a more limited range of measures than the difference favoring whites over African Americans. The sex difference in achievement appears to be related to a sex difference favoring males in terms of confidence in doing mathematics and, to a lesser extent, in the perception of the perceived usefulness of mathematics; no clear race difference has been convincingly documented for either of these attitudes. Neither the attitude of enjoyment nor the achievement-related behavior of persistence has been studied extensively by mathematics educators.

The seventh-grade mathematics class we studied

We spent 45 days studying a seventh-grade mathematics class. The class was part of a coeducational middle school with a student population that included African American students and white students from a variety of socioeconomic backgrounds. The class was taught by an African American male, whom we shall call Mr. Martin. There were 17 students in the class, including 5 African American females, 3 African American males, 5 white females, and 4 white males. We took field notes and made audio recordings of the 45 class sessions, systematically coded teacher–student interactions, gathered artifacts during the classroom observation, studied permanent school records, administered student attitude questionnaires (Fennema & Sherman, 1976), and conducted interviews with the teacher and with each student. Both of us observed almost all of the class sessions; we were not regular participants in daily activities but did on occasion interact with Mr. Martin and his students.

Mr. Martin's teaching style and some of its consequences
for students

Mr. Martin was a sensitive, caring teacher who wanted all of his students to do well and who believed that they all could do well. His general teaching style was to assign pages of work at the beginning of the period and help individual students as needed. Indeed, Mr. Martin interacted a great deal with the students in his class. There was a mean of more than four and one-half interactions per student per day; most of the interactions were academic (2.04 per student per day), followed by procedural (1.74), behavioral (0.43), and social (0.36).

Mr. Martin rarely conducted lessons with the whole class for the purpose of explaining content. Occasionally, if many people needed help, he would interrupt the individual seat work in progress in order to explain an idea to the whole class. Mr. Martin explained in the interviews that he believed this teaching style was appropriate for this class of students and for the content they covered. The students were labeled "high-average" (the second-highest ability group) by the school, and the content of the course was essentially a review of arithmetic.

As we observed Mr. Martin's classroom and conducted interviews with the students, we found that a number of the students expressed concern about the clarity of Mr. Martin's teaching. Mr. Martin was not as clear as he might have been in a number of areas. The main area they cited was in giving directions about classwork and homework; he was also inconsistent in how he followed up on assignments. For example, based on the questions students asked as they left class each day, we inferred that not only were they often confused about whether homework was assigned, but they were also confused about the specific content of assignments. There were also times when Mr. Martin assigned a particular page for the students to complete in class without clarifying exactly which exercises he wanted them to do; the students knew that only some of the exercises were to be completed, but were not certain which exercises had to be done. And there were times when, after Mr. Martin assigned particular exercises from a given page, he later changed the assignment, or at least responded differently to different students' questions about what had to be done. In one specific instance, after Mr. Martin had assigned the even exercises on a page, Bob, a high-achieving white male student who was not sure about the assignment, asked Mr. Martin what had to be done. Mr. Martin answered, "Do them all if you want to." In one of our interviews with Mr. Martin, he stated that he intended to be less than specific about assignments because he wanted his students to develop more responsibility and independence. He wanted students to do their assignments out of a desire to gain more knowledge of mathematics, not simply because they were told to do the work. He felt that comments like his response to Bob would foster such responsibility and independence.

Another of Mr. Martin's classroom behaviors that appeared problematic, but for which he had specific reasons, was his approach toward working with Henry, an African American male. In a class where the teacher interacted regularly with students, Henry received relatively little attention and what he did receive was predominantly negative in tone. The smiles and laughter that characterized many of Mr. Martin's interactions with students were rare in his interactions with Henry. Mr. Martin most often talked to Henry about completing assignments and threatened to call Henry's parents about his lack of effort. In interviews, Mr. Martin explained to us that he interacted as he did with Henry because he was concerned that Henry not fall victim to the "athletic syndrome." Mr. Martin's experience as a black student-athlete in college made him more sensitive to the academic risks involved in an interest in athletics. He was afraid that Henry's early success as an athlete might make him neglect academics. Mr. Martin was convinced that African American athletes were capable of performing well in the classroom but that, too often, they neglected academics because they expected to become professional athletes. He expressed some bitterness about the treatment he and other African American athletes received in college and wanted to be sure that the students he worked with recognized the importance of academic success for their futures. Mr. Martin clearly stated that some of his interactions with Henry were a result of his concern that Henry not fall victim to the athletic syndrome.

Ironically, Mr. Martin's intended lack of clarity in giving assignments, combined with his concern about the athletic syndrome, tended to make life in his classroom difficult for Henry. Henry was not able to deal well with Mr. Martin's lack of clarity. Most students in the class kept asking questions about assignments until they got an answer acceptable to them. In interviews, they told us about coming in after class to ask Mr. Martin again about the homework assignment, or calling each other in the evening for clarification. Henry did not demonstrate any of these compensating behaviors for Mr. Martin's lack of clarity and ended up in a cycle of not knowing assignments, not completing assignments, and being reprimanded by Mr. Martin.

We do not want to overstate the importance of Mr. Martin's intentions in working with his students, because he did not have an intentional way of interacting with all of them. A good example is Cathy, a white female. Cathy received almost no attention from Mr. Martin, in part because she rarely sought attention from him or asked him questions. For most of each class period, she worked independently on mathematics assignments. After completing an assignment, Cathy would quietly get out a library book and begin to read. When Cathy did interact during the class period, it was usually with Wendy, the white female student who sat next to her. There were times when Wendy, who sought only a little more attention from Mr. Martin than did Cathy, would go to Mr. Martin's desk to get help, return to her desk, and answer a question from Cathy about the same topic. During the times when Mr. Martin walked around the room helping students with their seat work, both Cathy and Wendy, on those rare occasions when they asked for help, were content to sit quietly with their hands in the air for extended periods of time, while Mr. Martin helped those students who demanded his attention by calling out to him.

In an interview with Cathy, we found that she was not at all concerned about the relative lack of attention she received from Mr. Martin. She was, in fact, very positive about his teaching style because she liked the fact that she did not have to sit through teacher explanations she felt she did not need; Cathy preferred to go ahead and work on her own and was delighted to read the library book she had brought with her to class when she finished an assignment. In one of our interviews with Mr. Martin, however, he worried that Cathy was one of the students who might need more structure than he was providing, and he expressed some concern about his lack of interactions with her. Mr. Martin gave no indication that any of his interactions with Cathy were intended to achieve a specific goal. He clearly saw her as being a very capable mathematics student, saying she was one of two students from his class who may have been able to succeed in the highest mathematics ability group. But he said nothing about the need to spark a competitive urge in her or to keep her from doubting herself, which were the concerns he expressed about Tim, a white male and clearly the most dominant person in Mr. Martin's class.

Tim received a great deal of positive attention from Mr. Martin and was often at the center of classroom interaction. When the class went over assignments, Tim consistently was called on for answers and called out his evaluations of answers given by other students. Although the other students expressed annoyance with Tim's behavior, Mr. Martin never reprimanded Tim for interrupting other students with his evaluative comments. Mr. Martin did on occasion reprimand Tim for goofing off with Bob, the white male student with whom Tim often interacted, or for packing up too early near the end of the period; however, the reprimand was always given with a smile or a laugh. In fact, just the mention of Tim's name in class and during interviews made Mr. Martin laugh affectionately. Near the end of our last interview, he even referred to the class as "Tim's class." When the class had difficulty with a mathematics problem and Mr. Martin wanted a member of the class to explain how to do it, he most often looked to Tim for an explanation. In many ways, Tim was a living "teacher's guide" for Mr. Martin.

Our interviews with Mr. Martin indicated that he saw much of himself in Tim and that he intended to interact with Tim in the way that we observed. Mr. Martin did not seem to consider or be concerned about the consequences for the rest of the students of Tim's role in the classroom. When we explicitly asked if Tim's actions might have a negative effect on what the other students learned, Mr. Martin could not identify any such effect. He clearly saw Tim as the best mathematics student in the class, even in the face of his own evidence that Bob's class average (including tests and homework assignments) was higher than that of Tim. He explained Bob's performance as a function of his relationship with Tim, not in the sense that Bob "copied" from Tim, but in the sense that Bob benefited simply by sitting next to Tim and being motivated by him. Mr. Martin chose to view the negative responses of other students toward Tim not as a sign that Tim might be having a negative impact on their learning, but as a normal response of people to those who do well. In fact, he accepted the negative responses to Tim because he saw them as a source of motivation for Tim to do even better. Mr. Martin was much more concerned about the effect of classroom events on Tim than about the potential negative effect of Tim's actions on his fellow students. He consistently mentioned his goal of motivating Tim to perform at an even higher level and of not having Tim doubt himself.

Another dominant person in the classroom was Katrina, an African American female. Like Tim, Katrina received much positive attention from Mr. Martin, but of a very different sort. Mr. Martin laughed and joked with Tim, and the topic of most of their interactions was mathematics. He also laughed and joked with Katrina; however, their interactions were often about nonmathematical topics. For example, Mr. Martin and Katrina talked about his work as a free-lance photographer. He often shared anecdotes of his personal, out-of-school activities with Katrina, but he almost never did so with Tim. Katrina and Mr. Martin did interact about mathematics, but most of this was a result of Katrina asking for help, which she did more often than anyone else in the class. There were contradictions in Katrina's behavior. On the one hand, as leader and member of a group of four African American females, Katrina was both independent and assertive. On the other hand, as a learner of mathematics, she was very dependent on Mr. Martin and rarely worked on her own longer than 5 minutes without asking him a question about the assignment. Tim, unlike Katrina, rarely asked Mr. Martin a question about mathematics or anything else.

During an interview, Katrina expressed some of the strongest disapproval of Mr. Martin's teaching style that we recorded. She referred to her mathematics teacher from the previous year as having the kind of teaching style she preferred. According to Katrina, this teacher began each period with a whole-class review of previous work and explanations of new work. We observed, however, that, unlike Cathy, Katrina and the other three African American females in her group received a significant amount of teacher instruction in mathematics, primarily because they demanded help from Mr. Martin. In a classroom where Mr. Martin generally allowed students to select and arrange their desks as they wished, members of this group sat closest to him, often got up and walked to his desk to ask him a question, and carried on an ongoing dialogue with him from their desks. In most cases, Katrina represented the group in interactions with Mr. Martin.

Katrina, therefore, was like Tim in the dominant role she played in the classroom; she was like Cathy, however, in that Mr. Martin's interactions with Katrina and Cathy were not of the same quality as his interactions with Tim and Henry. For example, we learned through the interviews that he did not purposely focus so many of his interactions with Katrina on social topics; furthermore, he said nothing about Katrina's mathematical dependence on him and seemed to be unaware of it. On the other hand, Mr. Martin did express concern about the limited number of African American students in advanced mathematics classes and, in the case of the four African American females who sat together, said that he wanted them to provide a peer support system for each other. However, his concern about a support system seemed to focus only on these four female students and not on the other four African Americans in the class, one of whom was female.

As exemplified by Katrina, Cathy, Tim, and Henry, the situation in Mr. Martin's classroom was extremely complex. Katrina's practice of constantly seeking help from Mr. Martin perpetuated her mathematical dependence on him, while giving her more instructional time with him. Cathy demonstrated a great deal of independence while receiving very little instructional time. Tim's independence, combined with his constant demand to be the center of attention in the classroom, led to consequences very different from Cathy's more passive independence. Henry demanded and received little attention. Like Cathy, he did not appear to mind the lack of attention (especially since what attention he received was predominantly negative); unlike Cathy, who suffered because of what else she might have been able to accomplish, Henry suffered because he needed help in order to complete the work at hand. We view these four students not so much as typical of their race-sex groups (in fact, within their own classroom they were not typical), but more as archetypal mathematics students. We cannot dismiss the race and gender of each of these students as we discuss their characteristics, but we should not conclude that all students within a particular race-gender group are adequately described by a particular configuration of characteristics.

Achievement, attitudes, and achievement-related behaviors in
Mr. Martin's class

We evaluated the achievement, attitudes, and achievement-related behaviors of the students in Mr. Martin's class.

Mathematics achievement. Six measures of achievement were used in our case study, four classroom measures (Grade 6 final grade, Grade 7 November test grade, Grade 7 January test grade, and Grade 7 second-quarter grade) and two standardized achievement measures (Grade 6 Iowa Test of Basic Skills [ITBS] overall mathematics percentile and Grade 7 American Junior High School Mathematics Examination [AJHE] score). On all six measures, the mean for the white students in the class was higher than the mean for the African American students, with the differences on the two standardized achievement measures greater than one-half of a standard deviation and the differences on the four classroom measures less than one-third of a standard deviation. The achievement results comparing boys and girls were mixed. On the first three measures (Grade 6 ITBS overall, Grade 6 final grade, and Grade 7 November test), the female students had higher means than the male students. On the last three measures (Grade 7 AJHE score, Grade 7 January test, and Grade 7 second-quarter grade), the male students had higher means than the female students. Again, the differences on the standardized achievement measures were greater than one-half of a standard deviation, and the differences on the classroom measures were less than one-third of a standard deviation. Therefore, the achievement by race and by sex in this classroom (i.e., whites higher than African Americans, sex results mixed) reflected, in general, the achievement pattern for the nation as a whole.

What we found most important in the classroom we studied was the pattern of achievement among the race-sex groups. Grade 6 final grades (maximum score 100) showed African American females highest (88), followed by white males (87), white females (84), and African American males (80). On the three Grade 7 classroom measures, white males and African American females scored highest (with white males having a slightly higher score on two of the measures), followed by white females and African American males. The standardized test scores were somewhat different. On both the ITBS and AJHE, white males scored highest, followed by white females, African American females, and African American males. On the ITBS, the African American males stood out with a particularly low percentile compared to the other three groups (a percentile of 57 compared to percentiles in the 70s for the other three groups). On the AJHE, the white males stood out with a score higher than that of the other three groups (a percentage score of 33 compared to percentage scores in the low 20s). The consistent pattern on all measures was that white males scored higher than white females, and that African American females scored higher than African American males.[1] Our data compared with at least one study (Yando, Seitz, & Zigler, 1979) that reported African American females achieving at a higher level than African American males.

Confidence in learning mathematics. In our classroom, results from the Fennema–Sherman confidence scale (1976) showed African Americans scoring higher than whites (with a difference of more than one-half of a standard deviation) and females scoring higher than males (by less than one-third of a standard deviation). We found, however, that looking just at race or just at sex was misleading. What stood out in the Fennema–Sherman confidence scale results was that the African American female students scored so much higher than any of the other three groups, almost a full standard deviation higher than the next-highest group, the white males. Furthermore, reflecting the achievement results, the sex differences in confidence were in opposite directions in the two racial groups. White males scored almost one-half of a standard deviation higher than did white females; African American females scored more than a full standard deviation higher than the African American males. The student interviews were consistent with some but not all of the results from the Fennema–Sherman scale. For example, both the male and the female African American students spoke confidently about their ability in mathematics, confirming the difference in favor of African Americans that we saw on the paper-and-pencil instrument. Unlike the result from the Fennema–Sherman scale, which showed the African American females standing out from the other three groups in a positive direction, the interviews led us to conclude that the white females stood out from the other groups as being less confident in their mathematical ability. This conclusion from the interviews is especially important in light of the fact that all four groups demonstrated a substantial amount of confidence on the Fennema–Sherman scale (i.e., the mean scores for all four groups were higher than any mean reported by Fennema and Sherman [1978] in their study of middle school students).

Even though, of the four race-sex groups, the white females had the widest range of achievement scores, what bound them together was some doubt about their ability in mathematics. During our interviews, one of the white females described herself as "not that smart in math"; another said she had "a lot of trouble" with mathematics. Even when the white females expressed confidence, it did not always come out in a positive manner, as when one said, "I'm not *not* confident." Wendy is an example of a white female who was a very capable mathematics student, based both on her achievement scores and on our observations of her, but whose confidence level did not match her achievement level. She said she was "pretty bad" in mathematics and claimed that just adding, subtracting, multiplying, and dividing confused her. She said she worried a lot about tests and believed she was lucky to do as well as she did because, in her words, "I'm not good at math." However, we do not want to paint an exclusively negative picture of Wendy's confidence. For example, when asked whether, in the end, she could figure things out, she said, "Yes, I am good at figuring out things, but it takes me a little while in math." Wendy believed that doing her homework, studying a lot, and keeping her notebook neat covered up for some of the problems she perceived herself as having.

Perceived usefulness of mathematics. As they did on the confidence scale, the African American students in our classroom scored higher than the white students on the Fennema–Sherman perceived usefulness scale. Unlike the confidence results, the boys scored higher than the girls on perceived usefulness. In both cases, the difference was about one-third of a standard deviation. Once again, the sex differences were in opposite directions in the two racial groups. African American females scored higher than African American males by less than one-third of a standard deviation. White males scored higher than white females by more than two-thirds of a standard deviation. Among the race-sex groups, the white females stood out in a negative direction, being more than one-half of a standard deviation below the next highest group, the African American males.

The interviews did not provide information that would confirm or disconfirm the paper-and-pencil results as much as they showed how little these seventh graders could say on their own about the usefulness of mathematics. This result is particularly interesting in light of the uniformly positive ratings of the usefulness of mathematics that all students gave on the paper-and-pencil instrument. In fact, an African American female with one of the highest scores on the usefulness scale could find virtually nothing useful to say about mathematics in the interview. She said she had not thought much about what she would do after high school, was not sure whether she would use math, and was not sure why she had to study it. All the other students either gave examples of how mathematics was useful or at least said that it was useful. However, most of their perceptions of the usefulness of mathematics were limited. For example, students said they needed mathematics to know how to count, or to be able to figure out the cost of something at the store, or to be able to balance a checkbook. Other examples were more closely linked to particular careers the students were contemplating. One student, who wanted to be a photographer, said he needed math to see "how big the pictures are." Another who wanted to be a pediatrician said she needed math "to do my bills." The girl who wanted to be a dentist gave a bit more detail. She said she needed math to measure teeth and "times that by a certain amount and make that much." The girl who wanted to be a veterinarian said she needed math to figure out how many stitches animals would need. Some students gave more global statements of the usefulness of mathematics, claiming that math is all around us, that you use it every day, and that most jobs today have to do with numbers. But no one was able to clearly substantiate these common slogans about the usefulness of mathematics. The point is that although the paper-and-pencil results differentiated among groups of students, the interviews did not allow us to confirm those differences; even more important, they indicated how shallow an understanding the students had of the usefulness of mathematics.

Enjoyment of mathematics. We used two items from the Fennema–Sherman effectance motivation scale as measures of enjoyment: "Math is fun and exciting" and "I don't understand how people can enjoy spending a lot of time on math." Ratings were adjusted so that high means indicated high enjoyment. Consistent with our other attitude results, African Americans scored higher than whites on both enjoyment items, by almost three-fourths of a standard deviation on the first item and by almost a full standard deviation on the second. The boys in the class scored higher than the girls, with the difference being more than a full standard deviation on the first item and only about one-fourth of a standard deviation on the second item.

The white females stood out in a negative direction from the other three race-sex groups. They were the only group whose average on each item indicated that they disliked mathematics. (An average rating of 3 on the 1–5 scale would be neutral; the white female averages were 1.60 and 2.60.) The difference between the white females and white males was more than one and one-half standard deviations on the "math is fun and exciting" item and more than one-half of a standard deviation on the "don't understand how people can enjoy" item. The African American males indicated enjoyment of mathematics that was greater than (by more than one-half of a standard deviation on the "math is fun and exciting" item) or equal to (on the "don't understand how people can enjoy" item) that of the African American females. The enjoyment items, therefore, were the only attitude or achievement measures on which the African American females did not score higher than the males.

The student interviews were consistent with the paper-and-pencil results. In particular, the white females as a group expressed greater dislike of mathematics than did the other race-sex groups. One of the five white females indicated some enjoyment of mathematics when she said she liked it because, unlike her experience in sixth grade, she knew what she was doing. But mathematics was not a favorite subject for her; in fact, she said she did not have any favorites. Another of the white females said she liked math a little bit but was not all that fond of it. Others expressed more negative feelings, including one girl who said math was her least favorite subject and one who said "I hate math; I simply hate math."

Persistence in doing mathematics. We used two items from the Fennema–Sherman effectance motivation scale as indirect measures of persistence: "If I can't solve a math problem right away, I stick with it until I do" and "I would rather have someone give me the solution to a hard math problem than to work it out for myself." Ratings were adjusted so that high means corresponded to high persistence. On both items, African American students reported more persistence than white students, by about one-third of a standard deviation, making the persistence results consistent with every other nonachievement quantitative measure. The sex results for the two items were somewhat mixed. The boys showed more persistence than the girls on the "I stick with it" item, by more than three-fourths of a standard deviation; on the "give me the solution" item, the girls indicated more persistence, by less than one-fourth of a standard deviation. In the race-sex groups, African American males stood out as higher on the "I stick with it" item than any of the other groups, with a mean that was almost a full standard deviation greater than that of the next group. On the "give me the solution" item, African American females had the highest persistence rating, about a third of a standard deviation beyond the next-highest group.

We found it difficult to form conclusions about student persistence based upon our interviews, another indirect measure; and we found it even more difficult to link the indirect quantitative and interview measures with our classroom observations. What was most striking about the persistence results was the number of inconsistencies within and across measures. For example, an African American female whom we saw in our classroom observations as one of the most persistent learners in the class had very low ratings on the two paper-and-pencil persistence items and indicated moderate persistence during the interview. Tim, who was viewed not just by Mr. Martin but also by his fellow students as the best mathematics student in the class, had the highest possible persistence rating on one item and the lowest possible rating on the other. In the interview, he said his response to a difficult story problem was "I can do this" and that he never gave up. During our observations of him, he did give up at times. This kind of inconsistency led us to reconsider the definition and importance of persistence in the classroom.

Conclusions

Our discussion of attitudes and achievement-related behaviors will focus on two main conclusions. First, the constraints of the mathematics classroom require a reconsideration of the meaning of persistence: A distinction must be made between persistence and independence, if the relationship between persistence and achievement is to be fully understood. Second, an analysis of the attitudes of both groups and individuals leads to the conclusion that there is no simple and clear relationship between a specific attitude and achievement. This conclusion does not diminish the importance of studying attitudes; it means, however, that the relationship between attitudes and achievement is more complex than correlation coefficients can express and that we may need to look closely at the particular configurations of attitudes demonstrated by individual students.

The role of persistence in the mathematics classroom

Both the paper-and-pencil items and our classroom observations pointed to the problems of defining persistence and determining the relationship between persistence and achievement in the mathematics classroom. In the classroom we studied, it was easier to find examples of students quickly giving up on a problem than it was to find positive examples of persistence on one's own in the face of difficulty, because the students were given few opportunities to persist in this way. Tim is a good example. He strongly agreed with the paper-and-pencil item that said "I stick with it," but he also strongly agreed with the item that said "I would rather have someone give me the solution to a hard math problem." Although the responses appear contradictory on the surface, a closer look at the items in light of our classroom observations of Tim makes the responses appear reasonable and consistent with his actions, and demonstrates the problematic nature of persistence in the mathematics classroom.

Tim had the highest scores on both of the standardized measures of achievement and was at or near the top on the four classroom measures. He was viewed by his fellow students and Mr. Martin as the best mathematics student in the class. As we said earlier, Tim dominated class discussions, was called on most often by the teacher to answer difficult mathematics questions, and gave a running commentary during class sessions on the performance of his peers. He was a source of great annoyance to most of his classmates; they took special delight when he gave an incorrect answer to a problem. Tim did not challenge the authority of the traditional classroom methods of doing mathematics in the way that Grieb and Easley's (1984) "pale male math mavericks" did, but he did provide a challenge to the personal authority of the classroom teacher.

Tim did not continue in all situations to struggle with a problem on his own when confronted with mathematical difficulties; in fact, he was sometimes quite willing to give up. What was reflected in his effort was not so much persistence in solving mathematical problems on his own as it was an urge to get his work done as quickly as possible. When giving up on a problem and asking Bob or Mr. Martin for help would likely lead to finishing his work more quickly, Tim was quite willing to seek help. Persisting on his own was not always important to Tim because doing well did not only mean getting a good grade on an assignment. In fact, getting done quickly was consistently the most dominating factor for Tim, so much so that he would sometimes announce he was done even before he had actually completed all of the assigned work. So Tim may have interpreted the idea of "I stick with it" in the first paper-and-pencil item as getting the correct answer in any way he could and as fast as he could. This approach is quite compatible with his desire that someone give him the answer to a hard problem, his response to the second paper-and-pencil item.

This analysis of Tim's behavior in the classroom is a bit misleading because Tim rarely had to face a hard problem. He could quite easily handle almost all the assignments the teacher gave. So he had only rare opportunities to demonstrate his willingness to struggle on his own, but when this did occur, his choice was usually to seek out help in order to finish the assignment quickly. One reason for the difficulty in determining the relationship between persistence and achievement is that continuing to struggle on one's own in the face of difficulty is rarely encouraged or observed in mathematics classrooms, including the one in our study. It was easier for us to find examples of a lack of persistence than it was to find positive examples of persistence in the face of difficulty because the level and pace of instruction discouraged this kind of struggle.

Both the higher- and lower-achieving students in the class rarely demonstrated persistence. The higher-achieving students, such as Tim, had almost no opportunity to struggle with a mathematics problem because most of the work was easy for them; the lower-achieving students did face difficulties but had little opportunity to struggle on their own because of the pace of instruction. Furthermore, the students were never taught how to deal with difficulty other than to immediately ask for help. The goal in the class we studied was clearly not to learn through struggle but to get answers and complete assignments. The students did not really have to struggle to get an answer, especially on tests and assignments that were presented in a multiple-choice format.

In a classroom situation, persistence cannot be judged on the basis simply of whether or not children get an answer, because getting an answer is, in effect, required of everyone. However, we also should not judge children's persistence on the basis of whether or not they struggle on their own to get an answer, because that is not always the most intelligent choice in a mathematics classroom. Although persisting on one's own may be a virtue, the time constraints of the mathematics classroom and the pace of instruction can make this kind of persistence an impediment to achievement. Even in nonclassroom situations, when a student is given a task with no time constraints, this kind of persistence is not always constructive: It may be valuable to leave a problem for a while and come back to it later. But in a mathematics classroom, this typically is not an option for students. So an individual has to balance her or his urge to continue to struggle with a problem with the need to complete the page of problems and go on to the next assignment. Getting help, either from peers or from the teacher, may not, then, be a sign of lack of persistence as much as it is a reasonable choice within the constraints of the classroom.

It is clear to us that struggling on one's own in the face of difficulty needs to be encouraged in mathematics classrooms. However, our study of this classroom leads us to conclude that we may need to think of persistence differently, or of different kinds of persistence, because children and teachers will always have to deal with time constraints in some form. For example, we may need to make a clearer distinction between persistence and independence and look for persistent attempts to understand, rather than persistence in facing a hard mathematics problem. We could then attempt to judge the level of persistence demonstrated during interactions with others. We might ask whether a child is willing to struggle in order to understand a concept during an interaction, or simply wants to get an answer. Our classroom observations led us to conclude that there are important differences among children in how they act during mathematical interactions with the teacher and their peers, but we really did not focus enough on those different interaction styles to reach more specific conclusions.

The relationship between attitudes and achievement

Even when researchers have used paper-and-pencil instruments to isolate particular attitudes and provide correlations between attitudes and achievement, they have not been able to explain how attitudes affect achievement (or even how achievement might affect attitudes). In this section, we will discuss the apparent relationships between the attitudes of confidence, usefulness, and enjoyment, and the mathematics achievement of the students in the class we studied. We will also describe how these attitudes appeared to interact with each other, making it difficult to isolate their particular effects. Limited measures of achievement and unique configurations of attitudes of individual students further confounded attempts to link attitudes and achievement for groups of students.

Confidence, usefulness, enjoyment, and achievement. It was not difficult to see the necessity of looking at race and sex simultaneously in order to get some sense of the relationship between attitudes and achievement. Looking just at race, African American students scored higher than white students on all paper-and-pencil measures of attitudes, but lower than white students on all six measures of achievement. Looking just at sex, the mixed-sex differences in achievement made any claims about general sex differences in attitudes and achievement problematic. When we looked at the four race-sex groups, however, the relationship between attitudes and achievement was clearer though not definitive.

Confidence appeared to be the attitude most related to achievement among the four race-sex groups. For example, the sex differences in achievement and confidence were in opposite directions within the two racial groups, with white males and African American females demonstrating higher achievement and more confidence than white females and African American males, respectively.

Usefulness and enjoyment appeared to be related to the sex difference in achievement for the white students but not for the African American students. On the paper-and-pencil measure of usefulness, on the paper-and-pencil and interview measures of enjoyment, and, again, on all six achievement measures, the white males scored higher than the white females. Although the African American females scored higher than African American males on all achievement measures, the two groups were within a third of a standard deviation of each other on the usefulness scale, and the African American males demonstrated enjoyment of mathematics that was equal to or higher than that of the African American females.

The findings about usefulness and enjoyment are important for two reasons. First, they demonstrate that different attitudes may have different relationships to achievement for different groups. Second, even though the extent to which African American females and males enjoy mathematics does not seem to reflect the sex difference in achievement favoring African American females, it is still important and helpful to understand the enjoyment of mathematics felt by the African American males. Not only do we want students to enjoy mathematics, but knowing that a relatively low-achieving group has a relatively high level of enjoyment should inform attempts to help those students achieve at a higher level. Interventions to improve the mathematics achievement of the African American males would be different from those for the white females because of the different relationships between enjoyment and achievement of the two groups.

The interaction among attitudes. It was difficult to isolate the effects of a particular attitude because of the way in which attitudes seemed to interact with each other. We began to see this interaction as we tried to explain responses from the interviews that contradicted the paper-and-pencil results and that, at times, were contradictory from one statement to the next. Cathy provides a good example. She was the most successful white female student in the class; she also was described by her fellow students during interviews as being unpopular. Mr. Martin identified Cathy and Tim as the two students in the class he would consider moving to the accelerated mathematics group for seventh graders. On the paper-and-pencil measures of attitudes, Cathy had relatively high scores in confidence and perceived usefulness and low ratings on both enjoyment items. During the interview, Cathy indicated she did not enjoy mathematics; she gave contradictory responses to our questions about the usefulness of mathematics; and her confidence in her ability to do mathematics was difficult to separate from these other two attitudes. The interview gave us a fuller understanding of Cathy's attitudes because we were able to see them in interaction with each other. Her confidence and her perceptions of the usefulness of mathematics were not as positive as the scale scores indicated, and her level of enjoyment was low, but not as low as her ratings on the two paper-and-pencil enjoyment items. Put in another way, the total picture of Cathy's attitudes toward mathematics was not simply the sum of her scores on the paper-and-pencil measures.

When we asked Cathy during the interview how she would compare herself with other students, she underestimated her standing in the class, saying: "Sort of medium. Not really real super duper good. Not real terrible awful bad. Just sitting there, average." We asked her why she was average and how she could get to be above average and she said: "I could try a whole bunch harder and study a whole bunch more and maybe really cover the stuff." She said when she felt sure of something, she didn't bother to go back over it because it was boring to her, indicating both a higher level of confidence than the earlier comment conveyed and a lack of enjoyment of much of the mathematics that was studied in the class. This lack of enjoyment was confirmed throughout the interview. At one point she did say that she liked math a little bit, but then immediately said that she was not all that fond of it.

When asked what makes some people better in mathematics, Cathy said part of the reason is that some people have a "talent" for math, and later admitted that she had "maybe a little bit" of talent, again showing some awareness of her ability and more confidence. Cathy also said that some people are better in mathematics because they really care about it, and then indicated she really did not care, linking her lack of enjoyment with her belief that much of mathematics was not very useful: "I think in math you need to know the basics. Any more is a waste of time." Cathy was able to give some examples of the usefulness of mathematics and even said, "Pretty much you need math anywhere." But she also said, "You don't want to elaborate on [math] and learn all the stuff you're not gonna use." She ended the interview with the claim that, other than in computation, "you don't need mathematics much for everyday life."

We concluded, based on these responses from the interview with Cathy, that more important than her level of confidence was her view of mathematics as something she did not enjoy doing and that had limited usefulness. Because her level of confidence clearly interacted with these other attitudes, it is not easy to say exactly how confident Cathy was in her ability to do mathematics. The point is that Cathy's case is a good example of the failure of the paper-and-pencil attitude scores to describe attitudes fully; they did not show the extent to which her attitudes interacted with each other. Isolating a particular attitude is as problematic and as potentially misleading as it is helpful.

The problem of achievement measures. If we are correct in concluding that attitudes interact with each other and form unique configurations for individual students, it becomes even more difficult to describe clearly the connections between attitudes and achievement. Furthermore, traditional measures of achievement can actually hinder attempts to understand these connections. We can again use Cathy to illustrate this point. Even though Cathy was one of the two or three highest achievers in the class, it appeared to us, based on classroom observations, that her attitudes did, in fact, lead her to learn less mathematics than she might have. For example, when she finished a task, rather than letting the teacher know she was done, she was content to sit at her desk and read a novel she had brought to class. Mr. Martin often did not notice Cathy at such times and, when he did notice, allowed her to continue reading her book. He jokingly commented during an interview about the number of novels Cathy had read in his class, but he sometimes could not remember her name when we talked about her.

Again, despite the extensive amount of time Cathy spent not doing mathematics, she was among the highest achievers in the class. So her attitudes did not hamper her in successfully completing the tasks in this particular classroom. What we worry about, and cannot fully describe based on the case study, is the cumulative effect of her attitudes and the consequent neglect over time on her mathematics achievement. She was a student who appeared to us to be capable of a much deeper understanding of mathematics and who was exactly the kind of student who needs encouragement to continue to take mathematics courses.

A final note

We began our case study with the objective of looking at sex and race differences in mathematics attitudes and the achievement-related behavior of persistence. Notwithstanding that the African American students scored higher than the white students on the paper-and-pencil measures of attitudes and persistence, we found that the most productive level of group analysis required looking at sex and race simultaneously. Even this group analysis was limited by the extent to which individual students showed unique configurations of interacting characteristics, which confirmed for us the importance of considering archetypical students rather than just demographic groups. Our work points to the need to qualify group differences by studying individuals over time and their attitudes and behaviors in interaction, using multiple measures of achievement.

Note

1 The means on the classroom achievement measures were related to the number of total teacher–student interactions and academic interactions, and the means on the standardized achievement measures were related to the number of procedural interactions. African American females and white males scored highest on the classroom achievement measures and had the highest number of total and academic interactions. The order of means among the four race-sex groups for procedural interactions (white males, white females, African American females, African American males) was the same as the order of the means on the standardized achievement measures. Relatively large academic interaction differences were reflected in relatively small classroom achievement differences, and relatively small procedural interaction differences were reflected in relatively large standardized achievement differences.

References

Fennema, E., & Sherman, J. A. (1976). Fennema–Sherman mathematics attitudes. *JSAS Catalog of Selected Documents in Psychology, 6*, 31 (Ms. No. 1225).
    (1978). Sex-related differences in mathematics achievement and related factors: A further study. *Journal for Research in Mathematics Education, 9*, 189–203.
Grieb, A., & Easley, J. (1984). A primary school impediment to mathematical equity: Case studies in rule-dependent socialization. In M. W. Steinkamp & M. L. Maehr (Eds.), *Advances in motivation and achievement, Vol. 2: Women in science* (pp. 317–362). Greenwich, CT: JAI.
Leder, G. C. (1992). Mathematics and gender: Changing perspectives. In D. A. Grouws (Ed.), *Handbook of research on mathematics teaching and learning* (pp. 597–622). New York: Macmillan.
Reyes, L. H., & Stanic, G. M. A. (1988). Race, sex, socioeconomic status, and mathematics. *Journal for Research in Mathematics Education, 19*, 26–43.
Secada, W. G. (1992). Race, ethnicity, social class, language, and achievement in mathematics. In D. A. Grouws (Ed.), *Handbook of research on mathematics teaching and learning* (pp. 623–660). New York: Macmillan.
Yando, R., Seitz, V., & Zigler, E. (1979). *Intellectual and personality characteristics of children: Social-class and ethnic-group differences*. Hillsdale, NJ: Erlbaum.

Part III

12 Making inequality: Issues of language and meanings in mathematics teaching with Hispanic students

Lena Licón Khisty

How should we explain the disproportionately and consistently poor achievement of Hispanic students in mathematics in the United States? Recent data indicate that the general population of Hispanic students performs well below the average national level in this subject (Matthews, Carpenter, Lindquist, & Silver, 1984; Moore & Smith, 1987). In comparing recent National Assessment results with previous assessments, Matthews and her colleagues (1984) indicate that Hispanics showed only small gains in the lower cognitive areas of knowledge and computational skill and no gains in understanding or application. As we examine these data, it is important to bear in mind other demographic factors that relate to this population. First, the National Center for Education Statistics (1981) has projected that the school population of limited-English proficient (LEP) students will reach 2.8 million in 1990 and 3.4 million in the year 2000; Spanish-speaking students will constitute 71% of this population in 1990 and 77% in the year 2000. Second, although this population is growing very rapidly, educational institutions remain virtually static in their response to the issue. One in four teachers has LEP students in his/her classrooms, but only 3.2% of the nation's teachers has had the academic preparation to teach them (United States Department of Education, 1982). Through an analysis of these data, we begin to see a framework of inequities that suggest factors to account for the underachievement of Hispanic students.

Traditional perspectives on the general poor performance of minority students have focused attention first on factors related to individual characteristics and then on factors related to the cultural background of the student. Since the 1960s, the predominant paradigms that have guided investigations into this phenomenon have assumed that the problem resides, if not necessarily in genetic deficits, then in cultural deficits. Such models concentrate on pinpointing and describing what students do not know, what experiences they presumably do not have, or what language and behavior differences they possess that result in a mismatch with the norms of the school. Actions and policies consistent with these pathology models are

279

based, therefore, on changing the student and/or the family – on remedying the assumed imperfections.

However, we can look at the problem in a fundamentally different way. At the heart of this paradigm shift is the premise that there is a process of school failure that involves inadequate or inappropriate instructional decisions that de facto handicap poor and ethnic minority students. Moll and Diaz (1987) describe it this way:

> Although student characteristics certainly matter, when the same children are shown to succeed under modified instructional arrangements it becomes clear that the problems these working-class children face in school must be viewed primarily as a consequence of institutional arrangements that constrain children *and* teachers by not capitalizing fully on their talents, resources, and skills. . . . this conclusion is pedagogically optimistic because it suggests that just as academic failure is socially organized, academic success can be socially arranged. (p. 302)

The research presented here reflects this latter paradigm. In essence, it is based on the argument that the teaching and learning process consists of an interaction between persons for the purpose of developing and sharing meanings. It logically follows that language is crucial if the development and negotiation of meaning is to occur. Consequently, if we are to fully understand instructional dynamics – and obstacles that arise in the process that constrain minority children – we must examine not only curriculum and classroom activities, but also classroom discourse, that is, what is said and how it is said. In the case of students for whom Spanish is a home and/ or dominant language, language use in classrooms is naturally critical (e.g., Cazden, 1986).[1]

Furthermore, consistent with the contention that no pathology resides within the student, the focus of attention is on the discourse characteristics of the teacher. However, this is not to suggest blaming the teacher. Rather, it is the teacher who makes instructional decisions and determines instructional contexts; it is the teacher who explains new concepts and poses questions to stretch students' thinking and understandings; and it is the teacher who represents the element that completes our understanding of classroom processes and, more important, becomes the agent of change (e.g., National Council of Teachers of Mathematics, 1989).

In what follows, I first present the general results of observations of mathematics teaching in five classrooms with sizable populations of non-English (NEP) and limited-English proficient (LEP) students of Mexican descent. The teachers in these classrooms are fluently bilingual and are able to instruct using the primary language of the student. Next, I offer a closer look at the dynamics of teacher discourse in mathematics with two contrasting case studies. Just as the zoom lens of a camera provides more detail of the subject, the microethnography of just two classrooms provides detail that reveals how a simple concept such as talk becomes a political tool that either empowers students or disenfranchises them.

Background

This research has been informed by three major areas of inquiry. The first relates to the work by sociohistorical psychologists (e.g., Moll, 1990; Scribner & Cole, 1981; Vygotsky, 1978; Wertsch, 1985) on the critical role of social interaction in learning. Vygotsky (1978) in particular has offered a framework of socially constituted development of higher mental processes. Within his framework, there are many interrelated factors that must be present, one of which is an "enabling other." This is a more experienced person who embodies and, consequently, *models* the intended outcome for the learner. In this case, modeling corresponds to a traditional pattern of direct instruction and imitation, rather than to what exists in an apprenticeship, where the mentor exposes the novice to, and enculturates her/him with, new behaviors in a spontaneous and informal manner. In this mode of instruction, there is no artificiality of conversation, and, therefore, little loss of contact with the purpose of dialogue. Also, as in an apprenticeship, the enabling other gradually relinquishes a dominant role as the child internalizes the new cognitive behaviors. For all of this to be accomplished, the enabling other must provide a scaffold for the learner via dialogue that includes probing questions and cues that extend talk as well as the intellectual range of the learner. Let me illustrate this modeling-and-scaffolding process with an example taken from the work of Tharp and Gallimore (1988):

A 6-year-old child has lost a toy and asks her father for help. The father asks where she last saw the toy; the child says, "I can't remember." He asks a series of questions: "Did you have it in your room? Outside? Next door?" To each question, the child answers no. When he says, "In the car?" she says, "I think so," and goes to retrieve the toy. . . . Through this small domestic collaboration, the father is rousing to life significant cognitive functions. Such teaching – understood as assisted performance of apprentices in joint activity with experts – becomes the vehicle through which the interactions of society are internalized and become mind. (pp. 7–8)

Research on the role of modeling or assisted performance in the teaching of language arts supports the need on the part of students to have teachers model new concepts (e.g., Au & Jordan, 1981; Langer, 1987; Tharp & Gallimore, 1988). It also is clear that for the modeling to be effective, language use must be carefully considered, as in the situation just described, in which the father chooses to ask a series of questions instead of making a declarative statement that might have quickly informed the child.

The second area of inquiry consists of the work that has been done concerning effective instruction for bilingual or language-minority students. One of the most significant findings relates to the academic benefits that result from use of the student's primary language – in this case Spanish – in instruction, particularly when it is used in the teaching of concepts (e.g., Cummins, 1981; Garcia, 1988).[2] It is only reasonable that when new meanings are being developed, the language that the child comprehends best should be the one used. However, use of the primary language in instruction also provides the support needed while the student continues to develop proficiency in the second language, specifically as it is used academically in classrooms and textbooks. This proficiency in the cognitive academic language is not easily acquired and can take as long as seven years to achieve (Cummins, 1981). This suggests that English language development be integrated with academic skill development and that during instruction, attention be paid to students' acquisition of new terms for concepts, or simply new vocabulary and syntax modes (e.g., Tikunoff, 1985). Consequently, both the native language (L1), Spanish, and the second language, (L2), English, are used in instruction; however, the languages are kept separate and are not mixed.

In regard to mathematics, the use of the primary language may be very necessary in order to clarify confusions that result because of the differences between Spanish and English mathematical terms (e.g., Casteneda, 1983; Cuevas, 1984). This may be particularly important when Spanish is used at home by parents and other adults, and children may develop certain understandings that are not necessarily the same as those in school, where instruction is usually in another language. Without attention to making bridges between meanings and terminologies developed in the two contexts, that is, home and school, mathematical discussions could be less than effective and may even be incomprehensible.

The third area of inquiry concerns the nature of the language we use to communicate mathematical ideas or the mathematics register. This is not to be confused with the special terminology used in mathematics. Rather, the mathematics register extends to the use of the natural language in a way that is particular to a role or function (Halliday, 1978). In other words, it is a set of unique meanings and structures expressed through everyday language. The development of a mathematics register is accomplished in many ways, including reinterpreting existing words such as carry, set, face, point, or reduce (Halliday, 1978). Thus, the register can present many instances in which words have meanings different from what children expect, and this can be especially hazardous for LEP students. For example, it is easy to imagine limited-English-proficient students being confused by the mathematical meaning of the word *left* (as in, how many are *left?*), when commonly it is the directional meaning of the word that is stressed in the learning of English. It also would not be unusual for LEP students to be confused by words such as *sum* and *whole,* which have nonmathematical homonyms. Such words would not necessarily present the same kind of difficulty for native English speakers, since they do not have to deal with comprehension of the language in the first place, which makes it easier to identify the subtleties between the different meanings.

Comprehending mathematical talk is made more difficult because symbolically we can have one statement (e.g., 10 - 4 = 6), but verbally, we can express it several different ways ("ten take away four is six," or "four from ten leaves six"). Moreover, these expressions are often unthinkingly and freely interchanged by teachers as they instruct (e.g., Pimm, 1987).

The issue surrounding the mathematics register does not lie in the register itself nor in whether students should learn it for its own sake. Instead, the issue is one of identifying mathematics with its language. If Hispanic students do not know the language for, or have the means of expressing, mathematical ideas, they cannot, in essence, do the mathematical work; they are curtailed from participating in those activities that develop and enhance mathematical meanings and comprehension. The issue is compounded for students for whom English is a second language because they must contend with multiple language variables all at the same time. Therefore, the existence of the register needs to be brought to students' attention and its structure needs to be taught, along with the rest of mathematics, in order for students to develop sufficient control in its use as a way of communicating mathematically.

The importance of these points is that learning mathematics involves language in a way that appears to be much more crucial than previous studies of mathematics education with language minority students might suggest. If we accept Vygotsky's premise that the more able other (i.e., the teacher) has to model the desired cognitive behavior, and if we accept that learning is most effective in the child's primary language and that mathematics entails unique language use, then we have to explore further those verbalizations and development of meaning strategies the mathematics teacher uses.

Methods

As part of a larger project, school administrators, as well as bilingual and mathematics curriculum directors, were asked to identify teachers whom they considered effective in the teaching of mathematics with Hispanic students. Classrooms were selected from elementary schools with a significant population of Hispanic LEP and NEP students. Data gathered in five of these classrooms form the basis of the present discussion. Three classrooms are at the second-grade and two are at the fifth-grade level. Consistent with ethnographic methods, field observations were carried out at various times over a year and each classroom was videotaped intermittently for 7 to 10 hours when the teacher indicated that new concepts would be introduced and explained. In addition, an entire week of each teacher's mathematics lessons (e.g., introduction of new concepts, review, etc.) was videotaped to get a sense of consistency across the lessons, and one whole day was videotaped to get a sense of how mathematics related to the rest of each teacher's curriculum. Each teacher was asked a prepared set of questions regarding personal and teaching background, academic and language backgrounds of his or her students, and perceptions of teaching mathematics. Informal interviews were conducted with each teacher after a videotaped lesson, in order to identify and clarify instructional decisions that were made. Informal interviews were also used with randomly selected students to assess their grasp of the mathematical meanings presented in the lesson and to enhance the observations.

The analysis of videotapes, the primary source of data, focused on the following constructs: (a) the nature and use of a mathematics register; (b) the nature and use of L1 (Spanish) and L2 (English); (c) instances of language use for the negotiation of meaning, or for emphasizing rote learning; and (d) the clarity or ambiguity of language used in concept development. Triangulation among three independent observers was used to provide validation of the items deemed to be linguistically troublesome.

It is important to note that although all of the teachers for this particular discussion were bilingual, there were important differences among them. One had had all of her schooling (including higher education) in Mexico. Two other teachers were not native speakers of Spanish, but did have extensive academic training in the language and had lived in Spanish-speaking countries. The last two were Hispanic, had had most of their schooling in the United States, and had varying degrees of fluency in Spanish.

General results

As we look inside these five classrooms, two patterns of teacher discourse emerge that are particularly relevant to our discussion. The first relates to the differences among teachers in their efforts to attend to the language of mathematics.

Effective techniques used by some of the teachers included emphasizing meanings by variations in voice tone and volume, and by pausing either before or after a word is spoken in order to draw students' attention to it. Also, at times as a word was spoken, it was written or pointed to among a previously prepared list of words.

Another effective technique was the frequent "recasting" of mathematical ideas and terms. As Spanos and his colleagues (1988) have pointed out, mathematics has many linguistic features that present problems to students, including a semantic structure comprised of synonymous words and phrases that can be used to signal a single mathematical operation. The recasting observed in this study attempted to provide students not only with some of the synonyms relevant to the particular problem, but also with other ways of looking at the problem within the immediate context of discussing it. The following excerpt demonstrates this recasting technique.

In this episode, the teacher is giving directions to a second-grade class on how to make a paper cat that each student will use to illustrate his or her own story. The teacher is weaving the development of various geometric concepts into her directions that students will eventually follow on their own. She has just introduced the word "perimeter" as the concept of an outline of a figure.

Please note that dialogues in Spanish have been translated into English and the translations are in italics. However, it should be recognized that there are many instances in which the subject code switches between Spanish and English and uses the two languages within the same sentence or paragraph.

T: ¿Qué es un contorno? A ver tú.
        (*What is an outline? Let's see, you.*)
S1:   Ahm, un, una figura.
        (*Ahm, a figure.*)
S2:   Un rededor de figura.
        (*A line around a figure.*)
T: Very good! Good job, you are a good listener, I like you. Un contorno, el contorno es el rededor, el perímetro, la línea que encierra la figura. El contorno es el rededor de la figura. La figura puede ser una persona, un animal, una cosa, un pedazo de papel, un . . .
        (*An outline, the outline is the surrounding, the perimeter around the shape, the line that encloses the figure. The outline is the line surrounding a figure. The figure can be an animal, a thing, a piece of paper*)
S1:   Un jugete. (*A toy.*)

As can be seen, recasting during instruction provides students with a repertoire of mathematical talk and perspectives for comprehending the talk. In this case, the teacher provides not only synonyms but also examples of how the word is used in sentences. Moreover, this example suggests that it is not enough simply to provide a formal definition of a term or even to translate the item into English.

Clearly, if a student knows only one way of expressing a mathematical concept, it will be very easy for the student to get lost in a discussion when synonymous terms are freely interchanged. For example, in the following excerpt from a discussion in an upper-grade classroom, we can see almost the reverse of what occurred in the example just given. In this case, a student gets lost in the teacher's explanation because no attention is given to making sure students recognize the interchangeability of "three-fourths" and "three-quarters."

T: Now we can take three-fourths of this. OK, what's three-quarters of this number [pointing to a number]? Can someone tell me?
        [Chorus of correct and incorrect student responses]
S: Teacher, I don't understand. How did you get three-quarters?
T: Here [pointing to ¾ and proceeding to work out the problem].

In the interview with this student, it was found that he had understood "three quarters" to mean coins. He did not know that "three-fourths" and "three-quarters" were register terms for the same concept and were interchangeable. On the other hand, the teacher's response suggests that an assumption was made that the student had these terms in his cognitive repertoire and simply needed to be reminded. Consequently, the response, which was intended to clarify, was meaningless.

Less effective techniques were characterized by missed opportunities to establish and clarify the mathematics register. In an earlier paper related to this research (Khisty, McLeod, & Bertilson, 1990), my colleagues and I described a teacher's use of the Spanish word *decena* (meaning a group of 10) during an explanation of place-value and regrouping. This is a specialized word that would not be familiar to most young students; it is also very similar to the word *docena,* which means dozen. The two spoken words can easily be confused (as often occurs with "eights" and "eighths"), particularly if the teacher's accent is difficult to understand. During the lesson, no steps were taken to draw attention to the word *decena* and its meaning, nor to contrast it with the other word. As a result, students found the discussion incomprehensible since they were not able to make a connection between what they thought they heard as directions to form groups of twelve and what they saw in the teacher's demonstration of regrouping by ten.

In the following dialogue, we can see how another teacher gives care and attention to developing students' understanding of the mathematics register. The teacher is using the context of constructing paper houses to develop concepts of rational numbers with her students. She has just explained how each student will get half of a piece of paper to use in their projects, and now introduces the concept of a fourth and its relationship to a half. Notice that the teacher draws the students' attention to the fact that *cuarto* in Spanish can mean both "fourth" and "room," and she specifically clarifies which meaning is being used.

T: Y cada partecita se va a llamar . . .
        (*And each little piece will be called . . .*)
S1:   Fourth.

T: Fourth. Este es un cuarto y este es un cuarto [holding two pieces of paper]. No un cuarto de la cocina ni un cuarto de la casa. Es un cuarto del entero. ¿Si este lo doblamos . . . en otro, en una . . . en una mitad, este . . . medio, cuantos cuartos va haber en este medio? (*This is a fourth and this is a fourth. It is not the room as in kitchen nor as in a room in a house. It is a fourth of a whole. If we fold this . . . into a half, this . . . half, how many fourths will there be in the half?*)

This example also points out that the mathematics register is not language-specific. Each language has its own unique way of expressing mathematical concepts. Mathematical meanings, which can be confused in one language (e.g., *cuarto* for both "room" and "fourth" in Spanish, and "sum" and "some" in English), may not present confusion in another language. Consequently, we cannot assume that if you know the mathematics register in one language, you know it in another language. For LEP students, this means that attention must be given to clarifying confusions caused by both the Spanish and English mathematics register, and to making connections between ways of expressing concepts in both languages.

Thus far, we have looked at the various effective and ineffective techniques teachers used to clarify the mathematics register. We have seen how teachers may specifically draw students' attention to key words and phrases and make sure that students distinguish the specialized meanings of the mathematics register from alternative everyday meanings of the same words. I have also noted that teachers, on the other hand, tend to miss opportunities to develop the register; they either forget to do so, or they seemingly do not recognize its importance to student understanding. However, there were also several instances in teachers' explanations when they actually made errors in using mathematical terms and phrases. For example, let us examine the following dialogue from a lesson with upper-grade students. The errors in this episode are of two types: First, the teacher presents a dot completely out of context and asks for its mathematical meaning; second, the Spanish word for "one-tenth" is used to refer to all decimal numbers.

The teacher's objective in this lesson is to introduce addition with decimals to the students. The teacher has just completed leading the class in solving an ordinary whole-number addition problem and now puts a dot on a blank overhead screen:

T: ¿Quién sabe que es esto? Who knows what that is [pointing to the solitary dot]? ¿Quien sabe? Who knows? ¿Quien sabe? ¿Quien sabe? [The teacher is translating as he goes along.] [Students raise their hands and one is called on.]

S1:   Un décimo. (*A tenth.*)

T: Right, décimo (*tenth*). How do you say it in English? Decimal [with a very specific Spanish pronunciation]. ¿En español? Décimo. (*In*

Spanish? Tenth.) [Teacher and students are saying the key words, décimo and decimal, pronounced as in Spanish, in unison.]

Throughout the rest of the lesson, the solitary dot is referred to as the "decimal," and there is no further explanation of how it is used in the context of rational numbers. The significance of this lies in its potential to mislead because, mathematically, a dot is also used to mean a "point" in the geometrical context and to denote multiplication when it is raised above the line. In many countries, including those in Latin America, the dot is used in place of a comma to set off particular whole-number place values. Lastly, in this episode, the stage has been set for confusion by the free interchange of decimal, pronounced as it would be in Spanish, and décimo (one-tenth), which is not the translation for decimal. By the end of the lesson, students could be heard using the words interchangeably among themselves just as the teacher had.

The second pattern of teacher discourse to emerge from the data concerns the very little Spanish that was actually used in the mathematics context. This was true at both grade levels for all of the teachers except one, in spite of the fact that in all of the classrooms, there were students who spoke no English or for whom English was clearly a weaker language. The Spanish that was used fell into two categories, which I have chosen to refer to as "instrumental use" and "markers of solidarity." In the first case, teachers tended to use Spanish in a perfunctory manner as an "instrument" to discipline, to call students' attention to the subject of the lesson, or to punctuate a statement. In the second case, Spanish was used to give encouragement and to motivate the class. However, in these situations, Spanish was most often used as a shared but private mode of expression when a teacher worked individually with a student. In general, these uses of Spanish can represent appropriate applications of the language in teaching. In fact, a "marker of solidarity" can be particularly useful because it serves to draw students into classroom processes. The issue surrounding the use of Spanish in the ways I have described is that the language is not used in the context of making meaning in mathematics.

Overall, very few whole thoughts during mathematical explanations were conveyed in Spanish. Individual Spanish words or phrases were sprinkled in the teachers' talk, or sentences were not completed. In light of this, it is natural to ask whether Spanish was used more extensively at any other time or for any other subject. In other words, was Spanish particularly excluded from the mathematics context, or was this the general state of affairs for all instruction with these students? Observations of instruction at different times of the day revealed that Spanish was used more frequently to develop concepts related to reading and/or language arts instruction. This is consistent with the findings of others, which suggest that mathematics does not require as much consideration of language use or discourse as other subjects (e.g., Cazden, 1986). As I argue later in this discussion, however, this is not true. It also points to the tendency of bilingual teachers to see themselves as language and culture brokers. The implication is that there is an accompanying tendency to make Spanish relevant only in the areas of language development and cultural ties. Given additional curriculum and policy constraints, districts can be less concerned about developing concepts equally across all academic areas (Khisty, 1991). Therefore, it becomes easy to overlook the need to use extended talk and students' primary language in teaching mathematics. This is no small matter, since these techniques constitute critical links to success in the subject for Hispanic students.

However, interviews with the teachers suggest other contributing factors besides the inclination to give priority to language development issues above other areas. The teachers who used Spanish the least in a mathematics context had learned Spanish either in an academic setting or informally within their families. The teachers for whom Spanish was a second language did not have any training in the technical aspects of the language; this is to be expected, since few foreign-language programs address this area. In essence, they had not had access to the Spanish mathematics register. The other teachers, who had little or no formal training in the language, had been left to themselves to develop a Spanish mathematics register. In many of our observations of these teachers, it was noted that some English mathematical terms and phrases were directly translated into Spanish and, as a result, were not always correct. All of the teachers in interviews expressed a sense of helplessness about speaking mathematically; they recognized that there were times when they really did not have a command of the Spanish vocabulary needed to explain concepts thoroughly. On the other hand, for them, mathematics was also simply a difficult subject to explain (Khisty, 1991).

It should be noted that the only teacher to spend a considerable amount of time developing mathematics by way of explanations, questions, and cues to extend student talk was the teacher who used the most Spanish in instruction. Also, while some of the other teachers tended to use a concurrent translation method (switching frequently between Spanish and English), which often resulted in incomplete sentences, this teacher tended not to mix languages. She spoke in one language for longer periods of time and her talk stands out because of its pattern of complete thoughts, as contrasted with the other teachers' broken discourse. Furthermore, while she used a considerable amount of Spanish, this was balanced with the active development of English skills in highly contextualized situations. This is the same teacher who had had all of her schooling in Mexico. Moreover, from observations of her teaching, it is clear that her primary instructional goal was to teach concepts and not to develop language skills only.

The politics of talk

The foregoing discussion is intended to provide a general overview of teacher discourse characteristics found in the classrooms used for this study. As can be seen, in these environments there are clearly language strategies in instructional practices that are questionable because of their effect in constraining Hispanic students' learning of mathematics. If students are unable to understand instructors' presentations fully because words are used in such a way as to distort what is being said, or because instruction is simply in a language students do not understand or have to struggle to comprehend, then it is small wonder that Hispanic students have trouble developing proficiency in mathematics.

However, there is another aspect to learning in addition to simply comprehending words and phrases used in explanations and problems. It has to do with communication processes that encourage a sense of what it means to do mathematics, that foster the internalization of the subject, and that enculturate the learner into the world of mathematical activity. In essence, it has to do with minimizing feelings of alienation from mathematics.

The enculturation process is multidimensional and complex, and many factors contribute to it. But one crucial means by which students become enculturated is by having ample opportunities to talk about mathematics, to ask questions that test their understandings, to engage in debates about various mathematical processes, and, in general, to participate in the higher cognitive levels of the subject that accompany active dialogue.

Clearly, this is the process by which shared meanings are developed and advanced. It is also the means by which meanings become personalized. Without participatory dialogue, learning remains outside the person; it is something that is removed from personal experiences and mental connections, and it is elusive and difficult to hold onto (e.g., Bishop, 1991). Freire (1970) also suggests that the acquisition of the "word which names the world" is what gives an individual power to participate in the world. Talk, therefore, is the critical vehicle by which an individual internalizes meanings, becomes enculturated, and develops a sense of personal power in mathematics.

The following section is intended to illustrate how talk or the absence of talk results in either drawing students closer to mathematics or alienating them from it. The two subjects discussed here are experienced second-grade teachers who are very concerned about mathematics; they spend a lot of time teaching it and thinking about how to improve their instruction. Both are competent bilingual instructors, although one uses English considerably more than the other.

Teacher 1

This teacher generally presents information and develops ideas in English and then provides a more basic and less detailed translation in Spanish. The mathematics lessons seldom have a conceptual introduction to the day's activities that connects them to any previous or future activities. The classroom is arranged so that each table has a group of four to six students seated around it. However, students spend their time working quietly and independently on completing worksheets. The problems students work on are part of a currently popular manipulative-based mathematics curriculum. With this instructional arrangement, the teacher spends her time walking around the room answering individual questions, and students often spend a good deal of time waiting for the teachers' attention.

During the lesson described here, a group of Spanish-speaking students have been separated from the rest of the class to receive special attention. The teacher and four students sit around a table. The lesson is on chip trading and place value, and very closely follows the teacher's guide for this curriculum. The teacher and each student have square boards in front of them, and there is a basket of red and black plastic objects on the table. The teacher pulls out one red and four black objects, puts them in the middle of the table, and says something too low for anyone to hear clearly. Then, she begins again and as she points to each black object, she says: "Uno, dos, tres, cuatro" (*one, two, three, four*) and as she puts her finger on the red object, she says "manzanas" (*apples*), as a name for the collection. She then signals with her hand for all the students to join in and repeat the chant that she has just demonstrated. In unison, the chant is completed twice and then each individual child is signaled to take a turn. The third time through the group chant, one of the young girls makes a mistake and says "cinco" (*five*), instead of "manzanas." She is told to do the chant again. Once the teacher is satisfied that the routine has been mastered by everyone, she then directs each student to move the black objects as they are counted to one side of the board and when they come to "manzanas," the red object is exchanged for the others. This routine of regrouping in base 5 proceeds for several turns, and then the process is reversed in the same strict order. The only talk that takes place is the counting described. There is no discussion of why "manzanas" is used in place of "five," nor of the cognitive relevance of this activity to the nature of regrouping in general and to base 10 in particular.

Teacher 2

Just as English is the primary language used in Teacher 1's classroom, Spanish is what is most often heard in Teacher 2's room. Also, just as students spend most of their time working individually in the other class-room, in this room, they spend their time working in groups on various projects that integrate mathematical skills related not only to adding and subtracting with multidigit whole numbers, but also with basic understand-ings of rational numbers. They also spend considerable time sitting in a group on a carpet in front of the teacher, who sits on a small chair. In this arrangement, teacher and students engage in lively discussions focused on mathematics. By traditional standards, this class is very noisy. The follow-ing is an example of Teacher 2's lessons. Each student uses a slate for writing the problem.

T: Okay . . . write . . . one hundred and three, one hundred and three, ciento tres, ciento tres, . . . ¿Si digo ciento tres, cuantos lugares voy a tener ocupados?
        (. . . *one hundred three, one hundred three. . . . If I say one hun-dred three, how many places are going to be occupied?*)

Sch: Ciento tres, ciento tres!
        [Sch. indicates that many students are talking at the same time.]

S1:   Tres. (*Three.*)

S2:   Tres. (*Three.*)

T: Voy a tener tres lugarsitos. . . . ¿Van a estar los tres lugares ocupados?
        (*I'm going to have three places. . . . Will the three places be oc-cupied?*)

Sch: Si. (*Yes.*)

S1:   No.

S2:   No.

S3:   Yes.

S4:   No, porque esta un soldado.
        (*No, because there's a soldier.*) [Students use "soldier" to describe the zero place holder.]

The discussion continues with various students offering opinions, asking questions, and sometimes freely changing the subject. The teacher brings the students back to the original topic.

T: Okay, ciento tres, we have how many hundreds?

Sch: One.

T: Yes, one hundred. What do we mean when we say we have one hundred, what do we mean by that? [The teacher translates her statements.] ¿Que quiere decir . . . que queremos decir cuando decimos que tenemos una centena?

S1:   Una . . . una vez cien.
        (*One . . . one time a hundred.*)

Sch: Diez!

S2:   Yo deje . . . zero veces diez.
        (*I said . . . zero times ten.*)

A debate among the students ensues and a correct interpretation is arrived at with the help of the teacher, who both questions and explains. Then another multidigit number is offered and the discussions begin again.

On a subsequent day, the students are about to start a project of baking a cake. The project is intended to reinforce skills in reading and following directions, as well as basic concepts of measuring and rational numbers. The students are to work in small groups with each group having its own box of cake mix. Before starting the project, the students gather together on the floor in front of the teacher for overall directions on how to proceed. Shortly after the teacher begins, one of the students interrupts with a question about the picture of a slice of cake that is on the box. The student has recognized that the slice must be a fraction of the cake; the question has to do with what fraction is represented. The following dialogue is another example of how this teacher seizes opportunities to engage her students in mathematical talk and thinking.

S1: What is this? [The student is indicating the picture of a slice of cake on the box.]

S2: Son de chocolate.
(*They are chocolate.*)

T: What?

S1: Mira, le quitaron uno.
(*Look, one has been taken.*)

S3: De chocolate.
(*Of the chocolate.*)

T: Oh, I see, you guys, le quitaron un pedazo a la fracción, ¿verdad?
(*Oh, I see, you guys, a piece was taken that's a fraction, right?*)

Sch: ¿Que fracción es esta? [indicating the cake slice]
(*What fraction is this?*)

S1: Era un tercio.
(*It was a third.*)

T: ¿Creen ustedes que este es un tercio?
(*Do you think this is a third?*)
[The students all say yes.]
Pero está muy chiquita para ser un tercio. Miren el tercio que grandoso está allí [pointing to a picture on the wall of a pie-shaped third the students had made].
(*But this is too small to be a third. Look how big the third is over there.*)

S2: Un cuarto.
(*A fourth.*)

S3: Miren que tan chiquito [pointing to another picture on the wall of a pie-shaped fourth].
(*Look, it's too small.*)

S4: Teacher, teacher, si le quitan . . . un poquito del tercio.
(*Teacher, teacher, if you take . . . a little from the third.*)

The students continue offering guesses, making comparisons with what they already know about fractions, and justifying their own analysis. After a short while, one of the students finally asks: "How will we figure it out?" The teacher responds with a question that invites the class to offer ways to figure out what fraction is represented by the slice. The students accept the challenge and spend part of the afternoon trying to measure the cake slice instead of doing the baking project.

From these examples, we can infer each teachers' assumptions about the role and purpose of talk in mathematics. In Teacher 1's classroom, students' talk is controlled through the use of repetition and choral speaking. There is no room for personalization by a student, since deviations in responses are met with corrections and implicit herding back into the group.

Teacher 2, on the other hand, carries on active discussions with many instances of positive challenges to students to explain what they mean and to use what they know to solve a problem not encountered before. There are many variations in the student responses and clear indications that everyone can and has a right to offer his or her own idea or to ask a question.

In essence, what we can see here are two very different messages being given to Hispanic students via communication processes. In the first class, students are being told implicitly that they cannot really participate in mathematics, that mathematical knowledge is beyond them, and that this knowledge is something that someone else has to give them. In the second class, the implied message is just the opposite: Mathematics is participatory, it resides within each one of us because of universal experiences with quantities, and it is socially constructed, meaning that all students have equal chances in mathematics.

Summary and concluding remarks

Throughout this discussion, I have argued that there is nothing inherent about Hispanic students or their culture and family life that should handicap them to the extent indicated in recent national studies (Matthews et al., 1984; Moore & Smith, 1987). Instead, I have offered alternative hypotheses that focus on the nature of teachers' language use in the instruction of mathematics. I have pointed to issues concerning teachers' clarity of wording and choice of languages – that is, English or Spanish. I also have offered a perspective that connects the relatively simple concept of speaking with a more crucial and formidable aspect of mathematics teaching and learning related to the alienation or empowerment of minority students in mathematics.

I wish to conclude with a reminder of my opening remarks to the effect that consideration of a shift in paradigms away from students and toward school processes, including teaching, is not to suggest fault finding or cynicism about teachers. My position is that teachers are genuinely good hearted and concerned about providing the best instruction possible. In fact, as I noted earlier, the teachers in this study recognized their shortcomings with respect to explaining mathematics and being able to change their instructional practices. They also felt a sense of powerlessness when it came to acting on their intuitions about effective instruction.

What I am suggesting is that variables related to teacher discourse, learning environments that promote student talk, and educational policies that encourage and support instructional change in light of these variables have not gotten sufficient attention as we discuss Hispanic students' performance in mathematics. We have operated too long with the myth that mathematics teaching and learning transcends linguistic considerations. As I hope I have demonstrated, such a mythology is particularly detrimental to the educational advancement of high-risk students.

Nor are the issues I have put forth easily reduced to improving bilingual teachers' clarity of speech or engaging students in classroom discourse. We must begin to ask questions about the content of teachers' conceptual explanations and about teachers' abilities to use questions and cues to extend student talk and thinking, all in two languages. We must ask questions about how to carry out principles of teacher and student dialogues in those cases when the participants speak different cultural languages. We must ask questions about the use and quality of contextualized situations so that they genuinely engage minority students in higher-level critical thinking in mathematics rather than in superficial, and ultimately lower-level thinking. Most important, we should ask questions about our teacher-training policies and activities and how they affect and interact with the foregoing issues. Are *all* teachers provided with sufficient and specific opportunities to acquire appropriate knowledge and skills with which to implement effective instruction in mathematics in multilingual and multicultural contexts?

Last, what sets these issues and questions apart from a more generalized discussion of improved instruction for all students? Why is it not enough to assume that "good teaching is simply good teaching"? The answers lie in the implied assumption that we can ignore socially contextualized instruction, which considers the unique sociolinguistic and cognitive needs of language minority students. Improved instruction for Hispanic students in mathematics is grounded in the process of redefining teaching as creating learning environments that capitalize on students' home language and experiences rather than ignoring or devaluing them.

Acknowledgments

The research reported in this paper was supported in part by National Science Foundation grant number MDR-8850535. Any opinions, conclusions, or recommendations are those of the author and do not necessarily reflect the views of the National Science Foundation.

I wish to express my debt and gratitude to colleagues who assisted me along the way. I would like to thank the very dedicated teachers and students who allowed me into their classrooms and shared their time and insights with me; I promised them anonymity and so I must thank them collectively. I would also like to thank members of the research team: José Prado, who started work on the project as a high school apprentice and is now a confirmed college student; Kathryn Bert and Jennifer Cowgill, research assistants, who spent many hours videotaping and transcribing; Gilberto Cuevas, Hugh Mehan, and Alba Gonzalez Thompson, who served as consultants throughout the project; and Verna Adams and David Pimm for their thoughtful comments on earlier drafts of this work. Finally, but not least, I am grateful to Douglas B. McLeod, a special colleague and collaborator from the beginning.

Notes

1 The focus of the research and discussion in this chapter is on Spanish-speaking children of Mexican descent, to whom I refer with the generic term Hispanic. However, many of the issues and concepts discussed here pertain equally well to any group of students who are non-English or limited-English proficient.
2 For additional discussion and a comprehensive review of research in bilingual education, the reader is referred to L. W. Fillmore and C. Valadez (1986), Teaching Bilingual Learners, in M. Wittrock (Ed.), *Third Handbook of Research on Teaching* (pp. 648–685), New York: Macmillan. Also, a good review of successful programs and their characteristics can be found in S. Krashen and D. Biber (1988), *On Course: Bilingual Education Success in California,* Sacramento: California Association for Bilingual Education.

References

Au, K., & Jordan, C. (1981). Teaching reading to Hawaiian children: Finding a culturally appropriate solution. In H. Trueba, G. P. Guthrie, & K. Au (Eds.), *Culture in the bilingual classroom: Studies in classroom ethnography* (pp. 139–152). Rowley, MA: Newberry House.

Bishop, A. (1991). *Mathematical enculturation.* Norwell, MA: Kluwer.

Casteneda, A. (1983). Mathematics and young bilingual children. In T. H. Escobedo (Ed.), *Early childhood bilingual education: A Hispanic perspective* (pp. 139–147). New York: Teachers College Press.

Cazden, C. (1986). Classroom discourse. In M. C. Wittrock (Ed.), *Handbook of research on teaching* (3d ed.), (pp. 432–463). New York: Macmillan.

Cuevas, G. (1984). Mathematics learning in English as a second language. *Journal for Research in Mathematics Education, 15,* 134–144.

Cummins, J. (1981). The role of primary language development in promoting educational success for language minority students. In *Schooling and language minority students: A theoretical framework* (pp. 3–50). Evaluation, Dissemination and Assessment Center, California State University, Los Angeles.

Fillmore, L. W., & Valadez, C. (1986). Teaching bilingual learners. In M. C. Wittrock (Ed.), *Third handbook on research on teaching* (3d ed.), (pp. 432–463). New York: Macmillan.

Freire, P. (1970). *Pedagogy of the oppressed.* New York: Continuum.

Garcia, E. (1988). Attributes of effective schools for language minority students. *Education and Urban Society, 2,* 387–398.

Halliday, M. A. K. (1978). *Language as social semiotic.* Baltimore, MD: Edward Arnold.

Khisty, L. L., (1991). *Program and policy issues in the mathematics education of Hispanic bilingual students.* Unpublished manuscript. University of Illinois at Chicago, College of Education.

Khisty, L. L., McLeod, D., & Bertilson, K. (1990). Speaking mathematically in bilingual classrooms: An exploratory study of teacher discourse. In G. Booker, P. Cobb, & T. Mendicutti (Eds.), *Proceedings of the Fourteenth International Conference for the Psychology of Mathematics Education* (Vol. 3, pp. 105–112). Mexico City: CONACYT.

Krashen, S., & Biber, D. (1988). *On course: Bilingual education success in California.* Sacramento: California Association for Bilingual Education.

Langer, J. (1987). A sociocognitive perspective on literacy. In J. Langer (Ed.), *Language, literacy and culture: Issues of society and schooling* (pp. 1–20). Norwood, NJ: Ablex.

Matthews, W., Carpenter, T., Lindquist, M., & Silver, E. (1984). The third national assessment: Minorities and mathematics. *Journal for Research in Mathematics Education, 15,* 165–171.

Moll, L. (Ed.). (1990). *Vygotsky and education: Instructional implications and applications of sociohistorical psychology.* Cambridge University Press.

Moll, L., & Diaz, S. (1987). Change as the goal of educational research. *Anthropology and Education Quarterly, 18,* 300–311.

Moore, E., & Smith, A. (1987). Sex and ethnic group differences in mathematical achievement: Results from the national longitudinal study. *Journal for Research in Mathematics Education, 18,* 25–36.

National Center for Education Statistics. (1981). Projections of non-English background and limited-English-proficient persons in the U.S. to the year 2000. *Forum: Bimonthly Newsletter of the National Clearinghouse for Bilingual Education, 4,* 2.

National Council of Teachers of Mathematics. (1989). *Curriculum and evaluation for school mathematics.* Reston, VA: Author.

Pimm, D. (1987). *Speaking mathematically.* New York: Routledge & Kegan Paul.

Scribner, S., & Cole, M. (1981). *Psychology of literacy.* Cambridge, MA: Harvard University Press.

Spanos, G., Rhodes, N. C., Dale, T. C., & Crandall, J. (1988). Linguistic features of mathematical problem solving: Insights and applications. In R. Cocking & J. Mestre (Eds.), *Linguistic and cultural influences on learning mathematics* (pp. 221–240). Hillsdale, NJ: Erlbaum.

Tharp, R., & Gallimore, R. (1988). *Rousing minds to life.* Cambridge University Press.

Tikunoff, W. (1985). *Applying significant bilingual instruction in the classroom.* Rosslyn, VA: National Clearinghouse for Bilingual Education, United States Department of Education (1992). ERIC: Instructional features in the classroom, Part 3.

United States Department of Education. (1982). *The condition of bilingual education in the nation, 1982.* A Report from the Secretary of Education to the President and the Congress. Rosslyn, VA: National Clearinghouse for Bilingual Education. (ERIC Document Reproduction Service No. ED 262 555).

Vygotsky, L. S. (1978). *Mind in society: The development of higher psychological processes.* Cambridge, MA: Harvard University Press.

Wertsch, J. V. (1985). *Vygotsky and the Social Formation of Mind.* Cambridge, MA: Harvard University Press.

13   Equity in the future tense: Redefining relationships among teachers, students, and science in linguistic minority classrooms

Beth Warren and Ann S. Rosebery

Equity in science for linguistic minority children can have at least two meanings. Cast in the present tense, calls for equity mean providing linguistic minority children with the same educational opportunities currently available to children in the educational mainstream: the same science, the same mathematics, and so forth. Cast in the near-future tense, calls for equity express a critique of current mainstream practice. What is needed, these critiques say, is not more of the same, nor even a more efficient version of current practice, but an entirely different kind of science and mathematics practice. This point of view is tied to the science and mathematics education reform movements, although more implicitly than explicitly, because the documents representing these movements (American Association for the Advancement of Science, 1989; National Council of Teachers of Mathematics, 1989; National Research Council, 1989) unfortunately do not deal assertively or deeply with issues of equity for linguistic minority children (Meyer, 1989).

Secada (1989, and personal communication, August 4, 1992) uncovers part of the dilemma embodied in these two meanings of equity by making an analogy to a "moving target." He argues that if we take current practice as the object of equal opportunity, then we are committing to the view that current practice in science and mathematics is worthy of emulation. He argues that it is not. Therefore, equity must be conceptualized in the future tense, with science and mathematics envisioned as something other than the textbook and demonstration-based curricula they currently are.

But we believe the dilemma runs even deeper. If we target the near future and involve linguistic minority children in different, "progressive" forms of scientific and mathematics educational practice, the children are still accountable – at least for the present – in the terms set by current practice (e.g., standardized tests). Delpit (1986, 1988) frames the argument as follows. Progressive pedagogies – which she defines as emphasizing meaning over form, process over product, contextualized learning over decontextualized learning – may actually undercut minority children (she is speaking

298

specifically of African American children). African American children, she argues, possess meaning and fluency; what they need to develop are the skills – control over specific written and spoken discourse forms – that middle-class children learn at home and get to practice at school. Delpit advocates a more reasoned interaction of skills and process, meaning and form, one that would allow for the representation of "multicultural voices" in determining the shape of progressive educational practice. She also argues for the explicit teaching of the "culture of power" (e.g., ways of talking, writing, interacting, and valuing) to children outside that culture (e.g., poor, nonwhite, non–English-speaking children). Without such explicit teaching, she maintains, minority children will not acquire the discourse patterns, interactional styles, and spoken and written language codes they need to succeed in the larger society.

We believe, in accord with Secada's (1989) position, that equality of educational opportunity in science cannot be achieved by importing mainstream school science into linguistic minority classrooms. However, in defining a new kind of science practice, we also seek to respond to the dilemma articulated by Delpit. We believe, as we think Delpit (1986, 1988) does, that we can redefine science in schools so that it admits diverse sense-making practices, carries with it more egalitarian values, and ensures that linguistic minority students acquire the mainstream literacies they need to succeed in school and beyond (Rosebery, Warren, & Conant, 1992; Warren, Rosebery, & Conant, 1994). Our view is that mainstream literacies, rather than defining how science is practiced in schools, must be embedded in an entirely different kind of practice.

In this chapter, we describe our work with linguistic minority children and their teachers – one goal of which is to create scientific sense-making communities in the classroom that parallel in some important respects science as it is practiced in the world. In particular, we explore the question, "What conditions are necessary to create classroom communities of scientific sense making?" by focusing on our work with teachers of linguistic minority children. We believe that the teacher, whether a bilingual, English as a second language (ESL) or science specialist, is critical to creating such communities. By presenting a case study of one teacher's experience learning science in order to teach science, we aim to illustrate the nature and complexity of the learning process that undergirds the creation of classroom communities of scientific sense making. As background to the case study, we explore current classroom practice in science, outline what we mean by a sense-making perspective, provide examples of students' scientific activity, and summarize what they learn in a sense-making culture.

A critique of current practice in science education

Why is current practice in science, which emphasizes textbook and demonstration-based learning, a bad model? Quite simply, because it does not work. Numerous reports testify to the sorry state of science education (Mullis & Jenkins, 1988). One recent publication reports that three-fourths of American high school graduates do not take science after the 10th grade (National Science Teachers Association, 1992). Except for a narrow elite, most students are put off by science, with its emphasis on assimilating textbook knowledge, answering known information questions, and making abstract connections in decontextualized situations.

This estrangement from science is exacerbated in the case of minority students. In general, they have less access to science, owing to stratification processes and resource limitations (Kozol, 1991; Mehan, 1991; Oakes, 1985, 1986). But access alone does not guarantee equal opportunity. As numerous studies have shown, the ways of knowing, talking, interacting, and valuing of low-income, African American, and linguistic minority communities differ from those evident in the mainstream science classroom (Au, 1980; Erickson & Mohatt, 1982; Heath, 1983; Michaels, 1981; Michaels & Bruce, 1989; Philips, 1972; Scollon & Scollon, 1981). School science as currently constituted privileges mainstream, middle-class ways of knowing (even if it does not succeed in engaging the interest of most middle-class children).

Furthermore, as Gee (1990) argues, schools may be good places to *practice* mainstream ways of talking and knowing, but they are not good places to *acquire* them. In current science classrooms, this problem is particularly acute because students do not often get to use scientific language themselves to construct meaning. In his study of the forms and functions of classroom science talk, Lemke (1990) reports that the predominant form of classroom science talk conforms to the pattern "teacher question–student answer–teacher evaluation," or triadic dialogue. Forms of talk involving authentic conversation ("true dialogue" and "cross-discussion" in Lemke's terms) are rarely found, except when the subject is not science but some nonacademic topic such as classroom business. Moreover, even in cases where students do get to use language to construct scientific meaning, the sense they are making may not always be understood if they talk science in nonstandard ways (Lemke, 1990; Michaels & Bruce, 1989). As Michaels and O'Connor (1991) suggest, teachers may privilege those students whose ways of talking are the same as theirs. One result is that students who talk science in nonstandard ways may be judged "not smart enough" to study science, let alone become scientists.

As Lemke (1990) argues, two sets of beliefs about science undergird mainstream practices and judgments about who can and cannot do science. One has to do with the "ideology of the *objective truth* of science" (p. 137), namely, that science is about facts that are indisputable and authoritative, based on observation and experiment, and independent of theory. Science appears as something other than the human, meaning-making, and intensely socially constructed activity it is (Knorr-Cetina & Mulkay, 1983; Latour & Woolgar, 1986). The other set of beliefs Lemke calls the "ideology of the *special truth* of science" (p.138), by which he means that in schools, students learn that science is a truth accessible only to experts, utterly opposed to common sense. According to this view, scientific knowledge is not only fixed and authoritative, but is constituted of the work of extraordinarily gifted individuals. Science, so the ideology goes, is such a difficult subject that only the specially talented can ever hope to master it. Those who cannot just aren't smart enough and either opt out of science or are selected out by stratification processes (Mehan, 1991; Oakes, 1985, 1986).

No one points out that science is taught only in very restricted ways. The restrictions tend to insure that only people whose backgrounds have led them to already talk a bit more like science books do, to already learn in a particular style and at a particular pace, to already have an interest in a certain way of looking at the world and certain topics and problems, will have much chance of doing well at science.

It is not surprising that those who succeed in science tend to be like those who define the "appropriate" way to talk science: male rather than female, white rather than black, middle- and upper-middle class, native English speakers, standard dialect speakers, committed to the values of North European middle-class culture (emotional control, orderliness, rationalism, achievement, punctuality, social hierarchy, etc.). No one points out that science has been done very effectively by other sorts of people in other kinds of cultures, or that science might look a little different in its models and emphases if its recent history had come at a time when other cultures had been politically dominant in the world and in a position to command more of its resources (say Italy, or China, or India). (Lemke, 1990, p. 138)

To summarize, school science as currently enacted is not just bad science practice; it also marginalizes those students who do not already represent mainstream ways of knowing and talking. As we have noted, it also appears that, except for a narrow elite, many middle-class students are put off by school science. In the face of this reality, the equity question then becomes one of how to make science an activity in which all students can participate successfully. However, this perspective has its dangers, too. In fact, most, if not all, of the major reform documents in science and mathematics state their commitment to the education of all students (American Association for the Advancement of Science, 1989; National Council of Teachers of Mathematics, 1989; National Research Council, 1989). Nevertheless, they are consistently vague on how minority students are to be brought into the reform movement. How exactly will they participate? To what extent will reforms take into account their culturally based practices and specific educational needs? Typically, the details of reform are worked out in mainstream contexts, with the implication that they can then simply be imported into nonmainstream contexts (e.g., bilingual education). But, in fact, reforms rarely "trickle down" (Secada, 1989), in part because they have not been explicitly conceptualized in terms of nonmainstream contexts and concerns, and are therefore inappropriate. Other factors also impede reform in nonmainstream contexts. Cole and Griffin (1987) specifically point to the economic and political pressures on schools serving mostly minority populations to reduce dropout rates and improve achievement test scores:

> It is not surprising that educators of minority students are pressured to "do the basics" better and leave innovative educational practices to others. However, a continued imbalance in the educational mandates that guide the education of minorities and of white middle-class children deepens the problem: as schools serving minority children focus their resources on increasing the use of well-known methods for drilling the basics, they decrease the opportunities for those children to participate in the higher level activities that are needed to excel in mathematics and science. (pp. 4–5)

We have framed our work in light of these concerns. In seeking to define a new kind of scientific practice in the classroom, we have deliberately located our effort in linguistic minority contexts. In the next section, we elaborate on our perspective, its theoretical underpinnings, and its practical implications. We also provide examples of students' scientific activity and evidence of their learning.

A sense-making perspective on science

For the past 4 years in the Cheche Konnen Project ("search for knowledge" in Haitian Creole), we have been working collaboratively with classroom bilingual, ESL, and science teachers from the Cambridge and Boston, Massachusetts public schools to understand science as a sense-making activity. Together, we have been exploring means for creating communities of scientific practice in language minority classrooms (Rosebery et al., 1992; Warren et al., 1992), that is, classroom communities that parallel in some important ways science as it is practiced in the professional world. Our goal is to make school science more a way of working and meaning making than a static set of concepts acquired in the context of an abstracted and generic methodology.

In our research, we are exploring what, if any, connection might exist between scientific practice in professional scientific communities and in schools. We assume, first and foremost, that scientific practice in the world is heterogeneous rather than unitary (Latour & Woolgar, 1986; Lynch, 1985). In actual scientific practice, competent practitioners orchestrate a variety of mediational means (e.g., tools, discourses, or genres) to construct scientific meaning. Second, we assume that scientific practice in schools may not, and even should not, look exactly like scientific practice in the world. Nevertheless, we believe that there is much to be learned about what science in schools *can be* by examining science as it is practiced in professional communities. Understanding the relationships between these communities will help us ultimately to clarify what it means to "learn science."

What, then, is the nature of scientific practice? In trying to understand this, we have examined several sources: in particular, writings from the sociology and ethnography of scientific work and writings of scientists themselves (Feynman, 1988; Knorr-Cetina & Mulkay, 1983; Latour, 1987; Latour & Woolgar, 1986; Longino, 1990; Lynch, 1985; Medawar, 1987). A central theme has emerged from our reading of this literature: Scientific practice is *a socially and culturally mediated process of meaning construction and criticism.*

For example, the Nobel Laureate scientist, Sir Peter Medawar (1987), compellingly describes scientific practice as a particular kind of storytelling:

Like other exploratory processes, [the scientific method] can be resolved into a dialogue between fact and fancy, the actual and the possible; between what could be true and what is in fact the case. The purpose of scientific enquiry is not to compile an inventory of factual information, nor to build up a totalitarian world picture of Natural Laws in which every event that is not compulsory is forbidden. We should think of it rather as a logically articulated structure of justifiable beliefs about a Possible World – a story which we invent and criticize and modify as we go along, so that it ends by being, as nearly as we can make it, a story about real life. (pp. 110–111)

Medawar's use of the story metaphor represents a bold challenge, both to typical school beliefs about what it means to be scientifically literate, and to the larger culture's assumptions about the nature of scientific knowledge and work. First, he directly challenges the belief that science is, at bottom, the accumulation of factual information about the natural world. Second, he challenges the belief that scientists work according to a rigorously defined, logical method, known popularly as the scientific method. And third, through his emphasis on storytelling (by which he means theory building and criticism), he challenges the belief that scientific discourse – the construction of scientific meaning – is represented uniquely by forms of writing and talk that are thoroughly objective and impersonal.

Central to Medawar's vision is an idea of scientific practice in which creativity, construction, and criticism – rather than discovery – predominate. His language suggests that science is projective rather than objective: Scientists build stories about a *possible* world, they do not discover the truth that already exists just waiting to be uncovered. Further, he insists on the dialogic quality of scientific activity: fact and fancy, invention and criticism interacting.

Contemporary sociological and ethnographic studies of the nature of scientific activity in laboratory settings add an explicit social dimension to this picture (Knorr-Cetina & Mulkay, 1983; Latour, 1987; Latour & Woolgar, 1986; Longino, 1990; Lynch, 1985). These studies show that scientists construct and refine their ideas within a community in which they transform their observations into findings through argumentation and persuasion, not simply through measurement and discovery. The apparent "logic" of scientific papers – the very thing that gets modeled in many science texts as the scientific method – is really the end result of the practice of a group of scientists who, through informal and formal talk, graphs, notes, statements, drafts of papers, and published papers, construct accounts ("stories"), negotiate claims, put forward and defend arguments, and the like (Latour & Woolgar, 1986). When asked what they are doing, scientists claim merely to be discovering facts; but close observation reveals that they are actually writers and readers in the business of being convinced and convincing others. (It is hard not to hear an echo of Medawar's storytelling in this.)

How is this view of science realized in the classroom? In Cheche Konnen, science is organized around students' own questions and inquiries. Students design studies to explore their questions; collect, analyze, and interpret data; build and argue theories; establish criteria and evaluate evidence; challenge assumptions; draw conclusions; and, where appropriate, take actions based on their results. Much of the science that goes on (the "curriculum") emerges from the students' own activity, the questions they pose, the dilemmas they meet, the observations they make, the experiments they design, and the theories they articulate.

Over the past 4 years, students' scientific activity has encompassed different phenomena and taken various forms. Students from kindergarten through high school have investigated the ecology of a local pond, the acoustics of a traditional Haitian drum, their local weather, and the relationship between salt intake and physical fitness. In addition to ranging in age, the students are linguistically and culturally diverse (representing seven countries), and vary in educational experience. Most students are judged to be 2 or more years below grade level. Some cannot read or write their first language, let alone English. Some have never been to school before.

What does an investigation look like? One class of seventh- and eighth-grade Haitian students, for example, conducted a study that came to be known as the "Water Taste Test." The students investigated a belief widely held in their class and the other junior high classes in their school that the water from the school's third-floor fountain (where the junior high is located) was better than the water from the other floors. Using a series of blind taste tests, they determined that their belief was not supported by the data. Most of the junior high actually preferred the water from the first-floor fountain, a result that horrified them because "all the little kids slobber in it." This result, however, raised a new question: What was the source of the first-floor preference? They analyzed several possible causes and concluded that temperature was a deciding factor. The first-floor water was 20 degrees colder than that on the other floors. They also uncovered high bacteria levels in all the school fountains, which led them to contact the local water department (see Rosebery et al., 1992, for further details).

At the same school, three kindergartens – one bilingual and two monolingual (English speaking) – have collaborated in science for the past 3 years. In the first year they studied their local weather; in the second, sound; and in the third, trees. During their investigation of sound, the work in one of the monolingual kindergartens took an interesting turn when the children and their teacher decided to soundproof their bathroom. They were driven to this because the noise of the flush, which was magnified as it reverberated off the bare tile walls, so frightened some of the children that they refused to go to the bathroom. Using boxes of increasingly larger size (from standard shoeboxes to wardrobe moving boxes) and alarm clocks, the students explored the sound dampening properties of a variety of materials (cotton balls, sheet rock, Kleenex, styrofoam, bubblepack, egg cartons). To determine the relative "soundproofness" of these materials, they learned to read and interpret a decibel meter. Based on the results of their experiments, the children chose to cover the walls of their bathroom with foam rubber. This reduced the noise level from 89 to 76 decibels. (A jackhammer is approximately 95 dB; normal conversation is approximately 65 dB.)

These investigations had several characteristics in common with the work of scientists. They were generative and constructive in character; one question or problem led to others. In their work, the students explored the relationships among theory, observation, and evidence. And like scientists, they worked at constructing arguments and marshalling evidence to persuade others (students as well as teachers and other members of the school community) of their point of view.

In addition, through their investigations the students learned and practiced mainstream literacies: asking questions, taking notes, arguing different points of view, writing in various genres, and using mathematics in various ways to construct scientific meaning. For example, in the Water Taste Test, the students developed surveys, wrote reports, and publicly presented their findings. They also grappled with statistical issues of sample size, bias, and graphical representation. In the weather and sound studies, the kindergartners (both monolingual and bilingual students), learned to count to 100 by

1s and 10s, explore patterns in complex data, read and make graphs, and add and subtract as they became increasingly proficient with such measurement tools as thermometers, anemometers, and decibel meters. We believe that this kind of science represents an intellectually *and* linguistically richer enterprise than most current school science – one that conveys more clearly an image of what it means to do science and be scientific.

What do students learn when they participate in scientific sense-making communities of the kind just described? To answer this question, we interviewed students who participated in the Water Taste Test to find out how their scientific knowledge and thinking developed over the school year (see Rosebery et al., 1992, for full details). Students were asked to "think aloud" about how they would investigate and explain two realistic, open-ended problems. The problems were designed to explore students' use of hypotheses, experiments, and explanations to organize their scientific reasoning. One problem focused on pollution in Boston Harbor and the other on a sudden illness in a school.

We saw striking changes in the students' talk from the beginning of the school year (September) to the end of the year (June). Not surprisingly, students knew more about water pollution and aquatic ecosystems in June than in September. More important, however, they were able to use this knowledge generatively in thinking through real-world problems. One student, for example, described in detail the processes of chlorination and flocculation when asked to explain how she would clean the water in Boston Harbor.

We also found that the students' scientific thinking had deepened. At the end of the year, the students were using conceptual systems to generate hypotheses and experiments (e.g., linking man-made waste disposal systems and groundwater contamination to water pollution). This contrasts with the start of the year, when they either asserted information stated in the problem description or put forward "black box" conjectures having no explanatory power: "people," "stuff they put in," "a poison."

In addition, the students used hypotheses differently. In the spring, they used hypotheses to organize their scientific reasoning, going beyond the information stated in the problem to put forward testable conjectures. They treated the facts recounted in the problems as *symptoms* of an underlying problem in need of explanation rather than as the explanation itself, as they had in the fall. They also used hypotheses to give direction to their inquiry, to connect stated symptoms to something smaller and more precise than the phenomena described in the problem.

In the spring interviews, hypotheses also functioned as part of a larger inquiry process linking conjecture and experimentation. The students no longer conceptualized evidence simply as information already known (i.e., through personal experience) or given; rather, they conceptualized evidence as the product of experimentation they would undertake to confirm or disconfirm a given hypothesis. This contrasts with their fall interviews, in which they interpreted an elicitation for an experiment ("How would you be sure?" "How would you find out?") as a text comprehension question for which there was a "right" answer. In June, however, they showed that they were beginning to understand the function of and relationship between hypotheses and experiments. For example, they sketched out experiments that were designed to test their hypotheses directly. When asked to explain the "logic" of their experiments, the students showed that they were thinking through the deductive consequences of their hypotheses and understanding critical aspects of experimental design (e.g., isolating a single variable).

One final note about what students learned as they carried out the Water Taste Test. From September to June, we noticed a subtle but important change in the voice the students used to respond to the interviewers' questions. In September, much of their discourse was enacted through the omniscient third person ("they put," "they left"), with occasional uses of the first person to tell stories from personal experience. In June, in contrast, a different voice emerged: the first person dominated, but the "I" was distinctly different from the "I" occasionally heard in September. In June, the "I" was functioning authoritatively as the voice of an active problem solver.

Enculturating teachers into scientific sense-making practices

The teacher plays a pivotal role in orchestrating scientific sense making. Actually, the teacher takes on several roles: coinvestigator, mentor, facilitator, group leader, at times master practitioner, even occasionally lab assistant. This view of teaching is markedly different from the one enacted in conventional school science. In this section, we explore the implications of this shift in perspective for teachers.

How do teachers learn to take on these new roles in the classroom? How do they learn to shape and support students' sense making? We believe it is by appropriating the values and ways of knowing that are associated with scientific practice and linking these through reflection to teaching and learning. We address these questions in the remainder of this chapter, beginning with a description of the theoretical framework that underlies our work with teachers (and students) and concluding with an analysis of one teacher's experience doing science.

Socially shared cognition and situated learning are two terms being used in the research literature to describe a new conceptualization of learning (Brown & Campione, in press; Brown, Collins, & Duguid, 1989; Lampert, 1990; Resnick, Levine, & Teasley, 1991; Schoenfeld, 1992, 1994). Integrating perspectives on learning and cognition from Soviet psychology (Vygotsky, 1978, 1985), cognitive science (Collins, Brown, & Newman, 1989) and anthropology (Geertz, 1973, 1983; Lave, 1991; Lave & Wenger, 1991; Rogoff, 1990), this new view frames learning as an inherently cognitive *and* sociocultural activity. The learner, whether student or teacher, appropriates new forms of discourse, knowledge, and reasoning through his or her participation in socially defined systems of activity or *communities of practice* (Lave, 1991). As Resnick (1988) has recently argued, education may be better thought of as a process of socialization – rather than instruction – into ways of thinking, knowing, valuing, and acting that are characteristic of particular disciplines.

Central to this sociocultural view is the idea that concepts are constructed and understood in the context of a community or culture of practice; their meaning is socially constituted (Brown et al., 1989). Within this community, moreover, practitioners are bound by complex, socially constructed webs of belief that help to define and give meaning to what they do (Geertz, 1983). As Mehan (1993) has noted, members of a community can not make up meanings in any old way. Rather, they build up ways of knowing, talking, acting, and valuing – particular ways of interpreting questions, giving explanations, telling stories or developing evidence – that organize meaning making within the community. Within this sociocultural framework, the learner is conceptualized as one who appropriates new forms of knowledge through apprenticeship in a community of practice (Brown & Campione, in press; Brown et al., 1989; Collins, Brown, & Newman, 1989; Lampert, 1990; Lave, 1991; Resnick, 1988; Rosebery et al., 1992; Schoenfeld, 1992, 1994; Warren et al., 1994).

From this perspective, learning in school really means *appropriating whole systems of meaning* involved in such tasks as reading and answering questions about stories, talking to the teacher, taking tests, playing with other students in the schoolyard, doing mathematics, doing science, doing history, and so on (Gee, 1990; Michaels & O'Connor, 1991). From the perspective of the teacher, learning means appropriating new ways of thinking about science on the one hand, and about teaching and learning on the other: for example, the intellectual value of asking and pursuing a scientific question, arguing one's point of view by marshalling evidence, making sense of another's point of view in relation to one's own, and so forth. For us, the notion of appropriation is key because it casts the learner – whether teacher or student – as someone who is trying to find ways to take the sense-making practices of science, for example, and make them her own, tune them to his own intention or her own sense-making purposes.

But appropriating a new discourse is a difficult process, as Bakhtin (1981) explains:

Prior to this moment of appropriation, the word . . . exists in other people's mouths, in other people's contexts, serving other people's intentions: it is from there that one must take the word, and make it one's own. And not all words for just anyone submit equally easily to this appropriation, to this seizure and transformation into private property: many words stubbornly resist, others remain alien, sound foreign in the mouth of the one who appropriated them and who now speaks them; they cannot be assimilated into his context and fall out of it; it is as if they put themselves in quotation marks against the will of the speaker. Language is not a neutral medium that passes freely and easily into the private property of the speaker's intentions; it is populated – overpopulated – with the intentions of others. Expropriating it, forcing it to submit to one's own intentions and accents, is a difficult and complicated process. (pp. 293–294)

What makes appropriation so difficult is that discourses are inherently ideological; they crucially involve a set of values and viewpoints in terms of which one speaks, acts, and thinks (Bakhtin, 1981; Gee, 1990). As a result, discourses are always in conflict with one another in their underlying assumptions and values, their ways of making sense, their viewpoints, the objects and concepts with which they are concerned. Each gives a different shape to experience. Therefore, appropriating any one discourse will be more or less difficult depending on the various other discourses in which students and teachers participate.

Using Bakhtin's perspective, we can frame the challenge of teacher development as follows: How do we enculturate teachers into scientific sense-making practices and values so that they can appropriate them to their own intentions? The idea is not simply to inculcate a new set of teaching strategies or implement new curricula, as is so often done in the name of teacher development and instructional reform, but to involve teachers in doing science and thinking about science as a discourse with particular sense-making practices, values, beliefs, concepts and objects, and ways of interacting, talking, reading and writing. This insider's view of scientific practice can then form the basis for rethinking classroom practice.

The role of discourse appropriation

We have come to appreciate the importance of discourse appropriation as the basis of teacher education in part because of our own efforts early on in the Cheche Konnen Project. At that time we did not understand, either in theoretical or practical terms, that what is at stake for teachers is their *identity* (Lave, 1991; Scollon & Scollon, 1981) – the mostly tacit beliefs and values on which their pedagogical practice rests. As a result, we implemented a "model" of teacher development that focused on curriculum and instructional strategy.

For example, during the summer preceding the first academic year of the project, a group of four teachers participated in a workshop held in the course of several days. We walked the participants through a set of activities – essentially, an introductory curriculum – on water quality, activities they could take back to the classroom and do with their classes. The lessons were prescribed; they "led" the teachers through the "inquiry" process. (Note that this is a common model of teacher in-service education, one that is usually considered progressive.) We did not create a community in which the teachers were practitioners who did the work of scientific sense making. One consequence of this approach was that they did not have the opportunity to appropriate the values and practices of a scientific sense-making culture. This approach provided them with no reason to uncover, let alone work through, any conflicts between their own viewpoints and values regarding proper instruction for language minority students and those underlying a sense-making perspective in science, unless, of course, they were already predisposed to thinking of science, teaching, and learning in these or similar terms.

To illustrate the problems we encountered by using this approach to teacher education, we include a transcript from one of the teacher's classrooms. It is taken from research we carried out in a multicultural and multilinguistic high school class (Warren, Rosebery, & Conant, 1989). The class was part of a basic skills program within the school's bilingual program. It included those students who were not considered academically ready for the regular bilingual program. The students were in Grades 9 through 12 and represented five different language groups.

In the following lesson, which took place several months into the project, the teacher and students reviewed a homework assignment on acids and bases. (The students were previously introduced to the pH scale and pH paper in the context of an introductory unit on water quality.) The homework asked the students to answer such questions as: "Ammonia has a pH of 11 and baking soda has a pH of 8. Which is more basic? How do you know?" Because several languages were spoken in the group, the lesson was conducted in English. At the point we enter the transcript, the teacher had written on the board: "Ammonia has a pH of 11 and baking soda has a pH of 8." She asked the students for their responses to the question, "Which is more basic?":

Transcript 1

1 Teacher: Which one did you put? Between ammonia and baking soda? Ammonia,

2 ammonia? . . . You see ammonia is 11 and baking soda is 8, so we said ammonia is more

3 basic. Ammonia, OK, all right. Ammonia. I don't see it in here [pointing to a

4 student's worksheet], I don't see it in here. Which one is more basic? Which one?

5 Well, write it down there! OK, all right. Why? How do you know? Who can change

6 that sentence for me [pointing to the sentence on the board] to give me an answer for,

7 how do you know, for ammonia and baking soda, using almost the same words? How

8 can I change that sentence? Nanzie, can you help me? OK, OK, go ahead.

9 [Nanzie goes to the board.]

10 Teacher: Let's change it to answer that last question about baking soda and ammonia.

11 How can I change that sentence to answer, "How do you know about baking soda and

12 ammonia? Because the pH number of –"

13 [Nanzie changes the sentence on the board to read "Because the pH number of."]

14 Rony: Baking soda

15 Teacher: Hold it! Hold it! "Because the pH number of baking soda . . ."

16 [Nanzie completes the sentence on the board by writing "baking soda is 8".]

17 Teacher: Why are you saying what is the pH number? You're going to give it away.

18 Student: 8!

19 Rony and Nanzie [in unison]: is lower –

20 Teacher: I'm sorry. I'm sorry, "is lower than . . ."

21 Rony/Nanzie/Sofie: "The pH number of baking soda . . ."

22 [Nanzie now has written on the board "Because the pH number of baking soda is

23 lower than the pH number of baking soda."]

24 Teacher: What are we talking about here? How are you going to do that? Don't you

25 know? Maybe we should make this "higher" [pointing to the word "lower" in the

26 sentence]; if we say "higher" we have to say that the pH number not of baking soda,

27 uh of – ammonia, we should put "ammonia" right here, so we can use "higher" over

28 there. So don't change this. Yeah, put ammonia in there.

29 [T explains what she wants done in Haitian Creole; the language of about half of

30 the students, including Nanzie.]

31 [Nanzie changes the sentence on the blackboard to read: "The pH number of ammonia

32 is higher than the pH number of baking soda."]

33 Teacher: All right! So what did we say? "The pH number of ammonia is higher, not

34 equal, is higher . . ."

This is not an example of scientific sense making. In fact, it looks a lot like conventional school science. All the action is keyed by questions from the teacher and responses from the students. In addition, because this is a linguistic minority classroom, the attempt to teach science is confounded by the attempt to teach English, too. The teacher's confusion can be seen in the homework question that frames the main discussion, "How do you know?" By this question, does the teacher mean to probe the students' understanding of how different pH readings relate to one another? Or does she intend to have students practice the comparative form in English, as is actually played out in the class? The consequence of her confusion is that neither intention is achieved, as Nanzie's own work eloquently attests (lines 22–23): "The pH of baking soda is lower than the pH of baking soda." The teacher becomes as confused as the students. In lines 25–34, she switches from "lower" to "higher" in order to escape the redundancy of Nanzie's sentence. In the process, she ends up doing all the constructive work herself (lines 27–28), telling the students which words to use and where to put them as if they were pieces in a puzzle.

In this example, we see the form science can take when the teacher has not articulated for herself *what* it is her students should be learning in science (i.e., what it means to do science), *how* they can best learn science, and *why* they should learn science. In our workshops, we did not create the conditions that would foster this kind of deep reflection on scientific and pedagogical practice. As a result, the view of science as a sense-making practice we thought we were putting forward "remain(ed) alien, sound(ed) foreign in [her] mouth" (Bakhtin, 1981).

As a result of this initial experience, we radically restructured our work with teachers. We articulated our goal as follows: to create a community in which teachers can begin to (1) make sense of science conceptually, epistemologically, and pedagogically; and (2) interrogate science and their own deeply held beliefs about it and classroom practice from these points of view. Only by entering into this kind of critical dialogue can teachers begin to appropriate scientific ways of thinking and knowing to their own intentions. With this in mind, we now organize our work with teachers around three guiding themes: the teacher as learner, as practitioner, and as researcher (cf. Duckworth, 1987; Literacies Institute, 1989; Phillips, 1990). These themes highlight three interrelated perspectives critical to the creation of classroom communities of scientific practice: the need for teachers to (1) become involved with scientific phenomena and make sense of their own scientific activity; (2) experiment with new teaching practices derived from their activity as learners; and (3) make sense of (a) their students' understandings, how they emerge, and how they are expressed, and (b) the relationship between students' learning and teaching practices.

To achieve these goals, we have organized a seminar on scientific sense making. We are currently working with eight teachers – five bilingual teachers, two ESL teachers, and a science specialist. These teachers, along with TERC staff (including a biologist), meet every other week for 2 hours after school and for 2 weeks in the summer.

The seminar began with teachers doing science; currently, the group is studying aquatic ecosystems. Most of the teachers started by investigating individual organisms (leeches, snails, planaria), although this focus gradually enlarged to include questions of community ecology and evolution. The teachers' investigations were organized around their own questions:

- Why do snails suddenly stop mating? Do they have a reproduction cycle?
- Are snails born with their shells? How does the shell develop?
- Why do baby snails seem to develop at different rates?
- How big do snails get? What is their life cycle?
- Why do snails poop so much? How important is poop and other "muck" to the ecology of a pond/aquarium? Does anything feed on poop?
- How do snails and other aquatic organisms relate to humans?
- Why do baby leeches stay attached to the mother for so long?
- If we put leeches in with snails, would the leeches decimate the snails?
- How do plants grow without a root system? How does duckweed reproduce?

The teachers pursued these questions at home and in the context of the seminar. For example, each teacher maintained a simple aquarium at home containing snails, plants, and other aquatic organisms (e.g., leeches, planaria, ostracods, etc.). They used hand lenses, stereoscopes, and microscopes to observe the organisms in their aquaria. They read books and articles on aquatic ecosystems, freshwater invertebrates, adaptation and evolution, constructivist teaching and learning, scientific practice, and classroom discourse. In addition, each teacher kept a science notebook in which he or she recorded anything of interest including data (i.e., observations, drawings, measurements), notes from readings, questions, plans for further investigation, and reflections on their classroom practice.

In the seminar, the teachers pursued their investigations and shared their work with their colleagues, collectively trying to make sense of what they were finding by puzzling over dilemmas, posing questions, developing evidence, designing investigations, interpreting data, and evaluating observations. As part of their practice, they also explored at an epistemological level what science is, how scientific knowledge is constructed, where theories come from, what constitutes evidence, the relationships among observations, theory, and evidence, and the like. As the teachers began teaching science, the focus of the seminar expanded to include critical reflection on classroom practice and an explicit exploration of the connection between their work in the seminar and in their classrooms.

Pat: A case study of one teacher

To best illustrate the character of the seminar and what it means to appropriate a new discourse, we focus on the experience of one teacher, Pat. We look in particular at her talk at three different times during the year. We examine what Pat said and how she said it in order to uncover the beliefs and values about scientific practice on the one hand, and on the other, about the teaching and learning in which her talk and action were grounded.

First, a bit of background on Pat. She is an ESL teacher with 25 years of experience. She coteaches, with a Haitian bilingual teacher, a combined fifth–sixth grade of Haitian students and teaches ESL to a combined seventh–eighth grade. Pat describes her science background as typical of most elementary grade teachers educated in the 1960s. She took a few courses in college to meet degree requirements and taught science in Grades 3 and 6, mostly, as she put it, "from the book." She feels that it was through teaching science that she did most of her learning in science.

January 9, 1992

We begin with a transcript from a seminar that took place January 9, 1992. The group had met six times before for a total of 14 hours. At this point in the year, group members were for the most part working as individuals; there was not much give and take about what they were doing and not much co-construction of scientific meaning. The January 9 meeting was the first after the Christmas break. During the holiday, the teachers had pursued their scientific questions at home, observing snails and other aquatic organisms, and reading related texts. To open the meeting, Beth, one of the researchers, asked the teachers to briefly share their observations with the group. Pat began:

Transcript 2 (1/9/92)

1 Pat: I would like to know if any one identified, or how one, how people
2 identified the snails that we have. I had thought it was a Helisoma from the
3 pictures in here, did anyone else?
4 Laura [science specialist]: Yeah, but I didn't key mine out.
5 P: What did you think?
6 L: I remember looking at those pictures but I didn't get really involved in
7 trying to figure out exactly what kind of . . . I sort of figured out what it wasn't in
8 a way, some things that it couldn't be, but I never did really key it right down.
9 Beth: What, Pat, made you particularly interested in identifying the kind
10 of snail?
11 P: Uh, there are so many different types and from the reading it said you can

12 make it if you look at the snail's, um, if the opening is on the left side it is
13 one kind of snail and if it's on the right side it's another kind of snail. And,
14 and I was trying to draw, to draw it, and it just, it was identified. I would like
15 to identify it. It's like, it's like naming somebody, you know, giving a name to
16 something, I, I like doing that.
17 B: Did you find that your observations fit with the kinds of things you were
18 finding in the book?
19 P: Mmmhmm.
20 B: Or –
21 P: And also the reading was interesting to me. You know, I was able to look for
22 the beating heart and the teeth and so forth so, it just, it helped to guide me as
23 far as, um, looking at it, and trying to find out something and seeing how it
24 worked.
25 Gilly [biologist]: Could you see the teeth?
26 P: Yes, the little red thing.
27 G: Yeah?
28 P: Hmmhmm.
29 G: Yeah?
30 P: Hmmhmm. In some of them.
31 B: What, what kind of red thing? I mean what details . . .?
32 P: Well, there are lots, you know uh there are thousands of teeth and the
33 teeth break off and then they grow more teeth so you know they, they're back
34 and forth, I think, I guess I have to look again [referring to her notebook] . . .
35 the *radula*. Ahh, it moves back and forth very rapidly and grinds the food to
36 clean it in the roof of this . . . *buccal cavity*. I learned all sorts of vocabulary
37 words. [Laughs] That means stomach. [Laughs] There are so many words I
38 didn't know that I had my dictionary next to me looking up words.
39 B: Did you ever see a snail eating?
40 P: Sure.
41 B: Using its mouth?
42 P: Mmhmm, mmmhmm. You could actually see it with the hand lens or, ah, it
43 was kind of munching and that's what it even says, it's munching. And then
44 with all those teeth, there are thou– . . . [reading in notebook] the teeth may
45 number in the thousands! Pretty interesting. Who knows? [Laughs]

This episode is striking in the way that Pat, through her talk, revealed her
initial stance toward science and her perception of herself as a learner. She
reported only those things for which she had found authoritative validation
(i.e., in an external scientific source). When asked to report on the science
she had done over vacation, for example, Pat talked mostly about a passage
on snails she had read in a scientific reference manual on invertebrates. She
shared with the group bits of what she had learned from the book (lines 32–
38) and, referring back to her notes, used several technical words (radula,
buccal cavity) to explain how snails eat. Significantly, her first move in the
conversation (lines 1–3) was to see if others in the group, specifically Laura
(Pat was looking directly at her), the science specialist, had identified the
snail. Through her question and gaze, Pat was seeking confirmation from

a person in the group she deemed more qualified than herself to make scientific claims.

Pat was quite clear about her reasons for using texts as references. In lines 21–24, she explained how the book helped orient her observations ("You know, I was able to look for the beating heart and the teeth and so forth so, it just, it helped to guide me as far as, um, looking at it, and trying to find out something and seeing how it worked"). But Pat's personal observations composed only a small part of what she chose to tell the group. In fact, she shared only two things she herself had seen (line 26, "the little red thing" referring to the snail's mouth, and lines 42–43, "it was kind of munching," referring to the snail's chewing action), and these only when prompted first by Gilly (the biologist) and later by Beth. This imbalance in Pat's talk between personal observation and research from authoritative sources did not accurately reflect the work she had done during the vacation. In her science notebook for this period, she filled nine pages with personal observations of snail anatomy and behavior.

Pat is like many of the teachers with whom we have worked who are initially unsure of the importance, accuracy, and validity of their own scientific work. Reflecting traditional school practices and the larger society's values, they tend to place greater stock in the words of an authority (i.e., a text, an expert, the scientific canon) than in their own sense making. In her report, Pat emphasized what she had learned from a book because, at this moment in the seminar, she placed more value on what it said than on what she herself had seen. It carried more weight than did her own hours of work. In fact, in lines 42–43, Pat revealed just how important external, authoritative validation was to her when she said, "You could actually see it with the hand lens or, ah, it was kind of munching and that's what *it* (our emphasis) even says, it's munching." The "it" was the book she had been reading. Pat's focus on identifying her snails (lines 2–3: "I thought it was a Helisoma") and on acquiring scientific vocabulary also suggests that she was trying to put herself in contact with the scientific canon and the standard scientific register.

From a Bakhtinian (1986) perspective, Pat was struggling to appropriate scientific words, to sound scientific. As she told us later, at this point she did not really understand what it meant to ask a scientific question. In fact, in the transcript Pat called attention to her own uncertainty – about herself as someone who can do science and about the validity of any knowledge she herself had constructed – when, in the last line of the transcript, she rhetorically asked, "Who knows?"

As we see it, the struggle for Pat, as for all learners, lies in appropriating "words" (broadly construed to include ways of making sense, valuing, acting, and the core concepts underlying a discipline) for the purpose of constructing scientific meaning. In this episode, Pat used technical terms for descriptive purposes and, through them, tried to make contact with scientific knowledge and practice. She was, in effect, attempting to set up fixed, definitional equivalence relations (such as those found in dictionaries) between things and their names. As Wertsch (1991) points out, those who use this practice often assume that "meaning is grounded in closed, exhaustive systems of decontextualized sign-type–sign-type relationships, or 'literal meanings' " (p. 116). As a successful learner, Pat is a skilled user of books. Similarly, as an ESL teacher, Pat strongly believes in the power of words; a principal function of her job is to teach new words to her students. Knowing the words of a domain is one of the ways in which she assesses competence – her own and her students' – in that domain. Her use of texts and technical vocabulary is, therefore, highly strategic and, it turns out, effective. Through this strategy, she bridged from familiar, literalist ways of knowing to more interpretive, scientific ways, as the next two transcripts show.

February 13, 1992

The next transcript is taken from a meeting on February 13, 1992. Between the January and the February meetings, the members of the seminar investigated various aspects of snail life, including reproduction, development, and feeding habits. During the seminar immediately preceding the February 13 meeting, Gilly, the project biologist, looked at the contents of a petri dish and found a leech in it with many young attached to its stomach. Pat immediately showed interest in the leech and decided to take it home for observation. Between meetings, she observed the leeches along with the snails she had at home, and filled 15 pages of her notebook with observations of leech and snail behavior (e.g., their movement, anatomy, eating, and mating habits).

At the start of the transcript, Pat took her turn at sharing her observations from the previous 2 weeks. As she did so, a jar containing the leeches was passed among the other seminar members. As she described how one of the snails eluded the adult leech by going above the water line, Sylvio and Laura, two teachers, were looking at the jar and seeing exactly what Pat was describing.

Transcript 3 (2/13/92)

1 Pat: Yeah, an interesting thing is that I had those same leeches in a petri
2 dish for a few weeks and when the mother, the mother must have had, I
3 don't know how many, she must have had more than 15 babies attached
4 to her underbelly because we kept seeing them drop off at, if it were put
5 into heat, if I held them up to the light to look at them on the slide a few

6 would come off, we saw them come off here but none were living in the
7 petri dish and I actually saw twice the large leech with a baby leech in
8 its mouth, it was going in and out and then finally it was sucked in so,
9 and I could find no baby leeches living in the petri dish, so I think that
10 the parent, you know, the adults, were eating the small ones which
11 made me think they must be hungry so I fed them. I took a larger snail
12 but I killed the snail because they couldn't, the snail was able to
13 knock the leech off so that it couldn't get into it to eat. Also the snail
14 was so smart that it would go, the leech would be attached, the snail
15 would go above the water line so the leech had to drop off. So you
16 know they *knew* they were after them. In fact, Sylvio [Pat's teaching
17 partner] was asking why are those snails up on the top of the jar lid
18 so much and I wondered why. Well, they were smart. They tried, they
19 didn't want to be eaten. But once we put them into the larger, the uh,
20 the large, the deeper water and, um, and I gave them to Sylvio to keep,
21 uh, the um, the babies are growing now so – They ate snail and now
22 they don't have to eat the babies apparently. But that's a question. I
23 want to take, you all say you have some more leeches? So the
24 question is, I'll keep some in a petri dish with an adult, adults,
25 without food, well with the snails to eat, see if they eat them then. And
26 then still, like this, it could be the deeper water, it could be, I should
27 have three actually.
28 Ann [a researcher]: Do you want to take some home tonight?
29 P: Yeah.

By February 13th, Pat's talk was markedly different. In her talk, she intertwined observational, conjectural, and experimental modes in one unbroken string of reflection. She was thinking through her talk, ending her turn by spontaneously formulating an experiment, the goal of which was to deepen her understanding of the conditions under which adult leeches eat their young.

Perhaps most striking, in contrast to the January transcript, Pat now spoke as an authority. She was not talking *through* the texts she had read, seeking their authority either to guide her observations or to confirm them. Rather, she spoke distinctly as the *author* of her own observations, discoveries, conjectures, and experiments.

Her report took the form of a story, in Medawar's (1987) and others' (Ochs, Taylor, Rudolph, & Smith, 1992) sense, in that it is a kind of theory with a problem to be solved at its core: how to keep the adult leeches from eating their young. Pat did not just report her observations as a set of events; rather she theorized them, explaining how her observations led her to particular hypotheses (lines 7–11) and beliefs about how the organisms interact (lines 13–19), then to particular actions or experiments (lines 13–19). An example of this theorizing discourse is found in lines 9–11: "I could find no baby leeches living in the petri dish so I think that the parent, you know, the adults, were eating the small ones which made me think they must be hungry so I fed them." But she found that this plan didn't work because the snail eluded capture (lines 13–15): "Also the snail was so smart that it would go, the leech would be attached, the snail would go above the water line so the leech had to drop off." Her last move was unplanned (Ochs, 1979), following on an explanation she marked as tentative, not yet supported by what to her mind was satisfactory evidence (lines 21–22: "They ate snail and now they don't have to eat the babies *apparently*"). She immediately recognized at least one, and possibly two, questions implicit in her account (the conditions under which leeches eat their young; the conditions under which baby leeches can survive). Finally, she proposed an experiment intended to evaluate her tentative explanation (lines 22–23: "But that's a question. I want to take –''). Thus, she opened her own explanation to a possible internal challenge, mirroring the kind of criticism about which Medawar wrote. The quest for naming and identification characteristic of her talk in January gave way in February to theory building and criticism. Perhaps most important, Pat now had an answer to the "Who knows?" with which she concluded her turn in the first episode.

February 27, 1992

Two weeks later, the seminar met again. During those two weeks, Pat gave the leeches to Sylvio, her teaching partner, for observation and caretaking. Pat herself observed snails and several snail egg masses (jelly masses with several eggs lodged in them). The week before Ann reported that a teacher in another seminar had witnessed a dramatic increase in the snail population in her tank (150 by her count). This fact figures in the following episode.

Transcript 4 (2/27/92)

1 Pat: Well, my, my three snails weren't mating so I, I put them into
2 another container and, also the baby, I should have had 150 baby snails
3 by this time like this other woman and they weren't, I mean they were
4 hatching, they were coming out and just stringy masses around but not
5 many snails. So, I've been, I was looking in my jar to see what could
6 have eaten, you know, the snails. I figured they were being eaten
7 somehow and there are, I brought in a few little animals, you know, that I
8 looked at but, um, then I also put some baby, two, some baby snails in
9 a, those, what are those little, petri dishes with some of those
10 animals and left them in for a week and they haven't been eaten. So I,
11 I don't know what's happ– You know, I still have that jar and the snails
12 aren't in there so the water is becoming murky. It's a bit murky, but,
13 you know, it's kind of gross right now. But, um, I don't know what's, why
14 those snails, those baby snails aren't, are not living, so many of them, but my
15 other snails are all alive.
16 Ann: I'll tell you one thing that I've noticed in our tanks down here is

17 that, um, the snails seem to be laying a lot of eggs in the roots of the
18 duckweed, you know, that hang down. And the eggs look fine for a while
19 and then all of a sudden they get cloudy and they get kind of fuzzy
20 around the edges. And we took some of the eggs out and looked at it
21 under a hand lens and under a stereoscope and they seemed to be
22 covered with little tiny creatures. Somebody has said that they look
23 like paramecium. Somebody else has said that they look like, I mean, I
24 have no idea what they are, but they are these little white creatures.
25 Oh, at one point they looked like stentors, they were all over them.
26 They looked just like a huge breeding ground for stentors and so I
27 think that what's going is, it's exactly what you said, something else
28 is –
29 P: I figured last night –
30 A: There's something out of balance.
31 P: That, that, that, that maybe those things, those little things that
32 are eating away at the other things are multiplying at a faster rate
33 than the snails or something like that, you know what I mean? That
34 the balance, it's out of balance, something's out of balance.
35 A: Yeah, hmmhmm. Whatever used to be eating the stentors and
36 keeping them, if they're the ones who are doing the, eating the eggs,
37 whatever used to be keeping them in check, isn't there anymore.
38 Beth [researcher]: Although this issue of –
39 A: Maybe –
40 B: In balance and out of balance –
41 A: Yeah.
42 P: That's interesting.
43 B: Is kind of a weird one, maybe it's not out of balance –
44 Rachel (bilingual teacher): Maybe there aren't supposed to be so
45 many snails.
46 A: Yeah.
47 Someone: That's right.
48 R: And in the other tank where there's 125 snails, that one's out of balance!
49 A: That's right! That's right.
50 P: Think of how many cockroaches are killed, just imagine, and flies.
51 All the larvae that's laid every winter and then in the spring. If some of
52 those things aren't killed, wooo!
53 Laura [science specialist]: And you know that, that's even true for the
54 tank in my room when I think about it. You know, I complain about
55 how many snails are in that tank but when you, when you see how
56 many egg masses get laid on the side of the tank and if there's, you know,
57 20 or 30 baby snails in there sometimes, I pulled 12 egg masses out of
58 there today alone.
59 P: Oh my gosh!
60 L: And then, you know, but it's not as crowded as it should be because if
61 all of those things hatched and grew up –
62 P: I know there aren't even that many snails –
63 L: They should take over everything! And they're in there a lot but not
64 anywhere as much as they should be according to what's been laid.
65 P: Does that newt eat, eat snails?

66 L: I don't think so.
67 P: Snails eat other snails, I saw.
68 R: Yeah, snails eat other snails.
69 L: I have a lot of, uh, planarias in there now, I noticed, and I think
70 they're doing a number on the snails.
71 P: Uh huh.
72 Josiane: They're mean.
73 R: Yeah? What do they do?
74 P: Do you think that's what was eating your snails?

As in the February seminar, here Pat told another story with two problems at its center: why the adult snails weren't mating and why she didn't have more baby snails than she did. She again combined observational, conjectural, and experimental modes: (lines 5–10) "I was looking in my jar to see what could have eaten, you know, the snails. I figured they were being eaten somehow"; (lines 8–10) "I also put some . . . baby snails in . . . petri dishes with some of those animals and left them in for a week and they haven't been eaten." The difference here, in comparison to the previous transcript, lies in the fact that Pat was not able to solve her problem. As a result, in lines 13–15, she repeated the central problem at the end of her first turn: "But, um, I don't know what's, why those snails, those baby snails aren't, are not living, so many of them but my other snails are all alive." Ann interpreted this repetition as an invitation to help Pat think through her problem.

The rest of the episode is a kind of dialogic storytelling that contributes to the co-construction of a theory (Ochs et al., 1992). Sparked by Pat's dilemma and Ann's analogous observation, several members of the seminar began to construct a theory to explain Pat's observations and, by extension, their own. In the process, they not only worked through what might account for Pat's observations, but they also helped Laura, the science specialist, see the tank she had in her classroom in a new light. Each participant in essence functioned as a coauthor (Duranti, 1986; Ochs et al., 1992). Ann's story (lines 16–28) reinforced Pat's own observations. Pat overlapped with Ann just as Ann put forward the idea of balance as being somehow important in explaining the situations she and Pat had observed (lines 26–34). Pat elaborated this idea in her own terms: "I figured last night that, that, that, that maybe those things, those little things that are eating away at the other things are multiplying at a faster rate than the snails, or something like that, you know what I mean?" It is interesting that she appropriated Ann's term "balance" only *after* she had articulated her own idea. Unlike the January episode, in which she relied on the words of texts, Pat chose to say what she thought in her own words first. Ann replied in terms of her own example.

Beth then took a turn (lines 38–43), and posed a challenge to the budding theory, reorienting the frame for its discussion: "Although this issue of 'in balance and out of balance' is kind of a weird one. Maybe it's not out of balance." In lines 44–48, Rachel, a Spanish bilingual teacher, then operationalized this in terms of Pat's dilemma: "Maybe there aren't supposed to be so many snails and in the other tank where there's 125 snails, that one's out of balance!" Pat followed with an analogy to cockroaches and larvae (lines 50–52). At this point (lines 53–64), Laura, the science specialist, reflected on the tank she'd been maintaining: "And, you know, that, that's even true for the tank in my room when I think about it." Laura clearly marked her utterance as a new thought ("when I think about it"). In this instant, she understood the dynamics of her tank differently than before: "You know, I complain about how many snails are in that tank, but when you, when you see how many egg masses get laid on the side of the tank and if there's, you know, 20 or 30 baby snails in there, I pulled 12 egg masses out of there today alone, and then, you know, but it's not as crowded as it should be because if all of those things hatched and grew up, they should take over everything! And they're in there a lot but not anywhere as much as they should be according to what's been laid." The group, through co-construction of a theory, led Laura to this new perspective. The conversation continued as the group tried to figure out exactly what might be keeping the snail population in check. They began by considering the impact of other organisms and ended with questions regarding what might be reducing the snail populations, including other snails.

We see in this episode a particularly rich illustration of the notion that theory building is an interactionally achieved sense-making activity (Ochs et al., 1992; Sacks, 1972, 1974; Schegloff, 1972). Pat's dilemma became a shared dilemma. In the process, the group theorized about it, using analogies, accounts of others' observations, and shifts in perspective on the concepts being theorized.

The foregoing transcripts show that the seminar evolved into a community of science practitioners. Furthermore, the teachers' joint scientific work became the basis for a rethinking of classroom practice. Over time, their inquiry came to include, in addition to their own science, analysis of their teaching practices and how these practices relate to students' learning. In the concluding section, we explore connections between the teachers' scientific practice and their classroom practice.

Building scientific sense-making communities in the classroom

Through their reflective practice, the teachers are constructing a view of science as a socially constituted, meaning-making activity that includes rather than excludes linguistic minority children. This new view of teaching and learning is rooted in the teachers' own appropriation of scientific ways of thinking and knowing. In conclusion, we would like to illustrate one of the ways the teachers are building on their own scientific inquiry and reflective practice to create scientific sense-making communities in the classrooms.

Three months after the group's discussion of snail reproduction and survival rates (transcript 3), the teachers began to critique their teaching practice. They felt they had succeeded in creating classroom communities in which children's scientific questions were valued. However, they were concerned that they did not always know what to do with those questions. In particular, they felt they did not know how to help shape students' questions into scientific investigations. An event in Pat and Sylvio's classroom provided the group with a context for exploring this problem directly.

A student, Jimmy, had written the following question in English in his science notebook as he was observing snails: "Why little animals can make babies? It too little to make baby." This question became the focus of the seminar for several weeks. Among themselves, the teachers explored the possible meanings of Jimmy's question and uncovered unexpected complexities. For example, they realized that Jimmy's use of "little" was ambiguous. By "little," did he mean age, size, sexual maturity? Intrigued by their own interpretations of Jimmy's question, they designed an investigation to study the size and age at which snails reproduce. From their study, they concluded that snails 5 mm in length and up can reproduce. They were careful, however, to note that their data for shorter lengths were not necessarily conclusive (i.e., possible sampling problems; duration of study too short).

In parallel, Pat and Sylvio engaged their students in discussion about the meaning of Jimmy's question. The class then used this discussion as the basis for designing a year-end investigation of the question: At what size do snails make babies? The students designed their investigation so that each student had snails of one size (ranging from 1 mm to 9 mm) in a petri dish. They discussed the importance of providing each with a suitable environment and comparable food supply. They agreed to observe the snails daily to see if any had produced egg masses. They measured the size of each snail once a week to see if they had grown enough to require "reclassification" (i.e., transfer to another petri dish containing snails of the next-larger size). In the end, they decided that on the basis of their data, they could safely conclude that snails 7 mm to 9 mm in length are capable of reproduction. However, they ran into difficulty interpreting their data for shorter lengths because some students had mixed snails of different sizes. For example, they observed that a dish with snails 3 mm and 5 mm in length had egg masses but decided to disqualify it because it violated the design criteria they had established for their study.

During part of a 2-week summer seminar, the teachers continued to reflect on this episode, analyzing transcripts of their own talk about Jimmy's question as well as transcripts from Pat and Sylvio's classroom. Through reflection on their own scientific practice and that of the students, the teachers co-constructed a theory of scientific sense making that brought to light fundamental issues in teaching and learning. For example, they confronted the challenges involved in understanding what students mean by what they say. They realized that bringing to the surface the tacit theories, beliefs, and assumptions underlying students' questions is integral to scientific practice and to shaping scientific investigations in the classroom. They further realized that by making these dimensions of students' thinking explicit, teachers help students specify the parameters of the investigation they need to undertake in order to understand the phenomenon in question. Their reflections also led them to think more deeply about how to orchestrate scientific discussions, the effect of teacher revoicings, ways to investigate the different kinds of questions children ask, how to assess student learning, and ways to socialize students into more formal genres of scientific reading, writing, and talking.

We believe that in order to rethink teaching and learning in these ways, the teachers had to become participants in a community of scientific practice and appropriate scientific ways of thinking and knowing to their own intention. Building on this experience, they explored with their students ways to create sense-making communities in their classrooms. Through participation in these communities, their students, too, are beginning to develop an "insider's view" of science (Rosebery et al., 1992). Pat spoke to this point during the summer seminar:

It seems to me that . . . you're teaching a certain, or they're learning, or you're learning together a certain way of being, of making sense, or of learning how to be scientific, that children never did before, that none of us probably did before in class. So you have microscopes and you have pond water and you have all these things that you've never seen before, all this wonderment around you, and you're able to pick and choose, to ask questions, not have them answered but go looking for evidence, setting up investigations. . . . At least maybe in our classrooms they've learned a way of asking questions. . . . you know, there's this certain way of being in the world that they're learning, that's what I think.

In this chapter we have sought to illustrate the complexities of the process into which we, Pat, the other teachers and their students have entered – namely, to define a new perspective on scientific practice in the classroom that admits diverse sense-making practices, carries with it more egalitarian values, and ensures that linguistic minority students acquire the mainstream literacies they need to succeed in school and beyond. When Pat speaks of students "learning a certain way of being in the world," she is describing a new kind of relationship between students and science, one that is distinctly different from that enacted in conventional school science. Moreover, she sees herself participating in a new relationship with her students, as they jointly work out what it means to be scientific. From this perspective, the transformation of science education into a practice that includes rather than excludes linguistic minorities demands more than new curricula, new teaching strategies or, more broadly, "trickle down" reform strategies. Rather, we believe that the remaking of science education into a more egalitarian sense-making practice entails deep transformations of identity for teachers and students alike, transformations that empower them to think, talk, and act scientifically.

Acknowledgments

The research reported in this chapter was supported by the National Science Foundation (NSF), grant number MDR-9153961. The analysis and preparation of the manuscript was supported by the National Center for Research on Cultural Diversity and Second Language Learning, under Cooperative Agreement number R117G10022 from the Office of Educational Research and Improvement (OERI). The views expressed here do not necessarily reflect the position or policies of NSF or OERI.

The work described in this chapter is the result of a collaboration between researchers at TERC and teachers and students from the Cambridge, Massachusetts Public Schools. In addition to the authors, the TERC research team includes: Faith R. Conant, Josiane Hudicourt-Barnes, Eric Johnson, Gillian Puttick, and Amy Taber. We wish to thank all the teachers, especially Pat Berkley, Sylvio Hyppolite, Laura Sylvan, and Rachel Wyon. Pat Berkley, in particular, spent long hours in conversation with us about the material presented here and carefully read an earlier version of this chapter.

We also wish to acknowledge the thoughtful comments of several colleagues who read various versions of this chapter: Faith R. Conant, Shahaf Gal, Eric Johnson, Bud Mehan, Ricardo Nemirovsky, Gillian Puttick, and Walter Secada.

References

American Association for the Advancement of Science. (1989). *Project 2061: Science for all Americans*. Washington, DC: Author.

Au, K. (1980). Participation structures in a reading lesson with Hawaiian children: Analysis of a culturally appropriate instructional event. *Anthropology and Education Quarterly, 2,* 91–115.

Bakhtin, M. (1981). *The dialogic imagination*. Austin: University of Texas Press.

(1986). *Speech genres and other late essays*. Austin: University of Texas Press.

Brown, A., & Campione, J. (in press). Communities of learning and thinking, or a context by any other name. *Human Development*.

Brown, J. S., Collins, A., & Duguid, P. (1989). Situated cognition and the culture of learning. *Educational Researcher, 18*(1), 32–42.

Cole, M., & Griffin, P. (1987). *Contextual factors in education*. Madison: Wisconsin Center for Education Research.

Collins, A., Brown, J. S., & Newman, S. E. (1989). Cognitive apprenticeship: Teaching the craft of reading, writing, and mathematics. In L. B. Resnick (Ed.), *Knowing, learning, and instruction: Essays in honor of Robert Glaser* (pp. 453–494). Hillsdale, NJ: Erlbaum.

Delpit, L. (1986). Skills and other dilemmas of a progressive black educator. *Harvard Educational Review, 56*(4), 379–385.

——— (1988). The silenced dialogue: Power and pedagogy in educating other people's children. *Harvard Educational Review, 58*(3), 280–298.

Duckworth, E. (1987). *"The having of wonderful ideas" and other essays on teaching and learning* (pp. 122–141). New York: Teachers College Press.

Duranti, A. (1986). The audience as co-author: An introduction. In A. Duranti & D. Brenneis (Eds.), *The audience as co-author* [special issue]. *Text, 6,* 239–247.

Erickson, F., & Mohatt, G. (1982). Cultural organization of participation structures in two classrooms of Indian students. G. Spindler (Ed.), *Doing the ethnography of schooling* (pp. 132–174). New York: Holt, Rinehart & Winston.

Feynman, R. (1988). *What do you care what other people think?* New York: Norton.

Gee, J. P. (1990). *Social linguistics and literacies: Ideology in discourses.* London: Falmer.

Geertz, C. (1973). *The interpretation of culture.* New York: Basic.

——— (1983). *Local knowledge.* New York: Basic.

Heath, S. B. (1983). *Ways with words: Language, life, and work in communities and classrooms.* Cambridge University Press.

Knorr-Cetina, K. D., & Mulkay, M. (Eds.). (1983). *Science observed: Perspectives on the social study of science.* London: Sage.

Kozol, J. (1991). *Savage inequalities.* New York: Crown.

Lampert, M. (1990). When the problem is not the question and the solution is not the answer: Mathematical knowing and teaching. *American Educational Research Journal, 27*(2), 29–63.

Latour, B. (1987). *Science in action.* Cambridge, MA: Harvard University Press.

Latour, B., & Woolgar, S. (1986). *Laboratory life: The social construction of scientific facts.* Princeton, NJ: Princeton University Press.

Lave, J. (1991). Situating learning in communities of practice. In L. B. Resnick, J. Levine, & S. Teasley (Eds.), *Perspectives on socially shared cognition* (pp. 63–82). Washington, DC: American Psychological Association.

Lave, J., & Wenger, E. (1991). *Situated learning: Legitimate peripheral participation.* Cambridge University Press.

Lemke, J. (1990). *Talking science: Language, learning and values.* New York: Ablex.

Literacies Institute. (1989). *The Literacies Institute: Its mission, activities and perspective on literacy.* Technical Report No. 1. Newton, MA: Author.

Longino, H. (1990). *Science as social knowledge.* Princeton, NJ: Princeton University Press.

Lynch, M. (1985). *Art and artifact in laboratory science: A study of shop work and shop talk in a research laboratory.* London: Routledge & Kegan Paul.

Medawar, P. (1987). *Pluto's republic.* Oxford University Press.

Mehan, H. (1991). *Sociological foundations suporting the study of cultural diversity.* The National Center for Research on Cultural Diversity and Second Language Learning, Research Report No. 1. Santa Cruz: University of California.

Mehan, H. (1993). The school's work of sorting out students. To appear in D. Boden & D. Zimmerman (Eds.), *Talk and social structure.* Cambridge: Polity Press.

Meyer, M. R. (1989). Equity: The missing element in recent agendas for mathematics education. *Peabody Journal of Education, 66*(2), 6–21.

Michaels, S. (1981). Sharing time; Children's narrative styles and differential access to literacy. *Language in Society, 10,* 423–442.

Michaels, S., & Bruce, B. C. (1989). *Discourses on the seasons.* Technical Report, Reading Research and Education Center. Champaign: University of Illinois.

Michaels, S., & O'Connor, M. C. (1991). *Literacy as reasoning within multiple discourses:*

Implications for policy and educational reform. Technical Report No. 10. Newton, MA: Literacies Institute.

Mullis, I., & Jenkins, L. (1988). *The science report card: Elements of risk and recovery.* Princeton, NJ: Educational Testing Service.

National Council of Teachers of Mathematics. (1989). *Curriculum and evaluation standards for school mathematics.* Reston, VA: Author.

National Research Council. (1989). *Everybody counts. A report to the nation on the future of mathematics education.* Washington, DC: National Academy Press.

National Science Teachers Association. (1992). *The content core: A guide for curriculum developers.* Washington, DC: Author.

Oakes, J. (1985). *Keeping track: How schools structure inequality.* New Haven, CT: Yale University Press.

(1986). Tracking, inequality, and the rhetoric of school reform: Why schools don't change. *Journal of Education, 168,* 61–80.

Ochs, E. (1979). Planned and unplanned discourse. *Syntax and Semantics, 12,* 51–80.

Ochs, E., Taylor, C., Rudolph, D., & Smith, R. (1992). Storytelling as a theory-building activity. *Discourse Processes, 15*(1), 37–72.

Philips, S. (1972). Participant structures and communicative competence: Warm Springs children in community and classroom. In C. Cazden, D. Hymes, & V. John (Eds.), *Functions of language in the classroom* (pp. 370–394). New York: Teachers College Press.

Phillips, A. (1990). *What teachers need to know.* Technical Report No. 3. Newton, MA: Literacies Institute.

Resnick, L. (1988). Treating mathematics as an ill-structured discipline. In R. I. Charles & E. A. Silver (Eds.), *The teaching and assessing of mathematical problem-solving* (pp. 32–60). Reston, VA: National Council of Teachers of Mathematics and Hillsdale, NJ: Erlbaum.

Resnick, L., Levine, J. M., & Teasley, S. D. (1991). *Perspectives on socially shared cognition.* Washington, DC: American Psychological Association.

Rogoff, B. (1990). *Apprenticeship in thinking: Cognitive development in social context.* New York: Oxford University Press.

Rosebery, A. S., Warren, B., & Conant, F. R. (1992). Appropriating scientific discourse: Findings from language minority classrooms. *Journal of the Learning Sciences, 2*(1), 61–94.

Sacks, H. (1972). On the analyzability of stories by children. In J. Gumperz & D. Hymes (Eds.), *Directions in sociolinguistics: The ethnography of communication* (pp. 325–353). New York: Holt, Rinehart & Winston.

(1974). An analysis of the course of a joke's telling in conversation. In R. Bauman & J. Sherzer (Eds.), *Explorations in the ethnography of speaking* (pp. 337–353). Cambridge University Press.

Schegloff, E. (1972). Notes on a conversational practice: Formulating place. In D. Sudnow (Ed.), *Studies in social interaction* (pp. 75–119). New York: Free Press.

Schoenfeld, A. (1992). Learning to think mathematically: Problem solving, metacognition, and sense-making in mathematics. In D. Grouws (Ed.), *Handbook for research on mathematics teaching and learning* (pp. 334–370). New York: Macmillan.

(1994). Reflections on doing and teaching mathematics. To appear in A. Schoenfeld (Ed.), *Mathematical thinking and problem solving.* Hillsdale, NJ: Erlbaum.

Scollon, R., & Scollon, S. (1981). *Narrative, literacy and face in interethnic communication.* Norwood, NJ: Ablex.

Secada, W. (1989). Agenda setting, enlightened self-interest, and equity in mathematics education. *Peabody Journal of Education, 66*(2), 22–56.

Vygotsky, L. S. (1978). *Mind in society.* Cambridge, MA: Harvard University Press.

(1985). *Thought and language.* Cambridge, MA: MIT Press.

Warren, B., Rosebery, A. S., & Conant, F. R. (1989). *Cheche Konnen: Science and literacy in language minority classrooms*. BBN Technical Report No. 7305, Cambridge, MA: Bolt, Beranek, & Newman.

(1994). Discourse and social practice: Learning science in bilingual classrooms. In D. Spener (Ed.), *Adult literacy in the United States*. Washington, DC: Center for Applied Linguistics and Delta Systems, Inc.

Wertsch, J. V. (1991). *Voices of the mind*. Cambridge, MA: Harvard University Press.

14 Taking power seriously: New directions in equity in mathematics education and beyond

Michael W. Apple

In Arthur Conan Doyles's "The Naval Treaty," Sherlock Holmes and Dr. Watson report to the reader that

Holmes was sunk in profound thought and hardly opened his mouth until we had passed Capham Junction.
"It's a very cheery thing to come into London by any of these lines which run high and allow you to look down upon houses like this."
I thought he was joking, for the view was sordid enough, but soon he explained himself.
"Look at those big, isolated clumps of buildings arising above the slates, like brick islands in a lead-coloured sea."
"The board-schools."
"Light-houses, my boy! Beacons of the future! Capsules with hundreds of little seeds in each, out of which will spring the wiser, better England of the future." (Quoted in Donald, 1992, p. 17)

In this little vignette, we have nearly everything necessary to tell the story of schooling in our own society as well as in Holmes and Watson's earlier London. The school stands as a beacon of hope above the sordid conditions of poor and working-class neighborhoods. It provides the seeds for individual mobility. Yet, these are *isolated* clumps of buildings, unconnected to the daily lives of that "lead-coloured sea." It is their very symbol as above it all, as capsules, that allows them to plant the seeds that will bring a "wiser, better" future. Holmes and Watson's conversation speaks to the tensions in our understanding of schooling. It embodies the hope that all of us have as educators – the hope of a better future for all children. Yet, at the same time, it appropriates an uncritical acceptance of the myth of schooling, the myth that schools – as "neutral institutions" – will provide an equal starting point for all who wish to run the race. Quite importantly, it also includes a subtext: It is a *class* story. The world is seen from above. The metaphors create a vision of rising up, of solid "brick islands" standing strong against a tide of dirty turbulence. A good school is one that is disconnected from the lives below, that ignores the sea. Popular culture and real lives are "sordid."

329

Education and power

The vision just described is not limited to the world of fiction, nor is it held
only by train riders like Watson and Holmes. Rather, many people, including many educators, take a similar position. Anything popular, anything
from that sea, is "soiled." It is not quite serious knowledge. Because of
this, too often we assume that popular literature, popular culture, popular
mathematics and science, are *failed* knowledge, not quite real. Popular
knowledge is pathologized (Donald, 1992, pp. 55–57), at least in comparison
with the existing academic curriculum, which is seen as uplifting and neutral. Nevertheless, the existing curriculum is never a neutral assemblage of
knowledge. It is always based on an assertion of cultural authority (Apple,
1990, 1993a; Apple & Christian-Smith, 1991). The same must be said about
schools. Although there are many schools (and teachers) that are models of
vitality and richness, the vast majority of schooling for the children of that
"lead-coloured sea" – poor and working-class students, girls and boys of
color, and so many others – is not neutral, not in its means, and certainly
not in its outcomes. Perhaps the best description is still that of Jonathan
Kozol, who simply describes both the conditions and results as "savage
inequalities" (Kozol, 1991).

Yes, that sea may seem sordid; but who controls the economic, social,
and educational conditions that make it so? Whose vision of schooling,
whose vision of what counts as real knowledge, for whom, organizes the
lives in classrooms in that sea?

One is reminded here of the French sociologist of culture Pierre Bourdieu's comments about how elite visions of the world, elite culture, habits,
and "tastes" function in our cultural institutions. Bourdieu (1984) puts it
this way:

The denial of lower, coarse, vulgar, venal – in a word natural – enjoyment, which
constitutes the sacred sphere of culture, implies an affirmation of the superiority of
those who can be satisfied with the sublimated, refined, disinterested, gratuitous,
distinguished pleasures forever closed to the profane. That is why . . . cultural
consumption [is] predisposed, consciously and deliberatively or not, to fulfill a social
function of legitimating social difference. (pp. 23–24)

As he notes earlier, these cultural forms, "through the economic and social
conditions which they presuppose . . . are bound up with the systems
of dispositions . . . characteristic of different classes and class fractions"
(Bourdieu, 1984, pp. 5–6). Thus, cultural form and content function as
markers of class (p. 2). The granting of legitimacy to such a system of
culture through its incorporation within an officially recognized curriculum,
then, creates a situation in which the markers of "taste" become the markers of people. The school becomes a class school. Holmes and Watson's
conversation speaks to this in hidden but no less powerful ways. Under-

standing this requires that we see schools – and the curricula, teaching, and evaluation that go on in them – in ways that do not make these connections between what we do as educators and the larger relations of power invisible.

In some fields of scholarship – the history of science comes to mind – a distinction is made between internalist and externalist analyses. In the former, we understand a phenomenon through the history of the development of the internal characteristics of a discipline itself. In the latter, we must see the connections between the development of a theory or area and the larger social relations that create either the need or conditions for such developments.

Most discussions of the content and organization of curricula and teaching in areas such as mathematics have been strikingly internalistic. Or, when they do turn to "external" sources other than the discipline of mathematics itself, they travel but a short distance – to psychology. There seems to be a strong assumption that by coupling better mathematics with new psychological theories, most of the issues of educational achievement and equity will be solved. This continues a very long history in education of borrowing our basic paradigms from a very limited range of disciplinary frameworks. The psychologization of educational theory and practice – though it *has* brought gains with it as some of the new mathematics programs, described in the chapters by Silver and Nelson, by Carey, Fennema, Carpenter and Franke, and by Khisty in her thoughtful, even more social-psychological analysis of language use demonstrate – unfortunately has also had a number of crucial limiting effects. It has, profoundly, evacuated critical social, political, and economic considerations from the purview of curriculum deliberations. In the process of individualizing its view of students, it has lost any serious sense of the social structures and the race, gender, and class relations that form these individuals. Furthermore, it is then unable to situate areas such as mathematics education in a wider social context that includes larger programs for democratic education and a more democratic society. Finally, because of these factors, it leaves us with eviscerated visions of *critical* practice (Apple, 1990, 1992a). Although perhaps not quite as uncritical as Holmes and Watson, all too often it does not include any systematic analysis of what Secada, Fennema, and Adajian call for in their introduction to this book, "the kinds of inquiry that will enable us to understand how opportunity is unequally distributed in this society, the role that mathematics and education play in that stratification, and how we might reclaim the aegis of educational reform to include the creation of a fairer social order as a legitimate goal."

It is for these very reasons that new, more critically oriented, "externalist" approaches to mathematics education are so important. For without a recognition of the socially situated character of all educational policy and practice, without a recognition of the winners and losers in this society, without a more structural understanding of how and why schools participate in creating these winners and losers (Apple, 1985), I believe we are doomed to reproduce an endless cycle of high hopes, rhetorical reforms, and broken promises. The essays included in this book signify the growing recognition among many mathematics educators of the importance of these issues.

As with any volume of this size and diversity, the individual chapters incorporate this recognition to varying degrees and with varying levels of success. A few simply add a layer of what might be called "social responsibility talk" to relatively traditional psychological and pedagogical aims and approaches or assume that because their focus is on the achievement of girls or children of color in mathematics that they have met the challenges articulated in the quotation I cited from the Introduction. Others base their entire approach on a critical reappraisal of the multiple ways in which differential power works in this society through the everyday activities of schooling and through the social and epistemological assumptions this entails about knowledge, about the relationship between knowledge and social practice, and about the role of the educator herself or himself in challenging these assumptions. Although my sympathies lie more with these latter articulations of critical educational approaches, there is no doubt in my mind that most of the contributions represented in this book push us – in their own ways – to take more seriously the relationship between equity and education. At the very least, they provide cogent attempts at placing teacher–student interaction at the center of curriculum practice.

In a review of this length, I cannot deal in detail with every chapter, though much could be said about each one. Instead, I will focus on a number of issues that need to be highlighted. My aim here is to push all of us a little further in thinking about mathematics education *socially,* so that we can stand on the shoulders of these contributions and then go further. Because of this, I shall say less about the very interesting work in science and mathematics education of some of the contributors than might otherwise be deserved. First, I want to highlight one of the major contributions these chapters make to how we think about teaching socially and about its connections to students' understandings. In the process, I will then examine the connection between academic knowledge and popular – or practical – knowledge that I noted earlier was so crucial a topic. As you will see, I do not believe that a sufficient answer lies in simply making the mathematics curriculum more connected to practical issues. Finally, I shall raise some critical cautions about where socially committed educators might go to make a real difference in schools and the larger society.

Countering the de-skilling of teachers

For those of us who are used to seeing mathematics as a field dominated by traditional pedagogies and curricula, and by conservative social and pedagogical aims, it may come as a surprise that some of the leadership in current curriculum reform movements comes from within the mathematics education community. Given its history as an area of what Basil Bernstein (1977) has called "strongly classified" and "strongly framed" experience (mathematics as pure and uncontaminated by the real world and taught in a strictly teacher-directed way), one would not necessarily expect it to be at the center of some of the most interesting educational transformations that are occurring in schools and universities today. Yet, as the chapters included here signify, this is a time of considerable ferment in mathematics education, both pedagogically and socially.

Despite all of the rhetoric about teaching and professionalism, about enhancing teachers' power and respect, the reality of many teachers' lives bears little resemblance to the rhetoric. Rather than moving in a direction of increased autonomy, the daily lives of teachers in classrooms in many nations are becoming increasingly controlled, increasingly subject to administrative logics that seek to tighten the reins on the processes of teaching and curriculum. Teacher development, cooperation, and "empowerment" may be the talk, but centralization, standardization, and rationalization are the tendencies.

Over the past two decades, the inner world of education – the actual processes by which teaching and curriculum planning go on – has been transformed in very damaging ways. Not only have the goals become increasingly conservative, but there has been a rapid growth in the adoption of reductive procedures of standardization and rationalization. This has been especially true in urban schools, although it is not limited to them. In school system after school system, teaching methods, texts, tests, and outcomes have been taken out of the hands of the people who must put them into practice. Instead, they have been legislated by state departments of education, state legislatures, and central office staff, who in their attempts to increase "the quality of educational outcomes" are often markedly unreflective about the latent effects of their efforts.

Some of these negative effects have been widespread. The tendency for the curriculum to be rationalized and "industrialized" at a central level focuses largely on competencies measured by standardized tests, and encourages the use of an escalating number of predesigned commercialized material written for those states that have the tightest centralized control over teaching, texts, and tests as well as the largest guaranteed market (Apple, 1986). The most obvious result here is the *de-skilling* of teachers. When individuals cease to plan and control a large portion of their work, the skills essential to doing these tasks well and self-reflectively atrophy and are forgotten. The skills that teachers have built up over decades of hard work – setting relevant curriculum goals; establishing content; designing lessons and instructional strategies; individualizing curricula and teaching based on an intimate knowledge of students' desires, needs, and culture;

and working closely with the community on all of this – are lost. In many ways, given the centralization of authority and control, and given the pressures on schools to define their primary goal as only economic utility, they are no longer needed (Apple, 1985, 1993a).

In the larger economy, this process of separating conception from execution, this de-skilling, has been appropriately called the degradation of labor. Importing these procedures into the school under the banner of supposedly improving educational quality can have exactly the same impact it has had in many industries: a loss of commitment and respect, bitter battles over working conditions, a lowering of quality, and something else of great importance to mathematics teaching in particular, the loss of skill and imagination. In the economic workplace, this process has also ultimately reduced the power of employees to have any significant say in the goals and procedures of the institutions in which they work. All of these characteristics run directly counter to what we are beginning to know about those factors that lead to effective and responsive curricula and teaching in schools (Apple & Beane, in press; Smith, 1993).

None of this, of course, is by any means new. It is quite similar to the situation lamented by Margaret Haley – one of the leaders of the first teachers' union in the United States – at the beginning of this century. In her campaign to have teachers continue their efforts to create an educational system that was more truly democratic in both means and ends, Haley was quite clear about one of the most important ingredients in her platform. De-skilling – or as she so cleverly called it, "factoryizing" – had to be overcome. Haley and so many of her teaching colleagues believed that teachers had to organize to alter conditions in which they were expected "to carry out mechanically and unquestioningly the ideas and orders of those clothed with authority of position and who may or may not know the needs of the children or how to minister them" (Fraser, 1989, p. 138). As a teacher, Haley clearly recognized what was at stake in terms of skill, autonomy, and the lives of children if such "factoryizing" approaches took even greater hold. As a *woman* teacher, she also realized the political fact that, since the majority of teachers were and are women, they had to work even harder to gain respect and legitimacy for their skills and power (Apple, 1986).

To raise this example is not to suggest that we are at the stage we were 90 years ago. Of course we are not (though one wonders what Haley might say if she saw the standardized, tightly controlled, and overly text-based models now in use in so many classrooms in this nation). Indeed, as many of the chapters in this book indicate, there are schools in which immense gains have been made. However, we are in danger of losing the collective memory of how many years it took and of the many sacrifices that were made in order to achieve these gains. In the process, we may witness a slow but steady return to conditions that stimulated the de-skilling of both teachers and students[1] and in which subjects such as mathematics were unlinked to the daily lives of students, thereby reproducing the racial, class, and gender divisions of the larger society.

This very issue of de-skilling and its attendant losses for students and teachers is what makes the chapters in this book that describe less routinized and more interactive curricula and pedagogy – chapters that pay close attention to social difference – so interesting and necessary. The interventions discussed by Silver and Nelson, by Keynes, by Carey, Fennema, Carpenter and Franke, by Ladson-Billings, by Frankenstein, and by Warren and Rosebery, and the research of Khisty, all begin with a very different picture of what the teacher and the appropriate interaction between teacher and students should look like. All assume that subtle skills and critical dispositions need to be more than slogans, and that they must be put into practice by teachers and students. In their different ways, all are based on a recognition – sometimes overt, sometimes unstated – that mathematics and science are crucial forms of knowing that can make a difference in people's lives if, and only if, the environment of the classroom is based on an awareness of inequalities and on an educational process that seeks to deal with students and teachers as capable of sophisticated reasoning about their daily lives inside and outside of classrooms. It is for this reason that these efforts deserve our support, not "only" for what they say about mathematics education but also for how they enable us to rethink the dominant models employed in other curriculum areas as well.

But rethinking *dominant* models requires that we pay attention to the two senses of that word. Dominant can mean something that is long lasting and accepted. However, and of great importance in our own deliberations about education, it can also mean having illegitimate power over others so that the benefits of one's actions flow in undemocratic directions. This is where questions of equity come to the fore and where the socially situated character of all educational activity, especially given the current growth of conservative social and educational policy, needs to be recognized.

The practical and the critical

Although they constitute the focal point of this book, words such as equity are sliding signifiers. They do not have an essential meaning, but – as Wittgenstein (1953) reminded us – are defined by their use in real social situations with real relations of power. What equity actually means is struggled over, in the same way that concepts such as democracy are subject to different senses by different groups with sometimes radically different ideological and educational agendas (Apple, 1993a). This is quite clear in the chapters themselves, since, as I noted, for some authors equity is largely about raising the achievement scores on what academics and some groups in the larger society have defined as high-status knowledge, whereas for others it entails a much more thoroughgoing reconstruction of the ends and means not only of education but of the relations of domination in the larger society. Thus, behind each of these chapters – even if only tacitly – is a social theory about what this society "really is" and what it is necessary for educators to do to participate in changing it. These theories or social visions may be in conflict.

We are in the midst of such conflicts today, and education sits at center stage. Of course, not everyone or every group has equal power to define the terms of these conflicts or to move their resolution in progressive directions. In fact, as I have argued in my analysis of the *Curriculum and Evaluation Standards for School Mathematics* (National Council of Teachers of Mathematics, 1989), it is the conservative agenda that seems to be having the greatest impact in education today and that, unfortunately, may provide the direction for a good deal of "reform" (Apple, 1992a).

In the early days of Margaret Thatcher's first government in Britain, she spelled out the evangelical aims of her political program. "Economics is the method," she said. But this was not all. "The aim is to change the soul" (Donald, 1992, p. 122). And the soul was to be changed in strikingly conservative directions. Although Thatcher spoke for Britain, much the same could be said for what has happened in the United States.

I have discussed critically the attributes of the conservative restoration at considerable length both in general and in mathematics education elsewhere (Apple, 1992a, 1993a, 1993b), and I have no wish to totally recapitulate my arguments here. However, the aims of the conservative agenda are all around us. Let me mention four major tendencies for "changing the soul" of education: (1) proposals for "choice," such as voucher plans and tax credits to make schools more like the (thoroughly idealized) "free market" economy, while budget cuts force draconian measures on local school districts; (2) the movement in state legislatures and state departments of education, as well as at a national level, to mandate both teacher and student "competencies" and "outcomes" and to establish statewide and national curricula and testing, thereby centralizing even more control over teaching and curricula; (3) the increasingly effective assaults on the school curriculum – and on teachers – for a supposedly antifamily and anti–free-enterprise bias, for "secular humanism," lack of patriotism, and neglect of the "Western tradition"; and, most powerfully, (4) the growing pressure to make only the needs of business and industry the primary goals of the educational system (Apple, 1993a, p. 20).

I do not believe that taken together these constitute a wise set of policies. But, in my mind, any discussion of transformations in mathematics education must be evaluated in light of where it stands vis-à-vis these issues. At the base of each issue is one question – Who benefits? – and it must be asked continually. Perhaps my fourth point, regarding the pressure on education to orient to the needs of business and industry, can provide a paradigm case.

Let me take as an example something that is clearly present in a number of the descriptions of programs in this volume. I refer to the call to develop mathematics curricula and strategies of teaching that are more closely connected to what Holmes and Watson saw no need for – the "lead-coloured sea" of daily life. For part of the conservative agenda is itself critical of schooling that limits itself to elite "academic" knowledge. Because of this, our analyses must be more subtle than simply decrying the neoconservative emphasis on a return to older visions of academic study. The solution is not simply to call for the "practical," and for a curriculum that is more engaging to students, though these elements may offer parts of an answer. Some chapters – such as those of Warren and Rosebery, Ladson-Billings, and Frankenstein – recognize the issues to which I shall point here.

Few people who have experienced the levels of boredom and alienation among our students in schools will quarrel with the assertion that curricula should be more closely linked to "real life." This is not the issue. What really matters is the question of *whose* vision of real life counts. Take, for instance, a mathematics curriculum that places at its center a goal of "mathematical literacy" for flexible job performance. This construction of "real life" – preparation for paid work – is usually totally uncritical. It pushes to the margins any real concern with the actual and declining conditions under which so many people labor. It ignores the steady movement toward low-wage, part-time, nonunionized, no-benefits, service-sector employment for millions of American workers. Absent the integration of these kinds of issues directly into mathematics curricula, the goals of using mathematics to prepare students for "real life" is not only a partial fiction, but it institutionalizes as official knowledge only perspectives that benefit the groups that already possess power in this society (Apple, 1986).

Compare this to John Dewey's own reappraisal of the dangers of defining education as a narrow practical activity supposedly designed to prepare one for the "world of work." Such an education, centered around a particular definition of "the practical," severed the connection between daily activity and critical understanding that was so necessary in any education worthy of its name. Thus, when Dewey argued for vocational education (redefined and for all people), he saw it as being constituted by "the full intellectual and social meaning of a vocation." Speaking in the language of his day, he insisted that this had to include "instruction in the historic background of present conditions; training in science to give intelligence and initiative in dealing with material and agencies of production; and study of economics, civics, and politics to bring the future worker into touch with the problems

of the day and the various methods proposed for their improvements"
(Dewey, quoted in Jones, 1989, p. 104). The "practical," then, could never
be divorced from historical, ethical, and political understanding without
losing something in the process. Schooling should never be seen as simply
training for industries' needs.

The danger residing within a totally practical emphasis for the children of
the poor, dispossessed, and working class was recognized by the noted
Italian political theorist and activist Antonio Gramsci. He leveled a with-
ering critique at school officials who saw their job to be only satisfying
"immediate, practical interests" under the guise of egalitarian rhetoric. Behind the democratic slogans, he warned, was a neglect of the utter import
to develop in students the capacity "to reason, to think abstractly while
remaining able to plunge back from abstraction into real and immediate life,
to see in each fact or datum what is general and what is particular, to
distinguish the concept from the specific instance" (Gramsci, quoted in
Jones, 1989, p. 104). By limiting school curricula to only the practical
problems of daily life, such schools left access to the skills of critical
reasoning only to those who were already in power (Jones, 1989, p. 104).

These points illuminate a very real tension in any educational program
that seeks to treat equity in more than rhetorical ways. On the one hand, it
is very important to take seriously the following question and answer:

"How do you get somebody to understand an abstraction? By relating it to the
reality that it is an abstraction of" (Judith Williamson, quoted in Jones, 1989,
p. 182).

On the other hand, we need to be very careful that these new educational
strategies are not pedagogies of *individual adaptation* rather than pedagogies of social change. "Progressive" teaching and curricula are not always
socially critical. In a highly stratified society such as the one in which we
live, "experiential, affective and emotional learning can shape dispositions
and loyalties" just as easily in directions favoring the powerful, rather
than the least advantaged. It can inhibit, not enhance, the development of
dispositions of rigorous critique (Hargreaves & Reynolds, 1989, p. 22). We,
thus, need to ask the authors of each chapter in this book whether their
analyses and proposals are indeed linked to the development of such critical
dispositions. Many of these chapters will stand up very well to this scrutiny.

Students themselves are often quick to determine whether a focus on real
life is serious or not. If it does not connect in powerful ways to their daily
experiences, many students will simply return to the "cynical bargain" of
doing just enough to get by that Linda McNeil (1986) has shown charac-
terizes so much of their school experience. This makes Gloria Ladson-
Billings's accounts of how teachers connect their mathematics teaching to
the realities of students' lives and material conditions even more important,
since it is clearly guided by a critical appraisal of how so much of the
schooling offered to African American students in this society has the effect

of disqualifying a majority of black children, especially in times of severe economic and social dislocation (Apple, 1985; McCarthy & Apple, 1988).

This critical appraisal is equally evident in other parts of the book as well. There is a recognition, in a number of the chapters, of the power of the economic crisis and what it means for the present and future of those people who have historically been less well served by the dominant institutions in this society. Tate, for example, is perceptive in his assessment of how voluntary mathematics standards will make it nearly impossible – simply for economic reasons – for poor urban districts to have enough money to support them. Frankenstein bases much of her discussion of her proposed mathematics curriculum on the social and economic disparities that provide much of the deep structure of this society. And Keynes, who is less overtly socially critical in his account of the development of a university-based mathematics program that includes "disadvantaged" students and young women, still points to the fact that, because of the budget crisis, the program to which he is so committed is getting declining support.

As I have come to expect from his work, Walter Secada also has a nicely nuanced appreciation of the multiple uses of educational and social discourse. He is especially insightful on how the understandable demand to focus on "doing something now" can lead us to ignore the larger conditions that generated the problems we may currently face. These points lead me to make a suggestion to the readers of this book. We should read the chapters that describe real-life curricular interventions through the eyes of these more general chapters that ask us to stand back to ask once again "who benefits?"

Some critical cautions

"Who benefits?" may seem like an easy question to ask, but answering it can be quite complicated, for social and ideological interests and beliefs are not only found in what and how we teach. They also are fused with the deep structures of how we understand mathematics and science. As we are beginning to understand, part of the problem rests with the epistemological groundings that stand behind not only our definitions of knowledge and knowing (Harraway, 1989), but also our own attempts as researchers to understand these issues in the lives of students, teachers, and ourselves (Gitlin, 1994). Damarin's presentation of many of the counterassumptions of feminist positions is valuable here. She takes important first steps in this direction in her clear discussion of the conceptual/political principles underlying feminist-standpoint epistemology. While her description is a bit too brief to carry the weight of such an epistemological challenge, it does bring such material directly to bear on the core questions surrounding the nature of mathematical teaching and knowing.

This does not mean that our accepted ways of developing knowledge are still not crucial tools, if they are reconstructed around alternative social uses. This is made very clear in Marilyn Frankenstein's discussion of how statistical understanding can provide a powerful tool in helping students become critically literate about the nature of class relations in this society.

Although I am very supportive of the efforts of Damarin and Frankenstein, because I am committed to similar approaches I want to raise a few collegial cautions so that other readers who also find their discussions of considerable interest can have some food for thought. I do this because parts of mathematics education do not have as long a tradition of socially critical work as other areas of education have. There is a long history in educational scholarship of borrowing perspectives from other disciplines – taking them out of their self-correcting context. Thus, we are then unaware of the debates over their conceptual, empirical, or political status and, hence, may risk importing these dangers into our own activities and research. A prime example here, of course, was the domination of behavioral and competency-based approaches in curriculum development for a long period. When these first appeared in curriculum theory in the early part of this century, they were based on F. W. Taylor's work in industrial management, work that was hotly contested at the time for its antiunion and antiworker implications. In fact, at the same time as it was being imported into education, its basic approach – based on time and motion analysis – in essence was being outlawed by an act of Congress for use in federally funded work because of the unrest and dislocations it caused (Noble, 1977).

In its later guise in the 1960s and 1970s, such reductive and even stricter behavioral approaches entered into the mainstream of curriculum development nearly a decade after most psychologists have concluded that they were based on simplistic theories that misconstrued the complex nature of human knowing. Hence, the growth of the constructivist theories that are so much in evidence in this volume. Yet, even with the emergence of such constructivist approaches, the dominance of the earlier, less subtle influences could have been avoided if education had paid considerably more attention to the internal debates within the area from which they borrowed. For this very reason, I shall briefly note a few of the controversies that we should pay attention to when we appropriate – as I think we must – the perspectives that stand behind Damarin and Frankenstein's important contributions.

Take as an example Damarin's appropriation of important perspectives from feminist and poststructural work. At the theoretical level, though she herself does *not* slide into this, there is a danger here of lapsing into a total epistemological relativism. In its most egregious forms in educational theory, not only is this at times conceptually naive, but it is often based on questionable politics as well (see Apple, 1993a; Best & Kellner, 1991; Connell, 1993).

Counterposing Frankenstein's and Damarin's chapters is useful here. Both are grounded in the personal. Both see mathematics education as an activity that is linked to real relations of power. Frankenstein is considerably more structural in taking the approach that class and economic relations are largely the engine that drives our society. Damarin chooses to focus on the conceptual/political assumptions that undergird patriarchal relations. Although the former, for all its power, can be reductive (class and economic structure "determines" all), the latter at the same time can enable powerful insights into the masculinization of our logics and practices, and yet fail to appreciate some of the most compelling structural relations in which we all exist. Taken too far, the former can be essentializing (McCarthy & Apple, 1988); the latter can be uncritical about some aspects of postmodernism (Palmer, 1990). Taken too far, both can give too little attention to the debates over their respective positions.

Do not misunderstand me here. I would make the Frankenstein and Damarin chapters required reading for all mathematics educators and researchers. They are both important contributions. However, I would ask the readers of these chapters to go further – to inquire into the debates over each position, into the dangers of forms of class reductionism (while still being clear about the very real power of class relations) that may limit our appreciation of the utter power of racial and gender dynamics and relations on the one hand, and of an uncritical acceptance of all postmodern assumptions and approaches on the other. These dangers are *not* inherent in Frankenstein's and Damarin's contributions, but they can easily arise if we are not reflexive about our own critical approaches. Thus, a double reflexivity is needed – one that is critical of dominant approaches and agendas, and another that is constantly self-critical of the alternatives we propose.

There are resources within the book that are helpful in this regard. The cogent analyses of race by Tate and Ladson-Billings serve as effective counters both to a totally class-based understanding of how this society operates, and to one that can at times ignore the material practices of the state and economy (see also Dale, 1989; Omi & Winant, 1986).

All of this, of course, means that we need to be much more sophisticated in our analyses of power. It is not just "society" that causes x to occur rather than y in mathematics education or any other part of schooling, but a complex assemblage of relations of power, some occurring at a macro level, others occurring at a micro level. And each of these is complicated and sometimes contradictory (Apple, 1993a; Popkewitz, 1992).

Take class as one example. As Basil Bernstein and I have pointed out, it is too easy to trace much of the power behind education policies and practices back only to the workings of economically dominant groups. Surely these groups are indeed powerful, but class relations are complex. Fractions of the middle class play important roles here. Furthermore, ideological alliances between dominant, middle-, and working-class groups have been formed to support parts of the conservative social and educational agenda that I mentioned earlier. Gender and race dynamics play a significant role here as well. Any complete analysis of this requires a profound understanding of the utter complexity of these alliances (Apple, 1992b, 1993a,b; Bernstein, 1977, 1990).

Patriarchal relations provide yet another example. Like Damarin, but in different ways, Leder and Campbell also recognize the patriarchal structuring of mathematics. Leder is useful, though perhaps somewhat too brief, in reminding us of the gendered past upon which current mathematics education stands. Campbell, by raising the issue of mathematics as a male domain, is clear that the problem is not "girls," but mathematics teaching and how mathematics is situated in the larger society. This is a good reminder, yet it could have been taken a bit further in Campbell's application to schools themselves. Thus, although she places on teachers some of the blame for poor mathematics curricula and teaching of "girls," this could have been made more powerful if she had then connected these claims to a recognition of the sexual division of labor in teaching and administration, something Margaret Haley understood was critical in dealing with issues of gender. Remember, 67% of teachers are women, and there has been a constant struggle by teachers, and female teachers in particular, against conditions that reduce their autonomy and respect, deny recognition of their skills, and standardize curricula, teaching, and evaluation in ways that de-skill teachers. Nearly all occupations that have been socially defined as largely "women's paid labor" have been subject to these conditions and struggles. For women of color, the situation has been even more difficult. Once again, a more structural understanding would have seen the complexities in teachers' lives, and might have placed more of the blame on the conditions under which so many teachers work (Apple, 1986, 1993a; Casey, 1993; Warren, 1989). It also would have recognized how state policies in education, as in so much else, are structured around gender dynamics in quite powerful ways, ways that may make it difficult to institutionalize more than a few small steps forward unless these structural dynamics are dealt with overtly and at the very beginning of our attempts at reform (Franzway, Court, & Connell, 1989; Kenway, 1990).

Being honest with ourselves

Everything I have said here requires that we place even our best efforts at educational reform back into the larger society. It assumes that whether our attempts to create more responsible curricula and teaching succeed is dependent on a realistic and critical assessment of the conflicting forces at work inside schools and in that larger society. I have claimed that our aim should be not only the formation of "critical literacy" in our students, but, in essence, becoming more critically literate ourselves. As I argued, too much of the literature on reforming education evacuates such social questions. Even the literature that expressly deals with some aspects of how schools may fail an increasingly large population of students does this by once again tacitly psychologizing the problem. The fact that a number of the chapters included here, in particular Khisty's analysis of the ways language functions in classrooms, base their social and psychological underpinnings on a Vygotskyan or similar perspective – a thoroughly *social* understanding of the situatedness of human knowing – acts as a counter to this tendency. The problem, though, does exist in the larger community of "reform"- minded educators who often do not "think the social" in critically adequate ways.

Take the language of reforms to assist "at risk" students, a language that lies behind a number of the programs discussed in this book. The social construction of what the "problem" is diverts our attention from some of the most important root issues. Michelle Fine (1990) articulates the point in the following way:

To position students as "at risk" bears potentially two very distinct sets of consequences. The benevolent consequence is that their needs could in fact be attended to. The notion of "at risk" . . . also offers a deceptive image of an isolatable and identifiable group of students who, by virtue of some personal characteristic, are not likely to graduate. As Foucault would argue, the image betrays more than it reveals. Diverted away from an economy that is inhospitable to low-income adolescents and adults, particularly U.S.-born African-Americans and Latinos, and diverted from the collapsing manufacturing sectors of the country, housing stock, and impoverished urban schools, our attention floats to the individual child, his/her family, and those small-scale interventions which would "fix" him/her as though their lives were fully separable from ours.
[They] divert social attention to individual children and adolescents, their families, and communities. . . . [While they do] indeed represent "real" issues, more dangerously, however, at the same time they are imaginary. They reproduce existing ideologies, shave off alternative frames and recommend as "natural" those programs of reform which serve only to exacerbate class, race, and gender stratifications. (p. 64)

Warren and Rosebery recognize this, as does Secada. They see that, in our responses to "at risk" youth, we tend to come up with simplistic solutions, plans that may be useful as part of a larger strategy of social and educational transformation but that, as an isolated intervention, founder on the shoals of the massive reality and depth of the problems education confronts. This can be seen, for instance, in the argument that greater involvement of parents is "the answer" to the problems of school achievement of "at risk" students in our urban areas.

Speaking of the issue of reforms aimed at parental involvement, though much the same can be said of many mathematics reforms, after deep involvement in and research on such programs, Michelle Fine again puts it well:

The assumption that empowered and involved parents produce educated students can be laid to rest. . . . Empowered parents . . . do not, in and of themselves, produce in the aggregate improved student outcomes in the areas of retention, absenteeism, California Achievement Test scores, or grades. Parental involvement is necessary but not sufficient to produce improved student outcomes. Without a serious national, state, and community commitment to serving children broadly, and to reconstructing schools in low income neighborhoods and their surrounds, deep parental involvement with schools will do little to positively affect – or sustain – low income students or their schools and outcomes. (1993, p. 691)

Fine goes on to argue that focusing only on any one element – here parental involvement – misses the depth of the problem and what may be necessary for lasting transformations.

As she notes, over the past decade, federal and state governments have tried to shift responsibility and blame for educational problems onto the backs of low-income parents. Individual parental-involvement projects cannot restore a rich, critical, and creative public sphere. Only with a powerful, supportive, and activist national agenda for children can parental involvement thrive, and only then if parental involvement provokes thoughtful, critical inquiry into public bureaucracy (Fine, 1993).

These points have very real implications for mathematics education and more general educational reforms. These attempts at partly democratizing educational decision making are occurring at almost exactly the "wrong" historical moment: This is a moment of severe public-sector retrenchment, not expansion. "School-based resources and decision making have been narrowed, not expanded." Thus, for instance, many school-based councils that have been formed to "empower" local teachers and parents feel "empowered only to determine who or what will be cut" (Fine, 1993, p. 696). Defending what is there, hence, often becomes more important than transforming curricula or expanding one's educational horizons.

Make no doubt about it: the new equity-based forms of teaching and curriculum development described in this book will take an immense amount of effort and time. Furthermore, this will have to take place in institutions where the intellectual and emotional labor of teaching is already increasingly intensified, and where resources to even keep buildings open the minimum number of days a year are often hard to find (Apple, 1986, 1993a).

Thus, for Fine – and I agree wholeheartedly – at the same time as we continue to strive for the best educational experiences we can provide for our children in every curriculum area, what is required is to couple this with "relentless attention to *systematic* power and critique" (Fine, 1993, p. 692).

Anything less may actually serve to hide the way existing realities of power systematically disenfranchise the least-advantaged members of our communities. Without combining these two projects, we may be left with Walter Secada's scenario: "Doing something now" may substitute for taking the larger issues seriously.

Conclusion

Asking about who will benefit from the hard work we are doing is a painful enterprise. All educators (one would hope) are deeply committed to making schools better places to be. Efforts to improve the curriculum and teaching that go on in these institutions – such as those reported in this volume – continue to be crucial. Linking them to more democratic conceptions of equity, to attempts to overcome the gender, class, and race inequalities inside and outside the school, is now more important than ever. The students studied in Stanic and Hart's interesting contribution may at least have a chance, since they are considered "high average" (but even there we can see how race and gender work). What of the millions of others in that "lead-coloured sea" who face the savage inequalities that so deeply characterize the commitments of dominant groups to the children of this nation?

In this regard, Tate raises one of the fundamental issues directly when he asks of one set of reforms in mathematics education, "How will changing the mathematics standards with a voluntary national assessment policy alter the philosophical, instructional, and/or financial capacity of an urban school system to educate African American students?" His answer is blunt, but I think accurate. "It will not." We have to be ready to face this answer squarely.

Do not misinterpret my comments in this chapter as implying that approaches that focus largely on new forms of pedagogy, curricula, and evaluation are not worthy. Indeed, as, say, the work of Carey, Fennema, Carpenter, and Franke, that of Silver and Nelson, of Khisty, and of Warren and Rosebery indicate, a good deal of very real progress is being made in building more thoughtful and socially and personally sensitive programs in mathematics education. Reading each of them taught me a good deal.

One of the elements that sets the programs described in this volume apart from much of the "normal" practice, not only in mathematics education but in many other curricular areas as well, is their conscious attempt to recognize, ratify, enhance, and enlarge the range of skills used by teachers (and students). They have expressly grappled with the issue of de-skilling and have sought to build solutions to its deleterious effects in practice.

For example, many of the efforts addressed in these pages, from CGI to the socially connected instruction specifically aimed at poor urban students of color, seem to offer important improvements by enabling students and teachers to reason their way through mathematics in disciplined yet creative and caring ways. As I noted earlier, these are light years ahead of the memorization, rote instruction, boring text and workbook-based models that unfortunately still play such a strong role in mathematics curricula and teaching. Thus, nearly all of the programs described in this volume are filled with progressive possibilities. Yet, for these programs to fully reach their democratizing potential and to have a truly widespread influence, educators who wish to make a real difference must continually ask critical questions, and must place these programs in their larger context. Only in this way will their definite progressive possibilities not be washed away, a fate that all too many democratizing initiatives have suffered in the past.

Thus, I am not asking us to embrace a fatalism that holds that it is impossible to change schools unless the social and economic relations of the larger society are transformed first. As public schools such as Fratney Street School in Milwaukee, Central Park East School in New York, the Rindge School of Technical Arts in the Boston area, and schools elsewhere daily demonstrate, it is possible to create an education that highlights and opposes social inequalities of many kinds, helps students investigate how their world and their lives have come to be what they are, and seriously considers what might be done to bring about change (Apple, 1993a). This also requires no small alteration both in the ways teaching and learning are organized and in the objectives that guide what the school is about. And many of the chapters included in this volume give us hope that these gains are indeed possible even in times of conservative triumphalism. However, for these changes to last and to grow, educators working in and with schools such as these need a much more searching, honest, and critical appraisal of this society, of how it is now organized to *deny* the possibility of large-scale success, and of what larger educational and social movements they can join to alter this (Apple, 1992a).

I take the attempts at building more equitable models of curriculum and teaching documented in this book – as well as the critically oriented ethnographic research that challenges dominant linguistic, pedagogical, and curricular practices – as crucial first steps, and I believe that they must be supported. But, like some of the authors here, I want to take some of the "fun" out of doing it. This is not to fill the role of Michael Apple as "Grinch." After all, there should be some measure of joy in working with students in schools and creating the possibilities for them to succeed. As someone who spent a number of years teaching in inner-city schools, I would never remove that joy. But let us not be romantic. Let us not act as if the problems of mathematics education can be "solved" in isolation from those of other subject areas and from those of schools whose *overall* structure is too often authoritarian in its relationship to students, teachers, and community members. Let us not act as if the main task is getting a few more students to do well on the cultural capital of elite groups or simply making mathematics more "practical." Let us not act in isolation from the larger social questions that give any serious concern for equity its critical edge.

Much can still be accomplished, as the chapters by Frankenstein, Ladson-Billings, and others document. But what gives them the right to call it an accomplishment is that – unlike Dr. Watson and Mr. Holmes – they've come down from the train and entered the "lead-coloured sea." And they have found that what looks colorless through the glasses of the "sublimated, refined, disinterested, and distinguished" riders on that train is instead a creative and moving river of democracy, of people wanting and struggling both for a better life for their children and for a society that no longer denies them the right to help determine the course of that river. Holmes and Watson are fictions. Equity, too, may remain a fiction unless we constantly connect it to these struggles for democracy.

Acknowledgments

I would like to thank James Beane, Elizabeth Fennema, Walter Secada, and the Friday Seminar for their helpful comments on this chapter.

Note

1 De-skilling is not the only process at work here. It is part of a larger, more complex, dynamic in which what counts as skills is struggled over and redefined. Further, as I have argued elsewhere (Apple, 1986), teachers are also being *re-skilled*. However, unlike what is detailed in many of the chapters included here, this process of re-skilling often involves the substitution of technical, management-oriented skills and the deemphasis of more creative and autonomous pedagogical approaches. In essence, "professionalism" is being redefined for teachers. It is increasingly equated with simply being a good technician.

References

Apple, M. W. (1985). *Education and power*. Boston: Routledge and Kegan Paul.
  (1986). *Teachers and texts: A political economy of class and gender relations in education*. New York: Routledge & Kegan Paul.
  (1990). *Ideology and curriculum* (2d ed.). New York: Routledge.
  (1992a). Do the standards go far enough? Power, policy and practice in mathematics education. *Journal for Research in Mathematics Education, 23,* 412–431.
  (1992b). Education, culture and class power. *Educational Theory, 42,* 127–145.
  (1993a). *Official knowledge: Democratic education in a conservative age*. New York: Routledge.
  (1993b). The politics of official knowledge: Does a national curriculum make sense? *Teachers College Record, 95,* 222–241.
Apple, M. W., & Beane, J. (in press). *Democratic schools*. Washington, DC: Association for Supervision and Curriculum Development.

348 M. W. APPLE

Apple, M. W., & Christian-Smith, L. (Eds). (1991). *The politics of the textbook*. New York: Routledge.
Bernstein, B. (1977). *Class, codes and control*. Vol. 3, *Towards a theory of transmission*. Revised ed. London: Routledge.
——— (1990). *The structuring of pedagogic discourse*. New York: Routledge.
Best, S., & Kellner, D. (1991). *Postmodern theory*. New York: Macmillan.
Bourdieu, P. (1984). *Distinction*. Cambridge, MA: Harvard University Press.
Casey, K. (1993). *I answer with my life: Life histories of women teachers working for social change*. New York: Routledge.
Connell, R. W. (1993). *Schools and social justice*. Toronto: Our Schools/Our Selves Press.
Dale, R. (1989). *The state and education policy*. Philadelphia: Open University Press.
Donald, J. (1992). *Sentimental education: Schooling, popular culture and the regulation of liberty*. New York: Verso.
Fine, M. (1990). Making controversy: Who's "at risk?" *Journal of Urban and Cultural Studies, 1*, 55–68.
——— (1993). [Ap] parent involvement: Reflections on parents, power, and urban public schools. *Teachers College Record, 94*, 682–710.
Franzway, S., Court, D., & Connell, R. W. (1989). *Staking a claim: Feminism, bureaucracy and the state*. Boston: Allen & Unwin.
Fraser, J. W. (1989). Agents of democracy: Urban elementary school teachers and the conditions of teaching. In D. Warren (Ed.) *American teachers* (pp. 118–156). New York: Macmillan.
Gitlin, A. (Ed.). (1994). *Power and method*. New York: Routledge.
Hargreaves, A., & Reynolds, D. (Eds). (1989). *Education policies: Controversies and critiques*. New York: Falmer.
Harraway, D. (1989). *Primate visions*. New York: Routledge.
Jones, K. (1989). *Right turn: The conservative revolution in education*. London: Hutchinson.
Kenway, J. (1990). *Gender and education policy*. Geelong, Australia: Deakin University Press.
Kozol, J. (1991). *Savage inequalities*. New York: Crown.
McCarthy, C., & Apple, M. W. (1988). Race, class and gender in American educational research. In L. Weis (Ed.), *Class, race and gender in American education* (pp. 9–39). Albany, NY: SUNY Press.
McNeil, L. (1986). *Contradictions of control*. New York: Routledge & Kegan Paul.
National Council of Teachers of Mathematics. (1989). *Curriculum and evaluation standards for school mathematics*. Reston, VA: Author.
Noble, D. (1977). *America by design*. New York: Alfred A. Knopf.
Omi, M., & Winant, H. (1986). *Racial formation in the United States*. New York: Routledge & Kegan Paul.
Palmer, B. (1990). *Descent into discourse*. Philadelphia: Temple University Press.
Popkewitz, T. (1992). *A political sociology of educational reform*. New York: Teachers College Press.
Smith, G. (1993). *Public schools that work*. New York: Routledge.
Warren, D. (1989). *American teachers*. New York: Macmillan.
Wittgenstein, L. (1953). *Philosophical investigations*. New York: Macmillan.

Index

349